Rediscovering the

Moral
Life

Frontiers of Philosophy

Peter H. Hare, Series Editor
(State University of New York at Buffalo)

Rediscovering the
Moral
Life

Philosophy and Human Practice

James
Gouinlock

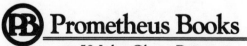 Prometheus Books

59 John Glenn Drive
Buffalo, New York 14228-2197

Published 1993 by Prometheus Books

97 96 95 94 93   5 4 3 2 1

Library of Congress Cataloging-in-Publication Data

Gouinlock, James.
    Rediscovering the moral life : philosophy and human practice / James Gouinlock.
        p.   cm.
    Includes bibliographical references and index.
    ISBN 0-87975-815-5
    1. Ethics. I. Title.
BJ1012.G665   1993
170—dc20   93-5169
                                                                            CIP

Printed in the United States of America on acid-free paper.

For Chrys

Acknowledgments

Several people had the generosity to read and evaluate a preliminary version of this book, and I owe them my great thanks. They include my colleageus at Emory University: Ann Hartle, Donald Livingston, and Donald Verene. I received helpful advice also from C. Michael Curtis and Richard Herrnstein. An anonymous referee had some excellent suggestions, most of which I incorporated into the final version. He turned out to be Richard Taylor, and I thank him as well.

Working with Prometheus Books has proved to be extremely satisfying. For this I am especially indebted to Steven L. Mitchell, the most cooperative editor with whom I have ever worked.

Finally, I wish to thank the University Research Committee of Emory University, which provided the funding for the released time that allowed me to inaugurate the research for this book.

Grateful acknowledgment is made to Harvard University Press for permission to make extensive quotations from the following work:

A Theory of Justice by John Rawls, Cambridge, Mass.: The Belknap Press of Harvard University Press. Copyright © 1971 by the President and Fellows of Harvard College.

Contents

Preface

Moral philosophy needs reorientation. As professional philosophers engage topics in the field with ever more sophistication, their analyses recede ever further from vital subject matter, and their conclusions wither on the vine of inconsequence. The present need is not to do even better what is already being done, but to do something different. That is the project of this book. This is not a plea for applied ethics, but for study of the fundamental conditions that give shape and urgency to all moral practice and pertinence to moral theory.

The persistent tendency of academic thought is to sustain the current professional literature for its own sake. The content of books and journals becomes the primary subject matter. But the subject matter that prompts the formation of philosophic disciplines is neither the published treatise nor language as such. It is the consternations, challenges, and aspirations of life itself, whether our aim be knowledge, action, or appreciation. Moral philosophy, accordingly, has its *raison d'être* as the response to the innumerable events and relations that inevitably grip us in human practice. We seek instruments of understanding and action to bring some kind of order and even satisfaction to the thousand perils and uncertainties of ordinary life. Hence moral philosophy would be born, not to become sophisticated in the convolutions of technical articles, but to investigate the salient characteristics of the moral predicament and the resources to contend with them.

Ultimately, I will argue, whatever constraint and resource there might be for our moral strivings must come from an examination of multiple features of the world itself, especially those of human beings and institutions. Whatever order and direction are available

11

to us can have no other source than these features and their real potentialities. The lessons might be uncertain, muted, unwelcome, conflicting. If so, it is because life itself is often this way: problematic, ambiguous, and disappointing; but with promises of good as well. In any case, it is the task of the philosopher to study real existence to see what can be learned from it, not to conjure away its most conspicuous traits. Presumably, its lessons can be given greater scope and definition than is found in pre-philosophic experience.

Philosophers today, however, look for the conditions of moral reflection in some cut-off and attenuated part of the relevant whole: in reason, intuition, language, or moral sense, for example. Indeed, they typically resort to fictions, such as a contrived and artificial definition of a rational agent or in some notion of "ideal" choice conditions. No such contrivance warrants concern in the actual toils of the moral life, where individuals, for the very life of them, must take account of a complex plurality of conditions. This book will examine the nature of these conditions and their import for human practice.

A prime demand made upon the reader of this study is to think in some unaccustomed ways. At least this is so for those who spend their professional lives trudging through the technical literature. The ideas to be articulated are not inherently difficult; obstacles to understanding consist largely in the propensity of specialists to think in the terms that are common currency in their own circle. Both questions and answers become conventional. When familiar conventions are turned aside, the difficulty in grasping the new point of view has nothing to do with the alleged incommensurability of systems of ideas, but with the human tendency to think in routine ways.

While I have deep misgivings about all currently influential forms of moral theorizing, my study is by no means a creation *ex nihilo;* it is a reconstruction of a number of prominent themes from the history of moral thought. For those who believe a restoration of basic subject matter would be salutary, and who would be alert to the means of discerning and appropriating its teachings, the following chapters might be a happy beginning.

Atlanta, Georgia   James Gouinlock
September 14, 1992

1

Introduction

Moral philosophy presents a curious spectacle: to most reflective persons it is a crucial inquiry, indispensable to an ordered and genuinely human life. There must be, so it is thought, principles of reasoning and acting to determine what such a life would be. Yet here we are three or four millennia into the subject with, apparently, rather little to show for it. Controversy on vital moral questions exceeds consensus. When we look to philosophy, religion, popular opinion, or the discourse of intellectual or political opinion makers, we observe impassioned disagreement; and even where we find consensus there is commonly disagreement about what warrants it.

The fact that disagreement is impassioned indicates how urgent such issues are. Depth of feeling, indeed, has a way of overcoming doubt; confidence and even certitude about moral questions exist in abundance. Those who despair of moral certainty are in a distinct minority. Yet a reasonably detached observer cannot but notice that all these conflicting certainties suggest a futility in the enterprise of moral reflection. If moral theory is to be intellectually respectable, the subject matter which theory addresses must possess constraints of a sort that would lead conscientious thinkers to a defensible consensus. But this has not happened, and the lesson is frequently drawn that there is something inherently undisciplined about moral thought.

Moralists are not easily discouraged, however; they persist in the quest for the philosopher's stone. It is problematic whether they will find it. If we look at just the last two decades or so, we witness a succession of allegedly demonstrative or otherwise conclusive moral systems, each one refuting—or just ignoring—the others. The eager student finds himself suspecting that seemingly rigorous systems of thought are contrived to support antecedently beloved moral and political postures.

The persistence of moral philosophy reveals a deep human need. We don't like to think that our moral convictions are unfounded and arbitrary. Life without an unshakable moral good, we think, is not worth living; and many are inclined to believe that the decay and degeneracy that mark so many cultures is owing in large part to the absence of clear, shared, and largely incontestable moral principles. Given such need, and such chaos in moral reflection, one might wonder how we have survived.

But survive we have, although it is a matter of standards of expectation as to how successfully. Sometimes we get along tolerably well, even in communities that don't exercise thought control to maintain a moral regimen. Such successes suggest that somehow there must be, after all, some durable and reliable sources of order and consummation in the moral life; there must be some discipline to be discovered in it. Indeed there is. Whatever direction and success we enjoy are not attributable to abstract philosophy. We have derived them from the teachings of life itself—inchoate, incomplete, and disorganized as they might be. Here are the sources of discipline. Rather than search the heavens of reason for immutable principles, philosophers might deliberately seek and articulate such basic lessons of mortal *life* as might exist, and thereby give voice to truly efficacious teachings.

Without minimizing problems of the persistence of moral disagreement, we may, I believe, find resources in the moral life that have received insufficient attention and hence too little appreciation and use. This book will attempt to identify them. There decidedly are constraints on thought and action in the nature of things. While they, like the gallows, can be understood in a manner to concentrate the mind wonderfully, they do not determine just a single precise line of thought or action; yet they still provide clear and potent direction in conduct. The nature of things by no means affords unlimited alternatives. To be mindful of the limitations and imperatives, the effective resources, the well-tested potentialities resident within the moral life brings focus and teaching to our aspiration.

Moral Life and Philosophic Theory

A basic assumption of my discourse is that moral *life* brings forth and incorporates moral philosophy; it is not derivative of it. Moral reflection occurs when persons undergo experiences that are troubling and demand action. They are often of a recurring nature, so *ad hoc* adjustments become policies. Troubles come in the form of conflicts, injuries, and uncertainties; or there are frustrations in the discrimination and attainment of ends. Effective reflection on these matters extends far afield and becomes a principal source of philosophy. We are led to speculate about what sort of world it is that contains human existence, what place human life holds in the world, what sort of conditions are provided in the nature of things to explain our calamities, yearnings, and successes. Systematic inquiry into the inclusive human predicament yields theories of reality, theories of knowledge, logic, axiology, philosophical anthropology, and social philosophy among others. Thus human effort and aspiration might become enlightened to answer to our deepest needs. A worthwhile philosophy must be broad in scope; it must take the moral life as its point of departure; and its merit can be discovered only by determining its efficacies in that life.

Perhaps it is a truism to say that moral philosophy is a function of the moral life, but one would get little hint of it by reviewing the efforts of philosophers over the last fifty years. *A crippling lack in recent theory is its drastically truncated subject matter.* Philosophers have largely confined themselves to conceptual analysis or (worse) to the coherent ordering of moral "intuitions," or to defining almost out of thin air what it is "rational" to do. They even put great store in the analysis of ordinary language. Moral philosophers take as their subject matter just the preceding sorts of things, rather than the moral condition itself. The product of their exertions can be no more than an artifice: a trim definition of rational agency, for example, when there are in fact no such agents. Such artifices do not merit attention in actual moral life, where real individuals must, according to their lights, take account of a tangled plurality of existential concerns. The conduct of life can prosper only when it is undertaken in awareness of the manifold and perplexing characteristics of real life conditions—human and worldly conditions—in their fullness and complexity.

The subject matter of the present inquiry is the nature of the moral life in its own right, including its plentiful resources for reflective conduct. Lived moral experience is polyglot, disordered, confused. One is inescapably a participant in it but may well be ignorant or confused about its character. Decisive relations are unnoticed, intricate, hidden, conflicting, and seemingly infinite in number. Accordingly, reflection on the moral life yields an analysis unavailable in pre-philosophic experience. The analysis aims at a pertinent general characterization of that life. We distinguish its most salient features and their operations. Thus we have an account of what I call the moral condition.

The moral condition is a discriminated object, grasped as the outcome of observation, selection, and analysis. It is not an idea or abstraction; we have an idea *of* it. It is a real condition: that which is determinative of the moral life and fateful for it. The realities that pulsate through our real experience must find their place in any adequate account of the moral condition. When we have formulated some general ideas about these realities, we can use them to make the moral life more significant, free, and powerful. We can give it direction and chasten its pretensions, when need be, with realism.

Yet statements about the moral condition do not represent self-evident moral truths, entail prescriptions, or yield verifiable definitions of moral terms. Contrary to the dearest wishes of many philosophers, they can do none of these things. This conclusion does not imply the abandonment of moral philosophy, but stimulates the formulation of a distinctly different conception of it. A moral philosophy might discern the realities of human nature and the encompassing world that are pertinent to our strivings and likewise contrive methods of thought and action appropriate to them. Such a philosophy produces no universal prescriptions; but it places indispensable assumptions and instruments at the disposal of persons already caught up in the moral life, where they can be utilized to address its typical predicaments with improved chances of direction, harmony, and fulfillment.

Historic Investigations of the Moral Condition

Many philosophers have already searched the nature of things with moral intent. To most persons, indeed, what is chiefly engrossing in the history of speculation are the varied attempts to decipher the nature of reality and to see what it holds for human existence. Minds of the highest rank have supposed that in doing so they might produce or discover an objective warrant for conduct and aspiration. In effect, they have addressed the moral condition, and many of them have deeply engaged the moral interest by discerning its remarkable traits. Perhaps a cosmic order is identified that includes a highest good; or they have found in human nature, or in reason, inherent principles of action. These philosophers have likewise examined social relations to see whether they disclose implicit rules of behavior and have reflected upon the intellectual and practical means that nature makes available for the conduct of life.

The classic renditions have enthralled and inspired countless readers. Searches in various philosophies answer to many of our heartfelt questions. We want to know what are the ends and relations in life that might afford genuine well-being, what forms of human development are most auspicious for the ways and means of nature, what disciplines and methods we might adopt to enlighten and implement our choices. We must be wary of temptations and corruptions that are apt to befall us, and with all this we must have some reliable sense of the capabilities and limitations of human nature and institutions. These are the questions that draw most people to philosophy. What is urgent in, say, Aristotle or Marx are their conceptions of the ills and ideal fulfillments of human existence, rooted in the very nature of things. Such philosophies are more absorbing than Jeremy Bentham's utilitarianism or G. E. Moore's intuitionism precisely because they present such engaging hypotheses about human possibilities, about which Bentham and Moore are virtually silent, hence failing to excite the moral imagination. One may speculate as to whether a given moralist—Marx, for example—was a utilitarian, but the wisdom of such persons is hardly exhausted by discerning in them a decision procedure for ethics. Our moral interest is far deeper and more comprehensive than that.

Although we do not possess unfailing criteria of judgment and action, we are immeasurably aided by assessing information about the fateful circumstances of mortal existence. We treasure philosophies for addressing this concern with resourcefulness, scope, and penetration. Plato is the grand master of such ventures. How many souls have trembled at his matchless intimation of the path to complete human consummation? There is a principle of being, he says, and in each of us an innate longing and capability to achieve union with it, by which we attain wisdom, order, and happiness.

> For surely, Adeimantus, a man whose thoughts are fixed on true reality has no leisure to look downwards on the affairs of men, to take part in their quarrels, and to catch the infection of their jealousies and hates. He contemplates a world of unchanging and harmonious order, where reason governs and nothing can do or suffer wrong; and, like one who imitates an admired companion, he cannot fail to fashion himself in its likeness. So the philosopher, in constant companionship with the divine order of the world, will reproduce that order in his soul and, so far as man may, become godlike. . . .[1]

The cosmic order, we are told, is eternal and unchanging, and with the proper education it can be replicated in the philosopher, completing, unifying, and perfecting his inherent nature. Once known, the same order might be reproduced in the state, making it wholly just and virtuous, and making the state the vehicle for the perfection of all its citizens. Moreover, Plato admonishes, the further we deviate from conformity to the order, the further we fall into discord and misery. Ideas to conjure with, and conjure we have! If something like Plato's vision might be true, the search for it makes life unspeakably exciting.

Plato's project and those like it founder in many ways. If the characterization of the order of being is itself found wanting; or if an alleged good, such as Plato's ideal of human nature, is inherently controversial, our hopes are crushed. Or the philosopher might speak in timeless accents when, in fact, it may be that change is a fundamental trait of being; so we could never know a moral principle impervious to history. For post-Humeans, if there is no logical relation between statements about what exists and those about what we ought to do, the philosophic system fails to give proof for propositions that would direct our effort. Perhaps, indeed, moral judgments have no intersubjectively confirmable meaning.

If one finds all the sorts of objections in the preceding paragraph convincing, then he is suffering from an intellectual hardening of the arteries. Most philosophers of the last half century, however, have been stricken with such an affliction. Philosophers, of all people, have been prone to tunnel vision, and their narrowness has been such that they do not nourish our moral interest. There *are* several objections to Plato that are telling, but in crucial ways the general ambition of his philosophy is of permanent worth and pertinence; and the import of his thought is not compromised by, say, the persistence of the "is/ought" problem. The constraints and consummations of his system do not lie in the verifiable meanings of his moral vocabulary or in the logical relations between declarative and normative statements. *They lie in the nature of the reality that he portrays,* insofar as that portrayal is accurate. Would anyone have any hesitation about how to conduct his life if the nature of things would be responsive to us in the manner that Plato declares? This is not to deny the importance of accurate reasoning; it is to assert the paramount importance of *what reasoning would disclose:* the actual traits and possibilities of the human circumstance.

That particular portrayal is probably not accurate. The moral condition might be radically unlike what Plato thought it to be. It might have imperatives and promises of quite a different order. It might, indeed, be much more permissive—so permissive in fact that it harbors no constraints at all—or it might be subject to significant change. It might be simply unknowable, or not knowable in an uncontroversial form. In any case, a succession of philosophers has given alternative, often compelling, descriptions of the decisive elements of the inclusive environment and of the portentious involvement of human nature with them. We have pored over the implications of these accounts, and have revised, rejected, and supplanted them. Consider all the thought, anguish, and hope that have been stimulated by the Augustinian belief in the one transcendent God, the fallen nature of man, the necessity of divine grace for eternal salvation, and the threat of infinite punishment.

We can easily think of further examples: Epicurus, Aquinas, Spinoza, Hobbes, Kant, Hegel, and Nietzsche are among the company that readily comes to mind. It would be a great mistake to regard the work of these philosophers as nothing more than the attempt to provide the logic for perfect principles of conduct. Regarded in that light, indeed, all of them are failures. But they also produced superb characterizations of the resources, limitations, and possibilities of human life, so far as such could be determined in a given historical situation.

It is not so much the logic of, say, Hobbes's *Leviathan* that addresses our moral interest, but his dramatic account of the natural condition of mankind. If Hobbes is right, then we really have no choice but to settle for a social order that is a strictly enforced nonaggression pact. Like other conglomerates of matter, human beings can only stampede after their objects until thrust aside by superior force. The alternative to the pact is a war of all against all, and human beings may in any case aspire to nothing more than "a restless desire of power after power that ceaseth only in death."

While, according to Hobbes, there is no sanctuary in mortal life, Spinoza understands the world to be a place that offers peace and beatitude. His world view recommends the cultivation of human powers that have neither place nor worth in Hobbes's world. We can come to perfect knowledge of our place in the natural order and thereby be released from the slavery of passion. Knowledge of nature also provides the means to abiding human kinships. It would be important, to say the least, to know whether Hobbes or Spinoza is closer to the truth; we would conceive radically different ends and instrumentalities of life.

While lacking the beatific vision of Spinoza, Locke had a somewhat more genial idea of human nature than Hobbes: it is rational, industrious, remarkably self-sufficient, and knows its own good. All common endeavor may be well pursued on the basis of voluntary agreement. On such assumptions, we need not look to long-practiced custom, hallowed tradition, or trusted authority to guide our lives; and it is impertinent and destructive of human enterprise for the state to interfere in human activities, except to prevent fraud and violence.

Locke is not deserving of the last word. Further accounts of the relation of human striving to the nature of things could be multiplied, citing Vico, Kant, Hegel, Nietzsche, Royce, among others. In any case, the systems of philosophers insist that the realities of the world are not equally permissive to all forms of conduct. Certain kinds of behavior are rewarding and cumulatively enriching; others are frustrating and hurtful. More or less specific demands are made on us by the conditions of our existence. We have fairly definite resources for contending with them; we could even learn from philosophers how to deal with change in a deliberate and constructive manner.

The variety of philosophies is daunting, however. The formulation or adoption of a tolerably correct and morally usable world view seems a task of great difficulty, and we should acknowledge that legitimate controversy will persist. These are, nevertheless, cognitively meaningful inquiries, subject to various tests, criticisms, and revisions. Needless to say, some of these inquiries have now devolved into the care of such specialized fields as physics, psychology, biology, and social science; philosophers must (critically) incorporate the results of specialists into their theories.

On the other hand, the dimensions of the task needn't be exaggerated. I shall argue in due course that there are features of the moral condition that militate in favor of at least a minimally adequate way of life, and that they are relatively few and unobscure. One might elaborate or add to them in a variety of ways, and hence envision still richer possibilities, without rejecting the most fundamental lessons. It might be objected that even a carefully elaborated account of the moral condition would not yield enough detail or constraints to provide the direction we need to cope with the controversies and perplexities that haunt the moral life. That remains to be seen. In any case, the quest for minute detail and impeccable accuracy in rules of conduct is one of the great vices of moral philosophy.

The moral condition, then, is what is set forth in a philosophic analysis of the moral life. To use the language of William James, it is a *vision* of the moral life, with its demands, resources, and limitations. If I were to speak incautiously, I would call it a metaphysics of morals. I do not pretend to anything so splendid as a complete metaphysics of morals, yet I expect to say enough about the moral condition to exhibit some of its major practical lessons and its pertinence to moral theory. I will in part be parasitic on others, illustrating how they have, in effect, clarified or obscured vital features of the moral condition.

Absolutism, Relativism, Pluralism

One of the main theses of the following inquiry is that our choices in moral theory are not exhausted in defending, on the one hand, rational certitude in matters of principle or, on the other, complete despair for finding any order or harmony in the moral life. Acknowledging that they come in various forms, I call these alternatives, for the sake of simplicity, *absolutism* and *relativism.* There is a third choice, *pluralism,* which recognizes an irreducible plurality of moral criteria, with neither a fixed order of precedence among them nor an uncontroversial interpretation of what they imply for conduct in particular situations. Pluralism by no means implies anarchy, however. It is integral to a conception of the moral condition that supports the possession and exercise of a few conspicuously precious *virtues,* or dispositions to act. The determination and analysis of these virtues is an experimental process, predicated upon a study of the real constraints and opportunities of the moral life. None of these dispositions entails explicit and invariable rules. They preclude absolutism and at the same time provide highly potent resistances to the slide into relativism. Pluralism issues in a way of life. After the manner of many ancient and some modern moralists, a way of life, rather than specific rules of deportment, is suggested.

There are several ways of guiding conduct. One is by means of prescription. This has been the preferred mode for most philosophers, especially those of absolutistic pretensions. Another way is that of setting forth the conditions and potentialities of human endeavor, whether in the large or in reference to particular circumstances, so that individuals can respond to the existential constraints and opportunities that confront them in the moral life. This has also been widely practiced, but recently—by the attempt to reduce it to decisionism—it has been dismissed as a form of nihilism. To paraphrase Dewey, this method of moral guidance consists in the revelation and articulation of the meanings of experience, making them coherent and perspicuous.[2]

Just as in the examples of philosophies already presented, Aristotle's vision of the good life, Marx's description of alienated labor, or Dewey's characterization of the organic connection of growth and community each calls forth a highly affective response and inspires specific inquiries and plans of action. Thoughts about the prospects of life and programs of implementation vary as our belief in the adequacy of such images varies. In due course I will argue that the prescriptive method must collapse into the method of articulating the meanings of life experience and that this method provides us with ample means for the conduct of life. We need not lead the moral life by subscribing to a set of putatively omnicompetent principles. We may cultivate a more or less well-defined cluster of practices and dispositions that seem well suited to meet the distinctive demands and promises of moral experience. They will neither be uniformly fixed nor invariably coherent with one another, and they will not free us from tragedy, error, and regret. Such a condition is beyond all human resource. Yet we fashion a manner of life all the same, adjusting it, if we can, as the lessons of experience, learning, and analysis demand. Such education may be well suited to the moral condition.

Pluralism, as we shall see, does not require absolute fixity in one's convictions; hence it is not refuted by failure to establish a given judgment beyond reservation. It is therefore incompatible with dogmatism and intolerance, yet it is anything but permissive regarding a very wide range of human conduct that is destructive of life and happiness. An adequately articulated pluralism can provide us with legitimate confidence in many of our convictions—sufficient to trust in their worthiness; to exult in them; to live and, if need be, to die for them. There is no philosopher's stone, but that leaves us with more than sand.

Pluralism has never been fully articulated and defended. Still less has it been studied in a manner to yield a way of life.[3] The almost invariant concerns of moralists have been with absolutism and relativism. A prescription for moral behavior that will be proof against all rational assault has been the fascination of many intellects. Somehow a rule or principle of action shall be determined that will make it clear, exact, and unarguable what ought to be done; or specific rights will be certainly established with precisely determined implications for conduct. Individuals must accept the moral claim as binding on them as surely as they must accept *cogito ergo sum.* Plato is commonly regarded as engaged in such a venture, and perhaps he was. Kant clearly belongs to this camp, and so do many of the prominent current writers. This quest is typically distinguished by the search for a single and all-decisive moral norm, such as the form of the Good, the commandment of a deity, the nature of a rational agent, the determination of ideal conditions of choice, or—however implausible it might sound—the inherent logic of our moral vernacular.

It is also characteristic of this school to assume that if the search for the Archimedean point fails, judgment becomes capricious and arbitrary, and we really couldn't speak of morality in the strict sense at all. In the sixth book of the *Republic,* Plato writes,

> For you have often been told that the highest object of knowledge is the essential nature of the Good, from which everything that is good and right derives its value for us. You must have been expecting me to speak of this now, and to add that we have no sufficient knowledge of it. I need not tell you that, without that knowledge, to know everything else, however well, would be of no value to us. . . . (trans. Cornford)

Likewise for a contemporary writer of note, Alan Gewirth, nothing less than a logically necessary supreme moral principle stands between us and chaos. Lacking such a principle

> would mean that behind the claims to correctness found in differing moral judgments there are only insoluble conflicts, and that the only recourse is to a radical relativism in which the conflicting judgments made by different persons or groups are left at that: they are made by different persons or groups.[4]

There is a clear tendency, accordingly, to say that moral philosophy has to be given up altogether if such an enterprise fails. Thus absolutism and relativism are the Janus faces of the same assumption. (If Gewirth is right that our alternatives are either apodictic certainty or utter chaos, and if we have heretofore lacked the ultimate moral principle, then how has it happened that we have so often avoided chaos?)

Absolutists, of course, have been subjected to familiar sorts of criticism, and so have the relativists. The dogged absolutist, determined to produce some sort of moral science, resists the nihilism of his kindred adversary. For his part, the relativist has little else but to assume a reactive posture: he skillfully punctures the pretensions of his opposite number but has nothing positive with which to supplant them.

I will have criticisms of each camp, but they are not merely rehearsals of the struggles already carried on between the two. The artifices of the absolutist have been criticized by the relativist, but not *as* artifices. The relativist will focus on the failure of the absolutist, for example, to provide the true definition of rational agency. The relativist, apparently, would accept such a definition if it were shown to be conclusive. I contend, by contrast, that the whole process is wildly impertinent. My objections will have a distinctive quality imparted by the character of pluralism. Ultimately, I evaluate from the standpoint of an articulated account of the moral condition. In this, as in other ways, my notion of pluralism is distinguished from others by reference to primary characteristics of the moral life.

Most recent philosophers have labored without a subject matter of much consequence. Hence many of the concerns of traditional moral philosophers, and of their devoted readers, have been rejected as futile or irrelevant. The attempt to formulate basic assumptions about the relationship between man and the world (going beyond merely epistemological inquiry) is at issue. The following chapters will resurrect some of these concerns, in perhaps unconventional ways, to indicate not just their respectability but their importance. Indeed, chapter 2, "Philosophy and the Moral Interest," is offered as a prime exhibit of the moral significance of such basic inquiries. It presents some of the principal contributions of some philosophers from the classic period in American philosophy: William James, George Santayana, and John Dewey. I have no thought to provide thumbnail sketches of their supposed ethical theories, as would typically be done in reference to such thinkers. These are generic philosophies, directed to a discernment and understanding of the salient characteristics of the human scene, and they were intended to fortify practical effort. These philosophers elucidated the moral condition and thereby added to our power to address moral perplexity, to distinguish the values most suitable to our situation, and to realize them in conduct. In this undertaking, they engaged more inclusive and compelling interests than are dreamt of in current academic philosophy. Some of these ideas will be incorporated into my own accounting of the moral condition; but more than this, the reader will acquire some fuller sense of what it means to explore the moral condition and search out its lessons for thought and aspiration.

No one doubts that, somehow, facts and values are vital companions in the moral life; but recent philosophic discussion of them has been exhausted in trying to figure out whether normative statements have any logical connection to descriptive ones. Chapter 3, "Knowing and Valuing," urges that this is an unhappy preoccupation. Such devotions shed no light on the moral condition and afford inadequate consideration of the ways in which our impressive cognitive resources can effectively bear upon real moral concerns. This chapter, the two succeeding it, and the concluding one include accounts of what the forms of pluralism are and why they are inescapable features of the moral condition.

Another familiar subject is that of moral language, which has by now become rather tiresome even to its devotees. Judging by the treatments it has received, the fatigue is understandable. But, despite the spinning of wheels of metaethical philosophies and their accompanying schemes of moral reasoning, it turns out to be a theme of highest moment. "Moral Judgment and Discourse," chapter 4, acknowledges that our power of communication is immensely important, but philosophers have scarcely identified the nature of its real efficacies in the moral life. I undertake to do so, emphasizing that the activity of discourse in concrete circumstances has unrecognized potentialities. In order for discourse to prove itself a consummate instrument of the moral condition, moreover, it must be conceived in a way to make it organic to the varied and multiform constraints and promises of the moral life itself.

Chapter 5 is on moral relations. Once again, the aim is to understand and characterize the moral condition with practical intent. Philosophers are understandably given to using moral conceptions, but their reflections tend to be directed at just these abstractions as such. To get some purchase on the moral life, however—on its real values, obstacles, perplexities, and opportunities—we must analyze the primary subject matter itself. In "Moral Relations" I undertake to characterize the range of typical life conditions that give rise to such talk of rights, duties, goods, justice, and so forth. Here, in the bowels of real existence, yearning for power and light, we are caught up in those natural relations that are denoted by distinctively moral predicates. Such relations of the moral condition must be recognized, studied, and appreciated, otherwise we are helpless to prosecute the moral life effectively.

A pivotal constituent of the moral condition is, of course, human nature itself. The old question "Wherein is morality by nature or by convention?" remains urgent. Yet it is scandalously neglected in the present age. Philosophers, indeed, hardly know what to make of the question. Accordingly, in the sixth chapter, "Moral Philosophy and Human Nature," I investigate the *various* ways in which our assumptions about human nature can legitimately be incorporated into moral philosophy. Lately, inquirers from beyond the tidy precincts of philosophy have had the good sense to engage these issues, but they have tended to be rather awkward in pursuing them. Perhaps my reflections would bring greater sureness and pertinence to their admirable efforts, and perhaps philosophers would find it respectable to join in. Although I am not so bold as to speak the definitive truth about human nature, I am willing to make at least a few confident assertions about where our knowledge of the beast can take us in addressing some fundamental moral controversies.

The study of some main features of the moral life will, at this point, have gone far enough to permit some systematic analysis of characteristic philosophies. That is, at the end of chapter 6 there is sufficient grasp of the moral condition to demonstrate its pertinence to an appraisal of some familiar theories and *modes* of theorizing. Hence chapter 7, "Prejudicial Simplifications of the Moral Condition." I begin with a classic archetype, Kant, and proceed to a selection of contemporary major offenders: John Rawls, Jürgen Habermas, and Richard Rorty. (I might also have treated of MacIntyre, who is not so much an offender against the moral condition but is still liable to serious criticism. I found it more pertinent to comment on his work in chapter 3.) My observations about these thinkers do not follow the ruts worn by other critics, whose reflections are sometimes incisive; my point is to evaluate philosophies insofar as they proceed in ignorance of the moral condition and would do violence to many of its precious values.

At the beginning of the final chapter, "Ways of Life," the moral condition has been portrayed with enough fairness and thoroughness, I judge, to reach some reliable conclusions about what instruments are most appropriate to it. Universal and invariant moral principles are inapt for our generic moral situation. Rather, the cultivation and exercise of certain *virtues* is maintained. These are rationality, courage, and respect for persons, each configured in a way that befits our condition. As they will be characterized, they are well suited for conducting the *processes* of the moral life in all their variations, uncertainties, and demands. They cannot give rational finality to, or bring an end to, moral predicaments. Nothing can do that. Any understanding of virtue that would pretend to such outcomes would compound our moral problems and drive us into warring sects. But virtues can be construed in such a way that, realistically, they can be both attractive and highly efficacious; and their exercise can give us a deep assurance of moral competence.

These topics may sound familiar, but I remind the reader that I do not address them from within contemporary paradigms of moral theory. My pursuit is in the direction of a usable moral world view. While this pursuit has many exemplars in the history of philosophy, it is generously informed with what I take to be the spirit of Aristotle and classic American pragmatism.[5] Some positions that I will advance are deliberately named for Aristotle or pragmatism, but my indebtedness is on the whole less specific. The emphasis on virtue is Aristotelian, of course (and virtue is more crucial for Dewey than most scholars are aware). Even more fundamentally, there is in Aristotle a determination to know the realities of the world, a determination that will not give way to easy pieties or wishful thinking. Especially in the magnificent *Politics,* he practices the mode of thought that would found human effort and bright hope on the most unblinking study of the conditions of natural life. Dewey, too, philosophizes much in this manner, but he is more inclined than Aristotle to let his enthusiasms run ahead of his evidence. Like both James and Dewey, I suffer deep tremors of uneasiness in the presence of philosophic abstractions. But what I find most valuable in the pragmatists is their intense recognition that we inhabit a changing and precarious world that offers a plurality of goods, promises novel dangers and opportunities, and affords neither certainty nor finality to vital belief. At the same time, the pragmatists formulated a conception of intelligence appropriate to this environment; and in this signal task they have exceeded all others, contriving a great human resource.

Whatever the amalgam of philosophies, my aim is not to recapitulate them but to seize hold of whatever wisdom I can to distinguish the most trustworthy instruments for the conduct of life. The intended result of the study, to put it in an abstract way, is to avoid the equally unattractive options of absolutism and relativism, while providing sufficient knowledge of the moral condition for individuals to act with intelligent and sustaining resolve. At the same time, I hope to make some contribution to reorienting the practice of moral philosophy to more apposite and engaging tasks. It might look for its appropriate discipline in concerns far more inclusive than those exhibited in its recent literature.

As I reflect on the program I have set forth, I am prompted to think how uncongenial it is apt to be to the contemporary sophisticate in moral theory. I am reminded of a remark of James. When introducing one of his extraordinary ideas, he muses on how unacceptable it will seem to the orthodox: "Regrettable as is the loss of readers capable of such wholesale discipleship, I feel that a definite meaning [for this idea] is even more important than their company."[6] Current moral philosophy is widely judged by its practitioners to be innovative and accomplished, and sometimes it is even taken seriously beyond the confines of academic departments. For my part, I take moral philosophy today to be largely in vain. Many other philosophers, and reflective people generally, are impatient with its artificiality and thinness, but they don't know what there is to take its place. Perhaps what I have to say will prompt some readers to look for more promising ways to conceive our moral life, reflection, and aspiration.

Notes

1. Plato, *The Republic,* translated with introduction and notes by F. M. Cornford (Oxford: Oxford University Press, 1945), pp. 208–209.
2. "We are weak today in ideal matters because intelligence is divorced from aspiration. The bare force of circumstance compels us onwards in the daily detail of our beliefs and acts, but our deeper thoughts and desires turn backwards. When philosophy shall have cooperated with the course of events and made clear and coherent the meaning of the daily detail, science and emotion will interpenetrate, practice and imagination will embrace. Poetry and religious feeling will be the unforced flowers of life. To further this articulation and revelation of the meanings of the current course of events is the task and problem of philosophy in days of transition." Dewey, *Reconstruction in Philosophy,* in *John Dewey: The Middle Works, 1899–1924;* volume 12: 1920, edited by Jo Ann Boydston (Carbondale and Edwardsville: Southern Illinois University Press), p. 201. All references to the writings of Dewey will be cited by giving title and volume number from *Early Works, Middle Works,* and *Later Works.* All are published by Southern Illinois University Press and edited by Jo Ann Boydston.
3. More or less recent examples of pluralism include Isaiah Berlin, *Four Essays on Liberty* (Oxford: Oxford University Press, 1969); Thomas Nagel, *Mortal Questions* (Cambridge: Cambridge University Press, 1979);

Bernard Williams, *Ethics and the Limits of Philosophy* (Cambridge, Mass.: Harvard University Press, 1985); and Charles Larmore, *Patterns of Moral Complexity* (Cambridge: Cambridge University Press, 1987). A recent number of *Ethics* (102, no. 4 [July, 1992]) is also devoted to this subject. These studies have in common a (laudable) desire to curb the pretensions of overweaning moralists. These pluralists do not, however, make a thorough examination of the nature and diversity of moral relations; nor do they make much of an investigation of the resources of pluralism for the moral life.

4. Alan Gewirth, *Reason and Morality* (Chicago: The University of Chicago Press, 1978), p. 7.

5. I would make a clear and sharp distinction between *classic* American pragmatism and the corrupt version propagated by Richard Rorty. See my "What is the Legacy of Instrumentalism? Rorty's Interpretation of Dewey," in the *Journal of the History of Philosophy* 28, no. 2 (April, 1990): 252–269.

6. William James, *The Principles of Psychology*, Vol. 2 (Cambridge, Mass.: Harvard University Press, 1981), p. 1223.

2

Philosophy and the Moral Interest

In a book highly critical of recent scholarship, the late Walter Kaufmann spoke of a work on Nietzsche by a well-known contemporary philosopher. Among the remarks Kaufmann made about the volume was that it "turned Nietzsche into a stammering Oxonian—and thus made him accessible to analytical philosophers."[1] Nietzsche's thought had been forced into a certain stereotype of what it is that philosophers are supposed to do; judged against that stereotype, it was found wanting. Nietzsche has not been the only victim of such philosophic analysis. In several fields the prevailing paradigms have served to obscure many of the main accomplishments of philosophy. Perhaps it is due to such paradigms that many contemporary philosophers appear to be unwilling or unable to learn from the history of their subject. In any event, they seem to have made little effort to find out what can be appropriated from the inquiries of their predecessors.

I have in mind in particular the disregard of the many dimensions of moral philosophy. Scholars who have written appraisals of the ethical philosophies of this century have failed to see much of what has been accomplished of permanent importance. Countless books and articles reflect similar neglect and misunderstanding. Although some writers are now showing more respect for their forebears, the results are still rather slender. Some will say that starting with the work of Rawls or Gewirth, moral thought has resumed its traditional responsibilities. This is true only in small part, for even the most recent paradigms suffer from making concepts or (obscurely conceived) intuitions, rather than the moral life, their subject matter. Many vital questions continue to lie fallow.

31

The Neglect of History

The lack of insight into what moral philosophy might contribute has left some weighty resources in our tradition unheeded. The most recent casualties are American philosophers of solid and striking achievement, men who understood the moral condition well and who exacted major lessons from their study of it. Yet within the past thirty years, five books were published that purported to review the principal accomplishments in ethics in the preceding hundred years, up to 1970; and none of them showed any recognition of these achievements. While none pretended to be a full-fledged history, they all claimed to cover the main issues and accomplishments. They are G. J. Warnock, *Contemporary Moral Philosophy;* Mary Warnock, *Ethics since 1900;* George Kerner, *The Revolution in Ethical Theory;* W. D. Hudson, *Modern Moral Philosophy;* and Roger L. Hancock, *Twentieth Century Ethics.*[2] Typical of all these authors, G. J. Warnock writes, "The aim of this essay is to provide a compendious survey of the moral philosophy in English since about the beginning of the present century."[3] All these discussions are principally concerned— one might say overwhelmed—with one issue: the meaning and use of moral language; that is, with metaethics, where the prize would be a solution to the is/ought problem. The concerns of philosophers like James, Dewey, and Santayana are nonexistent in this extra- ordinarily provincial and ignorant literature. Neither G. J. Warnock nor Hudson devotes so much as a word to such figures. Kerner devotes a single paragraph to one of them, Dewey. It is not clear that Kerner has read Dewey; he has read Morton White's influential article, "Value and Obligation in Dewey and Lewis,"[4] which he accepts without any suspicion that White's analysis might be in any way misconceived. Mary Warnock's chapter on emotivism deals at some length with C. L. Stevenson, and it is only for the sake of elucidating his position that she makes passing (and erroneous) reference to James and Dewey, whom she regards as among the sources of Stevenson's noncognitivism. Hancock has more interest than the others in San- tayana and Dewey, but his exclusive concern with them is to discern what metaethical position they evidently held.

The failure of these studies even to recognize the philosophic resources for the moral life developed by James, Santayana, and Dewey is total. Their failure to understand Dewey has been abetted by the authority of White and Stevenson. Both are highly reputed, and both have expressed high regard for Dewey, yet both have reluctantly concluded that his position is fatally flawed. But both interpreters are fundamentally mistaken. I have treated their analyses systematically in my article "Dewey's Theory of Moral Deliberation."[5] Fundamentally, White's problem is that he takes Dewey to be one of those pursuing a solution to the is/ought problem. Not only was Dewey not in that pursuit, he explicitly repudiated it as a throwback to the Platonic tradition. Stevenson's misreading complements that of White. He, too, focuses on the problematic character of Dewey's use of moral language, and he also says Dewey's ethical theory is too individualistic: Dewey has no way of addressing interpersonal conflict. This is said of the man who is frequently called the philosopher of democracy, the one who wrote so extensively on the sort of education and institutions that determine the habits and virtues vital to democratic life.[6]

In contrast to these accounts, I will review some of the accomplishments from the "golden age" of American philosophy, particularly those of James and Dewey. I will also give some brief attention to Santayana. Although he had much in common with James and Dewey, he was not a pragmatist. As a moral philosopher, he drew heavily from Aristotle, and this is a legacy worth preserving.[7]

The ideas selected to be summarized from these three are central to our grasp of the moral life and its resources; no fully comprehensive account of the moral condition would be adequate without consideration of them. For my own purposes, what I most want to appropriate is their conception of nature as the scene of both contingency and order, hazard and promise, resource and limit. But I do not confine the present exposition to just that. In any case, there is much wisdom to be found in them, yet one would get not an inkling of this achievement by perusing the pages of mainstream scholarship; so a precious heritage is little noted or appreciated.

These are not ethical theories. They are inclusive philosophies, possessed of moral insight and directed to an elucidation of the entire human estate. Their import is to aid us in understanding that estate in such a manner that we might prosper in it, so far as that is possible. To intimate some sense of their task and achievement, I will provide a summary account of their intellectual environment. This will be followed by a selective discussion of metaphysics, philosophy of experience, philosophical anthropology, philosophy of value, and philosophy of intelligence. These are distinctions of convenience. As we shall see, the issues in focus in any one grouping are inseparably related to those in others, giving evidence of the organic structure of their thought.

The Context of Classical American Philosophy

The challenges to philosophy that have arisen since the mid-nineteenth century are unprecedented. Consider a few of the changes that have occurred since 1859, the year of the publication of *The Origin of Species*. The theory of biological evolution affronted the values associated with beliefs regarding man's status in the universe and toppled the rational theology predicated on the harmonious relations between living beings and the natural environment. The downfall of Newtonian physics reinforced these developments, for it, too, led to the abandonment of the notion of individual, self-contained substances, each with its inherent essence (including a human essence). Likewise falling with the Newtonian and pre-Darwinian world view was the notion that there is a fixed and permanent order in the universe. Everything is in a process of change, and many earnest thinkers could perceive no underlying *telos* in this process. Change, accordingly, was meaningless. Nature was widely thought of as a lifeless, purposeless mass of atoms, themselves subject to transformation; and on this inconceivably remote and tiny planet, swarms of living organisms seemed to have no function but to struggle with each other to reproduce a pointless existence.[8]

While our conceptions of human nature and the world were being forced into drastic revisions, the human swarm struggled in unprecedented chaos. Social structures have been precarious and volatile, and change seems inevitably to be accompanied by war and further chaos. As if to corroborate the plentiful historical evidence, Freud inaugurated an inquiry that had the effect of giving scientific support to the notion that man is governed not by reason but by unruly passion.

This is also a period of astounding scientific and technological advance. (Dewey died in 1952, witnessing the onset of the nuclear age. At the time of his birth in 1859, we did not have radio, the telephone, the electric light, or a workable internal combustion engine.) Many could believe that science is the sorcerer's apprentice, and insofar as it led to a reduced self-image of man and to further doubts about his fate, science as such became an object of suspicion in many quarters. Many philosophies have reacted by taking the view that scientific inquiry is inherently limited: there are higher truths, inaccessible to scientific scrutiny.

There were a number of prominent philosophic ideas in this environment. They proved in time to be inadequate to the realities of experience, and they had to be addressed as part of the philosophic response to historical conditions. At the turn of the century, absolute idealism was the dominant philosophy in Europe, England, and America. It was also a moral world view, largely dedicated to preserving spiritual values. According to the idealists, reality is nothing but a rational system of ideas, the very being of which is constituted by the thinking of the absolute mind—the Absolute. Knowledge of the Absolute is attained, presumably, by a purely rational logic. Reasoning from any conceivable phenomenon of existence is compelled onward by alleged contradictions.[9] But contradictions, of course, are "really" impossible. We arrive at the Absolute by proceeding from contradiction to contradiction, incorporating ever greater syntheses. In the ultimate synthesis, all contradictions are reconciled in the whole, having, then, no real existence *as* contradictions. The essential nature of the Absolute is perfect, eternal, and unchanging.

The very existence of the temporal world is constituted by the self-knowledge of the Absolute. Inasmuch as the Absolute is utterly one and coherent, any event in creation is determined by nothing less than the entire system of reality as such. The whole is in every part, and each part is expressed in the very whole. Given the further assumption that rational essence is alone real—has being in the ultimate sense—then the Absolute alone has true being. Inasmuch as the really real is timeless, change and novelty—indeed, all deficiencies of being—are not, strictly speaking, real. They are excused from true being as mere appearance. By this thinking, evil and error are expunged from reality. All the processes of nature, in their plurality, incompleteness, imperfection, disorder, and conflict, are not what they seem. They are a *mere* seeming.

According to this philosophy, the good of man consists in conformity to the real, that is, conformity to an antecedently fixed and independent essence. Self-realization according to Bradley, for example, is complete identification with the Absolute. The highest *ethical* level of existence, he says, is conformity to "my station and its duties"; i.e., conformity to the social status quo. There are contradictions in the ethical, however. Complete self-realization is in the religious stage, Bradley continues, where conformity to absolute reality is complete, without contradiction, without lack.

Apart from idealism, which denies the real existence of matter, a main feature of the philosophic landscape was Cartesian dualism: the division of all being into two wholly different natures—thinking substance and material substance. The essential nature of one substance is utterly independent of the nature of the other, and the means of access of either to the other is opaque to human wit. Mind is impervious to matter and matter to mind.

Organic to the Cartesian legacy and common to all philosophies that were influential at the time, including idealism, was the assumption that experience is subjective. In other words, our experience is not of real things in the external world, but just of the content of our own minds. We can know the world, if at all, only by (a tortured) inference. The properties of the world, moreover, are not what they seem to be. According to one's philosophic predilections, nature is *only* a rational order of ideas, as supposed in the idealist reduction or, from the dualist position, it is matter in motion and *only* matter in motion. According to the latter view, nature has only the properties that can be described in exclusively mathematical terms; according to the former, nature is *just* rational. Either way, the other properties that nature seems to have are really "in the mind" and nowhere else. Experience, consequently, is an impenetrable fortress that imprisons each individual from direct converse with extra-subjective reality; and by itself it gives no clue as to what might be going on outside the walls.

Finally, this experience was thought to be comprised of a mass of atomic sensations. It occurs in little bits, and wholly unrelated bits at that. From any one atom of experience we can infer none other. This pulverized mass is put together not by any relations intrinsic to the properties of objective events, but by alleged mental laws of association, or in the mind of the Absolute.

Such characterizations of experience bear no resemblance to the experience that we mortals just have. In our nonphilosophic moments, we take for granted that we are participating in a world possessing a marvelous array of qualities and contingencies. The subtle play of colors on the water, the aroma of flowers, the warmth of a handclasp, the ringing of young voices, the kindness of a stranger, the wickedness of an official, the disorders and ruptures of nature—all are quintessentially real to us, and they provide us our motives for evaluation and conduct. We believe the occurrence of such events is dependent upon certain conditions. That is, there are real relations in nature, and they are discoverable. One event becomes significant of others and perhaps subject to deliberate enjoyment.

"So much the worse for experience!" chant the modern philosophers in chorus. In place of the exuberant richness, confusion, and significance of the real world, they insist on the dualism of subjective and objective. Nature remains a cipher, a blankness; over against it stands experience—meaningless, isolated, and impotent—and possessing no powers of action. Such was the philosophic view of things a hundred years ago.

A number of philosophers had conspicuous success in responding to this world, as presented in science, the arts, history, and philosophy. This experience called forth an extraordinary response from such thinkers as Peirce, James, Santayana, Dewey, and Mead, to name some of the most distinguished. They did not all respond in the same way or to the same events. Santayana, for instance, was more stimulated than the others by the state of religion, poetry, and literature. Their respective lifetimes were not identical either: James, for example, died forty-two years ahead of Dewey. Although there are noteworthy differences in their ideas, their inquiries took them to fundamental philosophic issues; their (sometimes varied) treatments of them do much to quicken the moral interest; and reflection on their contributions does much to enlighten human adventure. As noted earlier, attention will be given to James and Dewey, with some reference to Santayana. It could as well be more fully devoted to Santayana, or incorporate much of Peirce and Mead. My aim is not to produce a full-scale study, but to be selective and to illustrate the moral quality of their philosophies.

Worldly Metaphysics: The Traits of Existence that Matter

William James was repulsed by absolute idealism. It denied to reality the most conspicuous and fateful characteristics of existence. A world in which there are manifestly so many different, unrelated, and conflicting things going on doesn't seem to be systematic in the manner that idealism supposes. Natural processes are plural, unfinished, tending to uncertain outcomes. They are supportive of life in many ways and hurtful in others, and they are not dissolved into the "block universe," as James dubbed the absolutist conception.[10] Variations in the rings of Saturn have no bearing on the miseries of the inner city; the failure of the lettuce crop in Florida has nothing to do with the invention of the steam engine; the outcome of the World Series is unaffected by the birth rate in China; my scholarly research is unrelated to your stymied love affair; when a sparrow falls in England, the prime rate of interest in America pays no heed. The goods and bads of each situation do not implicate the entire universe; we may address our problems short of trying to move the Absolute. We participate in a diverse plurality of processes which, depending on human resolve, thought, and effort, might be directed to one end rather than another. For their part, however, the idealists tell us that reality is complete and perfect just as it stands, and that the Absolute, which constitutes the really real, is unmoved by human agency. We need only conform to it. James writes of idealism,

> It substitutes a pallid outline for the real world's richness. It is dapper, it is noble in the bad sense, in the sense in which to be noble is to be inapt for humble service. In this real world of sweat and dirt, it seems to me that when a view of things is "noble," that ought to count as a presumption against its truth, and as a philosophic disqualification.[11]

The idealist philosophy removed zest, adventure, risk, uncertainty, evil, and creative agency from the moral condition, leaving a pleasant but impotent apologetic in their place. For his part, James could not apologize for the very existence of the experienced world, much less explain it away. Rather, he was convinced that change, novelty, and the vicissitudes of human fortune are at the very heart of reality. Hence his devastating critiques of idealism, his formulations of pluralism and process, and his conception of a world in which disaster and triumph are equally real and equally possible. "I find myself willing to take the universe to be really dangerous and adventurous, without therefore backing out and crying 'no play.' " The genuine pragmatist, he continues, "is willing to live on a scheme of uncertified possibilities which he trusts; willing to pay with his own person, if need be, for the realization of the ideals which he frames."[12]

Dewey was inspired by James's critique of the block universe in particular and in general by his insistence of not obscuring or denying the realities of experience.[13] He advanced James's critique on a broader front, launching a wide-ranging reconstruction of what he called the classic tradition. A rich network of assumptions distinguishes the tradition, including its obsession with certainty, but Dewey was perhaps most disturbed by its denial of change—its conviction that the universe in its essential nature is fixed and changeless. It begins (at least) with Parmenides, but its all-time champion is Plato. In Dewey's formative years it found expression in idealism. As in idealism, change is relegated to an inferior and contingent realm of being or is regarded as an aberration of the eternal order.

Throughout the tradition, the moral imperative is that change be arrested or channeled to conform to the antecedently given nature of true being, or of changeless, autonomous reason. For Plato there is the heaven of ideas, eternally perfect and unblinking, knowable by unaided reason. Juxtaposed to the realm of the forms is the experienced world, the realm of change and contingency—of becoming. Processes of change are in themselves unknowable, but they are knowable in a derivative sense in relation to the forms, because events in the contingent world may be classified in reference to the ideal archetypes. The forms are likewise necessary for the act of evaluation. Experienced occasions can be unerringly judged as good or just by classifying them as somehow participating in the forms of the good and the just. Temporal institutions and the human soul attain their true end by being brought into agreement with the eternal.

This mode of thought has been manifested in various ways. Its stock in trade is fixed essences, perhaps lodged in substances, holding the nature of the universe in rigid order. In moral thought it is manifest not only in Platonism, but in various theological systems; theories of natural law and natural right; and of course in the philosophy of Kant, who believed that reason produces a single, universal, necessary, and omnicompetent imperative. The nineteenth-century theory that laissez-faire capitalism expresses the true order of nature is another example. A further claim in this assortment is the Marxian supposition that the seemingly heterogeneous processes of history follow a single invariant law. Dewey included utilitarianism in this manner of philosophizing, for it insisted on a single and unchanging end as the sole criterion of moral judgment.[14]

If there were this eternal and unchanging being, if it were knowable, and if its nature were also the standard of perfection, then the general aims of life would be fixed, clear, and luminously attractive; but if the basic assumption of the classic tradition is mistaken, belief in it would be hurtful. Adhering to the alleged standard would in fact be complying with the prejudice of a given time and place, given philosophic and/or religious sanction.

Dewey found the arguments in behalf of changeless being to be without warrant, and he deployed the evidence of the sciences to support the reality of change. (Moreover, the remarkable diversity of renditions of pure being is not reassuring to students of the tradition.) He did not deny the notions of order, permanence, and form altogether, but gave them a new ontological status. His analyses of these concepts were in fact highly sophisticated.[15] For our purposes, the most important point is this: there *are* constancies and uniformities in nature; *they are the correlations between processes of change.* Variations in one process are correlated with variations in another, and the correlations appear to be regular and predictable. There is a definite relation, for example, between the variations in pressure and temperature in an enclosed volume of gas; variations in the gravitational attraction between objects are correlated with variations in mass and distance; and so on. As the constituents in natural processes are varied, so, too, are their outcomes. Such changes are predictable insofar as we determine how a process is modified by the introduction of new conditions. Experimental science is the search for such correlations, and it typically proceeds by deliberate introduction and control of variations. Inasmuch as there are seemingly infinite variations that nature can undergo, its creativity and novelties are readily accounted for.

According to Dewey's analysis, order and contingency do not belong to disparate realms of being. In *Experience and Nature,* where they are designated generically as the stable and the precarious, they are understood as a function of the same natural matrix.[16] The stable refers, among other things, to established and known connections and correlations between events. The precarious refers to events that are threatening, obtrusive, unexpected, inexplicable, and the like—what Dewey more often refers to as the problematic. These are obvious and inescapable traits of existence that all persons must contend with. Life *is* precarious, highly precarious: from flat tires, spoiled milk, and unexpected visitors to disease, drought, poverty, and war. Such events do not occur miraculously, however, nor are they situated in a realm apart from order and regularity. They are continuous with the rest of nature. Each is part of a particular system of relations, a product of complex conditions. Each belongs, that is, to interdependent processes of change, the correlations of which are in principle discoverable.

To investigate an event in its continuities, accordingly, is to attempt to convert it to the status of the stable, to discover its determinate relations. There is no requirement for an ascent to the empyrean, which has no facilities for varying and directing the hurlyburly of natural events. If Dewey's conception of nature is correct, we might control natural contingencies in order to direct change to a desired end. We can work intelligently at healing the sick, establishing systems of production, allaying poverty, and preventing war. Generically, the problem of life is to function effectively *with* processes of change, rather than to evade them or arrest them to an antecedent fixity of being.[17]

If there is any merit in these views of James and Dewey, then it is critical to our fortunes to recognize that pluralism, change, and the continuity of order and the problematic are fundamental characters of the moral condition. I take it to be the part of wisdom to embrace such a view. Their discussion suggests that both James and Dewey regarded their explorations as fundamentally moral in intent—moral not in the sense of yielding specific rules of conduct, but in answering to the human concern with having an orientation to the fundamental qualities of existence so that one might determine how one should live.

Santayana's intent was likewise moral. Like James and Dewey, he judged the touchstone of any philosophy to be its assumptions about the generic human condition. "The first philosophers were accordingly sages. They were statesmen and poets who knew the world and cast a speculative glance at the heavens, the better to understand the conditions and limits of human happiness. . . . Such was philosophy in the beginning and such is philosophy still."[18] Displaying his particular temperamental bent, he writes,

> Against avarice, lust, and rancour, against cruel and vain national ambitions, tenderer and more recollected minds have always sought some asylum; but they have seldom possessed enough knowledge of nature and of human life to distinguish clearly the genuine and innocent goods which they longed for, and their protest against "the world" has too often taken on a mystical and irrational accent. . . . Every man is necessarily the seat of his own desires, which, if truly fulfilled, would bring him satisfaction; but the objects in which that satisfaction may be found, and the forces that must co-operate to secure it, lie far afield, and his life will remain cramped and self-destructive so long as he does not envisage its whole basis and co-operate with all his potential allies.[19]

In *The Life of Reason* Santayana fortified himself with a deep understanding of Greek naturalism and humanism, and with much of the philosophical anthropology that James had developed in *The Principles of Psychology*. His aim was to articulate the goods that are resident in human nature, art, science, society, morals, and religion, making them intelligible in terms of basic philosophic assumptions. The attempt to discriminate such goods was greatly assisted by what he calls the Aristotelian principle: the notion that everything ideal has a natural basis, and all natural processes are capable of ideal fulfillment.[20] An epitome of his principle is this comment about love: "Love is a brilliant illustration of a principle everywhere discoverable: namely, that human reason lives by turning the friction of material forces into the light of ideal goods."[21]

He eschews the dualisms that have plagued philosophy. The ideals embodied in art, science, philosophy, religion, and social practice are not derivative of disembodied minds or disembodied being; they are fulfillments of natural existence. He frequently looks to biology where sages had hitherto looked to special faculties or divine intervention. To achieve such ideals deliberately, we must understand their nature and sources. We would learn to understand nature as accomplice in our yearnings, and we would not look in inappropriate places for support of what a reflective person cherishes.

Particularly in *The Life of Reason,* but in many other works as well, Santayana disclosed the ideals of life that might be realized in the various phases of human converse with nature. In this he has had few equals in this century. His enterprise directly seizes the moral interest; but philosophers today, with their pinched stereotypes, would be essentially baffled by Dewey's judgment of *The Life of Reason:* "The most adequate contribution America has yet made, always excepting Emerson, to moral philosophy."[22]

Philosophy of Experience: Rejecting the Impotencies of Subjectivism

The question of the nature of experience and its relation to nature is freighted with moral interest. Here again the principal initiating force is James. While he left it an open question in the *Principles* whether experience might be systematically subjective, his *Essays in Radical Empiricism* undermine this notion; and in the *Principles* and thereafter he made a crippling analysis of the notion that experience is made up of unrelated atomic sensations.[23]

His analyses of various forms of sensationalism (or phenomenalism, as it was to be called later on) in the *Principles* were incisive and conclusive. Even if "simple ideas," "impressions," "sensations," "sense data," or what you will are brought into relation by some *deus ex machina,* they still would not be *experienced* as related. Sensations might occur in a definite order, but one could not experience them *as ordered,* for each atom of sense can, by definition, be experienced only as such, *as atomic.* But James saw no good reason to make the initial postulate that experience occurs in this atomic forlornness. After all, the evidence of immediate life is that we are engulfed in events in their relations; and if a philosophy is unhelpful in characterizing such experience, it is fundamentally flawed, an idle imposture.

James observed that experience occurs in a "stream," as he called it, and one event in the stream is experienced as a sign of other events. Different qualities in the nature of relations are themselves felt. "We ought to say a feeling of *and,* a feeling of *but,* and a feeling of *by,* quite as readily as we say a feeling of *blue* or a feeling of *cold.*"[24] One of the most important theses of *Essays in Radical Empiricism* is that experienced relations are of real events in the world. Abandoning the notion of consciousness as an entity, an entity within which experience occurs, James argues that experience is not consciousness of consciousness, but consciousness of the on-going world. The relations are properties of objective events.

These themes figured conspicuously in Dewey's philosophy. He argued that the notion of the subjectivity of experience is a product of the philosophic prejudice that the object of exclusively rational knowledge is alone really real. Since this knowledge is of essences, forms, or purely mathematical relations, all of the other qualities of nature are consigned to an inherently inferior level of being (as in Plato), or (as in modern philosophy) to a place removed from nature, the subjective mind. Thus the invention of mind as the sanctum for all the traits extruded from the rest of reality.

Experience is not a product of an antecedently complete subject, nor is it a property of an antecedently complete object. It is a function of the inclusive field of organism/environment. Giving up on the notion of self-complete substances, all existent things are regarded as functions of interrelated processes. No item of existence is self-subsistent, not the solidity of the Rock of Gibraltar, or the play of sunlight on the surf, or the soothing melodies of a lullaby. All are equally real. They are features of a distinctive *network* of events: in Dewey's words, "qualities *of* inclusive situations."[25] The nuanced and daunting array of properties that philosophers had read out of existence are restored to where they had seemed to the innocent person to be all along. The roar of cannon and the warmth of the lover are real, hosted by an objective situation. It is your *lover,* not a subjective event, that you experience. It won't do to say that roars and warmth wouldn't exist if it weren't for our sensory apparatus. Of course they wouldn't. Our senses are some of the necessary conditions for the occurrence of such qualities. Dewey observed that a property doesn't disappear into its causes. Everything that occurs is a consequence of many conditions, but occurrences are not thereby shuffled into nonbeing.

It would be hard to imagine anything more impotent in the conduct of life than experience as conceived in modern philosophy: just meaningless smithereens of sensation, giving not a clue to direct our strivings. If nature is nothing but matter in motion, moreover, it possesses no intrinsic value. Those events that actual people find to be precious, worth struggling for and cherishing, or, on the other side, that they find unwelcome or loathesome and struggle to resist, must be only subjective for any consistent sensationalism. They have no recognizable implication with nature and hence with natural science. Fact and value belong to orders of being utterly juxtaposed to one another. No wonder, then, that this idea of experience called out so many *ad hoc* postulates about the cognitive and moral offices of pure reason. What was a problem for dualists becomes a virtue for Kant.

The supposed dualism of fact and value constituted a dreary display. Dewey describes the characteristically oppressive view:

> When nature was regarded as a set of mechanical interactions, it apparently lost all meaning and purpose. Its glory departed. Elimination of differences of quality deprived it of its beauty. Denial to nature of all inherent longings and aspiring tendencies toward ideal ends removed nature and natural science from contact with poetry, religion, and divine things. There seemed to be left only a harsh, brutal despiritualized exhibition of mechanical forces.[26]

This "exhibition" had credence because all the objects of qualitative experience had been neatly removed from the objective frame of things. Restore experience to its rightful place, Dewey thought, and nature must be regarded as in full possession of those displaced qualities. He says of *Experience and Nature*, "I believe that the method of empirical naturalism presented in this volume provides the way, and the only way—although of course no two thinkers will travel it in just the same fashion—by which one can freely accept the standpoint and conclusions of modern science: the way by which we can be genuinely naturalistic and yet maintain cherished values, provided they are critically clarified and reinforced."[27]

Dewey's satisfaction with a highly enriched naturalism would not, of course, be shared by those with a persistent theistic bent. For that reason, it would not have been good enough for James. All the same, if we follow James and Dewey, we find no cause to believe that our experience surrounds us like a hall of mirrors, isolating us forever from each other and the world. It gives us access to the world and is the indispensable condition of knowledge. The events that we struggle with, aspire to, admire, cherish, groan and suffer with, belong to those plural and changing processes of nature. Their occurrence is too often precarious, but by recognizing that these events are not in a world apart, they fall within the purview of intelligent control. Such conclusions are invaluable additions to our knowledge of the moral condition, and they provide us with resources in the moral life that had been out of the reach of previous philosophies.

Philosophical Anthropology: Human Nature and the Moral Self

All the major philosophers of this classic period were united in their antagonism to Cartesian dualism. An assortment of their specific arguments against it might be given, but I will confine myself to the import of the issue for the moral condition. In his *Principles of Psychology* James went far, if ambiguously, toward a very different conception of human nature in the world than that of Descartes. Spurred by the work of Darwin, the thrust of James's thought was solidly in the direction of conceiving human nature as a function of the behavior of an active individual contending with an environment that conditions, promotes, and retards the interests of the organism. The formation of human nature is a function of activity in this environment. Ideas are not, as his predecessors had believed, representations of an antecedently fixed reality; they are primarily instruments for leading us from present to future experiences. "Mind is a fighter for ends," said James. The meaning of a present experience is what it portends for the life of an individual caught up in the processes of change.[28]

James removes the empirical self from the Cartesian cocoon, declaring,

> *In its widest possible sense, . . . a man's Self is the sum total of all that he CAN call his,* not only his body and his psychic powers, but his clothes and his house, his wife and children, his ancestors and friends, his reputation and works, his lands and horses, and yacht and bank account.[29]

He goes on to distinguish the material self, the social self, the spiritual self, and the pure Ego, the latter of which he finds to be nonexistent; but the others are eminently real. "Our father and mother, our wife and babes, are bone of our bone and flesh of our flesh. When they die, a part of our very selves is gone."[30] According to such a conception, the epidermis is not the boundary of selfhood. Rather, the self is the cofunctioning of features of the organism and environment. Elements of the environment are as indispensable and efficacious in feeling and conduct as are biological powers, and only an arbitrary simplification coupled with the weight of traditional thinking supports the notion of a self as an "internal" entity.

James struggled with the notion of selfhood, and his teaching is more mixed than my outline would suggest. Dewey, however, followed James's lead without Cartesian hangovers. He seized upon and developed the notion of *habit* with great effectiveness. Habits are dispositions to modes of behavior that are acquired and developed by the "live creature" in its converse with its environment. The latter, we must observe, is as much a determinant of habit as the former. We are all thinkers, workers, and lovers, for example; but the numberless variations in these activities are structured as much by the specific characteristics of the environment as by the capacities of the organism. Mere impulse, Dewey held, never provides a form of action. It does so only when it is incorporated within habit, the product of individual and the environment together. All thought and action are functions of habit, thus conceived. The habits constituting mind are principally a function of social interaction.[31]

Dewey abandons the notion of an encapsulated entity that is responsible for the functioning of human nature. An inclusive process of organism and environment is the "agent" of behavior. As individuals develop and refine ever more habits, they become more autonomous. The role played by the environment becomes, in varying degrees, less decisive in ongoing behavior than the already established fund of habits, which have taken on a distinctive and effective character. The process of the cumulative development of habits Dewey calls growth. As an individual continues to adapt to variations in his surroundings, new habits are formed and old ones qualified. Hence there is no fixed and final form of human nature.

Dewey's conclusions are subject to criticism and refinement in various ways. (He exaggerates the plasticity of human nature, for example, and minimizes the functions of genetic factors.) But if a view something akin to his is correct, then the Cartesian notion of self as thinking substance takes a mortal blow. A field of processes inclusive of the organism accounts for our nature and behavior.

The fall of Cartesianism was a great prize. There is immense moral import in ideas regarding the relationship of man and nature. The kinds, degrees, and causes of variability in human beings can only be determined experimentally. Dewey, as I have suggested, jumped to a conclusion in his assumptions about the degree of plasticity that we might reasonably expect. He attributed virtually all variations in human nature to variations in social relations.[32] Nevertheless, there *are* great variations in human capacities, emotions, conduct, and achievement; so the inquiry into their condition is of the greatest consequence. The Cartesian subject is substance. Its essential nature is impervious to its environment; with the best of intentions we still can do nothing to help people to be different from what they are. We may only throw up our hands and declare, "That's human nature!" Once again, it is clear that the explorations of James and Dewey open up new dimensions of the moral condition.[33]

The rejection of an atomic and fixed human nature has not been greeted with uniform thanksgiving. We tend to be defensive about the self and like to regard it as a thing apart. Its dignity resides, perhaps, in its being a divine creation set above all else in the natural world. Important as such beliefs are, I will not engage them right now. Rather, I will remark on some merits of thinking of the self as a product of and participant in inclusive processes of change. Again, James and Dewey are good teachers.

One of the phenomena of the moral life that has been regarded as most precious and yet difficult to account for is the capacity of individuals to subordinate their interests to a larger group, or perhaps to what they judge their duty to be. Some will insist, indeed, that such capacity is of the very essence of morality. Kant, of course, is the grand master of this view; but he can only give an account of distinctively moral behavior by postulating it of an unknowable supersensible will. Although Aristotle's conception of virtue had done handily without dualism, moderns have thought a radical bifurcation of mind and nature the only assumption to account for supremely moral behavior. John Stuart Mill, like Hume before him, struggled with this problem. His Benthamite predecessors had been reviled for holding that human beings act for no motive nobler than pleasure—indeed, their own pleasure. Mill flatly denied hedonistic psychology and agreed with alacrity that there are ends other than pleasure, and he insisted that individuals are entirely capable of exerting themselves on behalf of others in evident disregard of their own personal interests—and in fact sometimes do so. While acknowledging and praising this distinctive feature of moral experience, he had no conception of human nature that could make it intelligible, and he would not resort to such inscrutable notions as free will or divine grace. (Hume, too, lacked the assumptions to contend with this problem, confessing that the sources of altruism are unknowable.)

In his discussion, "What Self Is Loved in 'Self-Love,' "[34] James presented an analysis that takes the essential mystery out of moral heroism. With meticulous argument he had repudiated the various notions of the self as an abiding, unitary substance. The idea of the unitary and discrete soul-substance is sheer postulation. It is indifferently offered as the explanation of anything and everything; yet it cannot be used to anticipate any *particular* variation in behavior. Wickedly, James quotes the remark of Shadworth Hodgson, "Whatever you are *totally* ignorant of, assert to be the explanation of everything else."[35] He had also concluded, as we recently noted, that one's self is the system of relations that sustains the life and loyalties of the organism. Accordingly, what is loved is not a (mysterious) inner being, but some real feature of the inclusive world that is necessary or desirable for ongoing life. "To have a self that I can *care for*, nature must first present me with some *object* interesting enough to make me instinctively wish to appropriate it for its *own* sake, and out of it to manufacture one of those material, social, or spiritual selves, which we have already passed in review."[36] One loves to satisfy the craving for food, say, or for power. Food and power are objects of love, but so might many other things as well: the welfare of one's family and friends, and still larger goods, too. A person or cause might be so indispensable to one's life that he would prefer not to live without it. One can love many things. "I might conceivably be as much fascinated, and as primitively so, by the care of my neighbor's body as by the care of my own. The only check to such exuberant altruistic interests is natural selection, which would weed out such as were very harmful to the individual or to his tribe."[37]

Granted, there is interest satisfied in such aims, and the interest is one's own; but the interest is not in a mythical self, but in the object—one is genuinely interested in the other. What is crucial is not that the act is interested, but *what* it is interested in. "Then it's all a case of self-love after all!" is the reply. But consider the ambiguity in the use of "self" here. What is the self that is loved in self-love? What is at issue is the capacity of individuals to devote themselves to persons and principles beyond the epidermis, and James made this intelligible without resort to obscurity. This analysis does not imply that we may love equally and impartially all beings beyond our own skins, but we may love some of them, in varying degrees.

Dewey acknowledged his indebtedness to James's analysis. His conception of habit is especially helpful here. Habit, remember, is inclusive of organism and environment. It would then be literally true to say that particular constituents of the environment are an organic part of the self. They are *essential* to behavior and affection. On either James's or Dewey's analysis, it would not be a merely metaphorical statement to say, "When she died, part of my self died with her," for she was a crucial part of that complex of relations constituting the self. This is a legitimately edifying interpretation of human action, and it is unavailable to the view that subject is substance.

Philosophy of Value and the Good Life

James was a pluralist not only in his denial that the universe is wholly interlocked in "one unbending unit of fact." He was also repulsed by any morality that demanded universal adherence to its particular system of obligations.

> The elementary forces in ethics are probably as plural as those of physics are. The various ideals have no common character apart from the fact that they are ideals. No single abstract principle can be so used as to yield the philosopher anything like a scientifically accurate and genuinely useful casuistic scale.

> As a militant, fighting free-handed that the goods to which he *is* sensible may not be submerged and lost from out of life, the philosopher, like every other human being, is in a natural position. But think of Zeno and of Epicurus, think of Calvin and of Paley, think

of Kant and Schopenhauer, of Herbert Spencer and John Henry Newman, no longer as one-sided champions of special ideals, but as schoolmasters deciding what all must think—and what more grotesque topic could a satirist wish for on which to exericse his pen?[38]

James wrote little in a systematic vein in moral philosophy; but just the illustrations and digressions populating his writing on any topic exhibit qualities of intense moral experience. Many of his essays, likewise, explore dimensions of moral experience seldom if ever found in ethical treatises.[39] Both *The Varieties of Religious Experience* and *A Pluralistic Universe* exhibit the greatest possible interest in the yearnings and seekings inspired by our confrontations with the world, and they make judgments about their legitimacy and efficacy.

Dewey, also a metaphysical and moral pluralist, was a tireless expositor of the many dimensions of the moral life. His analyses of ends and change (as reviewed above, under "Worldly Metaphysics") are immediately pertinent to the moral life. There has been a variety of human ideals: that of Plato and Aristotle, or the Stoic, the Epicurean, the Christian saint, the Samurai warrior, the romantic artist, the Victorian lady, and so on. Each culture has certain stereotypes of what men and women are supposed to be—typically varying with class status. Such stereotypes are justified with the assumption that these are the true ends that nature has ordained for us, and deviation from them is somehow wrong. A like analysis is made of the social order. For Dewey, pluralism is again regarded as a more accurate and liberating assumption than monism. To reject the idea of static perfection is to deny that there is any "fixed end," as Dewey calls it, to the formation of human nature and society. He regarded fixed ends not as fulfillments but as impositions. The alternative is not a shapeless, directionless, existence; it is growth and unification with nature, which are congruent with his conception of nature as processes of change.

Yet, we might well think, Dewey's conception of the self sacrifices something of highest importance: isn't there a highest good which we entertain with such hope and passion? Are our yearnings of this sort in vain? Perhaps they are in vain, but perhaps also it is a yearning that does more harm than good. We are in a position to say something of Dewey's views about this issue. Inasmuch as it is a matter of surpassing moral interest, I will review it at some length.

The topic of self-realization goes back to Plato, but it is only the neglect of recent history that I am concerned with here, so I will begin with Mill. The merits and demerits of utilitarianism as an ethical theory have deservedly been the subject of much discussion. But Mill himself was concerned with issues in moral philosophy that are of great interest regardless of what happens to the debate about utilitarianism.[40] His theory of utility, indeed, was "grounded on the permanent interests of man as a progressive being."[41] These "permanent interests" are the "higher quality" values insisted upon in *Utilitarianism,* and Mill had something to say about these interests. There is, for example, his splendid chapter in *On Liberty,* "Of Individuality, as One of the Elements of Well-Being," which sets forth in outline a conception of self-realization. Mill urged a full and coherent, yet individualized, development and expression of human nature, accepting the passions as instruments of strength and growth. His analysis clearly surpasses any similar attempt in classical liberalism, for it is predicated on a much richer conception of human nature than had hitherto been advanced in that tradition. The main flaw in the theory, according to subsequent critics like Dewey, was that Mill's conception of the self was too individualistic, permitting him to ask the revealing question, "How much of human life should be assigned to individuality, and how much to society?"[42]—as if there were a necessary dichotomy between the development of individuals and their conduct as social beings.

Mill's conception of self-realization was not deliberately developed by his successors. T. H. Green and, even more so, Bradley were almost obsessed with self-realization; but their thought on the subject was derived from Hegel. In distinct contrast to Mill, they conceived of the self as attaining a unity with the cosmos. As the cosmos is already a perfect and harmonious whole, so the self likewise becomes perfectly harmonious. This unity and harmony would be effected by the individual's powers of cognition—the cognizing of the Absolute. For the individual who lacks such powers, self-realization is attained insofar as can be by coming to a sort of "instinctual awareness," as Green put it, of one's part in the organic whole of society. He becomes aware of himself as being an expression of the social whole, and he recognizes the social whole as expressing himself.[43]

When G. E. Moore undertook to criticize idealism in chapter 4 of *Principia Ethica,* he succeeded admirably in disclosing grave difficulties. He pointed out, for example, that if the supreme good is conceived as an eternal and supersensible reality, it cannot be affected by human action in time. Temporal action, then, can bring about no true good—quite an embarrassment for an ethical theory! For the most part in this chapter, Moore is incisive and effective in his criticism of the idealists. His discussion is also notable for the fact that he evidently shared nothing of their concern for self-realization. Likewise there is no evidence that he shared Mill's concern with individuality.

Contrast with Moore the way in which Dewey treated idealism. Dewey was likewise a trenchant critic, writing substantially more about the defects of idealism than Moore himself. But Dewey wrote with a view to preserving and enriching the best insights of the idealists by freeing them from those features of their thought that were distorting or erroneous. Sharing Green's great interest in self-realization as the moral motive, for example, he pointed out that Green's concept of the self-distinguishing subject was imcompatible with his concept of the self that comes into organic unity with the world. If we are to understand how the self can form a unity with the world, Dewey stated, we must abandon Green's concept of the self.[44] Primarily against Bradley, he argued against the conception of, as he called it, "a closed universe" that is essentially changeless and wherein no improvement can be brought about. Bradley's theory was not only false, but constituted an apology for the *status quo* as well. Dewey wanted to be clear about how conduct could be efficacious, and idealistic metaphysics fails to help.

While he separated himself from idealism, Dewey never gave up the idea of organic unities, so foreign to empiricism. Indeed, he continued to insist on the value of developing and integrating the self and unifying it with the environment. With a fervor equal to that of any idealist, he believed the experience intrinsic to such consummation is inherently precious.

Dewey dismissed the notion that the self becomes integrated with the indiscriminate totality of being. It can attain a harmonious integration with the affective environment and its continuities, but only temporarily, and this relation is achieved by highly selective behavior. Actual human conduct is confined to definite circumstances or situations that present their own obstacles and disruptions as well as promptings for success. Our typical task, Dewey says, is to convert situations from this problematic character to what he calls unified, or consummatory, situations. It is hence *situations* that become an organic whole; our powers as human beings are effectively engaged with the enviornment and fulfilled therein.

In the consummatory situation there is a felt unity of the self with its surroundings. Such consummations do not endure indefinitely; individuals fall out of phase with their environment and again they have the task of constructing a unification. Against the view of the idealists that there is a final and unchanging fulfillment, Dewey argues that fulfillments are always to be created anew. The conditions of unification with the environment change, and they do not endure indefinitely. Hence he substituted the notion of growth for that of self-realization, and the notion of the good of activity for that of a perduring condition in which the self finds repose.

Like Plato, Spinoza, and most other philosophers who attend to such matters, Green and Bradley had treated the process of establishing unifications of self and world as one of cognition alone. But the agencies of constructing consummations, Dewey objected, are at least three: creative and experimental intelligence, overt activity, and deliberate social cooperation. A creative intelligence formulates ways of dealing with the always variable problematic situations; it responds to each situation by conceiving alternative ways of reconstructing it to restore unified activity. These are plans of action. As experimental, intelligence treats these plans as hypotheses subject to test and revision.

Activity follows the experimental plan. One deals with a variety of conditions, demanding a plurality of skills and modes of activity. Accordingly, in addition to requiring habits of intelligence, the transformation of situations requires the agent to cultivate and possess multiple habits of conduct, not just of cognition. The teacher, carpenter, lawyer, farmer, and merchant each must develop pertinent capacities. As each develops more of such powers, he becomes more capable of creating integrally fulfilling situations.

Conduct often takes place in a social context, so problematic situations are typically shared situations. In order to transform their common predicaments, individuals must function together deliberately. Thus the third condition for constructing organic unities is social action. Effective social action, Dewey argued, requires deliberation that is public and social, which has *communication* as its indispensable constituent. Social deliberation is a process of sharing concerns; exchanging proposals for concerted activity; considering, modifying, uniting them (if it can be done); and trying to achieve as much consensus as possible regarding which one finally to act upon. Action is then more apt to be agreeable and coordinated. This process Dewey calls democracy as a way of life, or social intelligence. Social intelligence will not bring unanimity of decision, and it will not be free of abuse; but Dewey was convinced that whatever willing concert in social action of which we are capable will be more likely brought about by social intelligence than any other way yet devised. Individuals gifted in this method will attain more unifications in the complexities of conduct.

Recognizing, after Peirce, that scientific method is an inherently social process, he self-consciously adapted social method to moral problems. No doubt he overestimated the practicality of the method. In philosophy, every time a new method has been contrived, we have had wild enthusiasms over what could be achieved with it. Every man may be rational, so modern thinkers supposed, if only he uses the right method! Likewise Dewey and his rhapsodies about democratic method. But his rhapsodies were not altogether misplaced. The notion of social intelligence will reappear at further stages in the present volume. It is surely one of Dewey's greatest contributions to moral thought, yet it is not so much as identified in the scholarhsip.[45]

The topic at the moment is Dewey's transformation of the inherited notion of self-realization into that of growth. Growth is inseparable from the cultivation of open, trusting, and plural social relations. Dewey commends growth in just those activities that contribute to *social* ends, which can be inclusive of the ends of the individual. "The final happiness of an individual resides in the supremacy of certain interests in the makeup of character; namely, alert, sincere, enduring interests in the objects in which all can share."[46] In contrast to the notion that hell is other people, Dewey declared that "Shared experience is the greatest of human goods."[47] He spoke of such experience with religious accents. "And when the emotional force, the mystic force one might say, of communication, of the miracle of shared life and shared experience is spontaneously felt, the hardness and crudeness of contemporary life will be bathed in the light that never was on land or sea."[48] It would be hard to find a philosopher (I think, in fact, that there is none) who identified a more profound value in the experience of intimately associated life. He has no elaborate analyses of shared experience, no arguments, really, to defend it. He does point out that dualistic and subjectivistic philosophies cannot in their own terms even conceive of shared experience, and he believes that our feverish pursuit of diversion and even transcendence is a consequence of the failure of human association. In the main, he simply asserts the deep, persistent, and virtually all-sustaining value of true community. For example:

> That happiness which is full of content and peace is found only in enduring ties with others, which reach to such depths that they go below the surface of conscious experience to form its undisturbed foundation. No one knows how much of the frothy excitement of life, of mania for motion, of fretful discontent, of need for artificial stimulation, is the expression of the frantic search for something to fill the void caused by the loosening of the bonds which hold persons together in immediate community of experience. If there is anything in human psychology to be counted upon, it may be urged that when man is satiated with restless seeking for the remote which yields no enduring satisfaction, the human spirit will return to seek calm and order within itself. This, we repeat, can be found only in the vital, steady, and deep relationships which are present only in immediate community.[49]

Dewey suggests that the so-called religious need is, at bottom, a craving for close and loving relationships. But such relations are rare and difficult to achieve. It would not overstate his belief to say that those who possess them are blessed.

There are further dimensions of "religious" value. Consummatory experience might include the sense of oneness with an enveloping whole. In Dewey's philosophy we see how an individual can genuinely be in unity with the world—not in a wholesale way, but selectively. When dualisms and separate substances leave the philosophic menagerie, we may become sensibly aware of our continuities with nature. When his thought turns in this direction, Dewey sounds like a religious mystic. But his philosophy was wholly naturalistic; his reflections were intended to explain how, rid of supernaturalistic assumptions, a religious quality may pervade experience. He is rarely an eloquent writer, but he is at his best when he talks of the sense one can have of belonging to a whole.

Infinite relationships of man with his fellows and with nature already exist. The ideal means . . . a sense of these encompassing continuities with their infinite reach. This meaning even now attaches to present activities because they are set in a whole to which they belong and which belongs to them. Even in the midst of conflict, struggle, and defeat a consciousness is possible of the enduring and comprehending whole.

. . . There is a conceit fostered by perversion of religion which assimilates the universe to our personal desires; but there is also a conceit of carrying the load of the universe from which religion liberates us. Within the flickering inconsequential acts of separate selves dwells a sense of the whole which claims and dignifies them. In its presence we put off mortality and live in the universal.[50]

A further concern of those who seek the good is integrated selfhood, and Dewey is again worth hearing. There is no mystery about what an integrated self is. An individual whose habits are more-or-less supportive of each other, or at least consistent, is more-or-less integrated, unified, or "whole," as we might put it. One who habitually seeks to dominate others, yet also seeks friendship, suffers from an internal conflict, for the two traits are incompatible; while habits of honesty, cooperativenes, trust, and fidelity are mutually supportive. This sort of unity is not something antecedently given; it is an outcome, an achievement, that depends primarily on crucial features of the learning process. In principle, then, according to Dewey, integration of the self is attainable, given the right conditions—not including the all-sufficing Absolute.

After all, though, if there is no final form of the self to be attained, and if there is no absolute consummation in experience, then aren't the alternatives freighted with interminable frustration and meaninglessness? What, at last, is growth *for?* We need not despair, Dewey believed. Rather, activity can be of such a nature that it is intrinsically precious in itself; it may have qualities that are treasured on their own. One doesn't need an end that occurs after activity terminates. Dewey is well known for attacking the notion that there is a realm of being that lies beyond change. He scoffed at the notion that to abide in such a state would be a fulfillment of our nature. We deceive ourselves when we try to attain a condition that leaves all our troubles behind. There is no such condition to be had, and it is when we desire it above all that we suffer frustration and cynicism. We should not try to transcend problems, Dewey urged, but cultivate the habits that might make it intrinsically fulfilling to contend with them directly. A happy life will be found in cultivating a self that enjoys engagement with problems and possesses the habits of doing so effectively.

Some individuals are graced with the ability to love the ongoing *process* of life—the everyday tasks, adventures, and achievements, great and small—at home, on the job, and the like, day in and day out, right here and now. The pattern of life for such people is not that of enduring an obnoxious present for the sake of some expected reward, gritting one's teeth in anticipation of a better day (a day that is apt to turn out to be obnoxious, too). Their pattern is what Dewey sometimes calls the good of activity, and it can be one's salvation, especially when it is united with shared experience. It may well be the searchers for fixed ends who are more prone to misery. We live in a world of change, marked by the intersection of the precarious and the stable. Hence the good life is not one that seeks escape from this predicament. The problem is how to deal with processes of change, and the quality of the *process* of life becomes the good. This is an idea of the first importance.

No doubt his analyses are defective at some points and need refinement and supplementation at others. Human beings vary from one to another in what they need to sustain and fulfill them, in what they can regard as most firm and dear in their lives. I do not suppose that Dewey has all the answers or that he has even canvassed all the questions; many persons might even sneer at his ideal of shared experience. At least they might believe he expects too much of it. On the other hand, it might be that there is more worth to be found in human association than such people suppose. Perhaps shared experience, like so much else in life, is one of those consummate goods that we neglect simply because it has been there, right under our noses, so to speak, all the time, but undeveloped. The existential despair found in "deep thinking" philosophers might well evaporate like a mist in "the light that never was on land or sea."

It might be, however, that the sorts of democratic communities that Dewey envisioned could not be as efficacious or as common as he expected. Indeed, it might also be that such communities do not yield the closeness that he treasured as well as do some of the more traditional forms of association. He was surely carried away with the thought that communities of shared values need have no bounds. (He shares this faith with many utopians.)

Dewey's seems to be the philosophy *par excellence* for secular humanists, who are less apt to structure their lives in terms of Dewey's *bête noir,* fixed ends. But a life devoted to more-or-less predetermined ends needn't be so repulsive as Dewey supposed. Many persons find great satisfaction in a customary religious setting, for example, and there can be a profound sense of belonging and rightness in devoting oneself to the cultural, geographic, or ethnic traditions that have nurtured one's life. Just a life of consistent routine is sometimes found acceptable, affording feelings of safety and security. Persons engaged in such ways need not look enviously upon the life of the alienated intellectual (which is *not* Dewey's paradigm).

Despite such doubts, our concern for the growth and unification of the self is at least taken out of the realm of speculative metaphysics and into the domain of experimental inquiry. And there surely are enduring lessons in Dewey's views of the good life. His emphasis on the *process* of life, especially the life of shared experience, can be well taken by anyone, regardless of what such a person takes as ultimate. His teachings on intelligence, flexibility, open-mindedness, and the willingness to communicate are invaluable in the modern moral life. He advanced and enriched our knowledge of the human involvement with the nature of things well beyond the state in which it had been left by Mill and by the idealists. We all care deeply about the nature of the good. Whether we tend to adopt or to reject Dewey's conclusions, we cannot deny that they are of the keenest sort of interest. And his reflections are predicated upon a searching appraisal of the real possibilities of the moral condition.

Santayana was at least as absorbed with the multiform qualities of life as were James and Dewey. He has compelling observations about them, worthy of our attention. Although a materialist and an atheist, for example, he saw no reason to sacrifice religious values when they are properly understood. Religion cannot defensibly be regarded as a kind of superscience, laying out cognitive doctrines in defiance of natural science. Taken in this way, it is pathetic and groundless; but taken as an imaginative rendering of moral experience, it is a recognition of the most fateful traits of natural existence and an honoring of the ideals of mortal life. Religion is poetry. It conceives powerful images to distinguish the paramount values already resident in a civilization. As in the Homeric religion, for example, it symbolizes the crucial conditions and aspirations of a culture and thereby impresses their worth in a telling way on the community. Human aspiration does not require religion to justify it. On the contrary, religion is a way of *memorializing* and *celebrating* what is already most important in our existence.[51]

To take religious statements as literal truth, Santayana contends, makes them incredible. More important, it causes them to dissipate their moral lessons or even to convey something morally despicable. He was especially critical of the literal belief in the governance of the world by a perfect being. This belief entails the so-called problem of evil, with its tortured arguments and apologetics. Worse, a being palpably guilty of the utmost in moral barbarity is at the same time the object of both piety and worship. Santayana found polytheism a much better rendering of moral values, for it distinguishes some gods as representative of momentous natural powers and others as embodiments of ideal ends. Piety is "respect for the sources of our being" and spirituality is "devotion to ideal ends." Hence piety and spirituality, confounded in Christianity, do not have the same object.[52]

Philosophy of Intelligence

I have been discussing a few of the ways in which some American philosophers have told us much about the moral condition and thereby contributed importantly to the inquiries generated by our moral interests. American philosophy is identified principally with pragmatism, the import of which for the moral condition is poorly understood. It can be regarded as a philosophy of intelligence.

Pragmatism is recognized as a theory of meaning and truth, but to regard it as nothing more than a technical exercise in epistemology is to miss its significance.[53] Even as a technical theory of meaning, however, it performs no small service. Simply to require of any concept pretending to a legitimate role in discourse that it have sensible offspring is highly salutary. Empty talk has been the source of much that is worthless—or worse—in theology, metaphysics, ethics, and psychology. James's illustration, in reference to idealism, is delightful:

Affirming the Absolute Mind, which is its substitute for God, to be the rational presupposition of all particulars of fact, whatever they may be, it remains supremely indifferent to what the particular facts in our world actually are. Be they what they may, the Absolute will father them. Like the sick lion in Esop's fable, all footprints lead into his den, but *nulla vestigia retrorsum.* You cannot redescend into the world of particulars by the Absolute's aid, or deduce any necessary consequences of detail important for your life from your idea of his nature. He gives you indeed the assurance that all is well with *Him,* and for his eternal way of thinking; but thereupon he leaves you to be finitely saved by your own temporal devices.[54]

Pragmatists have perhaps been too stringent in their requirements for meaningful discourse. Neverthelees, their insistence on rigor in this matter has been entirely beneficial.

The pragmatists rejected the empiricists' notion that a meaningful idea is a composite of antecedently given sense data; they likewise rejected the rationalists' belief that an idea is somehow representative of an essence. It is only incidentally, if at all, an image. It is an anticipation of future events predicated on present conditions. Less abstractly, an idea is an anticipation of what something will do in relation to other events. The idea of a table is what can be *done* with such an object: put books or food on it, eat from it, decorate a room with it, make a gift of it to a friend, etc. The possessor of an idea of a table is empowered to act with objects identified as tables in a manner that will bring predictable results. But the example of a table is a bit academic. It doesn't capture, for example, the revolutionary excitement generated in James's *Principles of Psychology,* in which the pragmatic notion of ideas was generated not by poring over learned tomes, but by recognizing the vital character of experience. James perceives the active human being exercising wit and pluck to contend with the ongoing, changing, and uncertain events upon which life and fortune depend. Dewey's approach is precisely the same in *Experience and Nature,* where he articulates his theory of meaning, inquiry, and knowledge in reference to the generic demands and instrumentalities of the real world.

The differences in objects, in any case, are the differences in their conceivable functions, and the differences in ideas are the differences in what they predict. To find out the nature of any phenomenon, the inquirer neither passively accumulates sense impressions nor attempts to divine its essence by rational intuition. He manipulates the object in relation to other events. An idea, then, is preeminently an instrument of action. Ideas permit us to engage and deliberately use the events of our life experience. Experimental science is a highly sophisticated form of this procedure.

These are commonplace to the beginning student of pragmatism, but they were hardly commonplaces at the time they were introduced. Consider once more the contrasts to antecedent forms of empiricism and rationalism. Empiricism had caged the individual in a meaningless swarm of subjective sensations, and ideas were an amalgam of these antecedently given bits and pieces, effected by subjective laws of association. The empiricist theory left the nature and very existence of the world problematic; it could not coherently treat ideas as guides to conduct. The cage apart, taking an idea as nothing but a cluster of sensations is to render it impotent. Images, as such, predict nothing. One can't live with them. Platonic forms and Cartesian essences are equally impotent. They allegedly disclose the real nature of antecedent reality; they tell us what *type* of thing a substance is, but they say nothing about the correlations between processes of change. Hence they are not instruments for deliberate action with the changing world.

Dewey wrote of guiding conduct with scientific ideas. To scholars hopelessly addicted to the paradigms of the classic tradition (including those who claim to have repudiated it), this has meant that he wanted to deduce moral judgments from scientifically determined premises. This would be standard Platonic logic, precisely what Dewey found so inappropriate for functioning with processes of change. He demanded in its place an experimental logic, or theory of inquiry:

> Science has . . . affected the actual conditions under which men live, use, enjoy, and suffer much more than . . . it has affected their habits of belief and inquiry. Especially is this true about the uses and enjoyments of final concern: religious, moral, legal, economic, political. The demand for reform of logic is the demand for a unified theory of inquiry through which the authentic pattern of experimental and operational inquiry of science shall become available for regulation of the habitual methods by which inquiries in the field of common sense are carried on; by which conclusions are reached and beliefs are formed and tested.[55]

In a world of change, where heterogeneous processes are tending to uncertain and variable outcomes, we need to know the meaning of events. Thus we control the variables to produce a desired outcome. Experimental knowledge permits us to guide processes of change, to *construct* values, or goods. Strictly on the basis of antecedent philosophies, this was impossible to do.

Dewey's expression, the *construction* of good,[56] is significant. In contrast to the Platonic tradition, there is not a ready-made good. The fragmentary and changing events in which we are immersed are objects of love and hatred, hope and fear, promise and torment in numberless ways; they admit of varying interrelations and con-figurations. From these materials, if we grasp their meanings, we actively construct a good. Neither does this wholesome procedure bear any resemblance to the Sartrean program of inventing goods out of nothing but sheer volition. As Dewey recognizes, there *are* precious values in existence antecedent to choice. They must be selected, modified, and ordered.

He stressed the creative character of inquiry. New hypotheses may be formulated, calling for a novel reconstruction of existing conditions in order to produce an integrated and fulfilling situation. Hypotheses might predict, say, that if political, economic, judicial, or educational practice is altered in specified ways, then the result will be this or that increase in freedom, participation, wealth, growth, or learning, depending on what stresses exist in a given situation. Ideas might direct conduct in associated life in the same way that they do in the laboratory. The hypothesis predicts that if existing conditions are reordered in a certain way, the new relations will have a specific result. The experimenter proceeds to reconstruct conditions as directed in order to test the hypothesis, in order to produce the predicted result.

It might reasonably be objected that the projected outcome is itself problematic and controversial. The objection is weighty, and the manner of dealing with it is of great importance. Little will be said at this point, except to say that the judgment of morally problematic ends is not accomplished by deducing an "ought" from an "is," or the like. An irreducible plurality of criteria might be applicable to a proposed plan. Most moralists would wish to reduce the plurality to an incontrovertible order of precedence, but this is impossible. Moral disagreement is frequently a matter for social intelligence, embodying certain virtues, as we shall see in succeeding chapters. Some of its conclusions are apt to be a bit indecisive for the tastes of a Kantian. For Dewey's part, he witnessed the social convulsions of the twentieth century and our incessant trial-and-error confrontations with disaster and was profoundly convinced that we must initiate new and explicitly social methods for contending with such matters.[57]

Pragmatism breathes a new spirit—exemplified best of all in James—a spirit of challenge, adventure, and enthusiasm. The world is changing in any case, but we need be neither resigned nor powerless, nor hold desperately to the forms of existing institutions. With the intelligent and aggressive use of ideas, an open world is subject to constructive change, if only we can learn to do it. Perhaps they were unduly optimistic, but pragmatists looked upon these as heartening developments.

My concern in this chapter has been to give substantial examples of philosophies that responsibly address and attempt to satisfy some of the deepest interests possessed of reflective persons. They have, in effect, addressed the moral condition. But how quickly philosophy descends from the problems and possibilities of experience to a display of technical expertise! Hence this legacy has become all but lost due to the preoccupations of academic philosophers, and the moral interest has been left famished. The current return of normative philosophy is innocent of any nourishment it might find in the philosophies I have reviewed. We continue to alternate between giving up the moral life to its vagaries and attempting to reestablish the classic tradition, in which moral absolutes are excogitated by university professors. Both notions are undertaken in innocence of the moral condition.

The moral philosophers of the present day would have much to gain by absorbing this legacy. I do not suggest that the review of some of the achievements of James, Santayana, and Dewey exhausts all that they said, or that can be said, about the moral condition and moral philosophy; nor do I contend that the philosophers summarized are not subject to responsible criticisms; but I do assert that their neglect threatens to obscure potent understanding and resources of moral reflection. Regarding the project at hand, what I especially want to appropriate, as I have said, is the notion that the moral condition is fundamentally invested with the changing, ambiguous, and precarious, while at the same time it has rich sources of order, security, growth, and consummation.

Philosophy may take its point of departure from conspicuous and portentious forms of life experience—from the activities distinctive of human existence: knowing, valuing, aspiring, cooperating, struggling, fearing, rejoicing—all in converse with a world that is both resistant and supportive. Such a philosophy might formulate ideas about the nature of things that make this experience more luminous and coherent. Such ideas would make our lives less blind and oppressive. A philosophy might display or contrive instruments of reflection and action that would permit us to proceed more freely and happily. The succeeding discussions attend to further crucial characteristics of the moral condition. From that perspective some of the principal problems of the moral life and moral philosophy might be seen in a different and perhaps more sustaining light.

Notes

1. Walter Kaufmann, *The Future of the Humanities* (New York: Readers Digest Press; distributed by Thomas Y. Crowell Company, 1977), p. 69. The book at issue was Arthur Danto's *Nietzsche as Philosopher* [condescending title!] (New York: Macmillan, 1965).

2. G. J. Warnock, *Contemporary Moral Philosophy* (London: Macmillan; New York: St. Martin's, 1967); Mary Warnock, *Ethics since 1900* (London: Oxford University Press, 1960); George Kerner, *The Revolution in Ethical Theory* (New York and Oxford: Oxford University Press, 1966); W. D. Hudson, *Modern Moral Philosophy* (London: Macmillan, 1970); and Roger L. Hancock, *Twentieth Century Ethics* (New York and London: Columbia University Press, 1974).

3. *Contemporary Moral Philosophy*, p. 1.

4. *The Philosophical Review* 58, no. 4 (July 1949): 321–30.

5. *Ethics* 88, no. 3 (1978): 218–28.

6. For Stevenson's analysis, see his *Ethics and Language* (New Haven: Yale University Press, 1944), chap. 12; and *Facts and Values* (New Haven and London: Yale University Press, 1963), essay 6.

7. A scholar with considerable insight into the moral resources of American philosophy is John E. Smith. See his *The Spirit of American Philosophy* rev. ed. (Albany: State University of New York Press, 1983),

which attends to some of the same issues that will be treated in the present chapter. While more inclusive, this work excludes Santayana. See also Smith's collection of essays, *America's Philosophical Vision* (Chicago and London: The University of Chicago Press, 1992). The spirit of American philosophy is always present in the works of John J. McDermott. See his *The Culture of Experience: Philosophical Essays in the American Grain* (New York: New York University Press, 1976) and *Streams of Experience; Reflections on the History and Philosophy of American Culture* (Amherst: University of Massachusetts Press, 1986). A number of valuable insights about the moral bearings of pragmatism can be found in Cornel West's *The American Evasion of Philosophy* (Madison: the University of Wisconsin Press, 1989). West insists that pragmatism can be politicized in the pursuit of radical political action. I regard this as a deadly corruption of pragmatism. Whether a given pragmatist tends toward the left or right should depend on whether an analysis of the relevant subject matter discloses realities that support a given political orientation. Being a pragmatist should not be a question-begging operation.

8. Bertrand Russell's "A Free Man's Worship" (reprinted in *Mysticism and Logic* [New York: W. W. Norton, 1929]) epitomizes this view. For a summary of *fin de siecle* pessimism, see John Herman Randall, Jr., *The Making of the Modern Mind* (Boston: Houghton-Mifflin, 1940), pp. 580–98.

9. Donald Verene has pointed out to me that this analysis applies more to the British and American idealists than to Hegel. Hegel's *Phenomenology of Spirit* attends to the contradictions of metaphysical positions, rather than of propositions.

10. "Block universe" is used in "The Dilemma of Determinism," one of James's onslaughts against the monistic idealists. More thorough and systematic is *A Pluralistic Universe*.

11. William James, *Pragmatism* (Cambridge: Harvard University Press, 1975), p. 40.

12. Ibid., pp. 142–43. For Dewey, pragmatism "accepts life and experience in all its uncertainty, mystery, doubt, and half-knowledge and turns that experience upon itself to deepen and intensify its own qualities . . ." (*Art as Experience* [*Later Works,* Vol. 10: 1934], p. 41).

13. Dewey wrote to James to praise *The Principles of Psychology* for its success in emancipating experience from impertinent abstractions. "Many of my students, I find, are fairly hungering. They almost jump at any opportunity to get out from under the load and to believe in their own lives" in Ralph Barton Perry, *The Thought and Character of William James,* Vol. II (Boston: Little, Brown and Company, 1935), p. 517.

14. I have written on these and other aspects of Dewey's moral philosophy in, for example, *John Dewey's Philosophy of Value* (New York:

Humanities Press, 1972); *Excellence in Public Discourse: John Stuart Mill, John Dewey, and Social Intelligence* (New York: Teachers College Press, 1986); and the chapter "Dewey" in *Ethics in the History of Western Philosophy,* edited by Robert Cavalier, James Gouinlock, and James P. Sterba (London: Macmillan, 1989). Chapter 5 of *Excellence in Public Discourse* and "Dewey" give an account of Dewey's judgment of utilitarianism.

15. For an excellent analysis of Dewey's fundamental conceptions about nature, see Raymond D. Boisvert, *Dewey's Metaphysics* (New York: Fordham University Press, 1988).

16. See esp. chapter 2 of *Experience and Nature* (*Later Works,* Vol. 1: 1925).

17. See esp. *Experience and Nature,* chap. 9, and *Art as Experience,* chaps. 1, 3, and 8.

18. George Santayana, *The Life of Reason,* Vol. V: *Reason in Science* (New York: Collier Books, 1962), p. 155.

19. George Santayana, *The Life of Reason,* Vol. III: *Reason in Religion* (New York: Collier Books, 1962), p. 156.

20. George Santayana, *The Life of Reason,* Vol. I: *Reason in Common Sense* (New York: Collier Books, 1962), p. 26.

21. George Santayana, *The Life of Reason,* Vol. II: *Reason in Society* (New York: Collier Books, 1962), p. 13.

22. Dewey, *Middle Works,* Vol. 4: 1907–1909, p. 241.

23. In his critique of sensationalism, James was anticipated by the idealists, especially T. H. Green. Green, however, used the Absolute as a *deus ex machina* to relate sensations. James had no use for such devices. He would argue that relations between events are real, and they are experienced as such. For Green, see esp. his Introduction to *David Hume: Philosophical Works* (4 vols.) edited by T. H. Green and T. H. Grose (Aalen, West Germany: Scientia Verlag, 1964).

24. James, *The Principles of Psychology,* Vol. 1, p. 238.

25. Dewey, *Experience and Nature,* p. 203 (italics added). The best account of Dewey's philosophy of experience is Thomas S. Alexander's *John Dewey's Theory of Art, Experience, and Nature: The Horizons of Feeling* (Albany: State University of New York Press, 1987).

26. Dewey, *Reconstruction in Philosophy* (*Middle Works,* Vol. 12: 1920), p. 119.

27. Dewey, *Experience and Nature,* p. 4.

28. In a cognate vein, Peirce had said that every idea establishes a habit of action. See "How to Make Our Ideas Clear" (*Collected Papers of Charles Sanders Peirce,* edited by Charles Hartshorne and Paul Weiss, Vol. 5 [Cambridge, Harvard University Press, 1934], 5.358–387). Dewey frequently refers to ideas as plans of action.

29. James, *The Principles of Psychology,* Vol. 1, p. 279.

30. Ibid., p. 280.

31. For Dewey on habit, see esp. *Human Nature and Conduct (Middle Works,* Vol. 14: 1922), parts I, II, and III. On mind, see esp. *Human Nature and Conduct,* part III, and *Experience and Nature,* chaps. 5–8.

32. See esp. *Human Nature and Conduct.*

33. In this context, the work of George Herbert Mead also showed great accomplishment. See in particular *Mind, Self, and Society,* edited by Charles W. Morris (Chicago and London: University of Chicago Press, 1934).

34. James, *The Principles of Psychology,* Vol. 1, pp. 302–314.

35. Ibid., p. 329. James does not indicate the source of Hodgson's barb.

36. Ibid., p. 304.

37. Ibid., p. 309. James's analysis here draws upon the theory of natural selection. Recent biological studies have tried to explain the altruistic process in terms of the functioning of genes in one member of a species in a manner to preserve their duplicates in other members. This explanation is helpless to explain incontrovertibly altruistic behavior between creatures (including humans) who do not share the same genes. The hypotheses that would remedy this defect have been presented by Robert H. Frank in *Passions Within Reason: The Strategic Role of the Emotions* (New York and London: W. W. Norton & Co., 1988). In accordance with the principles of natural selection (including the principle that individuals, not groups, are selected) Frank gives great credence to the view that we possess inborn "moral sentiments," as he calls them. Remarkably, James's argument anticipates Frank's, at least in germ. In any case, the behavior of the individual is a function of many factors, and it remains an object of inquiry to determine what all the conditions of unselfishness are, and to what lengths an individual's unselfishness might go.

38. Both quotations are from "The Moral Philosopher and the Moral Life," in *The Will to Believe and Other Essays in Popular Philosophy* (Cambridge: Harvard University Press, 1979), p. 153 and pp. 154–55.

39. See, for example, "On a Certain Blindness in Human Beings" and "What Makes a Life Significant," both reprinted in John J. McDermott, ed., *The Writings of William James: A Comprehensive Edition* (Chicago and London: The University of Chicago Press, 1977), pp. 629–60.

40. I have argued in *Excellence in Public Discourse* that the richness of Mill's philosophy is better grasped if we do not think of his moral writings as a defense of utilitarianism, whatever Mill's own intent was. See esp. chap. 2.

41. John Stuart Mill, *On Liberty* (Indianapolis and New York: Bobbs-Merrill, Inc., 1956), p. 14.

42. Ibid., p. 91. Dewey's charge is overstated. See *Excellence in Public Discourse*, chap. 4.

43. In the United States the values of community and self-realization from the idealist perspective were expressed with great power by Josiah Royce. If an adequate history of the moral thought of the last hundred years is ever written, Royce will have a significant place in it. It is likely that Dewey was influenced as much by Royce as by Green and Bradley.

44. See Dewey, "Green's Theory of the Moral Motive," (*Early Works*, Vol. 3: 1889-1892), pp. 155-73.

45. For a systematic account, see chap. 5 of my *Excellence in Public Discourse*.

46. John Dewey and James H. Tufts, *Ethics* (*Later Works*, Vol. 7: 1932), p. 302. The lines quoted were written by Dewey.

47. Dewey, *Experience and Nature*, p. 157.

48. Dewey, *Reconstruction in Philosophy*, p. 201.

49. Dewey, *The Public and Its Problems* (*Later Works*, Vol. 2: 1925-1927), pp. 368-69.

50. Dewey, *Human Nature and Conduct*, pp. 226-27.

51. Santayana's view of religion is distinctively different from that of Feuerbach and Marx. The latter two saw religion as a form of alienation: all human power is conceived as foreign to the human and is invested in the divine. Religion can be that, of course, but it can also function to discern, praise, and solemnize fateful unions of human and natural powers.

52. See esp. chaps. 8-11 in *Reason in Religion*.

53. The most encyclopedic study is H. Standish Thayer's *Meaning and Action: A Critical History of Pragmatism* (Indianapolis and New York: The Bobbs-Merrill Company, 1968). An excellent analysis of Dewey's logical theory in relation not only to Peirce and James but also to "mainstream" logical theory is Ralph Sleeper's *The Necessity of Pragmatism* (New Haven: Yale University Press, 1986). John E. Smith's *Purpose and Thought* (New Haven: Yale University Press, 1978) is broader in scope than these two studies. It is extremely helpful in clarifying pragmatism as part of more inclusive philosophic assumptions. Broader still is Andrew J. Reck, *Recent American Philosophy* (New York: Pantheon Books, 1964), which is not confined to pragmatists.

54. James, *Pragmatism*, p. 40. Inconsistently, James later allows more significance than this to idealism. (With the help of Pamela Hall and Thomas R. Flynn, I translate *"nulla vestigia retrorsum"* as "no footsteps [lead] back [out].")

55. Dewey, *Logic: The Theory of Inquiry* (*Later Works*, Vol. 12: 1938), p. 102.

56. See esp. chap. 10 of *The Quest for Certainty* (*Later Works*, Vol.

4: 1929). This much misunderstood document is analyzed in my "Dewey's Theory of Moral Deliberation."

57. Marxism is also revolutionary in its treatment of theory and practice, making very effective criticisms of both empiricism and idealism. Marx, however, retained the notion of science as a summary of what is antecedently given, and he rejected the notion that experimental hypotheses can be used to direct processes of social change. He never fully tolerated the idea that the shape of the future might be contingent upon alternative reconstructions of the present. In brief, he was innocent of the experimental spirit. While this is a fault in his philosophy, he was nevertheless more realistic than Dewey in estimating the great resistances to change that are embedded in social forms.

3

Knowing and Valuing

Many philosophers suppose that the solution to problems in ethics is to be sought in the large question of the relations of facts and values. Somewhere in that welter of concerns might be discovered an objective and incontrovertible norm for behavior. There must be, one thinks, universal principles that can be established *as* facts, *as* truths (perhaps intuitively or self-evidently), or as unerringly derivative of ascertainable fact. Nothing subjective allowed here. Judgment cannot be just a matter of the vagaries of opinion and preference. Most commonly believed, perhaps, is that a divine being—possibly our creator—would fill such needs by its moral legislation.

A hardly less modest hypothesis for an objective ethics is that of Plato: there are eternal, perfect, and changeless archetypes of what is good and just. They are literally constitutive of the nature of things, and they are knowable by reason. It might be that inherent standards have a humbler role in the world order, performing nevertheless crucial moral functions. Kant's conception of reason is a case in point. Moore's indefinable, nonnatural property is another; but any form of value realism is offered with the same intent. In such theories, moral standards are part of the inherent structure of reality. The reality we inhabit is through and through a moral reality. In the way the expression is popularly and relevantly understood, there is no dualism of fact and value.

Establish the truth of such ontological theories, so it is supposed, and the basic problems of ethics are solved. If they remain unsolved, the failure lies either with ontological inquiry, or—to our lament— in the very nature of existence. To establish the reality of such a

71

moral world view would put in our hands a constant and undeniable rule of life, and perhaps much more; perhaps an assurance that in some large sense the universe answers to our moral aspirations. Life would be fundamentally justified.

To contend honestly with questions of fact and value yields crucial information about the moral condition. No serious philosophy can neglect them. We are engulfed and carried along by events that are alluring, frightening, hurtful, lovely, and in infinite variety and intricacy. This condition is also permeated by structures, orders, and continuities, subject to investigation and cognition; somehow the two sorts of phenomena are subject to some manner of correlation: we might rescue fragile and insecure goods by knowing something of the conditions of their occurrence. Recognizing this much, one's first reaction would not be to ask whether statements of evaluation are deducible from statements of fact. Some grasp of the existential correlations would presumably be our first concern—some trial at coping with the ordeals of real life. Nevertheless, the logical question must at some point be considered. If the issue turns out to be bogus, other sorts of investigation must be tried. With matters of choice and conduct pressing insistently upon us, we might ask whether our cognitive powers and accomplishments might still have some vital office. Especially if the conspicuous realities of conflict, tragedy, and uncertainty will not be explained away, we must assess the moral life for whatever resources it might really hold.

I choose to speak first of knowing and valuing, rather than of fact and value. The choice stresses distinguishable activities of human engagement with features of the world. It by no means ignores the objects of these activities, but it leaves consideration of them until later. Just to establish that neither activity—knowing or valuing—is reducible to the other will clarify the nature of the moral condition and thereby open the way to engaging its real problems and agencies.

Everyone agrees that knowing and valuing are pervasive traits of experience, but there is not much agreement about their respective natures and roles. Recall, for example, the difference between judgment as classification and judgment as experimental criticism, the contrast generated by the radical dissimilarities between classical and pragmatic conceptions of nature. There is a concomitant difference in regarding value as essentially changeless or as a function of change. In recent philosophy, much useful attention has been given to the interpenetration of knowing and valuing. We have been barraged, of course, with treatises that point out how moral prejudice invades the determination of alleged social facts (and even physical facts); it has been rigorously argued that the determination of concepts for cognitive inquiry involves selection—choice. James and the pragmatists, and many others, have observed that classifications are made for a purpose. Purposes may legitimately vary, and as they do, likewise the formation of concepts.[1] They also remarked that our evaluations are in part determined by variations in cognitive meaning. (If an object—say, a snake—is identified either as harmless or as poisonous, our judgments of its worth will vary accordingly.)

The present discussion is not a contribution to analyses of that nature. All that I wish to contend at the moment is that knowing and valuing are not the same. Knowing is *a value,* but it is not valu*ing.* Neither knowing nor valuing can be reduced to the other, and neither is dispensable in making moral decisions. The import of this thesis is of some consequence, for it means, as I will contend throughout this chapter, that moral philosophy and discourse are not reducible to science.

The Ambitions of Scientific Moral Philosophy

"Science," of course, has had many meanings. I intend by it not only to denominate the best authenticated and systematized knowledge (ignoring the meaning of "best"), but also—more liberally—to refer to any system of thought that is presented as rationally conclusive. *A "scientific" moral theory in this liberal sense would succeed in compelling assent among rational persons regardless of individual differences between them.* This characterization is more inclusive than "scientific" in its narrower sense, and it seems to capture much of what moralists would like to accomplish: they want somehow to adduce principles in a manner such that rational persons must consent to them, regardless of what idiosyncrasies might otherwise distinguish such persons. This rendering of "scientific" incorporates theories such as that of Rawls, for example. Rawls's procedure aims at a "moral geometry," as he calls it; the argument is intended to be "strictly deductive," but the first principle from which it is all suspended is a moral ideal. It is, Rawls claims, the ideal of the person implicitly held in Western liberal democracies; his argument, therefore, is presented as rationally conclusive for that population.

We shall see that such pretensions are categorically misconceived. To know (or to believe that one knows) that a certain condition exists is distinguishable from approving or disapproving it, admiring or condemning it, and so on for other affective states. Such states, moreover, are ineliminable from valuing or evaluating. If they did not exist at all (let us suppose), the condition under investigation could be assigned no worth. This is a position I will articulate and defend. On these assumptions, a determination of what morally ought to be done is inevitably, in the final analysis, a *response* to a wide and complex array of conditions. Given the variations in human beings, these responses cannot be identical, and sometimes they will be substantially divergent. *Reasoning* from true premises gives one and only one conclusion, but *response* to what is conveyed in such statements will not be universal. The existences cognized might, however, be of such a nature that the responses to them could be quite similar from one human being to the next. If Hobbes, for example, had his facts straight and complete, then his argument would be almost as compelling as a deduction. If the state of nature were as he described, our response to it might well resemble the behavior that Hobbes himself prescribed. But there is no reason to suppose it would be identical or uniform.

The distinction between reasoning and responding must be held. This makes clear why conscientious persons may disagree and supplies a main reason why we frequently should be tolerant or even admiring of the moral assessments of others. Of course, in the basic difference between reasoning and responding we see why there can be no moral science. Responding cannot have the intersubjective uniformity of logic, whether the response be to a given case or to an entire theory.

Grasping the generic difference between knowing and valuing has crucial, and difficult, lessons for the moral condition. To enter this argument, I will resume attention to the *ontological* questions with which I began, looking at some widely admired and emulated attempts to discover pristine moral principles or standards in the constitution of being, or in some part of it. Subsequently I will analyze some *logical* questions arising from the fact/value distinction. Then I will provide a sustained defense of the irreducibility of valuing to knowing. Our enriched, if not always reassuring, conception of the moral condition will give us insight into the obstinately plural forms of moral value and moral disagreement, and it will help us to be on our guard against the insidious blandishments of putatively scientific moral systems. It will help us to identify and deploy our pertinent cognitive resources and those of discourse as well.

The Ontological Status of Moral Norms

In the West, there have been several revolutions in our understanding of the world. The ancient Greeks imagined that the world is a cosmos, a definite and congenial order. The Christians, borrowing heavily from the classical model, also proclaimed an order designed and run by a perfect being, who looked after the personal destiny of each person, promising infinite rewards and punishments. All creation gives witness to His wisdom and goodness. All things that exist participate in the cosmic drama, each one striving to be perfect in its own kind as an essential part of the whole.

In the seventeenth century this world view was shattered. Nature came to be conceived as utterly mechanical and lifeless—matter in motion and nothing else. In itself it was bereft of qualities, ends, or a moral order. Each lump of being was thought to rush blindly on its purposeless way, propelled by impersonal force. Nature was in no sense a guide to conduct and aspiration. Its real nature was meaningless at best, alien to the human subject at worst. Revolutionary change also occurred in the nineteenth and twentieth centuries, but it has not been of a sort to resuscitate the old moral order. The Darwinian revolution, indeed, seemed to reduce human significance still more.

At the revolutionary turnings in man's understanding of the world, the immediate excitement has been with the new vision, as such. But a more profound problem soon becomes urgent: where or what is value in such a world? How, if at all, does it provide a guide to life and assure us that there is some worth in it? The intellectual revolution of the seventeenth century came up empty handed with such questions. In doing so, it at best obscured matters of value; at worst it made us keepers of an ashen truth. The Cartesian revolution emptied nature of moral consequence, either compressing all value into the private redoubt of the self, or catapulting it into a realm beyond nature. In the latter conception it has had an uneasy status: moral significance and direction become the province of the gambles of *a priori* reason or of religion—in effect, of prejudice or hope. In the former, they become the province, apparently, of mere subjective preference, bereft of any wider and more sustaining meaning.

David Hume was among the first to bring these problems to explicit focus, and he left us with the view that nothing in being external to the human is morally normative. He rejected divine law and argued with cogency that reason in and of itself, out of all relation to passion and sentiment, has no moral function. Experience, he believed, was wholly subjective in content and structure; it had no ascertainable correlation with external events. The mere existence of the latter, in fact, was conjectural.[2]

Hume authored the famous argument that from statements about any matter of fact or relation we can derive no moral judgment: there is no logical way to get an "ought" out of an "is." Evidently, it might seem, our knowledge of the world could yield nothing of moral import; and our moral judgments, accordingly, are at bottom expressions of whatever the subjective constitution of the passions happens to be. Hume was confident that there are innate, fixed, and universal moral sentiments. However, there is no intelligible reason in terms of his philosophy why he should believe they are more or less suited to overt behavior. According to Hume's philosophy, the natue of the constitution of the world in no way determines our subjective nature. The world just happens to be a place where there just happen (conveniently) to be events that are approved and disapproved by our innate sentiments—a very truncated view of the moral condition. For his part, believing in the universality of moral sentiment was enough for Hume.

Few moralists have been reassured. It is discouraging to believe that morality, at bottom, is only sentiment. Many have been unwilling to concede that ethical judgment teeters on such precarious support. Hume to the contrary notwithstanding, sentiment is fickle; in any case, it seems impervious to logic. Sentiments, as such, are neither true nor false. Most people, and most philosophers, continue to believe that if normative ethics is to exist at all, it can do so only as a kind of science—perhaps more than a science, if one is Kantian. To stand as a defense against moral chaos, a sure and austere morality must be demonstrated to be true.

The quest for an objective ethic often leads to human nature itself. It may be that invariant norms define our very nature. Hume's theory is a case in point, and so, in a way, is Kant's. Kant, of course, made an absolute distinction between human nature and rational nature, corresponding to his particular distinction between phenomena and noumena, appearance and reality, nature and things in themselves. Human nature, as such, is reducible to nature, while reason is noumenal. Moral authority resides exclusively with reason. Thus one might appropriately say that Kant's theory is not based on human nature. The fact to notice, however, is that human nature has direct access to reason; human beings happen to be possessors of it, and this condition is what makes them distinctively moral agents. Reason in and of itself provides the moral law. This alone is necessary and sufficient for the conduct of life. Kant resolutely insisted that our empirical, or natural, self is and must be utterly without normative significance. The passions, or any traits of human nature as such, have no moral worth. Reason, by contrast, is a creature of super-sensible reality. It is universal and invariant, and its nature owes nothing to the merely contingent fact that human beings happen to possess it. He believed it is in the very nature of reason that conformity to law as such, universality as such, is the one legitimate test for what is right.

This remarkable philosophy has many sources, but the most obvious is in Kant's acceptance of the idea that nature is fully described in the physics of Isaac Newton: the Newtonian world machine, matter in motion, governed by invariant law.

> The understanding can know in nature only what is, what has been, or what will be. We cannot say that anything in nature *ought to be* other than what in all these time-relations it actually is. When we have the course of nature alone in view, *ought* has no meaning whatsoever.[3]

Kant's announced reason for exiling moral value from nature is that there is no freedom there. Moral value exists exclusively in the free dictate of pure practical reason to conform to universality as such. As fine a reduction of moral worth as we are ever apt to see! But one suspects that with a different concept of nature Kant would not have pressed pure reason so urgently into service.[4]

These theories were hardly the first to advert to qualities pertaining to the person. The notion that compliance with our "true" nature is the standard of what is good and just has a long and absorbing history, but in Hume and Kant such qualities are the *exclusive* criterion. A similar body of thought—the moral sense school—detects a faculty in human nature especially equipped to discover antecedently existing moral facts; or—parallel to Kant—they believe we possess a faculty of such a nature that whatever is approved or disapproved by it is *therefore* right or wrong.

While some philosophers, such as those mentioned, have attempted to study the moral dimension of human nature in isolation, others have examined it as part of an extended field. Often, a discriminated form of human nature has constituted a standard, but the form has been understood—in Aristotle, for example, or Dewey—as organic to inclusive and decisive characteristics of the surrounding order. Such philosophers have thought it possible to conceive of the good of man only in terms encompassing man and world together. Think, too, of Spinoza, Hegel, or Nietzsche. The perennial fascination and inspiration that such philosophies hold for us is not so much in their formal structure as in the elaboration of the nature of the desired end and the conditions of its attainment. When the ideal self is ruptured from any context of moment, the resulting conception of the moral condition is thin and vain.

Included in such inquiries is the matter of the relation of individual to society. Is there a way of distinguishing them that will be decisive in determining rights or obligations? Depending on how we understand the individual/social relation, we might, with Locke and Mill, believe we can define freedom at its core in a nonsocial sphere of activity or, following Marx, as deliberate social activity.

The point of all these hasty references and allusions is to illustrate that the search for clear and binding moral norms usually takes the form of an inquiry into the nature of things. Philosophers are often convinced that it is in such inquiries, if anywhere, that fundamental solutions to moral problems are to be found. These questions are ontological; they are directed at discovery and analysis of what exists. Such inquiries might determine what, if anything, has distinctive and possibly supreme moral quality. Something in us and/or what encompasses us might be ascertained as truly existent and at the same time normative for conduct.

The Logic of Evaluation

Another sampling of questions regarding fact and value is primarily logical: that of deriving normative judgments from descriptive statements. These, too, come to a focus in the problems bequeathed by Hume. Solutions to the is/ought problem are commonly thought to rest on cognitive and logical operations alone. Statements about the way the world is would somehow entail statements about what we ought to do. The determination of such truths will be "scientific," possessing the superior cognitive authority of that enterprise. To deny such truths is to be convicted of some ascertainable error of fact or logic. In recent years, the problem has taken the form of asking whether moral language is reducible to descriptive language. If so, we will arrive at specific true statements about what we are morally required to do.

According to Bentham, for example, "good" and "bad" and presumably all moral expressions are defined in terms of aggregates of pleasure and pain. Seeming moral dilemmas are resolved by determining which action will promote the greatest happiness of the greatest number. Thanks to Moore, the attempt to define *moral* properties in terms of *other* properties (e.g., aggregates of pleasure and pain) is called naturalism.[5] Largely owing to Moore as well, the utilitarian reduction is widely judged a failure. Even if this is so, the task of producing intersubjectively verifiable definitions of moral words has been almost universally regarded as essential. We are repeatedly advised that without such definitions, normative ethics is nonsense. Moral claims must be cognitive. The is/ought problem must be solved! On this virtually all are agreed. The passion to believe that moral judgments are true seems to be exceeded only by the passion to believe in God, freedom, and immortality.

From the publication, say, of Ayer's *Language, Truth and Logic* in 1937 until quite recently, our moral philosophers have had nothing more edifying to do than to scrutinize the English language to see whether its moral words are indeed irreducible. Those who say so are called noncognitivists; those who deny it, following Moore, are termed naturalists. For both sides alike, the grand inquiries of traditional moral philosophy are forsaken. Gone are the absorbing questions of the moral implications of the nature of man and the world; gone is any distinctly moral motive for investigating those great subjects.

Ordinary language analysis applied to ethical discourse yields metaethics. In the early years of metaethics, one often heard that ethical judgments are nonsense, moral values arbitrary. Some analysts since then have believed that metaethics yields at least some substantive moral conclusions. It is asserted, for example, that the very concept of morality implies such behavior as giving reasons, being impartial, and testing reasons by extending their application from the particular case to similar cases: that is, by universalizing them.

Today, metaethics is no longer in the forefront. The quest for a scientific ethics has taken a new direction. It has been an ambitious quest in many ways, aimed at establishing one or another form of moral geometry. It shares with its predecessors the assumption that if normative ethics is to exist at all, it can do so only as a kind of science, perhaps even more than a science—possessing demonstrative certainty. It also assumes with its predecessors a very narrow conception of the materials that must be addressed to engage in moral theory. The new direction is highly rationalistic in both method and form. It gained great force with the publication of Gewirth's *Reason and Morality* and Rawls's *A Theory of Justice*. Ronald Dworkin, Robert Nozick, and David Gauthier are some more of its best-known practitioners. Its principal features will receive comment from time to time and will be more closely examined in chapter 7.

Disjunction of Logic and Ontology

Both the ontological and logical inquiries might be regarded as two parts of the same enterprise. Wouldn't the verification of the existence of the appropriate deity, or of Plato's Good, or Moore's, provide just the facts that would settle the question of objective morality? Possibly Aristotle's analysis of human nature, or Kant's, would suffice, if only their truth were established. Moral authority might, irresistibly, be found to be a function of specific properties of events. Perhaps more promising is that the existence of intrinsically moral ontological entities or intrinsically moral human traits might be verified. Perhaps the reason Hume could not logically produce evaluations in his conclusion was that he had denuded his premises of anything morally interesting. That is, his concept of nature was so empty and pointless that nothing of a normative character could be found in it. With a suitably enriched concept of the nature of things, perhaps including theological speculations, couldn't we derive evaluative conclusions from statements about an inherently normative structure of reality? Wouldn't inquiries of this sort, if successful, lay to rest the problems of definition that plague the controversy? An objective moral philosophy, if it were possible at all, would be contingent upon the correctness of the relevant philosophic theory of the nature of things. Philosophic and scientific concepts, of course, undergo change with the introduction of new discoveries and explanations. Similarly, moral language would undergo change, contingent upon successful inquiry and analysis.

It is not really obvious, however, precisely what the significance of the truth of such theories would be. One might easily believe that such conclusions about being or human nature would make moral philosophy a fully cognitive discipline. One might well believe that the problem is whether there really are such facts to be ascertained. Such an assumption would be premature. The establishment of the desired facts would *not* make a science of moral philosophy or moral discourse. The reason is that the determination of moral values—ends, principles, standards, judgments—cannot be reduced to matters of knowing. The element of evaluation, choice, decision, advocacy—call it what you will (for now)—cannot be eliminated from moral experience without making it indistinguishable from other modes of experience *and thereby rendering it of no service to the moral life.* The activities of favoring and opposing, loving, hating, honoring, respecting, serving, fearing, despising, and so on are the very substance of life; and without them distinctly moral experience vanishes. Such functions are what give rise to the specific problems of the moral life and moral reflection. We not only know things, but we are attracted and repulsed by them in endless variety and itensities. These responses determine for a live creature whether it lives or perishes, or lives well or miserably. Without such responses, life in any form literally could not exist.

Moral language must express these plural and varying noncognitive states in order to be *moral* language—to have any pertinence to the moral life. The noncognitivists are correct, then, in concluding that there is an irreducibly evaluative component in moral discourse, and hence such discourse cannot be through and through cognitive and hence scientific.[6]

Although moral philosophers are typically forgetful of the fact, moral philosophy is at the service of the moral life. Before there is philosophy there is real moral experience, which is often difficult. Our passions and affections are not often well served by our exertions; and one of our most typical predicaments is that of conflict. Were it not for the contentions that occur in the toils of social life, what has come to be known as moral philosophy would not exist. Now that it has been invented, however, its *raison d'être* is easily forgotten. A philosophy that argues for the reduction of the evaluative to the exclusively cognitive is forgetful. A fundamental problem of philosophy is to determine the coordinate functions of knowing and valuing, not to eliminate either one for the other.

Evaluation is a function of many conditions, including our existent likes and dislikes, expectations of others, anticipations of natural events, existing moral commitments, emotional and biological needs, traditional teachings, established loyalties. It is also a function of the regard in which we hold such things subsequent to reflecting upon them. Reflection does not abolish regard, but it might quailfy a given demand or aversion by disclosing its various functions. It might bring affecting events, including those we might think of as distinctively moral, to our attention in a manner hitherto unrecognized, and these new meanings would produce a new affect. Our moral decisions are necessarily constituted by more than the amassing of knowledge, no matter of what sort. Different moral theories and different moral judgments are strategies for producing different affects and subsequent action. Intersubjective agreement on cognitive matters does not, however, entail concord of evaluation.

The *subject matter* of moral discourse constrains and inspires our conduct. That is, the realities of the world in which we carry on our lives move us to act. The communication that occurs relevant to a given problematic situation, as well as empirical inquiries and imagination, bring these realities to our attention; we can imaginatively (sometimes fancifully) rearrange them toward rearranging them in fact. Linguistic behavior is a surrogate for the affective qualities of the life-world. By bringing these qualities into our presence, it *causes* us to make certain moral judgments; it does not *entail* them. I will have somewhat more to say about moral discourse in the next chapter. The lesson at this juncture is this: just as the realities that elicit attraction and aversion will not elicit quite the same attractions and aversions in different persons, the responses elicited by moral discourse likewise will not be identical. Moral discourse, then, does not uniquely determine moral action. There will be differences in the consequent behavior due to the differences in human beings.

Accordingly, the familiar experience of moral disagreement is not necessarily due to bad logic, ignorance, irrationality, or wickedness. There can be conscientious and irreducible moral disagreement. It is essential to recognize this feature of the moral condition. This does not mean that moral philosophy and discourse are therefore a useless passion. There are constraints and opportunities in the moral condition that militate against both absolutism and relativism. As we shall see in due course, a careful examination of the main features of the moral life dictates a form of pluralism.

For the present discussion, we may pass by distinctions within each class; i.e., different types of cognitive operations and different modes of evaluation. It is enough to see that there is such a distinction, no matter how difficult it might be to identify in various activities and to recognize its implications for the moral condition. The failure, indeed, to recognize implicit evaluations in moral theory and discourse accounts, in part, for the premature conclusion that ethics is, or could be, a science.

Those who suppose that evaluation is reducible to cognition and hence morals to science are unaware of the decisive evaluations implicit in their own experience. Hume's rightly famous argument makes more than a merely logical point. He says that the "ought" in the allegedly conclusive judgment is in fact put there by moral sentiment, even though we might not recognize the insertion. Hobbes, to take a familiar example, presents several cognitive claims about the nature of body, human nature, and the state of nature. These are thought to be deductively related. From these propositions he appears to deduce still further propositions about right conduct. Propositions with "ought" in them appear. But these prescriptions clearly are not deducible from the premises. Their source is the passions. The evaluation slipped into the argument so easily and innocently that no one recognized that the intruder had no validation from logic. The moral judgment is like the uninvited visitor at the party who is so genial and of good company that no one thinks to ask whether she has the proper admission. If the moral judgment were on the original "guest list," it would be so at the invitation of sentiment. If there are moral judgments in the premises, they are there only at the behest of moral sentiment.[7]

The validity of Hume's argument is not dependent on his ontology. Populate nature and the universe with whatever kinds of beings you fancy and adorn them with every conceivable property. We might acquire knowledge of them; it is a further step to evaluate them. We might judge the cognized beings adorable or loathesome in any number of ways. I certainly don't wish to deny that. I insist only that such epithets imply an irreducibly evaluative function.[8]

Sundry Attempts to Reduce Evaluation to Cognition

Have I made a blunder? Perhaps the element of evaluating doesn't really belong to morals. There is judging, of course, in the sense of determining whether the qualities of a given act are subsumed under a moral principle. But there is also, it will be said, distinctly moral knowledge, which is determined independently of our affective nature. We all speak in ways to suggest that we have knowledge of good and evil, or of rights and duties. We *know* what is good, and we teach it to our children. "I have knowledge of the Good, of God's law," etc. It is important to analyze such statements.

The Gods

Begin with the claims that most persons suppose would make moral norms not only cognitive and true, but also as compelling as they could be: knowledge of divine command. Assume there is a divine being and its commands are known. We are told, for example, to love our neighbors as ourselves. What gives such a command its moral authority? Why is it morally obligatory? Presumably because of its source: a morally perfect being. God is perfectly just, merciful, wise, and good. With that much established, the only impediment to a perfect morality, so it seems, is to have knowledge of the will of this being. But let us consider the grounds for regarding the divinity as perfectly just, merciful, wise, and good.

To understand how we come to impute such traits, imagine a universe populated by several deities, the behavior of each of which is different from that of the others. One of them may be consistently loving and partial to all humans; another may wish nothing but ill-fortune and torment for us. A third vacillates between protestations of love and justice on the one hand and the threat of infinite suffering on the other, regardless of what we do. Still a fourth remains utterly removed from humankind, leaving us to our own devices. Another imitates various human traits, but to exaggeration, being unusually lusty, vengeful, powerful, capricious, beautiful, artistic, skilled in the hunt, or wise.

To continue the fable, suppose each of these beings declares that it is morally perfect. Which one is really so? We can't take it on their own authority, for each makes the same judgment of itself, while each is drastically unlike the others. For our part, then, we would be in the unhappy position of somehow choosing from among the ranks of the gods. If we were to inquire of them what standards of perfection they employ, they would rightly dismiss the question as an impertinence. Each *constitutes* the standard. To admit to conformity to a higher law is to confess that one is not the supreme moral being.

We must, then, select from among the gods. But how? On what grounds? We can't ask *them*. I assume that if we were to look for divine authority under such circumstances, we would accept that of the god(s) or goddess(es)—if they have gender—whose morals are most congruent with what we take to be the imperatives and aspirations of our own existence. We would also necessarily have an eye to their good will toward us and their power in the scheme of things. I say this not because such a mode of selection seems highly probable. It is inevitable; there are no other standards by which we could proceed. My claim does not belong to the science of anthropology, however plausible it would be as such, seeing that different cultures have selected different gods. It is an illustration of the inescapable necessity of discriminating and selecting authorities according to human standards.

Divine command does not relieve us of choice. The matter is no different if we suppose there happens to be only one god, one who declares itself morally perfect. Were Satan that lone supernatural being, we would not accept him as a *moral* authority any more than we would a human tyrant who constantly threatened us with enslavement and torture. We might pay insincere homage and tribute to such a being, however, to try to propitiate it.

Nor does the argument depend on what the gods say of themselves.

Let them say anything about their moral qualities. We would worship and obey according to our interests, according to the way a given deity challenges, supports, or threatens human concerns. If there is an agency in the universe that is wise, benevolent, and powerful, that would be a supremely important fact; and belief in it would be very reassuring. We would do well to heed such direction as it might provide. That is, our evaluation of it would be very favorable, and almost everyone would share it. But it would be an evaluation. The thought is doubtless terrifying to anyone with the slightest fear of being displeasing to the powerful, but it seems to be inescapable.

If there is divine command, and if it is knowable, then the command is an objective fact. This knowledge as such does not settle the moral status of the command, which is still to be determined. Its *moral* status is not an object or fact existing independently of human evaluation. There is knowledge of whatever the god denominates good or evil. Once the divine will is assessed as *worthy* of obedience, however, *then* we can say we have knowledge of what to do; but the prior assessment is a necessary condition of counting the divine commands as objects of *moral* knowledge. The object of knowledge is the command itself—and, without doubt, what is believed to be contingent upon obeying or disobeying it. But there are all sorts of possible commands from all kinds of possible sources. The evaluation of the command is distinct from the cognitive act; without the evaluation, divine will as an object of knowledge is not yet a moral object.

An example of alleged moral knowledge less freighted with blinding emotion would make the point more accessible. One could say, "I know that kindness is good," but that would be possible only after kindness had already been confidently *esteemed* to be good. It is the same with God. It would seem obvious that a knowledge of divine will is permeated with the most acute hopes and fears imaginable. That and that alone is why such will is so important. But in fact it is not obvious, because everyone believes that divine will is morally authoritative quite apart from any human concern. Such refusal to recognize terrifying conditions is what psychologists call denial.

I am not just arguing that we cannot choose with other than human criteria. I am also saying that the criteria cannot be determined simply by the process of knowing. It takes cognitive inquiry to find out what traits of reality are crucial to human existence, but the criteria of "crucial" are determined by more than cognitive acts.

Platonic Forms

So subtle are the ways in which our evaluations are hidden from us that it will be salutary to consider some further examples. Plato's philosophy is another archetype of a supposedly impersonal basis for morality. Grant for argument's sake that there is a definite teleological order in the universe, determining the true nature and outcomes of all processes, including the human order. There is one ultimate *eidos* that determines the relations of all the others, including justice, courage, and temperance. This Plato calls the form of the Good. With knowledge of the Good, every act can be classified as morally good, just, etc., or as embodying a mixture of various forms. Surely *this* is unadulterated moral knowledge.

But Plato's company, too, includes the genial guest that makes her appearance in disregard of the announced criteria for admission. The ultimate form doesn't exist with *"To Agathon"* chiseled on it. Plato *gave* it that name of distinction. He did so for obvious reasons. To order both the state and the individual on the cosmic pattern is necessary for genuine happiness. The contemplation of the forms is itself a rapturous experience, and the Good is the condition of all that is valuable in human life. In calling this form The Good, Plato disclosed his conviction that the universe in its essential nature is friendly to human existence. This is not to deny that the form of the Good has value. It has value precisely because of its functions for human beings. Indeed, Plato himself refers to it in this way. Socrates asks, "Shall we further agree . . . that you and I must now try to indicate some state and disposition of the soul which has the property of making all men happy?"[9] And the inquiry, of course, leads to the conclusion that the desired state is knowledge of the Good. The Good *qua* good, then, is not just an object of knowledge. Its status in human esteem depends necessarily on human esteeming; its deservedly honorific status is not a product of cognitive and logical operations alone. Accordingly, even if there were a golden tablet affixed to the form, with *"To Agathon"* inscribed upon it, that in itself would have no more weight than one of the gods saying he is perfect. In either case, our proper response is "So . . . ? Tell me more."

It would also be misleading to suggest that its value is due to traits belonging exclusively to the individual. This would be to lead us to a conception of the individual similar to that identified in Hume and Kant, which makes the moral life something of a mystery. Obviously, they are perfectly objective traits and functions of the world that are valued. For example, to take the matter from the point of view of evolutionary biology, we recognize that the values of a species are a function of its intricate involvement with an environment. The structure of value is not determined by the individual alone nor by the environment alone. The argument here is that human affective responses are a necessary condition of evaluation. To take them as sufficient is a kind of philosophic blindness. We must look beyond human nature to complete an investigation of the moral condition.

I trust these remarks make it clear—if it has not been clear already —that what I am formulating is decidedly *not* a defense of sheer moral sentiment. Moral sentiment—evaluation unchastened by knowledge and intelligence—is one of the surest means of moral ineptitude, escapism, and charlatanism. An evaluation *is* an affective response, but it needn't occur in the void created by mindlessness. Likewise, what we call a moral judgment is not a cognitive claim, but the expression of an advocacy of some sort. But all advocacies are not equal. As countless episodes in daily life attest, there can be more or less informed advocacy, more sensitive or impartial advocacy, or deliberately obfuscating advocacy. We know the many differences between advocates.

Moral Faculties

Examples of the irreducibility of valuing and knowing could be multiplied. It is widely supposed that a characteristic human trait, or a set of them, defines our moral nature. That might truly be a useful distinction. Powers of reflection, impartiality, or compassion might be singled out. Again, however, this definition would not be merely cognitive; there is also a selection, a discrimination, of traits based upon what we take to be our interests. This interest might be conceived (implausibly) as rationality as such, but in any case there must be the interest. Surely the definition of our moral nature is not self-evident. On the contrary, it is obvious that we distinguish certain facets of human nature as being especially important because of *antecedent* moral experience.

The exclusively cognitive approach is not saved by arguing that we have a distinct moral faculty—say reason, conscience, or moral sense. *Why* is a given sense called the moral sense? What makes such faculties *moral?* We have many senses and faculties. A person would have to be dazed, gullible, or slavish to believe that there is, prior to our judgment of the matter, a self-evidently moral faculty within us, and all we need do is obey it. If an unknown stranger came to you and simply announced that he is your moral preceptor, no doubt you would scoff. If you were looking for moral advice from someone, you would first examine the credentials of the candidates very carefully. It is no different with the so-called moral sense or intuition. It is as a *consequence* of our moral experience tht we come to designate one or another of our powers as morally reliable. The predicate "rational" seems to have mystical powers, but it possesses them because we have already concluded that thought and action characterized as rational are much to be preferred to the irrational. An essential support of the rational is the sentimental.

We regard many of our traits admiringly. Philosophers have delineated various structures of human nature in a way to inspire devotion and effort. These are then called virtues. We speak of moral personality, human dignity, personal autonomy, and suchlike as treasured features of human nature, and properly so. But when we so discriminate, we have made an evalative recommendation. However much we would like to do so, we cannot thrust aside the reality of evaluative choice; and in no choice can we vault from a position free of an antecedent moral experience. Just as we define our gods to suit our experience, we likewise distinguish our moral powers.

The discrimination of moral and axiological traits could not occur except as a matter of selective interest and reflection. If you say such traits are discriminated *because* they are good, right, obligatory, etc., one would have to persist in asking why these traits and not others deserve such titles. Why are some objects of knowledge or intuition regarded as morally pertinent and others not? What are the properties distinguished, and what is their character such that they play a decisive role in judgment and conduct? To refuse to enter upon such an analysis is to be content with saying that they are good because they are good—a profound claim!

Moral Facts

It is testimony to the will to believe that G. E. Moore's assertions about a nonnatural property have been thought to have ethical significance. If the property does exist, we are not given *any* reason for its having moral status at all. For all we know, nonnatural properties of all sorts clutter the universe. Regions of the cosmos might also be populated with gods and Platonic forms. We can also speak of epigenetic rules, derivative of our genes, or of alleged transcendental conditions of discourse. *If any such entities are morally important, it cannot be so just because they exist, but because of the ways in which they enter into human experience and destiny.* We could not make a moral assessment of such things without knowing how they function for us.

If we were to take seriously a view like Moore's, we would have to make this cipher of a property the Archimedean point of moral choice. Inasmuch as it is literally decisive, if it qualifies a given event, that event is good, regardless of its other properties. The other properties could not determine the presence or absence of good without compromising good's uniquely decisive character and singular moral significance. When we wonder how to respond to a given phenomenon, we could determine all its natural traits and functions, but we aren't morally prepared to act, according to Moore, until we know whether it possesses the nonnatural property. In fact, that is *all* we would have to know. Take friendship, one of Moore's favorite examples of something good. Review its traits: sharing, intimacy, trust, caring, common adventures and trials, stimulation, loyalty, endurance, support, and so on. But these are not relevant to determining its moral value. We must still ask whether it is good! Moore gives us no reason why good should appear with these traits rather than others. If he did, he would give away his game, confessing that the *natural* traits of friendship were, after all, decisive.

I have heard it argued by serious philosophers that to ask why good is good is a foolish question. It is as silly as asking why yellow is yellow. Yellow just *is* yellow, and good, likewise, just *is* good; and that's all there is to it. This response, as anglicized philosophers used to say, is a muddle. Indeed, yellow is just what it is, and Moore's good is what it is, whatever it is. If we ask, however, why this color is *called* yellow, the answer is that we simply need a name to distinguish this property from others. Other than that, no moral consequence hangs on the selection of "yellow." The case is quite otherwise with "good." No one—including the defenders of a Moore-like position—would say that "good" is simply a designator and no more. On the contrary, it means that something very important is designated. Something is distinguished from all others due to its decisive value in determining moral conduct. Hence the question "Why is this property deserving of such a distinction?" remains altogether pertinent and altogether unanswered.

To take Moore's position seriously is curious. On the face of it, it is an affront to the qualities of, for example, friendship, and all the other properties of experience—a kind of nihilism or moral blindness. It might be only a failure of observation and reflection to identify exactly what it is that makes such things as friendship precious. Such failures distinguish all intuitionist theories: one item out of the entire panoply of experience is isolated, and this one item is regarded in its altogether exclusive existence as having definitive moral quality. This approach saves one the trouble of finding out why the item really is valuable, and it has the added virtue of dispensing with argument and permitting a dogmatic stance. "It's just right, that's all!" Moore's position is particularly bankrupt. We know what is good about Plato's Good, but Moore's is mysterious and impotent. In the present context, the point is twofold: Moore's type of value realism fails to make morality into a science, and it doesn't even present an ontology with any known relevance to morality.

Moral Intuition

The preceding comments about friendship prompt me to resume an earlier theme. They suggest one of the explanations for the initial plausibility of the interpretation of evaluative judgments as wholly cognitive. Some things are so deeply valuable that we rarely, if ever, make them an object of deliberate evaluation. Sometimes the most valued things are so taken for granted that we forget or ignore the reasons for their value. Such things, then, might seem to have their worth independently of our interests. To establish the value of friendship by reference to its constituent traits, we might think we are referring to nothing but simple cognition, of, say, loyalty, trust, and love. Clearly, however, it is because of our deep *affection* for such traits that we so prize friendship. The affective element is so deeply embedded in our experience, requiring no deliberate act of evaluation, that it is unnoticed *as* affective. So it is with other notions that acquire a seemingly axiomatic nature with regard to their moral status. It might seem self-evident that we ought to keep our promises, that we ought not to inflict needless suffering, that "we ought not to injure another in his life, health, liberty, or possessions," as Locke said, thinking he had delivered an intuitive truth of reason.

Some moral arguments appear to be so conclusive that we hasten to the further conclusion that the argument has to be exclusively cognitive. But distinctively moral considerations can be decisive in argument. The wanton mutilation of an innocent child is abhorrent to anyone who is not deranged, and the universal chorus that murder is wrong is not the consequence of cognitive considerations alone. More complex examples could be adduced.

There seems to be a kind of craving in human nature to forego inquiry into the meanings of experience. It is discomforting to our complacency and need for security. It is simpler to stand on habit, in effect, and proclaim intuitively obvious moral truths. When a Sidgwick or a Ross proclaims such "truths," he is actually drawing a dividend from the moral capital of his experience; and he (unwittingly) distinguishes an evaluation as a cognition. Such claims appear to be self-evident because the values to be realized are too extensive and precious to be outweighed in human experience by their alternatives. The claim might better be called insurmountable, meaning that the values to be realized are treasured well beyond those that would occur otherwise. Thus there is moral persuasion, not because ethics is a science, but because we inhabit similar environments and often have similar values. Unhappily, we get in the habit of crowning all manner of prejudice with the halo of intuitive truth.

Ordinary Language

There are further ways of arbitrarily foreshortening and misrepresenting moral experience and utterance. It is argued, for example, that the very concept of morality entails certain rules of thought and action. Accordingly, the support of this behavior might seem to be purely conceptual. It illustrates, however, that the notion of morality is itself morally determined. A brief survey of ethical theories discloses right away that there are and have been varied concepts of morality, and they incorporate varied value commitments. The merits of a given concept of morality are decided not by its correspondence to a paradigm laid up in heaven, but by the perceived merit of the behavior it prescribes.

The word "right" has no cosmic paradigm either. Even if it had, its meaning necessarily contains an evaluative component. The statement "What is right for me is right for others" is not a logical truth, for it *presupposes* in its utterance a commitment to the sense of impartiality expressed by the world "right." If one doesn't give a straw for impartiality, one is not obliged by the rules of logic to say "What is right for me is right for others." The statement is most intelligibly understood as a form of advocacy or as a declaration of one's position regarding impartiality. Consistency here is in moral behavior, not logical form; and this consistency is valued in making the utterance.

These remarks might be greeted with misgiving by those whose *métier* is the analysis of (allegedly) ordinary language. Perhaps our language does happen to be such that it possesses logical moral truths. In a sense, that might be true, but whatever truth it has does not challenge the theses I have been advancing. A very unlikely candidate for making ethics a science is that version of linguistic analysis which holds that some moral expressions are reducible to descriptive predicates. (This position can be called linguistic naturalism.) It might well be true that in the English language "good," for example, means, among other things, "beneficial to human beings." Implied here is a favorable evaluation of what is beneficial to human beings. The noncognitive component of "good" has not been eliminated.

This is the least of the problems of linguistic naturalism. It takes the *de facto* condition of the language, with the values with which it happens to be saturated, as morally normative. Disregarding the fact that a language is vague and ambiguous regarding the descriptive meanings of its moral expressions, there are in some cultures rather clear descriptive meanings that are morally repulsive to many others. What does "good" mean to cannibals or headhunters? To the ordinary Nazi, "evil" includes "Jewish," and "good" incorporates "domination of the world."

The Nazis in fact contrived and distributed a dictionary that defined crucial ideas in a manner to recreate ordinary German. This is reported in Ernst Cassirer, *The Myth of the State:* "Not long ago there was published a very interesting little book, *Nazi-Deutsch: A Glossary of Contemporary German Usage.* . . . In this book all those new terms which were produced by the Nazi regime were carefully listed, and it is a tremendous list."[10] In traditional German, for example, *Siegfriede* means peace through victory. In the *Glossary,* however (Cassirer reports), *Siegfriede* means peace through *German* victory. Another word, *Siegerfriede,* was revised to mean peace on the terms of the enemy; and there is no word that means simply peace through victory. Cassirer does not comment on how successful this venture into newspeak was, but if conditions were right, it might have transformed ordinary German.

Surely our moral evaluations must have some basis other than whatever has been petrified in the local idiom, but it is not clear that this *desideratum* has penetrated the obsessions of philosophers. Richard Hare's justification for universalization of prescriptions is that it is required by our language.[11] If one uses "ought," he is thereby committed to a universally impartial view. One may doubt that the logic of the native speaker is indeed what Hare claims. His view is that the language requires us to be not only perfectly impartial, but impartial regarding preferences when they are prudent and weighted according to their intensity. Very few users of English have realized this! The fact is that most persons are not universalistic in their moral outlook. Many who take a dislike or a moral repugnance to certain types of individuals will not believe that they are obliged to count the interests of such types equally; nor will they suppose that they must always be perfectly impartial between those to whom they are attached and others whom they don't even know.

Of more serious concern is the question of *why* it would be required by our language. How did it get that way (if indeed it did)? As the language evolved, Hare's argument was not available to its users and shapers. Evidently the language took shape as a *consequence* of various moral concerns, which found expression in discourse. Linguistic usage is steeped with values, but surely we don't want to count them as authoritative just because they are there. "Ordinary language," as Iris Murdoch observes, "is not a philosopher."[12]

MacIntyre on "Is" and "Ought"

Alasdair MacIntyre has long since given up on ordinary language analysis. He is now engaged in projects of greater scope and import. A central ambition is to reconceive human nature in a way that will close the gulf between "is" and "ought." He regards his attempt to reconstruct a sophisticated teleological conception of man as the means to derive judgments of what is good for human nature. The key to this feat is stated in chapter 5 of his *After Virtue:* If we recognize "man" as a functional concept, the trick can be turned— once we have the correct concept. Just as it follows from the functional idea of a sea-captain what a sea-captain ought to do, he contends, it would follow from the functional idea of man what a man ought to do.

While we wait for MacIntyre to produce this idea, we might observe that there are some severe problems with his argument. A sea-captain may be defined as one who navigates well and steams swiftly and safely. But he is defined in that way because we have already made the judgment that we prefer to take safe, speedy, and comfortable sea voyages; this antecedent evaluation informs the definition. The definition is not evaluatively neutral. In the same way, the argument about what a man ought to do would, in effect, be derived from a judgment of what a man ought to be.

MacIntyre announces the notion of functional concepts as if it were a great discovery, or rediscovery, recalling us once again to the *Nicomachean Ethics*. He forgets that for one formidable school of thought, pragmatism, *all* concepts are functionally defined. But that sheds no morally innocent light on the presumed logical relations of statements of knowledge and statements of advocacy. Concepts may be defined operationally, but evaluative judgments must be made in order to include a normative component in the definition. The question of what we should value remains as urgent as ever.

MacIntyre's work on human nature is suggestive, but it will not yield a logical bridge between knowing and valuing. Nevertheless, his work breathes more life than anything to be found in, say, Gewirth, Rorty, Nozick, or Dworkin; and he has helped to puncture prevailing stereotypes of the nature of moral philosophy. Still, he aims at a level of abstraction that could not be effective in the moral life. He wants to determine the most rational tradition of moral inquiry and practice (which would incorporate the most rational conception of man). Once the determination is accomplished, we presumably hold the solution to the is/ought problem, declare an end to pluralism, and deny the reality of tragedy. A truly Platonic ambition!

For his part, MacIntyre holds that some ongoing synthesizing of Aristotle, Augustine, and Aquinas proves most rational. Can he expect that conscientious inquirers will be compelled by the evidence to embrace this troika? One may doubt that there could be inter-subjective acceptance of the implied theology or of such claims to rationality, especially when normative conceptions (including "rational" itself) are integral to every tradition. In any case, I am enough of an experimentalist to give little credence to the proposition that the meaning of rationality can be determined only by reference to something so inclusive and vague as a tradition. (This is by no means to say that all traditions are equally rational.)

It is in the nature of the moral condition to make the achievement of MacIntyre's project impossible. In any tradition, however, we contend with the moral condition; so it is appropriate to characterize it as faithfully as possible. Such an analysis will disclose the generic resources and limitations available to us as moral beings, and it will disclose the virtues befitting that condition. These are virtues, we shall see, that find apt employment in the turmoil of the moral life itself.

Misbegotten Ambitions

According to my thesis regarding knowing and valuing, the very formulation of the is/ought problem is a misconception. The formulation presupposes that valuing is reducible to knowing—it is just a special kind of knowing. If, however, we recognize normative utterance as verbalization of advocacies, then the problem ceases to be even conceivably logical. From knowledge claims we can deduce further knowledge claims, but an advocacy is not the sort of thing that can be deduced from anything. Evaluations are elicited, never entailed. Alleged rigorous solutions to the is/ought problem do nothing but produce *someone's* "ought," *someone's* evluation—that of the author of the pretended solution. But it won't be everyone's "ought." Another someone will have another "ought." Yet the solutions are always presented as dispassionated and impersonal proofs. No one *appears* to the legislating for everyone else. The appearance is that we must succumb to logical argument, not to the values of a particular individual. It would be better to call the problem the is/out menace.

What is really at issue in philosophy's fixation on the is/ought problem? Did anyone ever adopt a moral position because it seemed to be deductively related to verifiable propositions? We acquire a morality as we grow up. Depending on how we are situated within it, we draw various lessons from the moral life. We are bombarded with moral suasion from a multitude of sources, and we might have the good fortune to have good teachers. As experience and knowledge (and misinformation) enlarge, we modify our morality—perhaps radically. We think about how it works; we live by it, more or less, and thereby continue to learn. In such a manner, most of us accumulate strong convictions and loyalties. If such a history has been fairly sincere and thorough, one can give a strong defense of his convictions; when he encounters further experience, action, and converse with others and reflects upon them, further qualification will occur.

Everyone but the sociopath has some susceptibility to moral concerns, as well as to outright emotional appeals of all kinds; we carry on our lives by articulating and criticizing such considerations. The reason-besotted philosopher supposes that we must get underneath all such things and justify them at large, or produce a princple that orders and trims the whole palpitating mass. An understanding of the moral condition dictates, however, that we can work only within it. We make our moral appeals, and others respond to them. They aren't waiting for the philosopher's stone, but they have this or that objection to our more-or-less elaborate advocacy, or they might have modifications to propose, or they suggest an alternative, and we respond in like manner. We might also identify arguments that are incoherent or inconsistent, that neglect alternatives or implications, that display ignorance of the facts, or distort them, or overlook crucial factors at issue. Hence the values at stake are vividly presented and can be recognized in their interdependencies and consequences. Thus our discussions are conducted, and at times they get somewhere. For right now, the point is that it is entirely permissible—indeed, unavoidable—to proceed with frankly moral advocacies.

If we are philosophers, however, we are apt to believe that this won't be enough. Moralists want more than this sort of reflection for ethical judgment. They want a claim that a particular kind of action is impersonally and categorically required or prohibited. The mere registration of the results of reflection is an impertinence, and moral discourse as a clash of opinion is contemptible. There must be a moral truth to which any personal inclination must submit, or morality is an illusion. So it has seemed to many. Philosophers will insist on a demonstration for moral belief, and they will present one to us!

The demonstration will be an imposture. We are confronted with moralists of strong convictions, developed out of their life history, which might have been highly educative. In one sense, that history has been effective: they do have these convictions. Due to the lessons of life experience, moral advocacy is already in place. Why, then, would they insist on ignoring the teachings of their moral history and attempt to substitute something for it that is utterly different in kind? They do not make a reflective analysis of the considerations that bring this advocacy; they contrive a new argument, out of whole cloth. The result of the alleged demonstration, rest assured, will not differ from the prior conviction. We have a marvelous ability to deduce the same moral propositions that we possessed antecedently to rolling out our logical artillery. With great ingenuity, philosophers and theologians produce a stunning and varied array of abstruse justifications for what we must do anyway, if life is to go on in some tolerable fashion. Why the vanity of the pretended demonstration?

Perhaps philosophers harbor the notion that without their cerebrations life would become quickly barbarous. It is well to remember here that there must be some powerful constraints and direction resident within the moral life itself, for it has managed to endure on its own and sometimes to prosper. We are not constantly enmeshed in adversarial relations. We have a great many shared moral commitments. It is partly because of this that disagreements are so conspicuous and vexing. What moral consensus we enjoy is due to our common experience—above all, social experience, which teaches us such virtues as telling the truth, keeping promises, respecting the concerns of others, being even-handed in our dealings, meeting our obligations, nurturing the young, and so on. These are massively important social functions, and there are fairly consistent rewards for honoring them, as well as punishments for betraying them. Admittedly, this is a rather unrefined consensus, and it leaves room for much diversity and uncertainty; there are many who search for strategies to get around such demands. All the same, their general necessity in the moral life is indisputable.

Very few of us—probably none of us—know just why we hold a good many of the moral convictions that we do. (Perhaps part of the reason for our convictions lies in our genetic code, of which we have little knowledge.) To approach that sort of understanding requires much reflection upon our experience. This is an extremely difficult task, however, and is easily set aside. Moreover, the resources that we might bring to reflection upon moral experience are not easily identifiable. We do know that we have strong moral views, never mind why. Better to cloak them in mesmerizing rhetoric, or authority, or to produce a deduction.

I have not dilated upon the question of the relationship between knowing and valuing just in order to refute mistaken arguments. What is significant is to contribute to our knowledge of the moral condition. Perplexity and conflict are perspicuous traits of the moral life. What are we to make of them? Typically, we wish to minimize them, but sweeping them under the rug of a putatively scientific morality is not a promising way to clean up the mess. A philosophy that cannot help us to understand and perhaps to alleviate this situation is an idle pastime at best. The relativist will leave it at that, while the absolutist, in effect, wants to stamp out moral disagreement, but can do so only by instituting some form of tyranny. Acknowledge, however, that evaluation cannot be melted down into cognition and it becomes easier both to understand why there is moral disagreement and to recognize a plurality of ethical values.

The common belief is that ethics is scientific or it is nothing. But there has to be something contrived in such a conclusion. The moral life persists in any case. We have moral communities that have endured by a variety of means—largely as a mtter of the trials and errors embodied in custom. With an added measure of intelligence and courage, communities attempt to enlarge and enrich their common life. Surely there is a role for sustained reflection to lend clarity and resource to this venture. Failure to attain scientific rules of conduct does not make all inquiry vain. We must learn to contend with our problems in a manner that is appropriate to the moral condition. Realism can be disappointing, but it also provides strength, emancipation, and direction. Not that the means of successfully contending with all our moral problems could ever be devised. That is the obsessive dream of would-be absolutists. Ethics cannot be a science, but there is a large and beneficent role for knowledge, intelligent discourse, and virtue in moral affairs. We continue to study the moral condition for its further lessons, whether chastening or revitalizing. The next step in the inquiry is to consider discourse, to see what resources it holds.

Notes

1. The classical pragmatists did not therefore conclude that such concepts do not trell us the way the world really is (unless "really" is freighted with rationalistic assumptions). A concept entails definite consequences, and if the consequences occur, the concept is validated. A concept is formulated to seek *selected* characteristics of the world, pertinent to a given problematic situation.

2. Hume was an extremely astute philosopher. His rejection of *a priori* moralizing is highly salutary; contemporary moralists should heed it. Donald Livingston's *Hume's Philosophy of Common Life* (Chicago: University of Chicago Press, 1984) does much to shatter the phenomenalistic stereotypes of Hume. Still, Hume cannot be altogether rescued from the charge that his philosophy of value is, in effect, confined to whatever the subjective characteristics of the human agent happen to be.

3. Kant, *Critique of Pure Reason* (A 547=B 575). Norman Kemp Smith translation (London: Macmillan, 1958), p. 473.

4. Kant's Third *Critique* offers quite a different portrayal of nature than the First, but his rethinking here evidently did not find its way into his moral philosophy.

5. This name (naturalism) has created a dismaying confusion, for it has led to simplistic renderings of, for example, Santayana and Dewey. Both of them referred to their philosophies as naturalistic, so current writers understand them to be singularly devoted to the logical problem of "is" and "ought" and judge them in reference to success or failure in that project. Then, inasmuch as the content of their moral vocabularies deviates from current usage, the entirety of their respective moral philosophies comes tumbling down and can be happily forgotten.

It is not easy to say with brevity what it means to call Santayana and Dewey naturalists, but it has nothing to do with the legacy of G. E.

Moore. Methodologically, it means an approach that is nonreductive and experimental, not only to be tested by experience but devoted to the elucidation and enlargement of experience, without deliberately forcing the facts of life into preconceived categories. Substantively, it means the attempt to understand the main features of human existence as derivative of and continuous with natural processes. Experience, mind, art, inquiry, knowledge, value, religion, and morality are analyzed as natural functions. (Needless to say, Santayana and Dewey did not always see eye to eye on the particulars of their respective positions.)

6. The noncognitivists reached this conclusion by means of analysis of ordinary language. I reach it by means of analysis of experience.

7. Hobbes's argument is meant to be deductive, but his premises include statements about the passions. His conclusions are "inferences from the passions." His argument presupposes the evaluations consituted by these passions. Hence the form of the argument would more correctly be regarded as hypothetical: if persons have such and such values, then this is what they would choose under the postulated conditions.

8. Hume's distinction between reason and sentiment rests on a quaint faculty psychology, but I take no recourse to any particular psychological theory. My point is only that the functions of knowing and valuing are distinguishable and irreducible.

9. Plato, *Philebus*, in *The Dialgoues of Plato,* Vol. 2, translated by Benjamin Jowett (New York: Random House, 1937), p. 343.

10. Ernst Cassirer, *The Myth of the State* (New Haven: Yale University Press, 1946), pp. 283–84. I am indebted to Donald Verene for calling Cassirer's discussion to my attention.

11. R. M. Hare, *Moral Thinking* (Oxford: Clarendon Press, 1981).

12. Iris Murdoch, *The Sovereignty of Good* (London and New York: ARK Paperbacks, 1985), p. 57. Richard Rorty's view is similar to that of the ordinary language philosophers. He thinks that moral judgments are true or false, but "true" and "false" are sociologically determined. That is, according to Rorty, our very notion of what "true" and "false" mean is nothing but a product of the company we keep, and there are no other possible criteria to invoke.

4

Moral Judgment and Discourse

To say that moral judgment cannot be reduced to cognition or moral theory to science are hardly the final points to be made about moral discourse, but more nearly the first. True, a number of reputations in philosophy have been earned by doing nothing better than analyzing moral language. With all these exertions, one might expect that our understanding of the subject would be greatly improved. The results, however, have been disappointing. This is due to a typically atomistic and reductive mode of analysis: the context of communication and action within which moral judgment occurs is wholly neglected.

We struggle with the swarm of contingencies in a moral situation, and we wish to deploy our best resources. Discourse can be one of them. What do philosophers have to say about this predicament? They are far more concerned with abstract reasoning than with communication, discourse. They reason, moreover, with abstractions (sometimes called intuitions) like passive spectators whose aim, at most, is to pass judgment on these conditions, not to participate in them to see what good might come of them. Participants, however, can find little use in these reasonings. Formal argument is often maladroit in moral contexts. Those engaged in conduct can be beneficially employed in *discourse*. They require communication that will record and convey the specific delicacies and urgencies, in all their variety, with which they would somehow contend. Conversation can take a variety of forms: honest, collaborative, informative, receptive; or threatening, deceptive, dominating, concealing. To reap its benefits, we must have some insight into its functions, appropriate content, and the virtues organic to it. To be a good reasoner, one requires no moral virtue. It is otherwise with discourse. Used wisely, it becomes one of the great instrumentalities of the moral condition.

Philosophers within the noncognitivist camp have confined themselves to pointing out what moral judgments evidently do in normal English usage. As irreducibly moral, such judgments don't make verifiable claims. Their emotive component has instead an illocutionary function. Judgments are employed to urge, warn, command, commend, and the like. Such judgments guide conduct in the sense that they provide a stimulus to act. They neither offer nor establish a truth claim regarding what is the morally correct thing to do. Reasons given to support the judgment are meant to persuade, not to verify.

The cognitivist is more ambitious. Moral reasoning is intended to produce true moral judgments, and moral philosophy is supposed to establish the criteria that make these judgments true. If philosophers can determine intersubjectively verifiable meanings of moral terms, then what we ought to do is decided by finding out which action satisfies the definition. Or perhaps a decision procedure—say, a contractual method, or the specification of rational agency—is advanced that certifies actions as morally right. From the point of view of the cognitivist, if such tests cannot be done, nothing can be done, and morality is a chimera.

In recent years philosophers have made much of an alleged incommensurability between different languages—between different vocabularies or conceptual schemes. The incommensurability pertains to scientific language and *a fortiori* to moral language. MacIntyre, for example, illustrates this thesis in regard to moral language by presenting several arguments addressing the issues of war, abortion, and private property.[1] All the arguments, he claims, are internally cogent, yet they all arrive at different conclusions. He ascribes this incoherence to the wildly incommensurate meanings of the respective moral vocabularies; he declares that the consequence of such babble is moral chaos in contemporary life. Such conclusions seem to support the noncognitivists, but for his part MacIntyre remains confident that a true theory of moral rationality can be expounded.[2]

I have argued that the analysis of the distinction between knowing and valuing leads to the conclusion that moral judgments, as such, are not verifiable; I agree with the noncognitivist position in that respect. Judgment is best understood as an expression of advocacy. Discussions of moral judgment, however, whether on the cognitivist or noncognitivist side, have suffered from a crippling limitation: judgment is not analyzed in the larger context of moral discourse.[3] Only a fraction of such discourse consists of moral judgments, and discourse itself takes place in an even more inclusive context, that of social action, which is itself constituent of a still wider environment: all those living and nonliving conditions with which we are enmeshed at every step of our lives. We must have some knowledge of the efficacies of lands, skies, waters, animals, insects, microbes, machines, and all manner of physical forces. Moral discourse cannot proceed in innocence of these fateful powers. In order to get some grasp of the resources and limitations of discourse, all these contexts must be given due recognition.

More recent moral philosophy—inaugurated by Rawls and aped by others—is vitiated by the same failing. For Rawls, moral judgments are irreducible intuitions. They are accepted or rejected on the grounds of their logical relations to *each other,* producing a charmed circle of intuitions. That they constitute such a circle establishes their moral validity. The emptiness of this approach will be indicated in chapter 7.

As we consider moral judgment in the context of discourse and action—in the context of the moral life, we might say—we shall find that fullness and accuracy of communication are fundamentally important. Given the noncognitive character of moral judgment, how is such communication possible at all? In fact it is entirely possible. To begin the analysis, I propose a method to determine the meaning of one's moral expressions on the occasion of each usage. I do not propose, however, to determine such meanings in a way that would rationally coerce agreement about their moral worth. I have in mind what have been called persuasive, or stipulative, definitions. Their being stipulative is no reason to ignore them. If they are appropriately formulated, they are indispensable for effective communication and action. Subsequent discussions in this chapter will explore further powers of discourse. The immediately following analysis favors Peirce in more ways than one.[4]

How to Make Our Moral Ideas Clear

Moral discourse is an organ of the moral life. It is whatever sorts of relevant talk or communication take place when we are engaged in morally problematic situations. I take it for granted that moral discourse has at least two functions. The first is descriptive: It denotes or characterizes the conditions that determine a situation. I use the term "descriptive" here to include predictions of how the situation would be expected to change contingent upon undertaking specified plans of action. The second function is normative: We must somehow render or convey our evaluation of the events described, our moral estimate of them. In brief, when a situation of moral discord occurs, we must clarify the nature of that situation and its prospects; and we must also gauge its worth in various dimensions.

Surprising as it might seem, our advocacy can be given an accurate operational measure. I shall argue that a traditionally pragmatic analysis of meaning will clarify both the descriptive and the evaluative content of moral judgments.[5] The most important feature of this method of clarification is that it permits us to establish an organic connection between moral ideas and worldly events. Moral *discourse* becomes inseparably engaged with moral *life*. This connection is absent in current discussion, in which the only contact that language makes is with antecedent intuitions, and intuitions are never chastened by exposure to worldly conduct.

Insofar as moral language, as such, is intended to satisfy descriptive and normative functions, it is notably ineffectual in doing so. Philosophers give this problem little notice, much less offer helpful suggestions. Perhaps, like Rorty, we readily assume that the moral vocabulary of a given community is perfectly clear to its members; the only problem is making it clear to others. But the situation is worse than this. It will be helpful to retrace the inadequacies of moral language before turning to a pragmatic analysis for help.

Our moral locutions are rather crude instruments of communication. Words like "good" and "bad," "rights" and "duties," "ought," "right" and "wrong," and so forth, generate more passion than illumination. Such words fail to capture fine distinctions, nuance, or complexity. Yet the qualities of moral experience are endlessly diverse and variable; our evaluations of them are apt to vary much as do the qualities themselves. The nature of a situation to be evaluated eludes characterization by such adjectives as "good," "bad," "right," or "wrong." Moral language seems an impertinence when we try to capture both the qualities of events and the gross and subtle variations in our estimations of them.

Consider the following judgments: "It was *wrong* of Jackson not to return his library books on time." "It was *wrong* of Alex to pull Jeannette's hair." "It was *wrong* of Jeannette to insult Alex." "It was *wrong* of Jones to misrepresent her deductions to the IRS." "It was *wrong* of Pol Pot to commit genocide." Suppose Jackson had tried very hard to return the library books on time, but just missed the deadline. Or suppose he missed it by two days. Two weeks? Or suppose he just let the books gather dust on his shelves indefinitely, while he remained utterly heedless of library regulations and the need for others to have access to books. Did Alex pull Jeannette's hair fiercely or gently? Did Jeannette insult him before or after he pulled her hair?

Such examples and their qualifications illustrate the point that moral words—in this instance, the word "wrong"—are not finely discriminating. Surely each of us would evaluate every one of these cases slightly differently, and our recommended remedies or punishments would be more or less different. If you protest that you would not call the act of the income tax cheater wrong in the same sense that you call Pol Pot's actions wrong, you grant my point.

The moral domain eludes simplification. If, to try a further example, Ms. Adams says, "I have a *right* to this property," what is conveyed by the word "right"? Do we know whether her claim is legal in nature and/or moral? Does she claim that her right is absolute, or is it negotiable in some way? Do we know whether she somehow *earned* the property in question? Or was it bestowed on her, and, if so, by whom? Perhaps she means her title would be bestowed by a Rawlsian decision procedure. Or might it be Nozickian? To what use is the property put? How does the utilization of the property affect others? Are there other claims to the property? What is *their* nature? Surely, if we are to understand and assess Adams's claim, we must know what she means when she says "right." It will be these answers that we require in order to respond to her claim. Even then, of course, each of us will not make precisely the same response, for the determinants of our moral judgments are not precisely the same. The point is simply to indicate the limitations of moral language in this typical context.

The discussion suggests that moral words are useful for expressing our preliminary feelings about some state of affairs. At least what we get from Adams is that she wants others to keep their hands off her possessions. Such expressions can also be useful for pronouncing a final resolution of one's deliberations. Once a matter has been thought out and a decision reached, we might pronounce the verdict: "That is her right."

It is also true that different kinds of evaluative expression suggest different kinds of moral experience or moral relations. When we say an act *ought* to be done, for example, we intend to give it a precedence in moral urgency over behavior that we would call good. However welcome and admirable a deed denoted by the word "good," it is not given the mandatory sort of status that we intend by referring to a deed that *ought* to be done. Likewise, it happens in moral experience that we wish especially both to encourage and to protect certain kinds of behavior. This is conduct that we would not lightly interfere with; and this kind of moral relation we call a right.

Moral language as we find it has these distinguishable functions, and others as well. Nevertheless, as I have remarked, it is a poor instrument of communication. At the same time, it is rich with meanings, however elusive. It is so because it encapsulates our moral experience and commitments. When Adams says "The state has no right to this property," her words might well express long and thoughtful experience. She doubtless means she is deeply opposed to an invasion of her property, but she could also be making reference to the entire web of behavior implicated in the preservation of private property. If asked what she means, she might discourse at length about the importance of the private sector, the menace of big government, the adverse effects of invasions of property on human vitality and individuality; possibly she will speak of her prior claim to the property. She might provide many historical examples illustrating what she takes to be the merits of private property and the liabilities of state control. Another person might give a different interpretation of "The state has no right to this property." He would cite page after page of Gewirth's *Reason and Morality,* perhaps, which has no recourse to experimental argument. Still another might say the state *has* a right and will fervently recount the evils of private property. The point is that to each speaker, his or her moral statements are extremely meaningful. They incorporate many of the person's deepest concerns and experiences, as well as many assumptions about the historical record, human nature, and the social order. It implies great apprehension regarding one set of arrangements and great devotion to another. Language sums up for each of us our moral values, our fears and aspirations as moral beings. The moral life throbs with beliefs and values, and these, presumably, are part of what we intend somehow to convey in discourse.

Philosophers have not been particularly good at analyzing moral language as a function of moral experience. The early noncognitivists, for example, are among those responsible for stupefying our sense of the meaning of moral judgments. They confounded our sense of reality in saying that moral language is altogether meaningless, and they made no attempt to indicate how the emotive force of moral judgment might be helpfully conveyed. "You ought to keep your promise" would mean something like "Hoorah for promise keeping!" or "I approve of promise keeping. Do so as well!" I wonder whether anyone has ever meant such a thing when saying "You ought to keep your promise." I wonder what the analysis would be of "Pol Pot was wrong to commit genocide."

Subsequent noncognitivists admitted a descriptive component in moral language, but said little about either its nature or its function; like their predecessors, they said nothing about how discourse might give accurate measure to evaluation. Their concern with ethical discourse centered on the verifiability of moral judgment.

Intuitionists have gone almost as far as emotivists to impoverish moral language. To assert, for example, that the words "good" or "right" refer to one simple property, and no more, is nothing short of larcenous. It not only robs words of their meaning, but robs us of any useful conditions of evaluation. It supposes our evaluations of the manifold, intricate, and vivid qualities of experience have nothing to do with those qualities themselves. This is what Dewey called selective emphasis, and here it is taken to its limit. Tragedy, suffering, triumph, love, loyalty, charity, and delight are not evaluated in themselves, but only as possessing some *other* distinct thing: good or bad, right or wrong *per se* (whatever *they* might be). These alleged moral properties are not just obscure, but valueless.

Whatever credibility such theories have derives from a conspicuous trait of philosophizing: getting so caught up in a dialectic of abstractions as to be forgetful of our very lives. Since we acquire a moral vocabulary early in life and use it more or less unreflectively thereafter, many persons are at a loss to say what they mean. The deontologist and intuitionist make a virtue of this failure. One says

" 'Ought' means 'what you must do' " or " 'what is morally binding,' "
or " 'what it is right to do,' " or even " 'ought' means 'ought.' " How
edifying! One must concede that intuitionism is a highly convenient refuge for those who are struck dumb whenever called upon
to explain what they mean. Are you unable to articulate your moral
convictions? Can you do no more than stammer, blush, and repeat
to yourself, "It just isn't right, that's all!"? Put an end to your embarrassment! Start talking about moral intuitions! Philosophers were
clear, if misleading, when they said moral language is nonsense, but
today they heave up moral intuitions as if they were self-evidently
meaningful, and communication is strangled with rhetoric.

Moral language is often, if not always, abundantly meaningful;
yet these meanings vary from person to person, sometimes to the
point of idiosyncrasy. This is evidently true even within a given
community. All communities are touched more or less with pluralistic
influences. (Consider just the debates within philosophical communities about the meaning, say, of the concept of rights.) Accordingly,
moral meaning is not well served by simple moral words; it is important
to determine a method to make our moral ideas clear without at
the same time denuding them of their richness. In the following pages,
I do not claim to offer intersubjectively verifiable definitions of moral
words. I intend a method for making moral usage *clear* and at the
same time *inseparable from the vital realities of moral life.* Moral
agreement is something that exists not antecedently to moral discourse,
but—if at all—consequent to it.

If an explicitly moral vocabulary is to be helpful, it must have
a way of referring to the changing, infinitely various, and unique
events of experience. At the same time, it must also be interpretable
in a way that will provide an exact measure of what is called the
illocutionary force of language. That is, both the cognitive and
evaluative functions must be satisfied in a manner that is clearly
communicable.

How is clarity to be found? Any use of moral language can
be explicated in terms of actual or anticipated conduct by actual
or possible agents. In this way, both the descriptive and evaluative
components of meaning can be thoroughly and unambiguously conveyed. Description, of course, for the pragmatist, is explicated by
indicating what consequences in experience follow from behaving
in a prescribed manner with specified existential conditions. Likewise,

we articulate our *evaluation* of a trait or an action in specifying the conduct that we will or would take in relation to it. The conduct we would take in the way of pursuing or avoiding certain events measures our evaluation of them.

To illustrate and elaborate, let us consider perhaps the most elusive word of all, the notorious "ought," with which Hume launched a thousand dissertations. How could we determine a clear meaning to judgments containing this seemingly indispensable auxiliary verb? "Ought" qualifies an infinitive phrase, such as "to keep your promise," "to help your friends," and the like, by designating the action at issue to be in some sense mandatory or highly important to do. There is at least a vague sense to such locutions. The conduct referred to is highly valued or precious in some way; it has a high priority relative to other actions, moral or otherwise. There is an importance in keeping your word that is not imparted in saying "It is good to keep your promise," or even "It is right to do so." That is, there is a genuine distinction in experience to which we try to give voice by using "ought." Beyond this, when we enunciate principles, like "One ought to keep one's promises," we are typically at a loss to render a clear meaning.

Within such a broad and vague sense of "ought" judgments, we can begin to make the meaning specific by reference to the sorts of actions to which the judgments are pertinent. If asked what it means to say "You ought to keep your promise," one can do better than declare that to promise is to guarantee performance and that to fulfill the guarantee is important. Recognizing that the constraints and inducements of conduct are ultimately in lived experience itself, one might well begin by furnishing a more detailed meaning of promising, which is crucial to understanding the value of this sort of conduct. It might proceed something like this: There is great interdependence of human conduct, and this interdependence is very much facilitated when the participants can count on specific behavior from each other. We depend on such behavior, and we trust in it most explicitly when participants declare a particular intent and give firm assurances that they will stand by it. That is, there is promising. In accepting your promise, individuals have vested you with trust; they are counting on your performance. Their conduct is now predicated on the assumption that you will do as you have sworn to do. Inasmuch as the conduct of individuals in common enterprises is highly dependent upon promised actions, the failure to keep a promise is typically injurious. Perhaps the aims of several persons are severely damaged by failure of one person to fulfill his oath. The persons damaged are additionally hurt simply because the faithless one could injure them so. It often hurts more that the pledge is trampled upon than that the promised behavior is not delivered. Breaking a promise strikes at the very heart of social action and the human bond.

So much, I take it, is a pragmatic account of the descriptive meaning of promising. What of the evaluative content of "You ought to keep your promise"? The kinds of behavior that are typically directed to the trustworthy and to the untrustworthy register the extent to which promising is valued. This will vary somewhat from agent to agent, but the general nature of the evaluation can be explicated by still further reference to the actions that are typically connected to promising. A characteristic response of those who are let down, for example, is to exact penalties of some kind from the one who fails them; and to exact a penalty is to express an evaluation, indicating that the activity is objectionable. The more fully these actions can be specified, the more fully do we have the measure of the values at stake. The injured parties might punish the offender in several ways; and one of the most hurtful is no longer to take him at his word, to withhold trust, to exclude him from further participatory conduct; in a word, to loosen or even break the social bond to him. This communicates the feelings they have toward the malefactor. Just as one suffers the penalty of a certain ostracism for breaking promises, he enjoys the rewards of trust, confidence, and respect when he steadfastly keeps them. Conduct is trusting, more fully shared, and cooperative. The social bond is strengthened, rather than loosened.

Most persons, of course, will accept some circumstance as extenuating. They will excuse or even praise the breaking of a promise under certain conditions, and the most crucial agreements will often specify the sorts of conditions that will release the partcipants from their commitment. All such actions, in well defined conditions, convey the measure of our valuation of that particular bond known as promising.

At a great level of generality, the meaning of statements, or principles, like "One ought to keep one's promise," cannot be explicated much more specifically than this. Just how much we are in favor of keeping promises is expressed by our conduct. As each of us strives to keep our promises through thick and thin, or fails to do so, and as we comport ourselves in relation to others who keep or fail to keep promises, and as each of us is more or less permissive or stringent in releasing others from their bond, and in rewarding and punishing those to whom we relate with promising, thus do we communicate quite accurately the worth we vest in keeping promises. If someone asks me, then, what is the value or importance in keeping a promise, I answer that it is measured in just the sorts of conduct indicated.

I grant that this interpretation of the principle is not universally shared, but I am at this point seeking clarity, not agreement. It seems a particular virtue of this method that it provides considerable definiteness to evaluative meanings. If the principle "One ought to keep one's promises" is to be given any intelligible sense, it would have to be by making reference to the relevant behavior. If one went through all this explication of meaning, I really don't know what would be left to be said. What else might someone to whom the principle is addressed need to know?

The conduct that measures the value of promising varies with different individuals. We do not all value fidelity equally. Conduct also varies with context: in many instances fidelity to one's word is vital; in others it isn't so much; and the rewards, punishments, acceptable excuses, and priorities will vary accordingly. Because of this variability, the general principle, "One ought to keep one's promises," has a vagueness that cannot be overcome by any method. *I* might specify what sanctions *I* tend to impose, but I speak only for myself and only in general. I can speak with even less reliability for others.

The individual who is given the general advice to keep promises will have his own particular response to the behavior organic to promising. That is, his own response will necessarily be evaluative, and the affirmations of trustworthy conduct will not be identical in any two persons. Normally the general response is congenial to such conduct, especially when the individual is reminded of how it affects his own activities when promises are kept or broken. Still more instructive is the universe of action. It is more instructive than the universe of discourse. One's evaluation of promising is most profoundly qualified when one actually undergoes the consequences of experience in the moral life—experiences ostracism or trust. We do not learn as effectively from discourse as we do from action. What discourse alone cannot accomplish might still be within the competence of life activity.

As we descend from high levels of generality, meanings can be made more exact. In a definite context, where a specific judgment is made, the meaning can be explicated with precision. If I tell my son, for example, "You ought to keep your promise to clean the garage," I can tell him, if necessary, exactly what consequences are contingent upon his succeeding or failing to honor his pledge. If he cleans it promptly and well, he will receive certain material benefits, and he will reinforce my willingness to rely on him and to share activities with him. If he breaks the promise, there will likewise be definite penalties. I might well tell him what would be acceptable excuses to me, thereby indicating the priority of the promised conduct relative to possible alternatives. I have made it as clear as possible what I mean when I say, in this instance, "You ought to keep your promise." At the same time, I have told him all that *he* needs to know in order for him to decide what action he will take. He knows exactly where he stands. I wonder what else he, as a moral being, needs to know of the statement "You ought to keep your promise" in order to make a decision. My statements are more helpful than saying only "You ought to keep your promise," or (imagine this) "Hoorah for promise keeping!"

This way of rendering "ought" judgments can be construed as making (perhaps elaborate) predictions: If you perform a given act, the consequences will be thus and so. If you fail to perform it, the results will be such and such. You will be excused from the act and its consequences only when particular conditions are satisfied. In such predictions, the gravity of the advocacy is registered in the gravity of the consequences and in the difficulty of satisfying conditions for release from the obligation.

Philosophers (and others) often understand "You ought to keep your promises" and suchlike as commands or prescriptions. I see no objection to that understanding, so long as we understand what is being said. If we take such utterances as commands, how are they to be analyzed? No differently, I would think. The command specifies actions to be accomplished; its verbal structure—and perhaps its source as well—implies that the actions are of the highest priority. If the actions are not carried out, certain consequences will ensue. Certain (but presumably few) contingencies will exempt one from the command. Commands or prescriptions are thus predictions, usually implicit predictions. They are often of unusually dire consequences for failure to perform the specified actions. Do this *or else*! If this analysis is correct, the notion of an unconditional imperative or command, as in the Kantian manner, is unintelligible. In the meaning of a command, there have to be stipulated consequences for obeying or disobeying. Without such an understanding, there is just another emotive outburst.

Judgments and commands are convertible to predictions. The prediction is verifiable, but it is left to the person to whom it is addressed to respond as he will to the predicted consequences. The statement "You ought to keep your promise" cannot be construed in a way that will coerce moral agreement simply by reference to facts and logic. Different individuals will place a different weight on the values contingent upon action. A person who is for whatever reason a utilitarian will keep a promise if it serves the greatest happiness. Another person might well regard a marginal increment in the general happiness as of little account compared to the suffering caused one or a few individuals by a breach of loyalty. That one or a few persons depend on him in a specific manner weighs more heavily with him than a little pleasure or even a little pain for a large number of other persons who have no reason to count on him in a specific way. Explicated meanings will often be found morally offensive, too. A person saying "You ought to keep your promise" might express the force of his demand by saying "I'll beat you to death if you don't!"—an unusually important circumstance for having a clear meaning of a moral judgment.

Other forms of moral advocacy can be given meaning by the same procedure. Such locutions as "good" and "evil," "just" and "unjust," "honorable" and "despicable," and so on can be clarified operationally by specifying patterns of behavior. One's articulation of exertions, rewards, punishments, and excuses conveys the evaluative component. If certain goals or possessions are designated goods, the descriptive and evaluative meaning of "good" can be translated into statements about what we would do to consummate certain experiences. As experience distinguishes and undergoes its endless variety of gross and subtle qualities, our behavior in respect to them likewise undergoes variation; and our selections and exertions give measure to our valuations.

Rights are in the forefront of moral controversy today. We are submerged in them. Demands for various services and protections are couched in terms of rights. Perhaps because of the centrality of that concept in current moral struggles, "rights" is evidently the most emotive of moral terms, casting mystical shrouds across the mind. How are rights made intelligible by reference to conduct? To say that someone has a right means that certain practices or services are guaranteed, almost regardless of what price must be paid to fulfill the guarantee. We use the word "right" in situations of that nature. To be clear about what it means to have a right in a given context, we would have to be explicit about what the assured conduct is, what actions will be taken to assure it, and by whom these actions will be performed; and we would have to itemize the otherwise permissible actions that will be sacrificed in order to make these assurances. The (presumably) few contingencies that would take precedence over these guarantees would also have to be articulated. This is what it means to have a right, and the value we place on the possession of a right stands forth in the actions that are required and those that are forbidden in order to preserve this condition and in the extreme nature of the exigencies that would supercede it.

We claim, for example, a right to due process of law. The meaning and value of due process can be explicated with clarity only by reference to the sorts of behavior that the right incorporates. There are carefully worked out procedures that must be observed if the right is to exist. Due process is treasured in our culture, for we wish to safeguard the innocent against deliberate or inadvertent injury, and we want people to be tried by impersonal procedure rather than to be at the mercy of individual authority. Our regard for due process is measured by the fact that we have severe sanctions for its violations, and we admit very few circumstances in which violations of due process would be excused. In addition, we are willing to pay a high cost for observing these procedures, including the acquittal on occasion of individuals who are in all probability guilty. According to a pragmatic analysis, this system of behavior is the meaning of "having a right to due process of law."

The only way anyone can sort out the rights claims being pressed today would be to strip them of their rhetoric and determine precisely what sort of conduct would be necessary to satisfy each one. We would have to stipulate who would provide this conduct and at what sacrifice of other modes of conduct. The exigencies that would suspend the guarantees would also have to be spelled out. I by no means suggest that such clarifications would by themselves settle the many conflicts involved, but at least we would find out what we are arguing about and what we are committing ourselves to in proposing a given right. Not the least advantage of this procedure, if it were used, is that the alternately absolutistic and emotive character of rights rhetoric would subside.

Not only do we hear an extravagant variety of claims for rights, but even verbally similar claims are dissimilar in their meaning—they call for different forms of conduct. A. I. Melden takes it as a fundamental principle, for example, that everyone has a right to the responsible pursuit of his interests.[6] Nozick is fully subscribed to the same principle.[7] To Melden, however, part of the meaning of the principle is that "society" has an obligation to assist individuals who lack the resources to pursue their interests; Nozick, however, emphatically rejects any such interpretation. He denies that individuals have any claim on unearned services from society or the state. Ronald Dworkin says that every individual has a right to equal concern and respect from the state. In addition to the question of what "right" means here, there is the matter of what "equal," "concern," and "respect" mean. As the reader of *Taking Rights Seriously* will find, they all mean whatever Dworkin decides they should mean.[8]

Such controversy has typically been approached as the attempt to establish a verifiable definition of what it means to have a right. The solution of the conceptual problem, as such, solves the moral problem. But it does not. The appeal to ordinary usage can hardly be adopted as the jurisdiction of last resort, and the appeal to intuition is obscurantist. A definition of the notion of moral rights is itself a moral enterprise. Hence the air is full of advocacy disguised as objectivity—evaluations disguised as demonstrations.

All such rhetoric could be expressed as demands for certain actions by assignable individuals or institutions. This procedure would not bring controversy to a close. To claim a right is not to conclude, but to initiate, discourse. The discourse would not be skirmishing over words or concepts. It would be addressed to what is really at issue in the moral life: relations to be adopted between individuals that would advance or retard their respective interests, moral and otherwise, including their interests in the concerns of others. *That* is what matters. Let's lay our cards on the table. Then and only then has the conversation found its pertinent subject matter, and it may proceed thereupon.

It is still important to ask "What do you mean?" Not many years ago, that question was asked as the prelude to an argument to the effect that you meant nothing, so people became weary of the question. More recently it hasn't been asked at all, and this is disastrous. When we read on and on in current books of philosophy, or in those of intellectuals who are advocates in the public policy debates of the day, we can become quite overwhelmed by the rhetoric. We read impassioned pleas for *fairness, community, autonomy, personhood, justice, rights, dignity, liberation, equality.* We are deluged by such stuff. Who can withstand it? We can easily become persuaded that we are morally defective if we don't embrace it all at once at face value. Who can be *against* such wonderful things? But they are not much else than appeals to our untutored moral sentiments. They play upon feelings unchastened by any reference to the intricate networks of behavior demanded of specifiable individuals or groups. Were such demands articulated, and examined for their implications for action, our responses to them might be quite different. It takes courage and intelligence to withstand the torrents of passion. A good beginning is to ask, "What do you mean?"

It might be thought that this method for bringing clarity to moral discourse, by expressing all evaluations in terms of conduct, presupposes a form of behaviorism, but no such assumption need be made. Presumably, someone with a radically free will intends to engage in various dimensions of moral conduct, and all that I am asking is that he specify the conduct he would pursue contingent upon certain behavior from others. Neither does this analysis of moral language prejudge who the moral agents are. If one frames the meaning of moral judgment in terms of conduct, it could include divine conduct.

Nor is my attention to action an implicit denial of subjective states. I have no wish to deny that we have moral feelings, desires, evaluations, commitments, approvals, disapprovals, and so on. Quite the contrary. I am trying to develop a clear way to communicate the practical import of these states. You can say, "I *approve* of being impartial," or "I *strongly favor* impartiality." "I am *devoted* to equal rights." "I *feel obligated* to my students," and so on. Put these matters any way you like. But how do you make them clear? If you say you approve of promise keeping, your statement remains vague until you tell us what behavior you're committing yourself to. Your statement would be particularly unhelpful in a concrete situation where promise keeping would be qualified by other values: You are in favor of promise keeping, but what behavior do you engage in relative to a person who has broken her promise because she was ill? You can say Jackson ought not to keep library books past the date due, and Jeannette ought not to have insulted Alex. Jones ought not to have deceived the IRS, and Pol Pot ought not to have massacred his countrymen. Such statements, taken in themselves, hardly begin to indicate the variations in conduct you would advocate or undertake relative to these different situations. Jackson might receive from you a mild admonition, while you might support massive commitments of resources and great risk of life to end an insane adventure like that of Pol Pot.

I see no obstacle to treating all moral words in the manner I have outlined here. No doubt there are many people who believe that moral words must somehow mean more than this, or less, or perhaps something quite different. Until they explicate the meaning they have in mind in some intelligible manner, I have to assume they are engaged in obscurantism. Our concern in the moral life is to conduct ourselves in various ways in respect to other persons and within a complex environment. There are both opportunities and constraints in these relationships. *Making our moral ideas clear is an essential condition of recognizing and utilizing these conditions.* Our fate is at issue here. To bet it on alleged moral intuition is simply mad. I do not suggest that such clarifications would settle the many conflicts and uncertainties of the moral life, but they are a necessary condition of any settlements that are not effected by authority. The fever swamps of moral rhetoric are clearly an obstacle to such accomplishments.

Admittedly, it is difficult to make our ideas clear in the manner proposed. It requires us to examine our moral experience thoroughly and honestly. One person's behavior is a response to that of another; in effect, it is an evaluation of it. But such behavior is a function of many evaluations and many traits of that person. We like a person in some respects, while having reservations or dislikes in others. We might be in his debt in some way, but find that he has also been deceitful to us. We might respond by castigating him and spurning his company, or perhaps only by voicing a mild reservation. No doubt such responses and their variations are a consequence of very complex conditions; they are not attributable to just one event. Hence it is difficult to determine just what our estimate of honesty is—difficult, but it is not impossible to make a workable approximation. Those who are sensitive to experience develop a fairly clear sense of what they prize, and why; they know what is important to them, and they can distinguish it in given cases. Their responses to the case are tempered accordingly. Those who cannot do so are emotional basket cases: they will have very unsatisfactory relationships, and if they have children, they will make basket cases of them, too.

Sometimes we use moral language without intending any action. We might, for example, say of a friend that he ought not to treat his children so harshly, but without intending to change our behavior in regard to him. Of course, we probably would do so, in subtle ways, but still, our judgment may be little more than an expression of mere feeling. As the case may be, these judgments will be more or less harmless—just because no action is forthcoming. To the extent that such judgments cannot be explicated in terms of anticipated conduct, their meaning dissipates into the merely emotive. We should neither take the case to be typical (much less universal), nor regard it as a virtue to use language in this way.

In view of the exotic array of interpretations of moral judgment, I must grant that this procedure is not one to which all will subscribe, but perhaps at this stage I can appeal to those who think both clarity and pertinence are important. They are conspicuously lacking in contemporary moral theory, and they are typically lacking in ordinary moral discourse as well. The nuances, complexities, and extremes of moral experience are not captured in conventional moral language, though they could be captured by the method I have presented. A poet might express experience more vividly or arrestingly, but not more accurately; and in moral practice, accuracy is hardly to be underrated. Fortunately, we rarely have to explicate our judgments in this compulsive sort of way; but at times of uncertainty, misunderstanding, or disagreement, it is salutary to do so.

The reasons for moral perplexity are many, but one of them—

the incommensurability (as distinguished from misunderstanding) of moral vocabularies—is surely not a major one. I earlier made reference to this problem, citing MacIntyre's thesis in particular. Though I cannot here indulge in a specific analysis of his examples, I am convinced that if all the moral claims used in them were articulated in the manner proposed here, there would be no difficulty in any of the parties finding out what the others meant. This is not to say that this new-found intelligibility would put an end to the disagreements at issue. It does mean, however, that the disputants cannot simply turn their backs on each other, pleading incommensurability. They need some other excuse to be intractable. Neither can any of them claim a special sanctity attaching to a specific moral vocabulary such that it is exempted from analysis. The analysis itself might well demonstrate that so-called absolutes are more variable even in the hands of absolutists than their champions suspect. If such a sobering experience were to occur, the parties to moral controversy might even be willing to consider some of the further possibilities for moral discourse.

Clarity in Evaluative Language and Moral Pluralism

There is a most informative implication of this analysis of moral language. Put to the test, there is probably not one moral issue about which any two readers of these words will have precisely the same assessment. It might be the death penalty, abortion, animal rights, marital fidelity, Eastern European policy—think of any case you wish. Those, for example, who favor abortion under some circumstances will differ concerning just what those circumstances should be. Even if there were rather close agreement about this, there might be significant variation regarding what measures should be taken in response to those who would violate the preferred guidelines. Even those who are adamantly against abortion will not be perfectly agreed. They might differ on just how severe a moral evil it is. This difference would show up in different prescriptions for preventing or punishing abortions.

Other cases will provoke similar differences. Setting aside the question of exactly what constitutes murder, we all regard the act as indefensible, but we differ on how seriously to treat it. We might reduce murder very greatly, for example, by permitting the police to detain anyone who looked the least bit suspicious. How far will we go in limiting freedom in order to reduce the incidence of murder? There can be no perfect agreement. We will likewise differ for various reasons about the severity of the punishment meted out to those who have committed such a heinous act. At least one reason consists simply in regard to how heinous one takes the crime to be. The lesson is this: when we specify the conduct that would give definite meaning to our advocacies, we will find that the specifications will vary, more or less; they will not be uniform. Given that advocacy is an individual's response to complex conditions, not the conclusion of a syllogism, this lesson should not be surprising.

It may well be, then, that words used in common like "right" and "wrong" mask real differences in moral judgment. In applying the theory that all meaningful use of moral language is reducible to statements about action, then it becomes evident that no two people have precisely the same meaning when they use moral language. When we must be specific about the actions that would express our evaluations in a given moral situation, it is unlikely that we would mark precisely the same actions. No doubt this is true even of self-proclaimed moral absolutists. What would they mean by saying that keeping promises is absolutely required or murder is absolutely wrong? They could be intelligible only by saying that there can never be any act that takes precedence over keeping a promise, no matter what; and any breach of the obligation would have to be met by the severest possible penalty, without qualification. No absolutist to my knowledge says this. They will advocate different exemptions and different penalties. Hence they will not literally be absolutists. To be precise, absolute absolutism is conceivable, but never seriously entertained. All moral "absolutes" are really dictates of very high priority, and even the absolutists are not in exact agreement about the priority.

This analysis discloses the inevitability of a certain pluralism in moral judgment. The next chapter will offer a depiction of the irreducible forms of moral relations, each of which possesses its own distinctive norms, for which there can be no invariant priority. Even pending that discussion, we may conclude that the criteria with which we adopt principles and make moral judgments are unavoidably diverse; so in this sense we recognize a pluralism that informs the moral life. Such recognition is one of the conditions that distinguish wisdom from fanaticism.

If it is true that we do not precisely agree about any moral issues, aren't we on the brink of moral chaos? Hardly. The obvious plurality of moral values need not be an impediment to an increase in moral accord. Even though we do not agree perfectly about anything, we are capable of constituting a more or less effective moral community. Our differences are not great enough to convert pluralism into mayhem. There is a simple reason for this: the benefits of mutual tolerance and cooperation vastly outweigh in most instances whatever benefits there might be in distrust and antagonism. There are very few persons who are absolutely intolerant of any moral values not identical to their own. We are all pluralists, differing only in the degree of our tolerance or intolerance. The pragmatic analysis of moral language puts this point in a conspicuous light. The exposure is not a liability, but an asset; for it might have the effect of reducing our absolutistic pretensions and making us more willing to engage in constructive moral discourse with one another, taking the real opportunities and limitations of our situation specifically into account.

How Does Discourse Guide Conduct?

Moral judgments presumably guide conduct; but what is it about them that guides, and how do they do so? Noncognitivists have assumed a neat, and untenable, division of labor: one use of language is merely descriptive, another is exclusively illocutionary. R. M. Hare says, "A statement, however loosely it is bound to the facts, cannot answer a question of the form, 'What shall I do?'; *only* a command can do this. Therefore, if we insist that moral judgments are nothing but loose statements of fact, [Why "loose"?] we preclude them from fulfilling their main function. . . ."[9] This is fairly typical, and typically misguided. We have seen that a command is either a disguised or implicit prediction of consequences, or it is merely emotive. Any moral judgment short of the emotive can be translated into a prediction; it is the response to the implied and predicted consequences that directs conduct.

The function of guiding conduct can be nicely fulfilled by statements of fact, whether formulated as predictions or not. One can articulate the meaning of keeping promises, with all the values organic to it, measured by the actions characteristic of such behavior. The meaning of promise keeping itself is a stimulus to act. There is no need to add an "ought" to the discussion to provide either direction or motive force.

What might "ought" add to the meaning, if anything? Possibly it contribues a favorable assessment of the practice by the speaker, or a warning to the hearer to heed the speaker's demand. We have seen, however, that favorable assessments as well as admonitions can be articulated as impending variations in the speaker's conduct, or in that of others: "This is what will happen if you don't keep your promise." These are simple statements of fact, and the facts are moving. Statements about existential conditions and possibilities have motive power because we respond to events as presented in discourse much as we would to the events themselves. "The house is on fire!" "War has been declared!" "The lake is icy cold." "Your daughter has been found." "Maggie loves you." And so on *ad infinitum*. When such remarks are made in a definite context, they can be extremely moving; given the feelings and instrumentalities operative in the occasion, the situation might suggest fairly definite actions to take. A specific moral judgment can be made clear in a manner to present the relevant contingencies directly to one's attention. To put it in the language of psychology, discourse guides conduct by specifying a schedule of rewards and punishments that will be contingent upon a specific act.

A moral judgment is often thought to prescribe a completely specific action, while the behavior that might be prompted by statements of fact is simply a response to the impending conditions. Hence it might be undirected and wayward. However, the action you want someone to take can be stated very precisely, and likewise the consequences for doing it or not. The agent to whom the statements are directed might not perform the action, of course, or might deviate from it somewhat. But agents have been known to reject obedience to sheer prescription, too.

Lest the preceding comments be misleading, I stress once more that I do not suppose that assessments of value are just a function of "our passional nature" and no more. Emphatically to the contrary. Judgment—advocacy—is not reducible to *either* knowing *or* valuing alone. The passions, the sentiments, do tend to be wayward; so it is of the highest importance that they be tempered and disciplined by the effects of knowledge and experience.

The isolated impulse is a loose cannon. When our response is not to an event in its immediacy, but to its meaning—its interconnections to other events—then it is more apt to carry our interests forward to auspicious experience and even to endow our conduct with wisdom. Our responses are learned in the experience of life activity, in the universe of doing and suffering. As we gain experience and knowledge, these reactions become more discriminating and refined, and we judge more and more in reference to the meaning of events, rather than to isolated stimuli. Inquiry into and reflection upon such meanings makes responses more judicious still, and conduct is more apt to be effective. Thus our responses are variously crude and refined. They constitute evaluations, variously crude and refined. Thus experience continues to tutor our conduct, and conduct tutors our judgment.

The meanings of experience are communicated in discourse. With the powers of thought and speech, we are beneficiaries of the knowledge and experience of others. Hence we may be spared many of the hazards of experience, and our conduct can also take into account the express wishes and intentions of others. When the qualities of experience are more conspicuously indicated and interrelated in discourse, our response will likewise be qualified. What happens to us in the ensuing action will qualify our subsequent evaluations still more. Hence discourse incorporates meanings more adequate to our circumstance. *Clearly enough, it is not discourse as such that guides conduct, but what discourse discloses.* Our involvement with the contingencies of life experience determines behavior.

In such discourse the intent is neither to produce demonstrations nor to discover some moral fact that defines a particular act as incontrovertibly right or wrong. The function of the information introduced is to condition, qualify, or reinforce the valuations that one has prior to the occasion for discourse, and ultimately to prompt conduct suitable to the occasion. The relation between cognitive beliefs and moral convictions is no more logical than that between stimulus and response. We are not, then, speaking of the formal relations between sentences; the concern is with how evaluations are generated, in part, by cognitive beliefs. Cognitive inquiries bring to our attention matters of value in their actual and possible configurations. In their capacity as syntheses and promises of life experience, inquiry and communication are functional in the formation and reconstitution of our values and hence of our behavior. You have, let us say, strong interests in the care and development of children. You believe that I have abandoned my child, and you morally condemn me for it, and perhaps you wish to take steps to remedy the situation. Maybe you take the step of consulting *me* about the case, and you learn that your understanding has been mistaken. Perhaps you discover that the child was not my own, and I was restoring her to the care of her parents; or perhaps the child has needs that I am not competent to meet, and I am putting her care temporarily in the hands of specialized and beneficent surrogates. Thus your evaluation of me changes; it might be that condemnation changes to approval. Strictly speaking, this has not been a *logical* process. By bringing your attention to relevant existential conditions, inquiry and communication have had the *causal* effect of bringing about a change in your estimate of me, which will show itself in changed conduct.

This is not to say that discourse will bring about evaluations that are uniform from person to person. When all is said and done, one person will not choose quite like another. One citizen might advocate that the state build a highway through the front yards of a residential neighborhood, and another will advocate that the state find an alternative, if more expensive, route. A third will call for the dismantling of the state. The decision of one individual does not constitute a norm that must be followed by another simply by virtue of his nature as a moral agent. As I have already indicated, this analysis is not tantamount to accepting moral anarchy.

It is feeble to think of discourse as self-sufficient. It occurs in a context of action, and the expectations of action are what give the discourse meaning and persuasiveness. Action, moreover, is more effectual in learning. One can be told that it is dangerous to fool around with another man's wife, but the admonition lacks the potency of an irate husband brandishing a pistol. Then we needn't be wholly discouraged if discourse fails to bring a moral change of heart. Experience may succeed where talk fails. (Talk, too, is more effective when others learn that we mean what we say.)

All of this is obvious, and I would be embarrassed to write it, were it not for the fact that what philosophers are most prone to overlook is the obvious, or the relevance of the obvious to their arcane meditations. We are guided by the meanings of experience, whether encountered directly or transmitted in language. Only in an elliptical sense can we say that the judgment as such directs conduct. The actual disciplines and opportunities are in the subject matter.

The Subject Matter of Moral Discourse

We often hear the expression that a moral code is *based upon* human nature, or *based upon* beliefs about the realities of the world. "Based upon" is vague. Given our predilection for supposing that disciplined moral theory or reasoning must be a kind of science, we assume that "based upon" means "logically derived from," "deduced from," "entailed by," and the like, or perhaps "verified by." Accordingly, a morality is, say, "based upon" human nature because it is entailed by facts about human nature; or moral claims are verified by alleged facts of human nature. Then, unhappily, when we decide that the is/ought problem is insoluble, we must conclude that moral principles are based upon nothing.

Such a conclusion has the immediate effect of banishing all of the great philosophical concerns from the domain of ethics. If nothing can be deduced from conceptions of man, nature, and the divine, then the moral pertinence of inquiry into such subjects disappears from before our eyes, like a lovely image. These absorbing subjects have been orphaned in compliance with the prevailing paradigms of moral thought. They are still absorbing, and we have misgivings about letting them go; but we don't quite know what should be done with them. Indeed, even with the present reassertion of scientific moral philosophies, these subjects have not been reclaimed. The current models of moral theory don't know how to utilize them. They harbor no adequate notion of what a reality-based ethic would be.

Suppose, though, that the relation between statements of knowledge and expressions of advocacy is not even conceivably logical. Then "based upon" can be intelligibly used to mean that an evaluation is *determined* by certain beliefs. A vague statement like 'My belief in democracy is based upon a theory of human nature' might be construed to mean that the speaker cherishes democracy because he believes it is especially suitable to human nature as he understands it. Democratic life is somehow appropriate to fulfilling what are judged to be important human abilities and aspirations. Clearly, his evaluation of democracy is in part based upon—that is, determined by—a cluster of verifiable beliefs. It is also based upon some further values, such as a selection of the human traits he regards as most worthy of support and expression. He believes that such values are apt to flourish in this system of social life; so his estimate of the arrangement is a function of his attachment to those values and to the verifiable proposition that such values are well sustained by these conditions.

When moral discourse is understood in the manner indicated, it becomes obvious at once that a vast array of information becomes pertinent to it. Any information that qualifies existing valuations can be introduced with varying degrees of relevance. The beliefs that evaluations are based upon can be investigated for their truth value, and the values at stake are at least subject to being modified through an analysis of their implications for conduct. Such indeed is the very stuff of moral controversy between the various stripes of socialists and capitalists, for example. A parade of beliefs about history, human nature, economics, class relations, and culture is disputed. According to one's belief, "bourgeois freedom" is attacked as an instrument of oppression or praised as the *sine qua non* of increasing emancipation. Likewise with "socialist equality." And there is some opportunity to see how these ideas work out in practice—to see what they really come to. Our allegiances are largely determined by these cognitive beliefs.

There can be no assurance that even if there were agreement about the verifiable facts, a nice agreement about the evaluations would ensue. It can hardly be doubted, nevertheless, that disputes about value, great and small, are determined largely by cognitive assumptions. If the adequacy of such assumptions were settled, the moral disputes would calm down appreciably—at least for serious persons. We won't persist in our prejudices or disguise blind tenacity as a "principled" stand. A measure of moral conscientiousness would be the extent to which one's judgments were emancipated from intuitions and were organic to the relevant bodies of knowledge.

Our topic is moral discourse. How it has expanded! It now incorporates as appropriate subject matter anything of human interest that is pertinent to the problem at hand. The orphaned children are returned to the fold. The grand inquiries into man and the world are again vitally important. The relevance of these cherished inquiries is not to produce premises for demonstrations, but to present intelligently discriminated objects of admiration, respect, thanksgiving, fear, love, and inspiration. Those who desire cognitive reductions of evaluation aim for logical proofs. In contrast, analysis of experience aims at education, vision, and enlightenment.

Principled Discourse

In such discourse there are also prominent roles for traditional features of moral deliberation and for cherished sorts of norms. We have moral principles, for example. They typically imply modes of conduct that are of widespread and enduring importance. The value of their observance is well tested. But it is imperative to understand their function. We do not serve the moral life by assuming that principles exist to be blindly followed, or that they are premises for deductions. Yet life requires good order, consistency, and reasonable predictability. Our principles are well regarded, then, as instruments for *distinguishing, ordering,* and *preserving* the multiple values of common life. "One ought to keep one's promises," we say. Promise-keeping is found to be of consummate value in human relations, and we spare ourselves from having to figure this out from the beginning on every occasion. We distinguish that particular *kind* of conduct; we note that it is typically of great consequence; we accordingly assert our advocacy that it should characteristically be honored, and we honor persons for their fidelity to it. The values that are distinguished, ordered, and preserved in its observance are not validated by the principle. Quite the reverse. The principle is validated by its efficacies in enriching and organizing the basic values of moral life.

In rationalistic reasoning, principles are introduced for the sake of dictating or justifying common practice. In discourse, by contrast, they serve as potent reminders that the conduct of life will be typically well rewarded if, through varying contingencies, we behave honestly, steadfastly, and the like. Accordingly, it is indispensable to keep principles steadily in mind. On occasions of reflection and discussion, their invocation reminds us of accumulated wisdom, of the long view, without which the many goods of experience are in greater peril. We can speak of moral standards and ideals in the same way. They are summaries of long moral experience and insight. They illumine the possibilities of conduct and discipline the imagination, and they typically weigh heavily in our deliberations.

Moral Discourse as Social

Discourse is by no means exhausted, then, in the explication of moral judgments. I now want to bring attention to another obvious point, and again one whose implications have been overlooked. This is the social context within which judgment occurs.

No one who writes on ethics fails to say that the function of moral inquiry is to guide conduct. It is commonly assumed that the philosopher attempts to come clean with the criteria in accordance with which persons in their private reflections may make correct choices. We seem interminably to find statements in textbooks to the effect that ethics attempts to answer the question (evidently posed to oneself) "What ought I to do?" Suppose, however, that we consider the problems of ethics to be those that have urgency in the moral life. Then we must immediately think of moral problems as social, *i.e.,* interpersonal. Morality has to do with the norms governing the way we treat each other. Its problems are not exclusively mine or thine, nor are its resources. Of course it is individuals who have these problems, but it is the social character of conduct that brings distinctively moral problems into existence. The nature of the moral condition is obscured by putting it as "What ought I to do?" Why not, "What assumptions and methods will tend to adjust and reconcile human conflicts and bring welcome ends into existence?" When we ask a different question, we invite different inquiries and search for different answers. We might look for social methods and resources to deal with troubles and prizes that are likewise social.

When individuals are engaged in situations where they must devise alternatives and choose between them, vital to their choice is knowledge of the behavior implied by a proposed alternative. The inquiry into the meanings of plans of action is on many occasions necessarily a social process. Actions are undertaken in concert with others, and they affect others. If we are to know how our behavior will affect others and how they will respond to it, promote or retard it, we must ask them, and they must reply. Their response, presumably, would include their evaluations of the issue, their perception of the rights, responsibilities, and deserts at stake, and their perception of the relevant facts. We can extend consultation to broader issues, about which other persons might have much greater knowledge.

This is the condition of each person in the predicament, and surely if common progress is to be made in dealing with it, short of the simple exertion of power, one person cannot decide the matter alone; he cannot decide for others. It is conspicuously a shared problem, and therefore communication is conspicuously necessary. There are many things to know about and to talk over. Moral issues have exceedingly complex ramifications, and there might be highly pertinent matters that we are unaware of or don't think to take into account. Consider the labyrinth of issues brought to bear on reverse discrimination, academic freedom, capital punishment, abortion, mercy killing, private property, egalitarianism. What good is it to talk just to oneself about these puzzles? For all of us but the most stubborn, we find that such communication frequently brings us to revise our judgments of what should be done.

Adherents of the classic tradition will say that it is fine to talk in this way, but the *moral standards* to which such information is subject are somehow beyond qualification by such a mundane process. Yet the claim that informed, sensitive, and intelligent discourse should not qualify moral standards merely begs the question. Not only the *means* of action, but the criteria for judging it are subject to discussion and analysis as well. Our standards of right and wrong, of good and bad and justice, cannot reasonably be thought to be beyond the reach of change or refinement; a seriously collaborative discussion of them might lead to welcome accord. It is more apt to lead to concord than is intransigent individualism.

Just as we differ in plans of action, we differ more or less in regard to the standards for judging them. Again, one individual can presume to have the definitive answers for the rest, but perhaps each feels entitled to that singular privilege. Unless we can establish our certitude, infallibility, and moral perfection, we are again in a position where such matters are open for consultation, discussion, and revision. Otherwise we are at a stalemate. Such communication is the life-blood of actual moral discourse. Perhaps a stalemate survives the process, but we resign ourselves to an exercise in futility if we presuppose such an outcome from the outset. We might get a more welcome result.

We seem to be habituated to a kind of moral solipsism, even among those whom we respect and trust. When we remember, however, that we sometimes change our minds about moral issues, and when we acknowledge that such issues are controversial, disputed by persons of knowledge and good will, then we might also acknowledge that it is not just the other fellow's convictions which are open to revision. We might even believe that we could learn something from each other. Rather than confining myself to private soul searching in a matter that concerns us both, rather than speculate about how I might feel if the roles were reversed, rather than wonder how you might feel about it, I might take the step of consulting you directly.

The consultative approach—*social intelligence,* in Dewey's nomenclature—has potentialities unavailable to other methods for contending with moral situations. It is not "value neutral." It is responsive to the vibrant hopes and torments of the moral life. (The idea of a morally neutral criterion with which to judge moralities is simply absurd. Moralities exist for *our* sake, not for some neutered sake.) Nor is this discourse easy to carry on. It requires virtue to exercise it and to resist temptations for deceit, manipulation, stubbornness, cowardice, evasion, and the like. Perhaps these virtues are worth the effort, however; and perhaps they are potentially, in some measure, within our competence. The topic will be resumed at later junctures, and the appropriate virtues will be considered in chapter 8.

In saying that moral discourse need not be reduced to talking to yourself, I by no means deny that soul-searching of some sort is a prominent antecedent of many decisions. Everyone, ultimately, reaches his own verdict and at his own peril; this condition cannot be discarded by an honest person. The discourse prior to choice is apt to be complex and wide-ranging, and it will often require information about which there is reasonable doubt. It can be soul-wrenching when we look at the alternatives and tragedies that crowd upon us, especially when these are given in face-to-face communication.

There is, then, a strongly individualistic phase in the process of moral decision, but accounts of deliberation that neglect its social character are blind to the realities and possibilities of the moral life. One of the most decisive features of prominent ethical theories is the assumption that the individual arrives at moral judgment exclusively by his own exertions. That is, a deliberate process of consultation is irrelevant to determining moral judgment. Theories regarding methods of arriving at moral decision have been strikingly individualistic. Equally striking is that such individualism has rarely been noted.

In speaking of an individualistic theory of moral judgment, I do not forget that philosophers get together and talk about moral theory, read papers at conferences, exchange letters, and publish books and articles. What I am talking about is that within the theories themselves there is rarely so much as a thought given to the possibility that moral discourse itself might be systematically and rigorously social.

The individualistic theory has appeared in various forms. As Plato had it, the true philosopher—should there ever be one—has a direct intellectual grasp of the forms, and by this knowledge he becomes an absolute authority on all moral questions. All persons and all activities of the state are disposed according to his wisdom.[10] Aristotle is less individualistic. Although he recognizes the man of practical wisdom as moral authority, he is reluctant to conclude that such a person is infallible or that all moral problems admit of unambiguous resolutions. In his discussion of justice in the *Nicomachean Ethics* and especially in the *Politics,* Aristotle notes that honorable persons will disagree. Hence he makes the remarkable claim in his *Politics* that the collective judgment of the citizens is often more to be relied upon than the deliverances of the individual of unusual virtue. "[I]f the people are not utterly degraded, although individually they may be worse judges than those who have special knowledge, as a body they are as good or better."[11] Almost as an afterthought, he had already made the striking remark in the *Nicomachean Ethics,* "When great issues are at stake, we distrust our own abilities as insufficient to decide the matter and call in others to join us in our deliberations."[12]

Aristotle's initiative went unrecognized; the Platonic alternative has been dominant. Although there is an acknowledged problem that some persons will have a corrupted reason, the tradition of natural law assumes that the individual with his unaided reason can discover what is morally right. Contractarian theories, classical and contemporary, might seem an exception. After all, do not such theories presuppose at least an *imagined* conclave of rational persons who reach an agreement about the principles that will govern their collective life? In fact, however, in such philosophies the contracting situation is a mere formality—one might say a superfluity, if not a sham; for the results of the contract are determined in advance by *individual* reason (or intuition). Hobbes and Locke, for example, were persuaded that any rational person must arrive at, or discover, the same principles as any other. One rational being, *qua* rational, can speak for all the rest. Rousseau's general will is of the same nature; it is the same for one and all, and anyone who has knowledge of it expresses the true will of all and rightly has moral and political authority. The general will is not the sum of individual wills, and it seems not to be a product of consultation. Indeed, concern with the interests of particular individuals and groups is corrupting. Rousseau declares, "If, when the people, being furnished with adequate information, held its deliberations, *the citizens had no communication one with another,* the grand total of the small differences would always give the general will, and the decision would always be good."[13] In this regard, Kant is most emphatic of all. The rational being consults only his own reason, which commands him absolutely regarding the right course of action: "Inexperienced in the course of the world, incapable of being prepared for all its contingencies, I ask *myself* only: Can I will that my maxim become a universal law?"[14] It has apparently never entered the head of a Kantian that moral discourse might be other than monologue.

Utilitarianism requires no social discourse either. If utility is the only valid test for morality, what is needed for the determination of policy is a legislator possessed of the ability to calculate the consequences of its implementation. He might need a public opinion poll to help calculate pleasures and pains, but the *moral* issue has already been decided.

The list of examples can be lengthened. Kierkegaard, Nietzsche, and Sartre make a virtue of extreme individualism in judgment. Nor is the determination of good according to Moore a social process. Moral qualities for any intuitionist are a matter of direct insight or inspection; they are not matters of a sort to be adjusted by deliberate social practice.

There are exceptions additional to the pregnant suggestion from Aristotle. Both Hume and Hegel rejected this sort of individualism and regarded our explicit moral norms as the product of custom and tradition. They were content that norms should remain just that, however. They advanced no deliberate method of moral discourse.

Marx was not an individualist either, but in accordance with his social thought, the reconciliation of moral conflict is impossible when there are economic classes; where there are none, the sources of serious conflict have already been eradicated.[15]

Chapter 2 of Mill's *On Liberty*, "Of the Liberty of Thought and Discussion," comes closer to advocating an explicitly social method than Mill's readers, or perhaps even Mill himself, realized. It is clear from the examples throughout the book that the main issues for which Mill demands free and open discussion are moral. The utilitarian standard itself, then, could not be accorded privileged status. On such issues (as well as any others) individuals should not regard their opinions as conclusive; and social discourse is the only means we can count upon to remedy the defects of our thought. This chapter might have been a great step forward in British theory of knowledge and ethical theory, but its implications for these fields were evidently unrecognized even by Mill. His *Considerations On Representative Government* also praises the virtues of discourse, but the explicitly ethical treatise *Utilitarianism* is innocent of the point of such notions for ethics.[16]

In Mill and in subsequent thought there is a bizarre dualism of democratic theory and ethical theory. Developments in democratic theory since Mill have stressed the importance of contriving a method of social decision that will acknowledge the realities of moral disagreement and at the same time assure the survival and effectiveness of the community while such disagreement persists. Shouldn't it be obvious that the problems of democratic life are an instance of more generic problems? Effective norms and methods of democratic decision would seem to be pertinent to the moral life in general.

It remained to a Hegelian, John Dewey, to be a constructive critic of moral individualism and to recognize that prevailing moral thought was anachronistic. Dewey's insights are nearly inaccessible to us today, for they are unreflectively interpreted as attempts to do what moral philosophers have always been doing. The procedures of social intelligence are familiar, however, in the everyday experience where we do not dictate to each other, where we do not resort to absolutistic or dogmatic ways. Voluntary human associations could not function without a certain tolerance and even respect for moral divergence. No marriage or friendship today could survive without something resembling social intelligence. In effect, we presuppose the irreducible variety of interests and norms generated in shared life. We have enough mutual respect to take each other seriously, to entertain differences in judgment as legitimate proposals, and to discuss our options in a civil and open-minded way. Typically, such discourse brings about qualifications, more or less, in our assessments and plans. If and when some sort of resolution is reached, everyone will not be equally happy with it, and some may conscientiously refuse to abide by it. Yet we often have good reason to stay with a collective judgment. It might be because we genuinely believe in the general virtue of our associates' judgment, and we might view our own position with something less than certitude. We might acknowledge that our own views have received an honest hearing, and we assume that in the ongoing activities we will continue to get such recognition. Our voice will be heard again; it will be respected and heeded. We also want to preserve the relations in which we are engaged, rather than disrupt or quit them entirely. From honoring such procedures we gain not only the benefits of "pooled intelligence," in Dewey's phrase, but the benefit of more satisfactory human relations as well.

This is the model of social intelligence. Need it be regarded as a too casual or somehow degenerate form of moral deliberation? Given the nature of the moral condition, it is perhaps the most sophisticated and promising mode of discourse. The notion is more fittingly described in the expression, "democracy as a way of life." It suggests certain dispositions of thought and action that we habitually exercise in our social transactions. It is not a simple counting of heads, which can lead to atrocious results. It must presuppose that the appropriate democratic virtues are more or less shared. Assuming the necessary conditions are present in sufficient measure, this is a model of discourse that is difficult to quarrel with. Of course the conditions frequently are not present. Hence Dewey's endless pleas that childhood education strain every fiber to practice and inculcate these features. He urged that the practice of democracy as a way of life be substituted for authoritarian procedures wherever possible, that the observance of its norms might become habitual.

Certainly the most pressing of the reservations to Dewey's theory consists in doubting his conviction that the conditions of social intelligence can be effectively extended. This is a most serious concern, and the applications of the method are surely more limited than he supposed. There are many obstacles to the effective exercise of intelligence, even among those who profess allegiance to it. Stubbornness, dogmatism, the closed mind, indifference, and defensiveness are sometimes useful to their practitioners. So are deception, intimidation, force, and silence. (Indeed, sometimes they are praiseworthy.) And there are fully conscientious moral absolutists, who will care little for the social procedure. Another potent limitation is our understandable reluctance to submit precious goods to social decision. We don't want to put many of our goods in jeopardy, so we would necessarily think of open moral discourse as having limits regarding what could be set at risk—each of us having our own conception of the appropriate limit. In some situations, too, recourse to collective deliberation would be an impertinence; in others a catastrophe. We must think realistically of what the limits of this particular form of civility are. All the same, as a critically conceived procedure, it is an ideal worth pursuing and struggling for. It is a matter, whenever feasible, of choosing civility over intransigence.

We should not assume that an ideal is worthy only if it can be universally accepted and practiced. Theoretical moral reflection need not be oppressed by the mad ambition to convince and "reform" everyone; it does well enough just to provide resources to those who grope for a better way of life. Social intelligence might be the most effective mode of deliberation of which the moral life admits; but that is not to say that it always, or even usually, admits of it.

The traditional moralist has hardly been unaware of the conspicuous phenomenon of moral disagreement, but his response has been to try to delegitimate it at large. He would advance a theory of right and wrong so cogent that it eradicates all rational objection. However rich the history of moral philosophy as characterizations of the moral condition, it is a wasteland of failures when regarded as successive attempts to settle moral questions definitively. Yet philosophers are still skulking about in their accustomed ways. No doubt they are moved in part by a genuine and reasonable anxiety: the fear of moral chaos. Hence they want to establish unarguable rules of conduct. Such rules would not automatically be followed—certainly not, but at least the moral legislator feels justified in demanding measures consistent with his principles to see that they be learned and obeyed. The thought of releasing the determination of moral conduct to a social process is enough to make almost anyone cringe. But social intelligence is not just any social process, and it is difficult to see how any cogent train of moral reasoning is threatened by intelligent conversation.

At issue at the moment is what I have called moral individualism, a method of moral decision. It has a certain plausibility if we regard individual reason to be endowed with appropriate powers, as in Locke or Kant, and if we suppose also that there are certain objects of knowledge that invariantly determine our moral evaluations. Then moral judgment is a kind of science—and a science, indeed, unlike experimental science, for it can be prosecuted by a single individual. Due to this legacy, there has been a preoccupation with moral *reasoning*, rather than moral *discourse*. Attention that might have been directed to discourse has been lavished on reasoning, where the latter is routinely taken to be something in which one may engage by oneself. These are concerns characteristic of the individualistic model: whether such reasoning is deductive in form, or inductive; maybe there is a peculiarly moral inference. What sort of logic is implied by the use of "good reasons"? What are the conceptual relations of evaluative words and moral judgments? What is one logically committed to when using "right" or "ought"? Are we logically committed to universalize a judgment with such words in it? And so on.

Such concerns hardly exhaust the resources of moral decision. Yet the vitally important topic of interpersonal discourse never arises. Perhaps it is the belief that morality is either reducible to a (lonesome) science or it is not a rational discipline at all that has hindered philosophers from identifying and exploring the resources of the moral condition. Philosophers have conceived moral inquiry not as colloquy, but soliloquy. They have reduced discourse to judgment, and they have reduced a social to an individual process. Naturally, the question of what might be the constituent elements of discourse has not been raised. Accordingly, the subject matter of discourse has been reduced to what can be incorporated into the prevailing conceptions of moral judgment.

The analysis of discourse in its full context discloses potencies of the moral life that have been unnoticed and hence unexploited in the philosophies of recent decades. Their default illustrates once more a perennial weakness of philosophy: the failure to engage fundamental subject matter. To engage it, however, is hardly to guarantee that the perplexities and pains of the moral life will disappear. We deceive ourselves if we think there are easy formulas for the conduct of life, just waiting to be discovered. If we find none that are entirely satisfactory, our failure does not necessarily represent a failure of philosophy. It is certain that the moral condition affords less than most of us would prefer.

At the same time, passivity is equally unrealistic. Growth in learning, wisdom, and efficacy is possible. Our moral convictions have been disciplined by the universe of action; but we need not regard them as but inert summaries of experience. The discipline can continue. Our basic conceptions of man and the world, chastened, one hopes, by worldly experience, can play a crucial role in determining our ideas about the fundamental aims and methods of the moral life.

Understanding of the moral condition does not prescribe solutions to a particular moral impasse. It does, however, have valuable lessons for the moral life. It can indicate what sorts of values are in vain and what are sustainable, more or less; and it can suggest what virtues for the conduct of life are supported and reinforced by the general conditions of existence. We are constrained by our understanding of the moral condition to accept a form of moral pluralism, to prefer an explicitly social method in the moral life, where practicable, and to advocate the cultivation and exercise of certain virtues. Succeeding discussions will show that pluralism has both its curses and blessings, but it is not moral anarchy or some other form of degeneracy.

The next phase of analysis will be to argue that associated life generates qualitatively different kinds of moral relations, but it does not generate a fixed order of precedence among them. Neither does it support differing moral relations with equal security of existence.

Notes

1. Alasdair MacIntyre, *After Virtue,* 2d ed. (Notre Dame, Ind.: University of Notre Dame Press, 1984), Chapter 2.

2. The nature of the attempt to make good on this claim is hinted at in *After Virtue* and developed further in *Whose Justice? Which Rationality?* (Notre Dame, Ind.: University of Notre Dame Press, 1988) and *Three Rival Versions of Moral Enquiry* (Notre Dame, Ind.: University of

Notre Dame Press, 1990); but by MacIntyre's own admission, he has not yet succeeded in producing the definitive account of moral rationality. If the arguments in this book are correct, he can't; for he is chasing his own version of a morality that would be science.

3. MacIntyre is an exception to this narrowness. In *Whose Justice? Which Rationality?* and *Three Rival Versions of Moral Enquiry*, he analyzes moral discourse as a function of a tradition. The rationality of discourse is a function of the rationality of a tradition. His analyses are of a different type, however, than that which I undertake. He is investigating the distinctive rationality of a tradition. In the present chapter, I am looking for the functional efficacies of discourse in specific judgments and actions.

Jürgen Habermas is also an exception. He presents an elaborately propounded communicative ethic. As we shall see in chapter 7, the crucial facts for him about communication lie in their supposed transcendental conditions. I will suggest not only that he is in error about such conditions, but that his assertions about their alleged moral functions are mistaken.

4. "How to Make Our Ideas Clear" is the essay by Peirce inaugurating the pragmatic theory of meaning. See *Collected Papers*, 5.388–410. No one has hitherto undertaken a pragmatic analysis of moral language in respect to the dual functions of describing and evaluating. Dewey suggests such an analysis in his frequent remark that a moral judgment is a plan of action. See also chapter 1 of his *Theory of Valuation* and the article "Corporate Personality" in *Later Works*, Vol. 2: 1925–1927, pp. 22–43.

5. I am not propounding a generic theory of meaning, nor am I saying what moral meanings ought to be or what they happen to be in ordinary English. I am proposing a way to make moral ideas *clear* and *pertinent*.

6. A. I. Melden, *Rights and Persons* (Berkeley: University of California Press, 1977).

7. Robert Nozick, *Anarchy, State and Utopia* (New York: Basic Books, 1974).

8. Ronald Dworkin, *Taking Rights Seriously* (Cambridge, Mass.: Harvard University Press, 1978). Equal concern and respect is organic to human dignity, he says, but that condition does not require property rights, for example. There is no curtailment of dignity if the state redistributes the fruits of your labor. "I would therefore not recognize the claim that some men and women want liberty as requiring any compromise in the efforts that I believe are necessary to give other men and women the equality to which they are entitled" (p. 268). Equal concern and respect *is* compatible with reverse discrimination, however. But are such claims *logical*? Is it *self-evident* that one does not offend against human dignity by extensive invasions of property, for example? Might this not be judged as coercive

and hence an *offense* against human dignity? Is it not arguable, too, that it *violates* equal concern and respect to deny admission on the basis of merit? It could be considered an *insult* to human dignity to admit a person to school on the basis of sex or race, especially if that person were intellectually under-qualified. My point in bringing up such questions is not to answer them, but to illustrate Dworkin's incessant practice of disguising his moral sentiments as derivations from axioms.

9. R. M. Hare, *The Language of Morals* (Oxford: Clarendon Press, 1952) p. 46. Emphasis added.

10. This is the orthodox reading of Plato. One is never quite sure, however, what Plato really intends. Socrates is usually represented as the man of dialogue. With him, moral discourse is social. On the other hand, as *The Republic,* for example, progresses, less and less of Socrates's time is spent in exchange of views. And for the historical Socrates, appeal to his personal *daimon* was evidently ultimate.

11. Aristotle, *Politics,* in *The Complete Works of Aristotle,* the Revised Oxford Translation, edited by Jonathan Barnes, 2 Vols. (Princeton, N.J.: Princeton University Press, 1984), p. 2034.

12. Aristotle, *Nicomachean Ethics,* translated, with introduction and notes, by Martin Ostwald (Indianapolis and New York: The Bobbs-Merrill Company, Inc., 1962), p. 61.

13. Jean-Jacques Rousseau, *Social Contract,* translated and with an Introduction by G. D. H. Cole (New York: E. P. Dutton, 1950), p. 27. Emphasis added. One can't help wondering what "adequately informed" could mean if consultation is not included in normal inquiry.

14. Immanuel Kant, *Foundations of the Metaphysics of Morals,* translated and with an Introduction by Lewis White Beck (New York: The Liberal Arts Press, 1959), p. 19. Emphasis added.

15. The status of the dictum, "From each according to his abilities; to each according to his needs," is not clear. Will the comrades in the higher phases of communism spontaneously adopt it? They had better think twice, for the first half of it has all the earmarks of oppression. *Must* one contribute to the limits of one's ability?

16. For a discussion of Mill's edging toward a social method in ethics see my *Excellence in Public Discourse,* chap. 2.

5

Moral Relations

The moral life has many dimensions and subtle variations. It would be difficult, if not impossible, to identify and characterize all the significant distinctions in moral experience, and such a rendering would be controversial in any case. Nevertheless, it is important to draw attention to some of the most distinctive traits of the subject matter. We have words that denote important, if crudely formulated, differences. "Bad," "good," "rights," "duty," "justice," and others differentiate prominent and recognizable variations in moral conduct. There are more or less definite kinds, or types, of behavior that are implied by such expressions. To get a fair grasp of the moral condition, these kinds have to be distinguished and analyzed.

Moral relations are not the invention of philosophers, nor do they exist prior to life activity. They are emergent of experience. Distinctive *kinds* of value-laden relations are struggled for, honored, and preserved in an uncertain balance. If we have some sense of the nature of these relations and their bearings on each other, we will have something of a survey of generic human values in their mutual reinforcements and resistances; that is, as they are functions of patterns of social behavior. These are the only values to which we can appeal in our moral predicaments.

By returning us to primary subject matter, such a survey might have some effect in demystifying both the moral life and moral philosophy. My concern is neither with concepts nor ordinary usage. Analysis of the *concept* of rights would attempt to determine the definition of the word, its "logic" in moral discourse, and its place among a cluster of concepts. But conceptual analysis must be the servant, not the master, of life experience. Many philosophers have believed that they conjure up basic moral distinctions from some arcane source detached from the exigencies and consummations of ordinary life. Sad to say, they often succeed in getting the unwary to believe them. But would anyone have even conceived the idea of rights, and vested it with moral dignity, if the distinctive conditions that go by that name had not already shown themselves precious in the conduct of life, or if there were not at least intimations of their real efficacies? Would Locke have adduced, *a priori*, rights in the state of nature, endowing them with ultimate value, if he had not already conceived their worth in actual existence?

What I have in mind, in contrast, is to identify and describe the sorts of experience that would prompt the formulation of moral concepts (such as rights)—to distinguish the salient relations and values that we would promote and secure in the moral life. Our subject matter—the subject matter that counts—is that life. What are the conspicuous relations that constitute it, and how do *they* tend to be knotted together? That is the knot that finally matters, not that of concepts, which might or might not reflect the dynamics of experience.

Although general classes of moral relations are distinguishable, they do not exist in mutual isolation. As complex patterns of social conduct, they are inescapably intertwined with other patterns. To realize one set of relations will require variations in others by way of sacrifice, compromise, conflict, exclusion, and sometimes creative union. Just as it is self-defeating to consider a single act in isolation from its continuities and alternatives, it is a distortion or neglect of the perplexities of the moral life to consider rights, for example, to the exclusion of obligations or of ends.

This sort of analysis resists the philosophic quest for final order and simplicity. As a consequence of this quest, we witness a war of ethical theories: some of them make utility the ultimate consideration, some are determined to define rational agency in a way that gives the last judgment, others stake everything on rights, and still others look for independent moral facts or qualities that will be decisive in moral choice—anything to avoid the anxieties of pluralism. Such monistic enterprises are bound to do systematic violence to the moral life. All moral conclusions do some violence to cherished values; this is unavoidable. However, it is not typically recognized by moralists *as* violence, and rationalistic sytematization fails to attend to the urgencies of the very experience that brings moral reflection into existence. Moral philosophy thereby dismisses the experience that legitimates its existence. We would not wrench typical moral values out of the context that gives them life and meaning. We would resist, in James's words, the efforts of philosophers "to substitute the content of their clean-shaven systems for that exuberant mass of goods with which all human nature is in travail, and groaning to bring to the light of day."[1] Of course we must seek order and economies in the moral life, and we can have some success in doing so. Philosophers pursue this goal to a fault. Hence legislation dispensed from the ivory tower runs the gamut from impertinence through condescension to indifference.

A further virtue of discriminating the types of moral relations is to see them as natural functions. In that capacity it is possible to make some assessment of what sustains them in being. Some are easily supported, others less so; and some are utopian. Reflection on the moral life will be ineffectual or even hurtful if we have no sense of what relations can realistically be introduced and maintained. We can pursue that sense only by undertaking something like the sort of analyses to follow.

I do *not* undertake what might be called a philosophic justification of the plurality of relations and interrelations to be examined. I want to indicate as well as I can what sorts of value are already prized and in contention in these relations. These are the values that would be ordered and preserved with reflective distinctions and thoughtful conduct. Analyses of the sort proposed must be preliminary to questions about what to do when the values are insecure or incompatible.

I trust the succeeding formulations will be helpful in suggesting the weighty intricacies of the moral life.[2] I will initially distinguish five types of moral relations. None of them seems to be reducible to the others, but each of them conditions the others. Some have subtypes. They are *ends, entitlements, requirements, service,* and *respect for persons.* For reasons to be indicated in due course, justice is not treated as one of the five. The social relations we might call "just" seem to be reducible to an amalgam, or function, of the others. Some vital constituents of this amalgam will be suggested. Initially I discriminate a given relation, with its own variations and problems, without much reference to other relations. However, it is just such reference, as we shall see, that makes the understanding of these relations both trying and important.

Ends

A conspicuous trait of moral experience is our concern for ends: a certain outcome, object, condition, or quality of activity is focused upon as being somehow preferable to others, and we want to undertake action to secure it. This is temporally our first moral experience, if at the beginning it can be called moral at all. Life demands that we possess various objects to fill the needs of the organism. In time, we reflectively consider ends for ourselves alone, for a few people, a community, or for the human race. We grade them as good, better, best; or bad, worse, and worst. We might pursue them by ourselves, but we also pursue them with the company of others, often in competition with still others, or in neglect of others.

We formulate ideal ends for people individually and collectively. Many thinkers have addressed themselves to determining the highest good. Knowledge of such an end, it has been supposed, might direct all our activities, individual and collective. Such a good might be a good for all; hence, the highest good would also be the common good. How simple and happy the moral life would be! Plato seemed to think it could be so ordered. In succeeding centuries the absolute good has been perceived many times. We are allowed to be skeptical about such perceptions, for their alleged object has shown great variation as it has been characterized by a succession of philosophers and theologians.

The utilitarians had a more modest goal. They said pleasure (or happiness—they made no distinction) is the only thing good as an end, and the only moral task is to learn how to maximize it, individually and socially. Unlike Plato, Aristotle, Augustine, Spinoza, Nietzsche, Bradley, Dewey, and many others, they have had (with the exception of Mill) little of an edifying or inspiring sort to say about the conditions of human existence that are requisite to happiness; in that sense the philosophy of the utilitarians is far less interesting than most other treatments of the good. (Only Moore is less interesting in this regard.)

Philosophers have been unwilling to concede that pleasure is all that is good as an end, much less concede that it should be distributed only in terms of general utility. We have diverse criteria for evaluating goods: quantity and/or quality of pleasure, conformity to law, compatibility with right, survival of the group, conduciveness to self-realization, personal excellence, possession of properties alleged to be intrinsically good, and so on. We may judge an end both for its own qualities and for its efficacy in further attainment.

The availability of ends—goods—is limited. Hence it is necessary to consider the question of the distribution of ends among different parties. There are competing demands for ends, and, perhaps wishing to avoid a free-for-all, we try to develop criteria for determining who should get what. It would be a mistake, however, to suppose that avoidance of a free-for-all is the only motive. We have relations of care and love; we identify to some extent with the condition of persons we don't even know. We come, moreover, to recognize that we must sustain certain behavior in order that it be reciprocated; sometimes we realize that our claims, simply because they are ours, do not have priority over those of others. Hence we want "to do right" by them, at least occasionally. For such reasons, and given the shortage and clash of ends, we must establish and honor *entitlements*. Some persons, at least, must come to some such recognition, and they strive to communicate it to others and support such behavior by means of education in the family, neighborhood, church, and school.

Entitlements

Social relations must be structured in such a way that we may pursue, achieve, and enjoy specified ends or conditions without interference from others; and in some cases their compliance, willing or not, is expected and enforced. At least this much is meant in saying that there are entitlements. Although, as the case may be, entitlements are not the same for different classes of individuals, and some individuals may have none, they designate indispensable relations in a society. Treading on uneasy terrain, I think it is fruitful to specify three distinct forms of entitlement relations that are all, unhappily, called rights, and a fourth, *deserts*. Following convention, the rights will be called *classical* rights, *welfare* rights, and *contractual* rights.

It might suit the ends of one person or many or the state to prevent other persons from speaking, associating, attending church, or preserving and disposing of their property as they see fit. Given the opportunity, these disruptions of human activity often occur. Hence pursuit of these acitivities is denied, and the prohibitions might well be resented. Why, one might naturally ask, should I be pushed around if I am making a contribution, or at least if I am doing no harm? I may have more than enough competence to carry out certain ventures without supervising authority. Why must someone in power decide what I can and cannot do with respect to my own life? Perhaps, too, the free exercise of certain human capacities is thought to produce a greater social good than would a command performance. Given both the love of freedom and the innumerable unpredictable contingencies of ordinary life, individual rights to initiative might prove remarkably effective in contrast to bureaucratic regulation. Reasons for advocating such entitlements might also include ordinary human concern for the impositions visited on others. There are many natural inducements, then, to want to guarantee various conditions, and they are given voice by declaring that human beings have rights: to life, liberty, estate, the pursuit of happiness, freedom of contract, equal protection of the law, and more.

There are obvious reasons for securing and maintaining social relations such that individuals are protected from different kinds of unwanted intrusion by one another and by institutional authorities. Within the confines of the classical conception, the only limitation on the exercise of such rights is that they not be used as instruments for invading the rights of others. Such an arrangement has been thought of as ensuring enlightened self-interest and the general welfare at the same time—a lovely dream! In any case, one of the glories of such rights is that it is not mandatory to exercise them. For the bearer of rights, they are not duties, but liberties and opportunities. The general notion of classical rights has the attractive feature of enabling, in part, free human enterprise.

Thoughtful students of rights relations do not accept them un-critically. They cannot think of rights as isolated things in themselves, to be accepted or rejected at face value. The list of rights is controversial, the more so as the list is lengthened, as the list of bearers is extended, and as incompatibilities occur. Such lists, indeed, will be rejected by a philosopher king who presumes to know the nature of everyone's true good. The American founders quickly discovered how difficult it is to determine rights and their limits, and the history of the United States Supreme Court substantiates the controversial character of rights claims, which proliferate left and right.

Rights are sometimes claimed to be absolute. Does this mean that they are impervious to all other moral claims? Are violations of rights never excusable? Can the conflict of rights be compatible with their alleged absolute character? Classical rights, whether claimed or actually embodied in law, conflict with each other: freedom of speech with due process, the right to life with the right of a woman to determine the use of her own body, the right to bear arms with the right to public safety. Some rights might be outright damaging to many persons. This is often said of property rights and freedom of contract: property rights license the owners of the means of production to exploit the working class. Depending on the nature of a right and its bearer, it could be a license to self-ruin or to the ruin, say, of the family—as some critics have argued of sexual liberation. Here a particular configuration of rights could mean the neglect of vital duties. I bring up such questions not to answer them, but to illustrate that rights, precious characteristics of social life, do not exist without their own vexations.

Another limitation perceived in classical rights is that their legal possession is not tantamount to having the power to exercise them effectively. Hence there is agitation, for example, for the provision of education. Traditionally, rights have implied only limitations on power and authority, guaranteeing freedom to engage in certain kinds of activity. More recently, there have been demands that rights also be provisions, that is, *welfare* rights. There are demands that people be provided with jobs, education, housing, medical care and the like; advocates argue that there is a right to such things.

Formerly, to satisfy a right meant only to refrain from interfering. Today, the satisfaction of many rights means that some assignable individuals or institutions are required to provide certain resources or services. "Rights" now becomes ambiguous, referring to two quite different situations. It is one thing to prevent a person from doing harm to someone else; it is quite another to require him to provide benefits for, in most cases, anonymous others. Satisfaction of the latter requires some compromise of the former and makes perhaps unwelcome demands on resources, both individual and collective.

Nevertheless, it is part of the experience of many to cherish a situation in which people who need help are given it, not as a consequence of the vagaries of charity, but as assured, and as required of definite persons, whether they like it or not. We might be agreeable to such an arrangement out of compassion, as well as from a potential reciprocity of treatment: we might well want such provision made for ourselves, our families, and communities, if we were down on our luck. Our sentiment for welfare rights gets a further impetus if we believe that persons are in need due to no fault of their own, and perhaps due to misuse by others.

Provision of welfare rights is clearly a function, in part, of the willingness and ability of the "community" to do it. If it is easy to do, there might be little to say against it. However, the issue becomes vexed when we ask exactly what these entitlements will be, which groups are eligible for them, and how much sacrifice from others is required. There are further questions: Why are the beneficiaries so much in need? Are they profligate, or have they been exploited by other groups? What will the effects be on the behavior of either recipients or providers? Will beneficiaries become more dependent? Will they lose self-respect? Or, in consequence of a helping hand, will they become such vigorous providers of socially valued goods that the aid is really an intelligent investment? What are alternative means, if any, for promoting the interests of those who are having a hard time of it? Simply to mention such questions is to suggest that it is at least as problematic to judge of welfare rights as of their classical antecedents. It is also clear that under any historical circumstances with which we are familiar, it is has been more difficult to introduce and sustain welfare rights than classical rights.

To many, another glory of rights is that they are, at first blush, indiscriminate: All persons, regardless of variations in their personal circumstances and identity, are entitled to such things as life, liberty, and the pursuit of happiness, and—if they are needy—to aid and comfort from others. They don't have to earn such rights; the differentiating characteristics of human beings are irrelevant to the entitlements. But even for those who hold this view, at least minimal qualifications are admitted. Should all rights be of this indiscriminate sort? How about the right to vote or to hold office, or the right to meaningful work? Are rights limited by geopolitical exigencies? Should we equip an expeditionary force to enforce the rights of Iranian women? To be utterly indiscriminate descends into mindless sentimentality.

A large class of rights arises only under special conditions: those stemming from some kind of agreement, contract, oath, or promise—what I am calling *contractual* rights.[3] These rights do not require extensive analysis in this discussion. Careful agreements establish definite expectations and responsibilities, definite excusing conditions, and definite rewards and punishments. Specified goods and services are owed to assignable individuals, usually in return for equally well-specified goods and services from other assignable individuals. To ask, then, "Does this contract give the parties particular rights?" betrays a love of the occult. Operationally, this is what it means to have contractual rights, and there is nothing elusive about why we bring these relations into existence. Name them what we will, they are indispensable for deliberate social intercourse. Many promises are of a more casual and imprecise nature. Hence the rights of those who are promised are indistinct, and the rewards and punishments organic to the act are likewise uncertain. Experience teaches that off-hand promising is not a good way to build social relationships.

Contractual rights have still other difficulties in their own nature. A routine, but certainly not universal, objection to them is that the parties to the contract often have unequal bargaining power. Those who are weaker must therefore accept an unsatisfactory arrangement because they haven't the alternatives they would have if they were more powerful. The laborer in an overcrowded market must accept poor wages or starve. A further problem is that agreements have serious effects on third parties, that is, on individuals who had no part in the contract. Should all contracts incorporate everyone who has an interest in the transaction? When a physician negotiates for a position in another city, should his or her existing patients have a voice in the decision?

It is essential to make a distinction between *deserving* something and having a right. Deserving pertains to a wider and sometimes different range of behavior. To judge someone deserving is a *deliberately discriminating* act. We have to qualify for desert, and we compete for it. We are not equally deserving, equally entitled to these rewards. Rights, moreover, pertain to the assurance of highly desirable conditions, while deserts pertain to both good and bad conditions, momentous and trivial. Someone deserves contempt, deserves to be hanged, slapped in the face, or ignored; deserves better pay, elevation to sainthood, the Wimbledon trophy, assistance from others, a little peace and quiet. In cases of desert, an individual or group is singled out due to particular qualifications. There is an implicit or explicit standard to meet or a test to pass; or—when one deserves a penalty of some kind—there is a test one is required or expected to meet and fails to do so. In an obvious sense, relations of desert are non-egalitarian. Desert is *merited,* and we are not equally meritorious.

In cases of desert, there is an assumption that meeting or exceeding the relevant standard earns—merits—certain rewards. Somehow, the reward is proportionate to the achievement. The person who accomplishes more deserves more: be it more praise, more money, more blue ribbons, more authority, more fame and honor. The reward for returning a lost cat is less than the reward for bravery above and beyond the call of duty. The just deserts of a pilferer are not those of one who absconds with the pension fund. The productive worker has contributed more; that person likewise deserves a greater benefit. Desert is a recognition or assignment of worth, of value. It is recognizing that one's activity is worth something relative to that of others. If one person's achievement is judged superior to that of another, yet that person receives the same reward, he feels cheated, and others will say that he was cheated.[4]

Why should it be this way? What are the values at issue in the institution of desert? Most obviously, they include those organic to an incentive system and to the process of learning; for these reasons alone, desert is very important. One is an advocate of certain deserts as a means to promote certain kinds of behavior and to discourage others. It is a means of discovering and developing talents, virtues, and exemplary deeds. Without differential rewards and punishments, such behavior would not be forthcoming. *It cannot be stressed too strongly that relations of desert are inseparable from learning.* It is catastrophic for children, for example, to be raised without rewards and punishments that are proportional to their deserts and are distinguishable from the deserts for different behavior. You can't get Johnny to put his toys away if there are no differentiating consequences, or if Billy gets the same reward as Johnny even if Billy ignores his assignments. Johnny will be utterly impervious to Rawls's difference principle, one assumes. Children (and adults) have to understand that they get a certain reward *just because* of the distinctive nature of what they do; if the reward does not in fact distinguish their behavior from that of others, the lesson from the reward is that it doesn't make any difference what they do.

We would be mistaken to reduce the values of desert to just those of incentive and learning, crucial though they are. What will function as an incentive is a factual question. What a person is worth is a normative question. We often believe persons deserve more than they get, even if whatever they get is sufficient to keep them at the wheel. Think of the devoted, effective, underpaid teacher. We might well think that a person who is rewarded only as an incentive, and only so much as is needed for an incentive, is being used. To declare someone deserving is to express our *esteem* for him. It is a measure of our regard for his virtue, achievement, artistry, or whatever. Desert reflects our desire to honor distinction, to bestow praise and gratitude for its possession.

We value the condition of being deserving over and above its work as incentive because we honor, admire, and prize excellence and achievement. We necessarily make distinctions of ability, virtue, beauty, accomplishment, and so on; we wish to mark them in some significant and distinguishing way. And individuals need such responses not only for the process of learning, but also, no doubt, because they cherish the experience of receiving and possessing these distinctions and their fruits; they are willing to compete for them. We need and seek such regard: we want a sense of achievement, of recognition, of contributing something valuable that is distinctively one's own. It is a fact of great consequence, moreover, that we respect the rewards of desert that are earned by others. We might envy, but we do not resent, the prizes that we judge to be truly merited. I might envy the literary prestige of a William Faulkner, but I don't resent it, because he deserves it.

Another value circumscribed by desert (that makes it similar to rights) is that of secure possession. What is bestowed as one's just desert is one's own, not to be denied or taken away for some other purpose. This is central in desert: it is precisely *this* achievement that is honored; it is *this* person, and not some other, who has been singled out. If the achiever has no title to the award, desert is negated. People who deserve what they get are not required, in the name of desert, to distribute it for the general welfare.

One can hardly guess how much ink has been wasted trying to justify *or* discredit desert at large. Many—including Rawls, apparently—believe it is an intelligible notion only if we postulate free will or an absolute subject of some sort. To say that a person has a deserving character, however, is to *evaluate* his character, not to make a statement about free will. The worth of anything does not evaporate when we learn that it has causal conditions. To judge someone deserving is to judge his worth, contributions, and attainments. The value of one's character is not predicated on the assumption that one deserves the antecedent conditions of that character, any more than the merits of a football team would be abolished if we learned they are all the consequence of causal conditions. In a competition, the judgment that one side is superior would not be invalidated by the fact that the winner began the contest with more ability and determination. Likewise, an individual seeking to meet or exceed a certain standard may well begin his or her exertions with greater skills or virtue than others; but that is not to deny that the person is deserving. The challenge was indeed met, and that is what is at issue.

To deny that such honoring and rewarding should take place is tantamount to saying we should not respond favorably to any excellence that we need, love, or admire. Should you withhold your love from your lover because he owes his charms to the "natural lottery"? And should you advise your lover not to love you in return because your lovable qualities have been caused to occur? When one is loved, she may well be grateful for everything that has caused her to be lovable, and she will be stimulated to cultivate these qualities. But surely she does not claim that the intrinsic goods of love, and all the behavior associated with it, should be forever abjured. She might believe that it is intensely sad that one person begins a competition with lesser capacities and resources than another, but this is not to deny that the greater achievement meets the standards of desert. To regret that some persons are less deserving than others is to introduce considerations additional to those that we employ in judging desert, and sometimes these considerations will prompt supportive action.

If we wish to retain the values associated with desert, then we must retain relations of desert. Relations of desert support values that are obviously treasured in human life. They are not contingent upon an assumption of free will, and to abolish them on such an assumption is an oppression. Aristotle made them the whole of distributive justice, saying no community could function without them. Locke, in effect, appeals to them in his defense of private property: if you do the work, you deserve the product.[5] Marx likewise appeals to desert: the worker is robbed of the product of his own labor. Students appeal to it when they complain about their grades. There are conceivable alternatives to the relations designated by this term, but there is no experimental evidence that a society can function without them.

This is not to say just what the standards of merit should be or precisely how they should be rewarded. Desert is a form of entitlement that is also liable to both dispute and misuse. What should be the standards of excellence (and failure)? Do they measure the sorts of excellence that we esteem? Who satisfies them? What prize is commensurate to the distinctive achievement? What is a fair day's work, and what is a fair day's pay? Who decides?

In addition to being difficult to determine in many cases, desert is not an omnicompetent relation. Never to permit its transgression would require typically heavy-handed and inefficient state intrusiveness in many instances. In other instances it would mean that large, though well-deserved, incomes could under no circumstances be touched by any kind of taxation. We typically accept forms of redistribution, however. Monomania in respect to one kind of moral experience to the exclusion of others is sure to be disastrous.

Requirements

A further distinct kind of moral experience is that pertaining to the fulfillment of certain kinds of social functions. The demands and opportunities of the moral life are such that we must place a very high priority on persons honoring certain norms and performing certain tasks, even when such persons have other things they would prefer to do. The strength of such priorities is manifest in our willingness to impose sanctions of varying strengths for failure to perform. In most instances, the reason for high priority is obvious: many ends require orderly and disciplined cooperation. The preservation of societies or of particularly valuable kinds of social relations is in the balance. Hence we have general and particular social *requirements*.

The existence of every form of associated life requires the performance of various functions. Participation in the group carries with it the assumption that one has certain roles to perform for the maintenance and protection of the association. There is a nearly universal assumption that sharing in the life and values of the group implies a loyalty to it which is to be expressed pragmatically in behavior. We typically believe that a person who refuses to make a contribution to the group is not entitled to its benefits, and we likewise believe that a person who is not a beneficiary of group activities is not under obligation to it.

I will subdivide requirements into obligations, responsibilities, and duties. While some requirements are specified and prescribed by law, others are not necessarily formalized or spelled out; they may be more-or-less variable and more-or-less mandatory. These I shall call *obligations*. The professor has obligations to the student, the parent has obligations to the child, husband and wife to each other, neighbor to neighbor, colleague to colleague, and so on.

There is variation in what these obligations are thought to be, and they may be determined by authority, tradition, custom, expediency, prejudice, or some combination thereof. This is hardly to say that they are arbitrary. The group must survive, and it aims to prosper. Nevertheless, the implicit requirements of group behavior are often vague and unsystematized; so one might dispute the exact nature of any obligation and its priority in respect to others. Today, for example, we agonize over significant shifts in the respective obligations of husband and wife.

Another class of requirements comes by way of explicitly stated arrangements that we are party to, approve of, or accept. For convenience in distinction, I call these *responsibilities,* rather than duties or obligations. We incur many of these responsibilities by way of our voluntary pledge, whether private (as in the case of personal promises) or specifically legal (as in the case of contracts). There is no mystery in responsibilities. Like their correlatives, contractual rights, they are vital to associated life. Also like contractual rights, they are subject to criticism regarding the relative bargaining positions of the parties to an agreement, and regarding the effects of such responsibilities on innocent bystanders.

Additional responsibilities are incurred by the sometimes vague procedure of consent or approval. We have, for example, the responsibility to obey the law. Of course, when and how we incur such a responsibility is problematic, for laws are often oppressive or inept. It is enough to say in the present context that when the *system* of law victimizes (ignoring the meaning of "victimizes") an assignable group, and the group has no legal recourse, members of that group are not typically judged to be blameworthy for avoiding or rejecting a purported requirement to abide by the system. No one consistently advocates that innocent persons cooperate in their own oppression.

What I have called obligations and responsibilities are discriminatory. Particular persons or groups are somehow distinguished as bearers of these claims on conduct, and the persons to whom the conduct is due are likewise specific. I have obligations to my children that I do not have to yours. I have a responsibility to a certain bank to make a monthly payment of a certain amount. I made a promise to Smith but not to Jones.

Many persons hold dear a relationship in which one owes a certain behavior to others on a less discriminating basis. This is the relationship of *duty*. Kant says we have a duty to obey the moral law *just because* it is universal, and many people have followed him in this. Anything that is truly dutiful, indeed, is owed to every rational being, as such. Hence my *duty* to my wife, friend, or countrymen is no different from my duty to anonymous persons around the globe. (One sees at once that to take duty as the *exclusive* moral relation exhibits no wisdom whatever.)

Kant gave voice to a not unusual moral sentiment, but there has been uncertainty about what such duties and their priorities are, and they make quite different demands on us. Some will say that we have duties to all human beings, or perhaps to all living things, to show them respect or concern, perhaps, or to be honest with them, or to refrain from doing them injury. We have a duty to serve God and our fellow man, to give each person his due, to avenge injustice, and so forth. Others speak of an abstract duty to aid the poor or the helpless, or the suffering.

In such cases, no prior agreement has been made; there need be no specific group relationship. Yet for many there is the vivid experience that other interests must be subordinated to meeting this sort of requirement. It is something one simply must do, a matter of human integrity, it is said; so it is called a duty. If such behavior were thought of as supererogatory, failure in it would not be admonished, condemned, or punished. But such measures are in fact taken or advocated in some quarters, and a duty is thereby asserted.

The gravity we assign to such duties varies, as indicated by variations in the penalties we might advocate. It is all very well to say we have duties, but what *action* do you advocate? Who, precisely, is to perform the duties in concrete circumstances? What do we do with conflicts of duties? Kant said we have a duty to tell the truth and to protect the innocent. If we can protect the innocent by telling a lie, how do we adjudicate the conflict? (Due to his blind faith in universal reason, Kant never even perceived the possibility of such conflicts.)

In much of the experience that calls for mandatory actions (requirements), there is a distinct consciousness of human ties. They are often of the strongest sort—those of love, loyalty, friendship, kinship—and persons so united feel a bond. (Hence it happens in many contexts that requirements on our behavior are not felt as constraints.) No doubt the metaphor "morally binding" draws on the experience of such bonds and gets much of its meaning from it. What is "binding" in morality are the demands, expectations, and reciprocations of the social fabric, as well as the fears of disapproval for not living up to them. "Bindingness" is not a property of judgments as such. To be bound by an obligation is to be implicated in an explicit relationship, with its own benefits and sanctions. Once again, the imperatives are in the subject matter, not in the conceptual apparatus that communicates them. In any case, there are precious human ties that must be preserved, enhanced, or created. This experience is distinct from that signified by classical rights. The latter are cherished for individual liberation and opportunity, as well as for the expected good of society. A sense of social bond is incidental, if not irrelevant. Especially relations of obligation have a communitarian quality lacking in individual rights.

As we move from the ties of obligation, those naturally generated relations of social life, through those of responsibility, of promising, contracts, and consent, to those of duty—to those requirements to humankind as such—the natural capacity and inclination of human beings to embrace these relations seems to dwindle, if not disappear.

In honesty, we must recognize that requirements are often burdensome in any situation. Think of the strife that occurs in families. If it were not for the normal sanctions of associated life, we would often slight or neglect our required roles, preferring to try our luck with benefits that might arise with different behavior. The loyalty to requirements attenuates the more distant we become from immediate rewards and punishments. We do not find that either acknowledgment or fulfillment of the more abstract duties is well supported in life experience. Moralists might demand them; they might exact strong penalties for noncompliance. But there are limitations to what can be accomplished by such measures. People will simply rebel if they are required repeatedly to subordinate their stronger interests to weaker or nonexistent concerns. Obedience to universal principle, if it exists at all, gives way to preference for family, clan, regiment, the old school, religion, race, class, or country.

In some quarters, however, there is belief that people can be socialized to accept almost any duty. If the belief is true, the desired reeducation of the populace might require a national crusade. If the belief is false, the crusade will be not only frustrated, but oppressive as well. The bonds of tradition, custom, familiar institutions, religion, ethnicity, and kinship are powerful. Here are the deepest feelings, the fiercest and strongest loyalties, the most stalwart virtues. One who wishes to grasp the disciplines of the moral condition would never dismiss such practices as "mere" custom.

I have adumbrated the nature of relations that prompt the formulation of concepts having to do with ends, entitlements, and requirements. Another highly significant type of experience is that which generates behavior that could be encapsulated in the notion of *service*.

Service

Service is not duty. The division between the two forever eludes precision, but for any particular individual it is marked at that point where he would not advocate penalties for nonperformance. In service we recognize our most obviously altruistic values. Human beings, in widely varying degrees, have genuine feelings of sympathy and compassion. They are generous and charitable; they want to help. Extraordinary acts of service are sometimes performed, and not infrequently these are at the expense of health, fortune, and even life. This can occur when neither entitlements nor requirements are at issue, but simply the desire to provide aid, relief, or comfort. Indeed, the desire to serve can become a passion, a religion. Perhaps several distinct kinds of passion might be enumerated, but I shall make no such attempt. Just let it be said that in any inventory of moral experience, altruism must be neither overlooked nor understated—nor overstated, either.

It might hurriedly be concluded that service is beyond reproach, an unmixed good, deserving of our unqualified admiration. That is not true. One might have cause to complain that particular services were ineffective, or even (by inadvertance) harmful, or that they were not provided to the most appropriate persons. Self-sacrificing service can, indeed, be sacrifice to evil. Think of the Hitler Youth! One might also believe that an individual did too much injury to himself in his devotion to service, or neglected his obligations. On a grander scale, Herbert Spencer was convinced that services to the weak delayed the perfecting of the race by maintaining incompetent individuals. Nietzsche believed that compassion was an insult to its recipient and had a debilitating effect on its possessor: one must celebrate excellence, vitality, strength, exuberance, self-command, and challenge. Absorption with the sufferings of others makes us pessimistic, and it diverts us from the truly redeeming possibilities of existence. Spencer and Nietzsche take objections to service to the unadulterated limit, but the nature of their objections is pertinent to any assessment of the moral life.

Another question related to service regards its motivation. A cynic believes the motivation is always self-serving, whether by way of gaining power, admiration, pity, reputation, or a smug sense of superiority. No doubt the cynic is frequently correct, but experience does not support this view altogether. We must acknowledge that some people really are charitable, generous, and "warm-hearted." They are indeed rewarded, often richly rewarded, in good feelings for the improvements they can effect for others; but we shouldn't hold their good feelings against them. Better to envy them. We can distinguish between the person with largely ulterior motives who makes a display of good works and the person who really does care about the welfare of others. The distinction is genuine, and we rightly honor those who tend to the altruistic side of it.

By insisting on the reality of altruism, we should not haste to the conclusion that self-interest is necessarily a bad motive. While some moralists have thought of enlightened self-interest as the source of all moral distinctions, others, equally plagued by a need for simplification, have regarded self-interest as the root of all evil. This contrast suggests that self-interest (a vague notion at that) is morally problematic. Many moralists have assumed that any interest is self-interest. The assumption is unfounded, and it gives the self a bad name. Any interest one has in moral relations are interests *of* the self, but not necessarily *in* the self, as James and Dewey point out so nicely. Moralists of the Kantian stripe hold that any act motivated by interest lacks moral quality—for many reasons a very dubious thesis. It leaves us either with the notion that morality is impossible or that there is some sort of self that functions without interest. The former notion begs the question of what morality is; it is also worthless in addressing the realities of life experience. The latter is a postulate contrived for the sake of saving the former. As Bertrand Russell observed, postulation has all the advantages of theft over honest labor.

The next type of experience I will treat is dauntingly complex and ambiguous; yet it is highly important, and not reducible to any combination of the preceding relations. I refer to the experience of holding persons in equal regard and esteem. They enjoy a type of moral equality, an equality of consideration, even if they are unequal in intelligence, power, beauty, talent, reputation, or wealth. We often call this *respect for persons,* and it is honored more in the breach than in the observance. Why the nature and meaning of this experience is so elusive, yet important, will become evident.

Respect for Persons

Many people want to show consideration for human beings as such, or they are advocates of so doing. That is, there is a concern for human agents, seemingly regardless of their individuating characteristics.[6] We say there is a dignity of man, and certain kinds of action honor it, while others desecrate it. The latter are "inhuman," degrading, dehumanizing. With some persons, at least, there is a sense of kinship to the entire race, a sense of some kind of bond with our own kind and a feeling that all members of this family, simply by virtue of being in the family, have the same moral status.

Respect for the individual, as I conceive it, does not imply specific duties. It is a readiness to regard others as moral equals without presupposing how the requirements of morality might be construed in any given case. As subsequent discussions will indicate, it implies a kind of impartiality that does not commit one *a priori* to a definite course of conduct.

Such concern for persons may be a consequence of our feelings of sympathy, of identification with the sufferings and hopes of human beings, coupled with a sense of impartiality. It also has a source in the wish of any individual to be treated on a moral par with others. A socialization process could be of a nature to give such feelings strong reinforcement. It would not be surprising if our general respect— whatever it is, and insofar as it exists—is in part a genetic characteristic. It might be that there is a biological trait of the species that makes itself felt in this manner. (If there is such a trait, it does not appear to be uniformly distributed, and it has obvious thresholds beyond which it is ineffective.) In any case, the experience is given conspicuous place in many philosophies and religions. It might be conceived in a manner to make it indistinguishable from duty or from universal and indiscriminate rights, or from service, but it has crucial meanings not captured by such notions. Indeed, I think we are searching for a moral relation that cuts across all such distinctions.

When we attempt to isolate just what it is in being human that is an object of respect, the picture becomes murky. There is something we find in the existence of human beings that we value. What is it? Answers are various: the possession of freedom, perhaps, or reason; moral capacity; the ability to love; the possession of a "true" self; being a child of God, good will; and possessing feelings, self-knowledge, and imagination are some. Although we are presumably seeking a common denominator, this review suggests that the traits comprising human dignity are a matter of selection and evaluation. We evaluatively distinguish characteristics we regard as objects of respect. Indeed, as the abortion controversy illustrates so grippingly, the very question of who qualifies as a person, or when, is heatedly contested. Respect might also be conditioned by dubious cognitive assumptions, such as belief in an immortal soul, free will, or the possession of an inherently impartial and universal reason free of historical contingencies. If we are worthy of respect, it might be that we will have to qualify with something of a more earthy nature.

Given such variations, the question of what constitutes respectful *treatment* is also open to dispute. If we were strict Kantians, we would respect rational nature *only,* and refuse, as moral persons, to cater to anyone's desires, as such, regardless of their object. If, on the other hand, we respect some other dimension of the person, our behavior presumably will be different. According to English liberalism, it is sufficient that all persons be equal before the law, regardless of their motivations.

Apart from the determination of humanness, it is often unclear in practice what constitutes respect. Does the policy of preferential hiring show respect, or is it patronizing? Does it show disrespect to those who are not in the preferred groups? Are people shown respect when they are denied differential deserts, and benefits are accorded by means of an overall plan of distribution? Are people shown disrespect when they are denied equality of result? Does the existence of hierarchies in the social order imply failure to respect persons? If we have, in some sense, equal respect for persons, how does this disposition aid in the resolution of particular moral problems? When there are conflicting values in the offing, we may have respect for all the parties involved, yet our choice means that we support some interests and compromises or reject others. On issues, say, of capital punishment, or the tension between freedom and regulation, or euthanasia, we are dealing with persons in each instance. We suspect that the specification of the nature of respectful relations is often tailored to antecedently held moral convictions.

It is certain that variations in respect are not equally sustainable. The tendency to equality of result, for example, is one that is mightily resisted by family attachments, love of liberty, love of status, normal competitiveness, demands for desert proportional to achievement, and for economic productivity. Even equality before the law rapidly loses universality. Equal protection of the law is accorded only to people of one's own nation; even then it is not equal. Liberalism did not initially think of women as persons in the same sense that men are. Kant enunciates a universal law for all rational beings, but he remarks routinely that the franchise is not to be accorded to "an apprentice of a merchant or artisan; a servant . . . a minor . . . all women; and generally anyone who must depend for his support . . . not on his own industry, but on arrangements by others. . . ."[7] We notice how readily the allegedly indiscriminate quality of respect tends to disappear when there is pressure from other values. These values are not necessarily reprehensible. Respect for persons is not an omnicompetent relation, and the moral life cannot sustain all goods equally.

I do not mean to suggest that respect for persons is a worthless idea. We can retain some notion of moral equality, or impartiality, and this is the distinctive, if vague, sense of respect that I wish to preserve and elaborate. (Chapter 8 will treat it as a central virtue in the moral life.)

Unquestionably, impartiality in some form is indispensable in the moral life. Without its occurrence at crucial junctures, life would be extremely uncertain and insecure. Just from the point of view of self-interest, we are each dependent upon impartiality, or fairness. We depend on some kind of impersonality and even-handedness in the social order, some sense that we will be treated with the same criteria as others. As with so many other moral relations, this condition is most vividly recognized in the family. If one child is judged by a different standard than another—or by inconstant standards—he will become deeply confused, incapable of trust, and quite possibly paranoid. We must have rules, and we want them administered disinterestedly. If there are, for example, stated conditions for advancement, and I meet the requirements, I am assured by the very statement of these criteria that I will be advanced if I satisfy the conditions. Impartiality, not the ambitions of one holding power, assures me of the new status. College students, like anyone else, would go mad if they thought their work was not judged in accordance with impartial criteria. Even within the privileged classes there is a desire for the consistent administration of rules. If one meets all the tests for elevation to knighthood, he wants the assurance that when the tests are passed he will indeed be knighted; he does not want to be denied because the queen doesn't like the way he grows his beard.

Without a kind of guaranteed even-handedness, most social relations degenerate into quarrel, fighting, and intrigue; they inspire no loyalty or devotion. The impartial administration of standards is a social necessity. Those who recognize it teach it to others, reinforce its observance, and penalize its infractions. We advocate them not only for ourselves alone, but also for those who are dear to us, and even for anonymous fellow citizens.

The demand for impartiality converts our merely personal interests into principles. This vital conclusion by no means settles the question of what these principles should be. Rather than struggle with that question, however, I want to draw attention to a preliminary issue: the very idea of impartiality. The notion turns out to be surprisingly ambiguous. If we follow the utilitarians, we will say that to be impartial is to treat each person as one and no more than one. No one has an inherently privileged status. If it happens, then, that it serves the greatest happiness of a given population to oppress a few of their number, then they may do so. The oppressed haven't been left out of the reckoning. Their pain has been put in the balance; and viewing all the available alternatives, their oppression turns out to be necessary for the greatest general happiness.

A different form of impartiality is to invoke one of the variants of the universalization test, which is descended from the Golden Rule and later given the imprimatur of pure reason by the categorical imperative. We would judge our own action impartially by determining whether we would approve of this type of act if the roles were reversed—if we, our friends, or our family were subjected to it in similar circumstances. If our answer is yes, our impartiality has been certified. We may ask whether we would advocate this type of action if it were a general principle of conduct, hence becoming subject to it at the hands of others. In moral situations, we act on a rule that we would universalize, that we would endorse no matter what our position.

This is a form of acting on principle, in which impartiality is consistency; but it does not assure consistency in the advocacy of principle from one person to the next. Consistency can be prejudicial in its way, depending on the nature of the principle. A military man might have no objection to universalizing the practice of doing two hours of close order drill every morning before breakfast. A health nut could universalize stringent diet and exercise. A person might show highly preferential treatment for the members of his own family—a kind of deliberate partiality—and be willing to universalize the practice. That would make him impartially partial, I suppose. In brief, this form of impartiality requires no consistency from agent to agent; so the "impartial" principles of one person might be prejudicial to those of another.

Resort to a hypothetical social contract is another strategy, and it presumes to remedy the deficiencies of the preceding form. We postulate undifferentiated human beings engaged in some kind of bargaining procedure. Since they are not specific persons, with their peculiar identities, commitments, and projects, they are not in a position to be prejudicial even if they tried. Or so it seems. The results of the bargain between faceless abstractions might be highly prejudicial to actual historical persons, each of whom enjoys and trusts in a certain panoply of rights, principles, goods, and obligations; the very life of such persons is built around their possession and endurance. Let Rawls try to tell a hard-working farmer that he doesn't deserve the product of his own labor! If the farmer stopped brandishing his pitchfork and paused to philosophize, he might well protest that *he* was no party to that mythical contract. Whose life *is* this?

Still another kind of impartiality, and at the same time another kind of respect, is to try to take all interests into account in morally problematic situations. This could take the form of actively consulting the parties involved, listening to the concerns, beliefs, and arguments of each in a serious way, encouraging conscientious inquiry and communication. It would mean not rejecting one another's ideas and concerns out of hand. Each is willing to listen and to be instructed and perchance to adjust his own convictions. For this form of impartiality to have practical effectiveness, the willingness to inquire, communicate, learn, and adjust must be mutual. In brief, it would be the accommodating impartiality of social intelligence. It is distinguished from other forms of impartiality by its respect for concrete individuals. The other forms are not necessarily communicative; they do not (or must not!) solicit information and advice from the persons actually caught up in the moral life. The homely impartiality of social intelligence must often determine and sustain principles, but it does not issue in rules that simply assume what is good or right for others, or what they "really" want. It is not obvious that the latter procedure is genuinely a respect for persons at all, rather than respect for an intellectual fabrication.

The respect shown in social intelligence can be given a modest, but affecting, interpretation. It can be taken simply as the acknowledgment that persons are bearers of sufferings and hopes, needs, self-consciousness, and keenly felt relationships; and they dearly want their condition to be taken seriously. They are insofar like us, we think, and that might be enough to take them in earnest.

The behavior implied in this respect would be something along the lines just indicated. At best, it would be moved by a certain attitude, a certain way of addressing individuals. Instead of prejudging them, fearing them, seeing them as hostile or intractable, we approach them with the assumption that they have a legitimate case to be made and something to contribute. This approach can have wonderful results. Address people as potential opponents, view them with suspicion, and they will very likely be moved to confirm your judgment. They see you as a threat, an adversary, and they will respond in kind. Approach them with a sincere attitude of respect, and they are more apt to welcome your consultation and participation.

There are many situations where these procedures will fail to avoid a stalemate, or where they are inappropriate. Some people *are* competitors or enemies; some are manipulators, liars, and exploiters. There are others who need authoritative direction. Nevertheless, we can approach others with the welcoming attitude until respect has been forfeited.

The virtues of social intelligence, however worthy they might be, are difficult to attain, and they possess no guarantee that divergences and antagonisms will be reconciled; but unlike other methods, they do not sidestep the very values and tensions that make an interpersonal situation problematic. Perhaps this attitude and approach should be called democratic respect. It claims no Olympian standpoint or finality, which many will see as a disabling fault. It is a demand for a workaday, contingent sort of moral equality. It tries to take into account the relevant conditions and relations of a moral situation, including the deeply held values, in all their complexity, discussed in this chapter. It does not suppose that the posture of respect for persons, in and of itself, provides prescriptions for conduct; it entails no specific principles. It is an attitude and a method that shows respect for real human concerns and attempts to construct a new situation out of just these materials—and, if a policy is needed, to formulate one. It might find support in the moral life precisely because it does not place our existing values immediately in jeopardy from *a priori* edicts. It gives everyone a chance for a fair hearing. (But no process will be acceptable if *all* values are to be subject to bargaining. Many of our goods are too precious for that.) It is, of course, a threat to dogmatists and absolutists, as well as to scoundrels of various sorts; so it will never be accepted by acclamation, we may be sure.

Interdependence of Moral Relations

Moral situations are complex. The existential setting is often one
of intricate interweaving of events; in this setting we typically find
the various moral relations mingled in uneasy tensions. Further insight into the nature of the moral condition can be won by a sampling
of the mutual reenforcements and resistances of these relations. I
have no pretense to be exhaustive and choose to concentrate principally on rights. The examples in this domain should be sufficient
to my purpose.

Rights are extremely valuable. As entitlements, they are a kind
of guarantee, but not a requirement. We may exercise them, but
we are not required to do so. In most instances, we are not required
to accept welfare rights or enter into agreements. Rights, then, allow
us to pursue and possess certain ends, but don't oblige us to do
so. This view is certainly preferable to the Platonic philosophy,
according to which there is one ultimate end, with lesser ends in
strict subordination to it, and each individual is assigned an end
in the all-inclusive hierarchy.

The existence of rights is united to other relations in ways both
delicate and profound. Many philosophers, however, think of rights
as having a virgin birth and possessing a purity unqualified by worldly
intrusions. John Locke thought that men had the property of having
a right like they had the property of being six feet tall or red-headed:
it is a simple fact about persons, taken in complete isolation from
social relations. Accordingly, there is no determination of rights
consequent upon an assessment of ends, obligations, social configurations, or historical contingencies. The view did not die with Locke.
Something much like it is held today by Gewirth, Nozick, and
Dworkin, among others.

What a remarkable coincidence, then, that the familiar, though
varying, laundry list of rights is highly conducive to ends—not to
all ends, but to *particular* ones! The rights to engage in religious
practices, to vote, to communicate without inhibition, to assemble
voluntarily, to engage in free contracts, and to acquire and manage
property do not require us to do these things, to be sure; but it
is assumed that we will do so to a great extent because the ends
attained in this behavior are particularly valuable. What a coincidence,
too, that peoples have struggled for religious freedom or the franchise

in the expectation that it would serve certain ends: relieve them of oppression, make worship without restraint possible, and permit them to conduct their political life in a manner more to their liking.

Indeed, a given form of conduct is a right, or end, or duty only as it functions in a distinctive kind of relationship. No act, taken in and of itself—taken out of relation to everything else—can even be identified as a right. Voting, for example, could be an *end*: it could be an attainment which we must earn, for which we must qualify. It could also be a *requirement*; it could be our legal responsibility to vote; and it could also be a right, an *entitlement,* granted just in virtue of living in the community. Likewise, say, with healthcare. It is always a matter of judgment to make these conditions ends, requirements, or rights. An unchecked proliferation of rights would bring tyrannical results down upon us just in guaranteeing and providing them. There could be such an epidemic of rights that maintenance of them would result in widespread coercion. Rights are guarantees; someone has to fulfill them, like it or not. When such a threat occurs, it would be much wiser to think of many conditions as ends, rather than as rights. In most instances, two weeks of paid vacation, an ample wardrobe, ownership of pets, possession of a home, are much better regarded as ends than rights. As circumstances vary, voting or healthcare—or conceivably even two weeks of paid vacation—might be treated as an end or a right. We would also like to be sure of the consequences for the possessor of many putative rights. The entitlements provided in our welfare program, Aid to Families with Dependent Children, have been disastrous for parents and children alike, rewarding the most self-defeating conduct.

Depending on variations in the constellation of rights that exists in a given society, there will be variations in the ends achieved, individual and collective. Depending on whether or how property rights are conceived, for example, the economic system will undergo massively consequential variations, and with it the whole system of government and the nature and function of private associations will likewise change.

Undoubtedly, variations in rights are correlated with variations in broad classes of ends: in human growth and excellence, learning and science, vitality in the arts, material productivity, social vigor, community solidarity, and so on. Depending significantly on what rights are possessed, communities will be egalitarian or libertarian;

individuals will tend to be individualistic, self-reliant, dependent, passive, selfish, rational, reliable, or communal. Often we are not sure just what these correlations will be; not unusually, they turn out to be surprising. But they are matters of the utmost importance to us and hence worthy of the most conscientious inquiry. To take rights seriously, we cannot take them in isolation, and certainly not as axiomatic.

At least we would not do so if we took the moral life as our subject matter, if we took our reflections to be in the service of moral experience. If we rest content with intuitions or concepts as our subject matter, on the other hand, it might well be at the expense of real human concerns. Intuitions are disguises or evasions, and we are easily beguiled by them. Locke tells us that we have inherent rights to life, liberty, and estate, and we nod agreeably. It sounds delightful to be so invested. When he adds that this determination is made by reason alone—independent, infallible, and universal reason—we might easily follow him in this, too. It all seems so obvious and so right. Clearly, however, we, like Locke himself, have been taken in. We nod and we follow only because our *experience* and *aspirations* are such that these rights appear to be invaluable for the moral life; but we do not realize that we nod for this reason. Supposedly, according to Locke, the lessons of history, sociology, and personal experience have no relevance to the assignment of rights. They are also irrelevant to analyzing and criticizing them, revising and adjusting them, if need be. Locke, like Dworkin or Nozick, was simply inattentive to moral experience and its functions in his reflections.

Rawls, Nozick, and Dworkin are more sophisticated than Locke. Their intuitions go through a much more elaborate screening process, but they do not cross the threshhold of experience. We get our intuitions in order first, answering all the basic moral questions; only then do we use them to legislate for experience. Nozick, for example, determines the "proper" nature of the state by asking what sort of state would occur on the assumption of absolute rights. He is evidently not interested in what varieties of actual concern and need have brought real states into existence. "A theory of a state of nature that begins with fundamental general descriptions of morally permissible and impermissible actions . . . and goes on to describe how a state would arise from that state of nature will serve our explanatory purposes, *even if no actual state ever arose that way*"[8] (emphasis in original).

The "rights philosophers" appear to be united in the conviction that there is something morally wrong about discriminating between the ends favored by different persons. To say that your goals are superior to mine is to deny me the respect due me as a human being. So long as we do not exceed the limits of an antecedently and independently existing framework of justice or of rights, we may pursue any ends we wish, and it is morally impertinent in this context to make comparative judgments. What is all-important, then, is to discover what our fundamental rights are and to determine what particular rights are derivative of them. The derivations are presented as exercises in logic. Ends presumably do not enter into the determination.

There is something remarkably naive about this procedure and no doubt something tendentious, too. Remember, rights are relations, and as such they are inevitably implicated in a myriad of further processes in the moral life.[9] It is not merely fatuous to determine rights independently of other relations; it is hurtful as well. Literally to forbid the government to discriminate between ends, for example, is to prohibit highly desirable public policies. Why must a government give equal respect to any and all ends? It is necessary for communities to require or encourage ends consistent with their survival and flourishing: national defense, education, the family structure, the integrity of religion, productivity, the thriving of the arts and sciences, prevention of drug use, and the like. If civic virtue is an end (as well as being a necessary condition of further ends), then, according to Dworkin, it is still a denial of the right to equal concern and respect for a government to facilitate the development of virtue in individuals in preference to other ends. A government may not encourage the formation and endurance of families, or discourage nonfamilial ways of rearing children. No, for that would be denying equal concern and respect to those persons who might wish for some reason—*any* reason, presumably—to discourage or oppose families. This, mind you, when we have before us the evidence of the catastrophic breakdown of the family. We have the strongest reasons to resist coercive government. *Requiring* persons to group in families would be intolerable; but even *encouraging* such ends—through tax policy, say—is a denial of right, in Dworkin's terms. We must maintain "equal concern and respect," though the heavens fall.

A philosopher afflicted with rights mania might attempt to circumvent such objections by selecting preferred ends, but thereupon declaring that individuals have a right to them, the right being primary, the end incidental. The strategy is disingenuous. It disguises its preferences for certain ends, maintaining the pretense that rights are determined independently of ends: particular entitlements are still, allegedly, derived from axiomatic fundamental rights.

Rights are also conditioned by requirements, and requirements by rights. Both are conditioned by ends, and by deserts, too, for that matter. And respect for persons cuts across all these relations. Some measure of moral equality is operative in them. The social relations that generate and sustain obligations eventuate in rights as well. Children, supposedly, have a right to be cared for and nurtured, but the right is not original or autonomous. It is a function of many conditions: parental love; regard for the feelings and welfare of the weak and innocent; and, above all, the need to sustain and enhance a civilization.

In examining such relations, we often say that entitlements and requirements (more popularly, rights and duties) are correlative. If someone has a right, someone else has a duty to honor, protect, or provide it; if someone has a duty, someone else has a right to its performance. This might be regarded as a conceptual truth; but if it is, it is a convention of recent origin. Historically, requirements come into existence before entitlements. Survival of the group is the first priority, and rights might be a luxurious afterthought.

Philosophers have asked whether, from the *moral* point of view, rights are prior to duties. Kant, of course, put duties first; but more recent writers give rights the first priority (while others still insist on utility). It is not an intelligent question. In the moral life, what we must be concerned with are the supports of, threats to, and adjustments in that entire and delicate fabric of values that constitutes the life of the group. If the tribe is about to be slaughtered, rights be damned. In happier circumstances, the right to free expression might be given priority over internal peace. But the point is, once more, that we not take these relations in isolation, or one at a time. Unless we are addicts of the classic tradition, we would not invariably subordinate ends, say, to rights, or rights to ends, or consider any particular moral relation as having invariant priority over others. Of course, abstract moral *theory* might be greatly simplified by the foundational approach, but it is not clear that the moral *life* would be a beneficiary.

Rather than look to conceptual relations for the answers to moral questions, we must be attentive to the existential patterns of action at issue: If certain benefits are guaranteed, to whom are they guaranteed? Who are the persons responsible for making good the guarantee? What do we require, specifically, of the guarantors, and what will be the sanctions imposed for failure? How is eligibility for rights and duties determined? In practice, might some people have most of the benefits of rights while others have most of the duties? Rights and obligations might be conceptually correlative, but in practice there might be much greater emphasis on one rather than the other. Persons might become obsessed with their rights and negligent of their obligations. We could have a "community" in which most members work at being receivers rather than contributors, or they can insist legalistically and unnecessarily on the possession of rights to the detriment of respect for persons in communal civility.[10] Such questions, along with many others pertaining to the "mosaic of value-relations," will determine our assessment of the claims before us, not conceptual considerations.

If rights are not omnipotent, neither are ends or requirements. Utilitarians are one class of offenders here. Like the rights philosophers, they are overly selective in their attention to the rich and subtle textures of moral experience, all of which must be subordinated to concerns of utility.[11] Desert cannot be taken seriously, for example. What you deserve must be hostage to the greatest happiness. But, it might well be asked, what claim do others have on a man's deserts? Perhaps they have not struggled and worked. They have no prior claim on the man; he owes them nothing. If we were strict Aristotelians, believing that justice consists in giving each man his due, the utilitarians must cast down our concerns; but surely there is *some* merit in the Aristotelian position, not least in obviating the incredibly *fussy* requirement to measure pleasures in the distribution of rewards. When we use desert as a criterion, it doesn't occur to anyone to question whether those who are equally deserving should be equally compensated with money, status, honor, or authority; but it never enters our head to distribute equal *pleasure*. It would be extremely difficult to accord a depressed person as much pleasure as a cheerful one. If the two are toiling side by side, yet the depressive receives twice the pay in order to help him get equal pleasure, the cheerful one—and no doubt anyone else but the obdurate utilitarian—would be outraged. Capitalism never spawned a proletarian revolution. Utilitarianism would. It is surely ingrained in human nature to assume that the individual is ultimately responsible for having pleasure. It is up to the person, with assistance from other quarters, no doubt, to decide how to employ just deserts for the pursuit of pleasure. Anything else would be an unworkable division of labor. Thomas Jefferson wisely referred to the *pursuit* of happiness, recognizing, perhaps, that pleasure cannot be the currency of the moral life.

It is wiser to consider the *conditions* of happiness; but even these could not be our exclusive concern. In the view of many, for example, utility gives insufficient protection to various entitlements and requirements, which are not readily to be turned aside for the greatest happiness. Why should we assume that pain and deprivation for some is legitimated by the augmentation of pleasure for others? *Many* relations in the moral life are important to us. A solemn promise, a specific bond and responsibility, will not lightly be breached to contribute pleasure to perhaps anonymous or undeserving persons. Deontologists express a widely shared value when they exclaim that it just isn't *right* to execute an innocent man for the sake of an increment in society's marginal utility. And is it humanly possible to count the life of someone we love equally with that of a stranger? Most people would think him a monster who would weigh utilities impersonally in such a case.

Contriving embarrassing cases for utilitarianism is a favorite indoor sport, and the utilitarian hasn't much reply except to beg the question, just as the defenders of other adamantine principles do. Nevertheless, it would be hard to defend a philosophy that did not take the general welfare, vaguely conceived, as a paramount concern. If respect for persons is taken seriously, then we must also be serious about the welfare of persons, and hence for the general welfare. In the name of simple realism about human nature, however, we cannot assume that people are always liable to some sort of moral censure if they are more devoted to local attachments than to humankind at large. Our concern for persons would extend to the moral values that they actually cherish. Inasmuch as very few persons are utilitarians, we would respect entitlements and requirements that are not reducible to utility. On the other hand, it would be difficult to support such sorts of relation that did not appear to have a usually favorable effect on human welfare. If they did not, they would be widely denounced for the harm they cause.

Although moral criteria need not be in a state of chaos, they are nevertheless frequently problematic; cruel uncertainties and conflicts will survive the most conscientious reflection and discourse. There are different kinds of demands and goods in moral experience; they are often incompatible; and impartiality of one kind or another seems to be insufficient to put them in uniform and uncontroversial order. It seems, then, that the rendition of "the general welfare" would best be cast in terms of what I have called the democratic version of respect for persons. This gives us no fixed plan of action or fixed ends, but it means that in moral deliberations we realistically regard the concerns of actual persons.

I have tried to distinguish the distinctive sorts of moral relations that occur naturally in life experience, and I have tried to perceive their peculiar *raisons d'être*. I have also made an attempt to see what is problematic about their exercise, including some remarks about how well their various forms might be sustained in the sometimes unforgiving light of reality. Finally, I offered some examples of the intermeshing of these relations in the moral life. My account is, of course, open to qualification. Nevertheless, I trust I have imparted some sense of the inevitable harmonies and dissonances of moral experience.

Justice

The critic will object at once: "What about justice? Isn't an account of justice what is needed in order to get our priorities precisely established and to promulgate incontrovertible criteria for settling conflicts?" If there is merit in the discussions of this and preceding chapters, then no definition of justice can be offered that is somehow scientific or morally uncontroversial. Any definition must be determined in part by irreducibly *moral* considerations. Claims for justice, moreover, must appeal to values and relations of the sort already presented. A review of the moral relations set forth suggests that each has problems in its own kind, and none is self-sufficient or omnicompetent. Any norms that justice might impose must come from the naturally generated values of experience, their modifications and interrelations. To declare that certain ends, entitlements, or requirements invariably and demonstrably take precedence over others is to beg the question, and it is done in a way that takes little, if any, account of the urgencies of the moral life.

I do not want to be understood to say that the notion of justice is useless or superfluous. Not in the least. The conduct of social life requires some ongoing order and integration of norms, and it requires stable and widely acceptable methods for adjudicating conflicts. Such order and method are derivative of the moral life, and they are subject to revision as they function more or less adequately to address its controversies and struggles. "Adequately," of course, is itself a normatively determined adverb. There seems to be no way to get outside of moral experience to legislate the norms of moral experience; and if there were, I don't know what merit such a transcendent perspective would have. It is precisely the values of *our* life, and not some other life, that are at stake. For *our* sake, these values need analysis, criticism, enrichment, and order; and they have to be enriched and ordered to address *our* needs and aspirations. If we think of justice as some kind of amalgam of the moral relations emergent of life experience, then we are more apt to contrive orders of justice that will do more justice to it.

It is a matter of the first importance to ask how we should go about determining justice. We can start from the postulation of rights, from the concept of a rational being, the ordering of "considered judgments," the ideal good, or a postulated social contract. Alternatively, we can look to the phenomena studied in history, anthropology, comparative politics, law, literature, and the behavioral sciences. Such studies tell us much about the moral life and the expedients that have been tried out in it, and how they tend to turn out for the weal and woe of the populations involved. Such resources are far more apt for the inquiry into justice than the *a priori* ruminations of philosophers. They might disclose moral structures that are suitable to the realities of the moral condition.

A natural response to my suggestion would be to assert that there are no helpful uniformities to be found; history and science disclose no such things in the heterogeneity of the human record. The conclusion is premature, perhaps even obscurantist, but that is not to say that such lessons are easy to discern. Nevertheless, there are many examples of political/social/economic successes and failures that admit of generalization. I confine myself to the sorts of relations presented in the immediate discussion. A conspicuous case is that of *desert*. There is abundant evidence from a wide range of sources that relations of desert are of paramount importance in considerations of justice. The notion is vague and variable in certain ways. This is a blessing, for the contingencies of the moral life resist final and invariant orderings. Yet there also seem to be identifiable family resemblances in the different renderings of desert. "To give each man his due" is the standard notion of desert and often of justice itself, but what *is* his due? How can it be determined?

In his familiar account, Aristotle declares, ". . . [T]he ratio between the shares will be the same as that between the persons. If the persons are not equal, their (just) shares will not be equal"; and he adds at once *"but this is the source of quarrels and recriminations,* when equals have and are awarded unequal shares or unequals equal shares. The truth of this is further illustrated by the principle 'To each according to his deserts.' "[12] He insists once more on the proportionality of equality shortly thereafter. "But in associations that are based on mutual exchange, the just in this sense *constitutes the bond that holds the association together,* that is, reciprocity in terms of proportion and not in terms of exact equality in the return. For it is the reciprocal return of what is proportional (to what one has received) *that holds the state together.*"[13] Aristotle is doing more than engage in the academic exercise of offering a definition. The italicized clauses express his conviction that the very endurance of the social fabric requires that relations of desert be upheld. No society can survive without them. A truly momentous claim! If Aristotle were right, our basic conception of justice would be uncontroversial, for no one would seriously defend an unmaintainable system.

And there is evidence that he might have been right. A field of inquiry has recently developed, *equity studies,* founded (inadvertently) by the sociologist George C. Homans. In his field studies on employee behavior, Homans found that persons invariably insist that they get what they deserve, and the failure to get it (even in getting *more* than they deserve!) brings about various forms of discontent and recalcitrant behavior.[14] In examining these relations, he discovered that they are of the very sort that Aristotle had already articulated, and he gives full credit to him. Following Homans, a number of researchers have conducted further studies, and they tend to corroborate Homans's conclusions.[15]

According to such inquiries, what a person is due is determined by a range of factors: work accomplished, of course, but also education and training, seniority, age, perceived talent, success in fair competition, or citizenship, as the case may be. Sometimes, too, such things as sex, class, race, or ethnicity are counted. As such factors vary, what one is entitled to also varies proportionately. What one is due is construed not only in terms of remuneration. When individuals are judged equally deserving, they also expect a correspondingly equal responsibility, status, and autonomy; they feel mistreated if there is not consistency with equals in all these conditions. I will feel cheated if I have the same accomplishment and seniority as you, and even the same pay, if you are accorded a spacious office and I am relegated to a cramped one. Like must be treated alike.

What this like treatment should be is of course arguable. We deserve equal pay, to be sure, and it should be more than that of an associate professor and less than that of the university president; but just what should that equal pay be? As Aristotle had acknowledged, the factors that determine desert are also more or less arguable. Accomplishment is surely among those that must be preserved, while race and sex are surely more problematic. But such questions do not eradicate the virtue of the relation of desert; they call for its critical adjustment and refinement.

Desert is found to compete with other criteria of entitlement, such as need and simple equality. These criteria qualify each other, but not equally. Under experimental conditions, for example, where two persons are found to be equally needy, yet one of them has struggled to succeed where the other has been irresponsible, observers judge the one who has struggled to be deserving of a greater share of a distribution than the other. (Sometimes the needy but irresponsible one is judged to have no claim at all. It is sometimes judged that even a *victim* is to blame for *being* a victim.) Simple equality is often thought to be appropriate in some relations, such as that of spouses; but it is found, in fact, (if we didn't know it already) that spousal relations founder when one or the other of them is perceived to be failing in their expected contribution. If the husband is a drunkard and the wife must take two jobs to maintain the family, the wife has little inclination to believe that she owes him an equal portion of her income. He should get what he deserves! Procedural justice, too, will temper distributive justice, but if the former threatens the latter in a major way, a different procedure needs to be adopted.

To my knowledge, none of the students of these phenomena doubts that cultural variations have a distinctive impact on who is judged to be deserving and what is judged to be deserved. Neither do they doubt that there are likewise variations in the weight given to need and equality, as well as to other contingencies. But they do not doubt that relations of desert permeate our many and varied transactions with one another and are indispensable to them. If they are correct, it would be simple folly to think of justice as excluding desert, as Rawls does.

Complementing equity studies is research into what is called "the belief in a just world phenomenon." Melvin Lerner's *The Belief in a Just World*[16] summarizes, systematizes, and advances this research, which finds a universal need in human beings to believe they live in a just world. Even persons who regard themselves as hardnosed realists, even cynics, repeatedly exhibit symptoms of this need. The point of this phenomenon for our concerns is that what is regarded as just is construed in terms of desert. Anyone who believes in a just world believes that everyone gets what they deserve. Those who fall lower in the scale of belief in a just world insist that people *should* get what they deserve. Lerner, along with some others, believes that the universal motivation of human beings is to get what they deserve—not maximization of pleasure, nor satisficing, but what they deserve.[17] If there is much credence in such claims, we could submerge desert as justice only with totalitarian measures.

The "just world" and "equity" researchers are confined, of course, to experiments on living subjects; they are not historians. But their findings are supported by such studies as *In Search of the Common Good*[18] by Charles J. Erasmus, an anthropologist, whose detailed and encyclopedic investigations carried him not only to many parts of the world, but to the study of many exemplary historical conditions, including monasteries and utopian communities. Erasmus did not set out to confirm an Aristotelian conception of justice, nor does he show any knowledge of "equity" and "just world" studies, but he corroborates, in effect, the Aristotelian position. He observed a wide variety of cultures and communities. Almost invariably, he finds that where some people receive equal shares for unequal work, the level of work of the more productive participants falls to the lowest common denominator, and hostility rises. According to this account, exceptions to Aristotelianism (an expression not found in Erasmus's research) are confined to deliberately utopian experiments, with their very unusual conditions, which drift steadily into Aristotelianism anyway.

Robert Owen's settlement in New Harmony is a well known case, as are the Amana community, Oneida, or the Israeli *kibbutzim.* Erasmus includes monasteries as well. Most such groups have tended to be communistic, but rarely democratic. In any case, they attempt to distribute benefits without recourse to desert. In those that have been moderately successful, one of the most conspicuous traits is that they are initiated with zealous religious commitments, and their intent is holiness and salvation, not secular success. They are typically comprised of a highly homogeneous population; they have very strict entrance requirements, and they have long and demanding probationary periods to qualify for full membership. Significantly, they maintain themselves with strict discipline. The sanctions for misconduct or underachievement in these associations are powerful. They include some combination of isolation, ostracism, humiliation, dislike, disgrace, physical punishment, excommunication, and the like. Even with a potent antecedent commitment to the scheme, severe authority and discipline are required to perpetuate it. The *kibbutzim,* moreover, were originally both a religious and political vanguard. In a most precarious environment, they were the heroic leaders of the sectarian movement known as Zionism, an excellent condition to preserve morale and dedication. The least successful of the groups mentioned was the Owenite. It lasted less than three years. Owen himself was nearly bankrupted in maintaining it, and he abandoned it in less than two years. A secular movement, New Harmony lacked what the others depended upon: a strong religious commitment. The lesson is this: the typical relations of desert are laid aside only with the most strenuous discipline and sanctions.

Some of these groups, such as the Amana community and the *kibbutzim,* have persisted rather well. But as they endure and progress, they tend to fall away from their original purity of resolve. In fact, they become joint stock companies in which shares are unequally owned and the members divide profits in proportion to their shares. Many members cease to participate in the labor of the community.

Outside workers are hired to do that, while members hasten to seek their fortune in the open market.

The recent study by Thomas Sowell, *Preferential Policies: An International Perspective,*[19] supplies still more corroborative data for the Aristotelian hypothesis. Sowell examined the effects of distributing reward with criteria other than those of merit in several different cultures and found the results uniformly disastrous. His research shows that economic losses were the least of the problem. "Group polarization has tended to increase in the wake of preferential programs, with non-preferred groups reacting adversely, in ways ranging from political backlash to mob violence and civil war."[20]

Such evidences give persuasive support to the fundamental importance of maintaining relations of desert. Many will sniff, of course, at the very idea of such studies, or they will cite different ones with different verdicts. I do not suppose that the question is closed. However, all attempts at creating egalitarian man have been failures, and we have paid an appalling price for the experiments.

The widespread (perhaps nearly universal) respect for desert might well be owing to its indispensable functions in the process of learning. As noted before, one of the requirements of effective learning is that rewards and punishments be proportioned to successes and failures. Moreover, these reenforcements, if you will, are most effective when they are consistent across the population being educated. Inconsistency brings hurt, failed learning, and maldevelopment. As participants in processes of learning, we may acquire great appreciation for conditions in which equal treatment is accorded for equal (but not unequal) accomplishment. It seems not outrageous to suppose that we possess something of an inborn bias that like should be treated as like. It might even be supposed that we *must* have such an inherent yearning in order to be offended *at all* when we get no more reward than the fellow who does less than we do. To feel offended in this manner, it seems we would have to have some sense of injustice already. Why should we howl with complaint when our reward for achievement is below that of others who have contributed no better? The howl is possibly no more than a demand for unlimited reward. However, the howling typically ceases when justice is done. These are speculations, of course. I offer them to suggest that the widely observed phenomena of desert are not necessarily unintelligible.

While some will find fault with desert because it is not egalitarian, it might otherwise be gratefully welcomed as a potent moral restraint on all manner of oppression, plunder, and the like, both petty and great. I am not speaking here of the *concept* of desert; I am referring to the possibility that such *relations* have natively strong, extensive, and uncoerced support. If they do, they constitute an inherent incentive for persons to abide by them, to resist infractions from themselves and others, and to teach and reenforce such observances. That would be a fact to celebrate! Given that there is so much bad behavior, one might be skeptical that such inner restraints exist, but that would be a premature conclusion. We have insufficient knowledge of what mixture of variables conspires to make us good or evil. It may be that something closely akin to the disposition described by Aristotle is more or less natural to us, and it might be morally indispensable.

Insofar as individuals believe in desert, moreover, they do not feel cheated or demeaned in a society that honors this relation. Nobody but the intellectual seems to find *deserved* inequalities demeaning. (But beware of intellectuals who think they are getting less than they deserve!)

The thrust of the mounting evidence is in favor of Aristotle. We should be sufficiently sophisticated, however, to recognize that desert itself is a relation that admits of significant variations, and it cannot be taken as an exclusive criterion of judgment without doing violence to other heartfelt concerns. It is by no means identical to the notion of universal rights, for example, nor with freedom of contract. We have obligations, too, that are justified by concerns other than those of desert. (Do I *deserve* my obligations to my family? Or aren't they *assumed,* or even *required* of me? Have my children *earned* the support that I owe them?)

My point here is hardly to say the last word about justice. I have no rational blueprint. My concern is to exhibit some of the complexities of the moral condition. All the same, a vital purpose is served by singling out desert for special attention. I raised the question of how we should think about justice, casting aspersion on philosophic abstractions. The human race has not done at all well in adopting the theories of distribution simply excogitated by philosophers, however "rational" or "just" they might seem in the abstract. On the other hand, the experience of the race seems to have expressed something of a verdict of its own. It is not for us to accept it uncritically, but it may be the part of wisdom to work cautiously *with* it: to refine and extend it, and to consider the possible integrations and conflicts of desert with other relations of deep human importance. Sowell reports that the widespread allegiance to status based on merit does not preclude a willingness to help disadvantaged groups prepare themselves to meet the qualifications for better positions. "[R]esource transfers designed to enable disadvantaged groups to meet standards are accepted while attempts to bring the standards down to them are overwhelmingly rejected."[21] It seems safe to assert that the laws and institutions of a just society would permit (not require) the flourishing of conditions of desert, yoked or supported as these conditions might be by other considerations.

There is no need to justify moral relations at large. They are given birth and nurtured by the needs and requirements of life itself. Philosophers have produced a truly luxuriant array of justifications for observing various norms of conduct. Whether Plato or Kant, Aquinas or Rawls, Bradley or Habermas, they have offered esoteric reasons for doing what we must do anyway. Take protecting the innocent, for example. No doubt there are several reasons why most people feel a deep horror at the victimization of innocent persons, but one of the most obvious is that the collapse of the distinction between guilt and innocence would mean the collapse of society along with it. If it really makes no difference to be innocent, then fewer and fewer people would take the trouble, and a rampage would rapidly ensue. We need no esoteric reasoning, no mythical contract, divine law, or categorical imperative to understand and support this position. Considerations of equal force support many other activities. Working cooperatively, caring for children, refraining from antisocial behavior, striving for fulfillment, abiding by rules, encouraging responsibility and industry—all will occur in the moral life anyway, due to its natural imperatives and promise.

There is also a never-ending demand born of that life to adjust and rework the interests that compete with each other or tend to reenforce each other. It need not be a labor of Sisyphus. As I have remarked several times, the failure to discover the Archimedean point does not destine us to a hopeless relativism. An understanding of the moral life might well lead to the recognition of a form of pluralism and to identifying the virtues most suitable for that condition. In concrete circumstances, our virtues and cognitive inquiries, informed by an understanding of the moral condition, might yet yield a good and orderly life, but not one ruled by (pretended) moral absolutes.

I do not ignore the fact that there are heroic attempts to prospect for the philosopher's stone. Some of the most representative will be considered in time. They founder in many ways, perhaps unearthing no more than fools' gold, but common to all of them is neglect of those very conditions that make moral philosophy a worthwhile enterprise.

Evil

Another critic might point out what seems a glaring omission: I have not treated of *im*moral behavior. Surely a task of moral philosophy is to show the clear difference of good and evil and to demonstrate the superiority of virtue over vice. Perhaps everything is bet on it. "Whatever be the theory of it, I am as certain that cruelty is wrong as I am that grass is green or that two and two makes four. If this certainty is merely contingent, then my whole universe is shaken."[22] This *is* an important issue, but in a way it is exaggerated and too easily cast in an obscurantist form.

If we insist on a cognitivist interpretation of moral judgment, or otherwise demand a rationally incontrovertible position in defense of moral norms, then our lives might be dashed in the failure to solve the is/ought problem. After all, the problem pertains not only to words like "good" and "right," but to "bad" and "wrong" as well. Hence, from the standpoint of this project, we would have to have some kind of scientific demonstration that, for example, murder is wrong. Lacking this, we must suffer interminable agonies of uncertainty as to whether murder is really wrong.

But isn't this a bit silly, after all? Is our moral experience really so indeterminate? If our concern is not with words or propositions, as such, but with what they convey about the realities of the moral life, then it is clear to anyone that murder must be detested, prohibited, and punished. We don't need to discover esoteric essences in acts of murder; and however we name the practice with moral predicates, it remains the self-same practice with the self-same consequences. If murder really had no sanctions, then all human life would come to a speedy halt. Most of us would not take the opportunity to start killing, but others would. Without law to protect us there are no prohibitions, no penalties. When we are threatened, we will have to defend ourselves. It will soon come to a matter of surrender or shoot back. For this and other reasons, murder is inimical to everything that is precious to us. Indeed, the person who passionately desires to prove that 'Murder is wrong' is true, is passionate precisely because he already abhors murder. His abhorrence is not held in abeyance until the proof is forthcoming; it precedes the proof, and with good reason. If someone were actually to refrain from action until his cognitivist scruples were allayed, he would show no regard for human life.

It may be said that the perpetrators of cruel acts do so with indifference to suffering, or even with relish; we dearly want to prove to them that their conduct is "immoral" or "wrong." This is a satisfaction we might or might not attain in a given case, and failure can be deeply disappointing. On the other hand, failure is no warrant for deciding that the acts are not really hurtful, antisocial, or indifferent to suffering. Nor is it warrant for concluding that our adversaries have a good case of their own. They might be palpably ill-willed. They might be sociopathic or unwilling to engage in honest discourse. If they spurn the burden of proof, if they will not venture to argue that the hurts they cause are somehow deserved, that is confession enough. Even when someone is up to no good, he typically presents himself in moral garb. He thereby puts himself in a position where he must be willing to engage in analysis and discourse, with all their respective resources. Few persons venture to justify callous or antisocial behavior *as such.* They disguise it with excuses, extenuations, and pleas that their victims deserved what they got. Some use lies and evasions; they perform somersaults of rationalization. Their mock justifications acknowledge, in effect, that some defense of their behavior is appropriate. Even Saddam Hussein does this. This behavior seems to constitute their recognition that morality is indispensable to social life. Accordingly, we should not assume that we must justify our own position in isolation from the alternatives to it. That assumption is a recrudescence of Cartesian thinking, which looks for self-sufficing truths. We have to judge a position in relation to its alternatives, and many of these will be without merit.

Problems that are really vexing are not constituted by juxtapositions of good and evil. We are more apt to suffer uncertainty when parties to a dispute are more or less equally motivated to do right, according to their lights, by each other. They defend different claims, but they do so conscientiously. Although we are given to doing so, we are misguided to take such cases as struggles of virtue and vice. The more typical engagement is that of parties who each sincerely regard themselves as advancing legitimate claims; no one is proposing deliberate evil. We are uncertain in the grip of conflicts of goods, rights, or obligations, each acceptable and sought after in itself but unable to coexist harmoniously with the others. One possible remedy for our uncertainties in such cases, if there is one, is communication and shared inquiry. This does not mean that we will have a shared resolution for action. The fact that consternation persists in such cases suggests something about the nature of the moral condition; it does not necessarily suggest that we have a conflict of saints and sinners.

In brief, the logical demonstration that an act or person is evil is not a crucial component in moral experience, although it would give us personal satisfaction to be able to prove even to the satisfaction of malefactors that they are *wicked*. Perhaps it can be proven to them on occasion that they are *malefactors,* and that might be good enough.

The moral condition is distinguished by a plurality of values. This very plurality is what makes moral concord and decision so elusive. Moralists would like to achieve concord by papering over this pluralism and installing one criterion as supreme. In effect, they take one of the values of the moral life and absolutize it, at the expense of the others. Nothing in our experience warrants the heavy hand of such claims of supremacy, and their inherently prejudicial character is betrayed in the profusion of absolutist philosophies.

A prime condition of moving in the direction of concord is convergence of belief regarding verifiable claims. Disputants in the moral arena typically predict a great array of benefits from adopting their particular principles. Capitalists and socialists, anarchists and fascists, hawks and doves, democrats and republicans, Platonists and Epicureans, whatever else they do, foretell a promised land contingent upon observance of their philosophy. Our belief in such predictions has much to do with our moral allegiance, in at least two different ways. First, and most commonly, we are *already* committed to the given philosophy, so we will be sure that its predictions are correct—

hardly in need of test, really, from our insiders' point of view. We have a plentiful supply of *ad hoc* hypotheses to save the original theory from embarrassment, come what may.

Second, as we find that the predictions of one camp or another turn out, as the case may be, disastrously or well, then we have good reason to join the one that really does have the welcome results, rejecting the others. Such predictions are in principle verifiable. They are often difficult to verify, and the testing process will be protracted. Still, some fairly confident conclusions can with time and diligence be reached, as Peter Berger has done, for example, in *The Capitalist Revolution,*[23] which presents a rich accumulation of data testing the disputed empirical claims of capitalists and socialists on many subjects, economic and political. (Since *glasnost* we have accumulated masses of damning information about social and economic conditions in the onetime Soviet Union and the Eastern Bloc. Evidences of these conditions had reached the West previously, but they had been disputed.) For anyone in earnest about addressing the problems of the moral life with some impartiality, it must be a fervent wish that the empirical claims of rival moralities and policies be analyzed and tested. It must be their hope that in time the lessons of history and of systematic inquiry will yield some verdicts, and that those verdicts will in still more time penetrate the skulls of ideologues and true believers of all kinds.

Perhaps the most decisive variable in formulating and judging these hypotheses is one's beliefs about the nature of man. Especially in recent years, however, insufficient attention has been given to this subject in moral philosophy. There are, in fact, multiple functions in moral theory and moral reflection for assumptions about human nature. Obviously, I have some convictions on the subject, but I am not so foolhardy as to think of trying to tell the whole truth about human nature. I have the more modest aim of surveying this multiplicity of functions and of indicating what is at issue for the moral condition in our alternate convictions about what sort of being we are.

Notes

1. William James, *The Will to Believe and Other Essays in Popular Philosophy* (Cambridge, Mass.: Harvard University Press, 1979), p. 153.

2. There is nothing new in the project of classifying values and of considering their actual and possible interrelations and priorities. Those between the instrumental and the final and between the right and the good, for example, are of long standing. But, again, I am not dealing with concepts. I am trying to identify relations *in rerum natura*. The analyses closest to the *type* ventured here are those of Stephen G. Pepper in *The Sources of Value* (Berkeley: University of California Press, 1970) and Dewey in Part II of Dewey and Tufts's *Ethics* (See *Later Works,* Vol. 7). Pepper discriminates seven specific "selective systems," as he calls them, each incorporating its own "natural norms." They are natural structures in life activity that call forth or elicit different sorts of human values and evaluations. One of the virtues of this analysis is that we have definite hypotheses about how nature generates specific features of the moral life. In this result alone we have an antidote to the conviction of some schools that our values arise as purely arbitrary choices. Another antidote gleaned from Pepper is to the compulsion to reduce values to just one type.

3. The idea that implied or express promising is the source of *all* legitimate rights is without merit. Historically, very few have arisen in this way, and it would take an alienated philosopher to deny that any of these have necessary functions in the moral life.

4. What has become the standard work on desert in analytic philosophy is George Sher's *Desert* (Princeton: Princeton University Press, 1987). My analyses here and in later chapters are rather dissimilar to his in both aim and content.

5. Locke expresses these values in the language of rights. *In effect,* desert makes right. His provisos aside, Locke says we are entitled to that with which we mix our labor only when the labor is expended on something that is not already owned. In cases where ownership has already been established, our just rewards are determined by contract.

6. When one of my daughters was about five years old, she couldn't sleep one night and came downstairs to sit on my lap. I was watching a television program about the treatment accorded to American Indians. She watched silently and with sadness. Shortly, she looked up at me and asked, "Daddy, aren't Indians people, too?"

7. Kant, *The Metaphysical Elements of Justice,* Part I of *The Metaphysics of Morals,* translated, with an introduction, by John Ladd (Indianapolis and New York: The Bobbs-Merrill Company, Inc., 1965), p. 79.

8. Robert Nozick, *Anarchy, State, and Utopia* (New York: Basic Books, 1974), p. 7.

9. A recent writer has examined these relations with insight. See Joseph Raz, *The Morality of Freedom* (Oxford: The Clarendon Press, 1986), esp. chap. 10. He understands rights as "important ingredients in a mosaic of value-relations . . ." (p. 255).

10. Quine comments on the degeneration of customary relations of obligation at Harvard: "Standards sank in various departments. The preliminary examinations for the Ph.D. had been the major hurdle in our department, and they were dropped by direction of the Students for a Democratic Society, who had found that the exams induced anxiety. Personal relations deteriorated. Professors who had shared their students' intellectual concerns in a friendly or paternal way were put off by the strident talk of students' rights and put to calculating their own rights and the limits of their obligations. The loss in rapport and fellow-feeling, as well as in academic standards, was not soon to be made up." (W. V. Quine, *The Time of My Life* [Cambridge, Mass.: MIT Press, 1985], p. 353.)

11. Actually, both act and rule utilitarians trade on other moral relations more than is commonly supposed. They do so, for example, in counting each person as one and no more than one. The shift from act to rule utilitarianism is prompted by a further demand for impartiality.

12. Aristotle, *Nicomachean Ethics,* translated, with introduction and notes, by Martin Ostwald (Indianapolis and New York: The Bobbs-Merrill Company, Inc., 1962), p. 118. Emphasis added.

13. Ibid., p. 124. Emphasis added.

14. George C. Homans, *Sentiments and Activities* (Glencoe, Ill.: The Free Press, 1962), pp. 61–75, 91–103, and *Social Behavior: Its Elementary Forms,* rev. ed. (New York: Harcourt Brace Jovanovich, Inc., 1974), pp. 241–69.

15. For a wide selection of writings on this topic, see *Equity and Justice in Social Behavior,* edited by Jerald Greenberg and Ronald L. Cohen (New York: Academic Press, 1982).

16. Melvin J. Lerner, *The Belief in a Just World: A Fundamental Delusion* (New York and London: Plenum Press, 1980).

17. Ibid., p. 175.

18. Charles J. Erasmus, *In Search of the Common Good* (Glencoe, Ill.: The Free Press, 1977).

19. Thomas Sowell, *Preferential Policies: An International Perspective* (New York: William Morrow and Company, 1990). For a more compendious account, see his "Affirmative Action: A Worldwide Disaster," *Commentary* 88, no. 6 (December 1989): 21–41.

20. Sowell, *Preferential Policies,* p. 15.

21. Ibid., p. 165.

22. H. J. Paton, "The Emotive Theory of Ethics," *Aristotelian Society,* Suppl. Vol. 22, p. 125. Quoted in Paul Edwards, *The Logic of Moral Discourse* (Glencoe, Ill.: The Free Press, 1955), p. 237.

23. Peter L. Berger, *The Capitalist Revolution: Fifty Propositions about Prosperity, Equality, and Liberty* (New York: Basic Books, 1986).

6

Moral Philosophy and Human Nature

In understanding the ways of man, we understand the most critical factors of the moral condition. It is urgently worth our while to consider in what way we, as moralists, can exploit whatever understanding we might attain. Isn't it remarkable, then, that recent philosophers give so little heed to these questions? The failure to pay serious attention to human nature accounts for much of the poverty of recent moral philosophy. The classic moral philosophers stirred the soul for many reasons, not least in their attempt to formulate a systematic anthropology, including attention to the continuities or discontinuities between man and world. The answer to the question, "What is man?" was thought to yield precious information about the constraints and possibilities of the moral life—and perhaps intimations of the highest good. The very conception of morality might be derivative of assumptions about our nature. Today, in our sophistication, such inquiries often seem not so much futile as pointless. But it routinely happens in philosophy that our prized sophistication is what gets in the way of contending with issues that really matter. The theme of the present chapter will be to consider how moral philosophy, if we learned how to take human nature seriously, might have some useful contribution to make to the conduct of life.

We know much more about human development and behavior than did our predecessors. Granted, much of our knowledge today consists in recognizing how inadequate the old assumptions were, and the study of humankind is rife with conflicting theories. Any moral philosophy that depends in crucial ways on beliefs about human nature must be insofar experimental. Better to be experimental than vacuous. The following discussions attend to the variable uses of the idea of human nature in moral philosophy. They consider as well the temptations of philosophy to ignore human nature, citing several examples. As we shall see, this (sometimes willful) ignorance can lead to calamitously wrongheaded normative principles. Thinkers from other fields have not been so negligent, and a sampling of their efforts is reviewed.

Uses of the Idea of Human Nature

A study of typical philosophies of the past indicates striking differences not only in the substantive accounts of what our nature is, but also in the ways in which these accounts are deployed in the respective moral theories. There are at least two generic questions here: What is man? and How might our knowledge of man be utilized in moral philosophy? So far as I am aware, there has never been a full-scale and concerted examination of the second question; but it suggests an important inquiry.[1] I will offer the merest sketch of it in order to indicate how distinctions within this subject matter might illumine the moral condition and moral philosophy. It turns out that the answers to the two questions are contingently—not logically—related. What we might expect a theory of human nature to accomplish depends significantly on what theory we hold. I will distinguish *ends, imperatives,* and *means* as characteristics of our nature.

Ends

A familiar use of a philosophical anthropology is to determine the end, or good, of human nature. Plato and Aristotle are classic instances. Human nature has a specific formation that constitutes its completion and perfection, and affords its highest happiness. The Greek notion is embedded in a larger theory: all natures have an inherent drive for actualization. They proceed from a determinate potentiality to their ultimate actuality. What is more, all actualities together constitute a perfect harmony, a cosmos. Hence the nature of man is such that when it is achieved throughout a community, that community thereby enjoys a consummate order.

When philosophers have been convinced that there is one end, or hierarchy of ends, that is appropriate to all persons, then they have no reservations about declaring that political society should be organized in whatever way is necessary to produce this hierarchy. Through the centuries, there have been many themes and variations in this at once edifying, complacent, and dangerous view. It is now in considerable disrepute, but the search for a personally and morally useful end for human nature remains deeply alluring. Notions of human fulfillment might be, and have been, developed that would preserve such a good without the threatening political implications; and general notions of human excellence might be developed with an eye to natural conditions that fall short of cosmic dreams. Dewey's enterprise was much of this sort.

Imperatives

Modern philosophy, giving up on teleology and hence also on that sort of ordering principle for society, provides an alternative moral function for knowledge of human nature: investigation of the nature of man yields certain imperatives or principles: moral *law*. Certain laws are organic to human nature, whether because of specific and changeless urges, or perhaps because of its inherent rationality. They are dictated by imperatives within our very nature, and they are clearly not to be regarded as ends. Hobbes's cautionary tale of man in the state of nature, for instance, excludes any developed notion of a completed human nature, but it concludes with the articulation of certain "laws of nature," that any informed person would accept, provided there were assurance of their enforcement. Our unfailing propensity to extreme egoism, competitiveness, and hostility, coupled with a fear of "wounds and violent death," demands no less. With Locke, laws of nature are laws of *reason;* and Kant takes this general approach to its limit. Deliberately leaving our contingent nature out of account, he declares that the nature of universal reason is such that it prescribes unconditional moral laws. It follows necessarily from the nature of reason that moral principle and judgment must be of a perfectly definite kind. The categorical imperative is a necessary expression of rational nature.

The idea that our nature includes pronounced and consistent propensities for both good and ill is no secret. There are native demands or inherent propensities of our nature in profusion; there is a natural drive to satisfy them. The satisfaction might even be a bad thing, but the demand must be acknowledged and reckoned with like any other natural force. Such drives typically incorporate an end—the satisfaction of the drive. It is important to know when satisfaction can be attained within a wide or narrow range of objects. The nurturing instinct can be fulfilled in varying ways, but not equally well. Can the desire to take care of one's family co-exist with large-scale redistributions of wealth and position? Must the reward of our competitive bent consist in hierarchies of power and status? Or are human impulses so plastic that they can always be satisfied with socially desirable objects?

The investigation of "laws" of our being needn't be confined to these urges as such. The notion of subjective imperative is ambiguous. There are innate demands—like those for sex, food, protecting, affection, domination, and so on—which we are apt to pursue with little prompting; if they are thwarted, we will resist, perhaps mightily. Such urges might or might not be morally supported, depending on the context. The structure of our nature, however, might also be such that there are only certain ways that particular goods can be attained; and these ways, too, can be thought of as laws or imperatives. Presumably, there is not an indefinite number of ways that virtue can develop, for example, or that the various powers and resistances in our nature can be channelled to socially desirable activities. Suppose it is a universal condition that children can develop the capacity for trusting and affectionate relationships only if they have a strong bond with a consistent and loving adult. Then we could take it as a *law* of our nature that the conditions of such a bond be given an extremely high priority in human arrangements. Such laws would be objective in the sense that any experimental law is objective, but they would count as a form of *moral* law only if they were discriminated as possessing distinctive worth. (In the given example, the evaluation could be set aside only at the expense of making human life intolerable.)

There may be many discernible laws, in this sense, that are inseparable from human nature. While such norms as telling the truth, keeping promises, and being responsible would be indispensable to social action for virtually any nature, there are surely many conditions native to our being that are necessary to sustain and enrich social bonds and individual welfare. I offered evidence in the preceding chapter, as an instance, that it might be organic to us to prefer that rewards be possessed according to desert. Human beings also need such things as love, nurturance, security, challenge, accomplishment, freedom, order, recognition, respect; and there is not an indefinite plurality of ways in which these conditions can be satisfied. Philosophers who are ignorant or indifferent to such laws moralize in a vacuum. The responsible moralist must be well acquainted with the actual powers and willingness of human beings to conduct themselves according to allegedly rational nostrums.

Perhaps in defiance of Dewey's objections, it should be noted that for our nature to possess a moral law, an imperative, in some useful sense would imply a fixity of sorts in it—something of a human universal, or some predictable regularities in behavior. Such laws would presuppose inherent tendencies or interests of a general kind. Or, when certain actions are uniformly vital to our survival or to our well-being, we could well say that their observance constitutes an imperative. Dewey himself, just in saying that growth is the moral end, implies that growth is a condition that human beings almost unfailingly cherish. He also said, "If there is anything in human psychology to be counted upon, it may be urged that when man is satiated with restless seeking for the remote which yields no enduring satisfaction, the human spirit will return to seek calm and order within itself. This, we repeat, can be found only in the vital, steady, and deep relationships which are present only in an immediate community."[2] Both sentences read suspiciously as though human universals are presupposed.

Means

Other forms of conduct might be of consequence only because they can be directed to some ulterior goal; they are *mere* means. Hence a theory of human nature can also be used in an exclusively instrumental manner. One of Dewey's most fundamental concerns with our nature, for example, was to understand it as integral with inclusive processes of change. How do human traits come into existence and undergo change in relation to variations of environmental conditions? How does learning happen? When such inquiries are successful, we would possess the means to educate effectively, and we could discriminate and control the conditions upon which treasured ends depend. More broadly, we might determine the means to a happier and more harmonious human being capable of more fruitful and fulfilling interchanges with the contingencies of natural existence.

The nature of the inquiry does not in itself suggest whether the means of human nature tend to be fixed or variable in their operation. We might have many options or few. In any case, such attentions to human nature are difficult to quarrel with, but they cannot stand alone. They must be complemented with some reflective treatment of ends and principles. To *what* ends should human nature be a means? Are there imperatives in our nature that determine the choice of means? The ways that human nature might function as a means are not reducible to imperatives. The inventory of behavior that is *possible* for us is very wide. There are different forms of social organization of which our nature is capable, for example; but the choice between them is not indifferent. At least this is so if there is merit in the notion of persistent ends and imperatives. The succeeding section will contend, indeed, that the failure to maintain such distinctions leads to highly dubious conclusions about the nature of community; and there will be still more examples in subsequent discussions.

Not the least important function of knowledge of human nature in its instrumental bearings is to determine what moral demands can realistically be made on us, and how we can develop the capacities to meet them. It is characteristic of some moral systems to make demands that cannot be met; of others, to be insufficiently demanding.

The preceding illustrations suggest that the peculiar employment of a theory of human nature depends largely on its content. The investigation of the moral bearings of human nature tends to one emphasis or another—to its ends, imperatives, or means—as these are thought to be especially distinguishable and potent. If we fail to identify, say, any significant ends or imperatives intrinsic to our nature, then moral reflection must proceed without them. As theory of man is modified and enriched, likewise with its applications.

All the philosophers mentioned did not confine their studies of human nature to an exclusive use. On the face of it, it would seem helpful to the moral life that some kind of working coherence among the ends, imperatives, and means of human nature be effected. Intensely conscious of the ontological difference between potentiality and actuality, and devoted as they were to self-realization, the classic

Greeks were deeply concerned with the means of education; yet their teleological theories, by their particular nature, had little to contribute to developmental psychology. Formal causes as principles of explanation have fallen into ill-repute (but an echo of their importance might one day be recovered in the study of genes).

For Hobbes, who denounced the distinction between potency and act, there can be no education that would transform human nature from something as it is potentially into a form of perfection. When we contemplate the plundering character of man in the state of nature, and we ask how to improve it, Hobbes replies, "We can't. What you see is what you get. Your ambitions are in vain." As for Kant, rational nature as such is a brute and universal given. Rational nature *qua* rational nature does not depend on contingent circumstances of human nature or the environment, and its only "end" is to conform to universal law.

The modern conceptions of man had, then, limited but highly important functions. Dewey's thinking on human nature has more versatility. His notion of integrated growth as the end is at the same time a theory of learning: habit formation is at once learning and growth. The moral question lies in the discrimination of alternative forms of growth. In an obvious way, then, his conceptions are more inclusive and instructive than those of classical teleology.

In spite of the historical precedents, the distinctions between the ends, means, and imperatives resident within the human frame are sometimes difficult to make, but they are nonetheless important. What is taken as an end, for example, might also be taken as either a means or an imperative. Virtue is surely an end, but it is a means as well. It might justly be regarded as an imperative, too. It can be a *moral* imperative, of course, but it might also be an imperative in the sense of being a felt *urge* to certain kinds of conduct.

To acknowledge that there are some contextually determined differences between ends, imperatives, and means does not suggest that these distinctions be abandoned. All behavior occurs in a context, great or small. To distinguish pertinent functions of human nature within each is essential to effective judgment and action. Unmistakably, there are ends, or goods, of human nature, and they are not endlessly variable or accessible. But we don't know enough about them. Intelligent men and women pursue a wide variety of ends, many of which turn out to be less satisfying than expected. No doubt part of the problem is that ends exist in a varying mosaic of relations, which is sometimes unknown or inscrutable; so the attainment of a given end will occasion unanticipated sacrifices, failures, and disappointments. Failure is also owing to simple ignorance of human nature, disabling contextual analysis.

No one doubts either that there are powerful propensities in human nature, but there is no uniformly accepted census of them. Especially when we raise the question of when they are native and when acquired, controversy becomes very heated. We have deep emotional and practical investments, for example, in convictions about the innateness of good and evil. On this topic an economist, Robert Frank, has provided a suggestive argument to the effect of resurrecting something like Aristotle's theory of virtue. That is, he believes that we possess native moral drives. Frank attacks the prevailing theories of motivation, which suppose that "rational" behavior is in deliberate pursuit of utilities for the agent. There is much behavior that simply does not fit that paradigm. Individuals do many things intentionally that are perceived *by themselves* to be injurious to their utilities. They stick to agreements and commitments, for example, when they could cheat on them with impunity. They are vengeful when vengeance is more costly than letting matters stand, and they reject negotiations that would be profitable when their share of the profit is judged unfair. How could such things happen? Inherent sentiments, emotions, or dispositions—as Frank indifferently calls them—are the answer. Such traits would be selected in the evolutionary process, because they *do* tend to be beneficial to their possessors. When individuals are perceived to possess such characteristics, then other individuals will desire to be in league with them, will be wary of cheating them, and will be less apt to try to push an inequitable agreement on them. These are not universal traits, of course. That would not be an evolutionarily stable state; the opportunist would thrive in a population possessing so much virtue that its members do not test the virtues of others. Hence there is a certain distribution of "immoral" sentiments as well. Frank does not face any hard questions about what the limits of the moral sentiments might be, but such research tends to give the lie to the notion that the moral life is created *de novo* as a convention. Such studies might, in time, tell us much about variations of moral behavior.[3]

The very heavens shudder when sexual differences are in dispute.

Steven Goldberg, for example, has surveyed the evidence from several fields of inquiry, concluding that male dominance is both universal and inevitable.[4] These investigations have made him enormously unpopular. Yet such inquiry is vitally important. Suppose, as many investigators believe, that the male brain and central nervous system are different from that of the female in such a way that males tend to exceed females in mathematical and other forms of abstract thought. Then the dominance of males in these areas cannot be attributed wholly to prejudicial discrimination. If the truth of such a matter were established and disseminated, we might be saved from lamentable social controls that would enforce equality of representation.

If we believe, however, that human nature is indefinitely socializable, we can employ it as a means to just about anything—no utopian arrangement would be in principle out of reach. At the same time, however, we would have to know much about the principles of socialization in order to know how to achieve such ends. Lacking such knowledge, even more lamentable experiments would be undertaken. Or, if there are powerful limitations to socialization, recognition of what they are would constrain philosophers in their contriving of moral systems.

The utopians' dream of the indefinite malleability of the human spirit is founded more on ideology and wishful thinking than candid thought and observation. While there are obviously innate and widely distributed human traits, it remains an object of responsible inquiry to distinguish them carefully and to determine their variations, functions, urgencies, and interconnections.[5] Such inquiry would also recognize the variable means and powers of education, which in many instances will be potent. Perhaps some features of behavior are almost entirely constituted by education; in other cases, socialization may function effectively only in league with innate propensities.

I do not mean to suggest that our only resources in such inquiries are provided by the behavioral sciences. Consider the riches in literature and the arts, not to mention one's own honest gaze on the human scene. Pertinent historical knowledge, too, might prove to be abundant. Where peoples are not prevented from exercising their preferred forms of conduct, various uniformities in patterns of life across cultures are exhibited: *e.g.,* family life, religion, tightly knit local groups, hierarchical structures, and observance of relations of desert. In the masterful fashion of Aristotle's *Politics,* we could undertake comparative studies to attain insight into how human harmony and well being wax and wain under varying conditions.

Indeed, it is not premature to believe that a resurrection of Aristotle's inquiry into morality by nature would be illuminating and practical, though not likely to be so omnicompetent as Aristotle supposed, nor so complacent as his assumption that whatever is by nature is good. Properly understood, the idea of morality by nature is wholly intelligible. It simply means that there are fairly definite talents, ambitions, imperatives, aversions, and allegiances characteristic of human beings, individually and collectively. These traits will not be equally distributed; they will characterize some groups more than others, and they will be more or less fixed or variable. *But they exist.* We do not deduce moral judgments from statements of their existence, and we do not take them as constituting invariable patterns of conduct. We take them deeply into account, however, in considering the reasonable expectations we can entertain about each other; we are on the lookout for the ill effects for feeling and conduct that accompany institutional arrangements that prove adverse to their fulfillment and exercise; we consider the ways in which the destructive traits can be resisted with minimal collateral damage; and we look for the social structures and moral relations that might allow the possessors of such traits to coexist and conjoin according to their nature and even to flourish.

What more classic example is there than the family? It is not a mere convention, a mere agreement. It exists by nature. It is so not only because of the nature of our genetic endowment, which strongly disposes us to favor those who possess duplicate copies of our genes. It also seems to be uniquely capable of nurturing the traits of character indispensable to civilized life. In addition to the fact that domestic life affords profound joy and meaning, it is a most demanding responsibility: hard work, dedication, and sacrifice day in and day out, year after year, often with pain and disappointment. It is not to be undertaken lightly. The devotion and energy that it requires cannot be conjured up by mere agreements or conventions. It is a matter of nature. That is, there must be a strong and enduring propensity to sustain it. (The fact that adoptive families can be highly successful does not refute this point. The parents must have a fundamental and abiding drive to *be* parents.)

Family structure is crucial for moralizing children. Young males are especially prone to antisocial behavior if they are not reared properly, and adult males undergo improvements in character when they marry and rejoin a family order. In the example of the family we see at once the inseparable interaction of both genetic imperatives and acculturated differences. Just because their treatment by their parents is so massively important to children, the parents have it largely in their power to turn their offspring into miserable, friendless sociopaths or into trusting, loving, and responsible adults. Because of the natural intensity of its relations, the family is the most effective milieu for such degradation or growth to occur. Hence the imperative for good families.

Families go wrong; spousal relations go wrong. Family relations are not analogous to the law of gravity. A husband *can* become a libertine; but in so doing he sacrifices a far greater good. He puts the good of his children at grave risk, and he deeply threatens the relationship with his wife that might otherwise sustain them both, and sustain them well, for a lifetime. If all these relations were merely by convention, there would be no reason why the children must have a responsible father. Perhaps a day worker could come in to play with the kids instead, and to discipline them. He could be counted upon to do this for years, or perhaps the kids would do just as well with a succession of day workers. For her part, the wife could just decide that it is irrational of her to insist on her man's fidelity, and the two of them could proceed lovingly as if nothing had happened, or they could part without recrimination or hurt.

In an obvious sense, the husband as libertine is also acting according to nature. Nature has many ways, but they are not equally generous or rewarding. Typically, it is deeply in our nature to need abiding love, trust, and accomplishment, and to work and sacrifice for them. Men especially are often willing to risk these profound satisfactions for the transient thrill of illicit adventure. But it *is* recognized as a risk: the former condition is the truly cherished one. Stresses, hurts, and frustrations are organic to any family life, but we are fitted by nature to endure them and contend with them responsibly. That is, the need for family has potencies not found in other associations. *Of course* there are legitimate controversies about family morality, but to regard the institution as subject to unlimited tinkering—as mere convention—is adolescent fantasy.

The Neglect of Human Nature

Morality by nature: what a vital subject! We do not know how much the inquiry into the ends, imperatives, and means of human nature might yield. Moral philosophy would be much simpler—but much less pertinent to the urgencies of the moral life—if there were not at least these three functions of knowledge of human nature to consider. We could speculate only about ends, or only about law. Where the moral end is posited independently of human nature, as in cases like that of Moore, we need speculate only about human nature as a means. Moral philosophy would be simpler still if we ignored all three functions, or chose not to consider them with earnest rigor. What such a philosophy would have to contribute to the moral life is another matter.

Since the time of Dewey (at least in the English speaking world), the last two options—taking human nature as a means, or just ignoring it—have been virtually the only ones in evidence. There seem to be several reasons for this, and it will be instructive to survey some of them.

Captured by the Is/Ought Problem

If we assume that valid normative discourse hinges on a solution to the is/ought problem, then oceansfull of knowledge about human nature would be in vain. At any rate, we would have to keep that knowledge in abeyance, or treat it as a curiosity, until such time as the problem were solved. Philosophers who are bound by this conception of moral philosophy must, I have argued, wait forever. Certainly most philosophers in recent times have been bound in this way; so most of them, as philosophers, have had their own reason for leaving the investigation into human nature out of account.

The Authority of Intuition

Another reason for neglecting human nature is to proceed by the way of intuition. We may simply collect our intuitions together, under suitably defined conditions, and retain only those that are logically coherent with one another. ("Our" and "suitably" are already morally loaded terms; but that's another issue.) I have already objected strenuously that this is an insidious and finally impotent approach because it amounts to an appeal to moral sentiment unchastened by critical awareness of the existential conditions of conduct. To their possessors, at least, intuitions seem to have perfectly obvious meanings, but they are not construed as predictions of existential events. Their formal relations to *each other* seem to be the only concern of the philosopher, who has thereby returned us, in effect, to a subjective cage of some similarity to that of pre-Jamesian empiricism. If the final constraints and opportunities of the moral life lie in the structures and contingencies of the real world, then the way of intuition is not so much futile as dangerous. The strengths and weaknesses of human nature are conspicuously important examples of such real-world conditions, but they may be serenely overlooked so long as we regard our intuitions as sacrosanct.

Kantianism

Where contemporary theory is infused with Kantianism, human nature must be shunted aside. The theory of rational choice, often making use of game theory, postulates an ideally rational agent and determines what principles such an agent would choose. These principles are then regarded as normative for the real-world population. It is not impertinent to remark that not one of this population comes close to satisfying the preferred definition of rationality. A single uniform abstraction is substituted for the varied and heterogeneous historical persons who populate real communities. It would be more accurate to call the abstraction an invention or fiction. Not surprisingly, the fictions of, say, Rawls, Gewirth, or Gauthier don't resemble each other much, and they eventuate in very different systems. Reality? Who cares? In the hurly-burly of social experience, we find devoted socialists, libertarians, fascists, and liberals and conservatives of every stripe. Utilitarians, deontologists, neo-Thomists, existentialists, pragmatists, moral skeptics, and legal positivists are all vying for attention. Ardent defenders of animal rights, women's rights, fetal rights, children's rights, gay rights, sexual rights, property rights, and the like crowd our attention. If anything should be obvious in the moral life, it is that these positions are not easily modified, much less relinquished. Champions of these stances, as well as many humbler people, do not resemble the moral paradigms used in rational choice theories. Their motivations, moreover, are determined by a striking array of loyalties, antagonisms, sympathies, ambitions, anxieties, and moral dispositions. Are all these variations to be rejected out of hand, rejected to suit the *a priori* definitions of rational agency? These are people's *lives* at stake, not the abstractions of theory. At what (frightening) costs could these lives be forced into the mold? It is a massive problem of the moral life to address its plural, diverse, and powerful tendencies and to go some way to reducing them to manageable orders. The theory of rational choice is not a good candidate. Human nature, among other things, must be studied more concretely.

Free Will and Responsibility

A more interesting and enduring shortcut is that of postulating free will. The great exponents of free will—from Augustine to Sartre—have typically, if not invariably, also talked of other dimensions of human nature and have given them significance in conduct. Nevertheless, it is not clear that they can do so consistently. If there is something called will, and if it is not in the last analysis conditioned by desires, compulsions, passions, and interests possessed by the actual human being, then it chooses and acts, somehow, independently of all that. If the will is, after all, constrained by these impulses, then how is it free? To introduce the notion of insurmountable constraint is to rob the will of its reason for being. If, as the free will advocates declare, it is always possible for a person by virtue of free will to have acted other than he or she did, then there is no reason why the will should not be fully efficacious in *every* instance. To speak of a struggle of the will and the flesh, where the flesh sometimes triumphs, is to confess that the will *cannot* always do otherwise. If it is free, it *can* triumph; and if it can, it will. Otherwise we are returning behavior to the complex medley of motivations studied by psychologists.

A consistently held free will position makes further reference to human nature in the moral life superfluous. At the same time, it makes it possible to create illusory expectations about the competence of moral beings: all we have to do, one thinks, is concentrate the will, and no moral requirement can be excessive. Likewise, we would be justified in exercising sanctions on behavior that falls short of such requirements.

There are many reasons why people have been attached to the notion of free will, some of them merely sentimental. Arguments in its favor have tended to be be aprioristic and, in the pejorative sense, metaphysical—without means of verification. As James was fond of pointing out, arguments against it tend to be of the same sort. James would be intrigued, and most readers surprised, to learn that a very substantial experimental literature on this topic has developed in recent years. There had been many experiments with human subjects under laboratory conditions in which behavior had been accurately predicted, but there was no general principle of prediction. This lack was evidently remedied by R. J. Herrnstein in his so-called matching law: a set of equations by means of which behavior can be predicted in a manner to plot it along a definite curve.[6] (The curve, incidentally, is not one of utility maximization.) This law is presently under experimental scrutiny in the relevant community of inquirers. Its validity would do more than support determinism at large; it would be a determinism that permits behavior under controlled conditions to be predicted with remarkable exactitude. This form of determinism does *not* imply that human beings can be conditioned to do anything that the proverbial men in white coats want them to. There is a finite range of rewards that will function as reenforcers to human nature, and there are individual differences between human beings that limit the range still more. What functions as a reenforcer for a given individual depends on *his* existing nature. That constitutes a crucial initial condition for any prediction.

Although it is possible that the matching law will in due course be falsified, tests of it so far have been corroborative. Verification of the law would be extremely dismaying to many, but dismay is not warranted. For those willing to listen, Daniel Dennett's *Elbow Room* ought to take the fear out of determinism.[7] I want to enlarge on Dennett to observe that the *values* associated with free will are much better understood and enhanced from a deterministic perspective, a perspective that has to take human nature far more seriously than do the indeterminists. I will focus on the related issues of personal responsibility and efficacy of conduct.

It is a fundamental confusion to take the vindication of reward and punishment as a peculiarly elusive problem. It is of the greatest importance that persons behave in a generally responsible manner: that they be dependable and reliable, that they meet their obligations and can be counted on. This is a condition of inestimable worth. Therefore it is of equal importance that persons be held responsible for their acts, for this is how they learn to be responsible. Being responsible is an outcome, an achievement. Nothing is easier than to justify the judicious meting out of consequences for conduct. Holding persons responsible, by way of praise and blame, reward and punishment, is precisely the way in which they *become* responsible; and their becoming responsible is the aim to be cherished. We learn to do certain kinds of acts and to avoid others. Hence reliable patterns of social action are established and sustained; persons can be counted on. Societies couldn't exist without widespread behavior of this sort.

To be thought responsible is a great credit to us; it typically brings welcome benefits: we are respected and trusted. Without doubt, some people are more responsible than others, and many tend to be irresponsible. The latter are a burden on their fellows, who don't take the burden cheerfully. It is a virtue most people desire to possess and surely need to possess, and we do a cruel disservice to deny them the conditions of becoming responsible. Rather than first establish a responsible nature in order to warrant punishment and reward, we must first establish punishment and reward in order to create a responsible nature. It is an imperative of our nature. We *must* nurture responsibility.

This is a familiar and vital process, and it is hard to see how free will has anything to do with it. The differences between the more or less responsible and more or less negligent seem to be a function of variations in learning, although constitutional factors have something to do with such variations. Mostly through natural reactions and crude educational techniques, the young are taught by their elders to be responsible. All too often, we do a poor job of it. To do the job well, we need to understand how human nature works; we need to know much about the learning process. (And we also need to apply it consistently. Educators must be responsible, too.)

As in any theory of responsibility, we also must make crucial distinctions about what sorts of conduct persons should be held accountable for. We must consider what sorts of excellence we wish to stimulate and nurture, what sorts of deficiencies to discourage. We must have some sense of human capabilities, individual and collective, and some reliable ideas about what the conditions are that will prompt individuals to cherish the discriminated virtues and to disdain vice. (I take it that, in general, excusing weak behavior does not help to minimize it.)

Such knowledge not only comes to our aid where the indeterminist is helpless, it is also of the first importance in response to theories that are widely regarded as dissipating the notion of personal responsibility. One of the fears generated by Marxist theory is that "history" robs the individual of responsibility for his acts; likewise one can argue that society, and not the individual, is responsible for behavior. Freudian theory is similarly viewed with alarm, for in it the deliberate individual seems to vanish within the folds of the unconscious.

The appropriate response to such seeming threats is simply to recall that people *must* be held accountable as part of the process of growing up, and when they are, they become responsible. There are limits to the process, of course, and these are to be determined by inquiry. We need to investigate how—not whether—variations in life conditions are correlated with variations in conduct. That there are such variations cannot be doubted, but knowing how to bring them about is the pressing concern. That is, again, we find out what sort of learning in fact makes a person capable of carrying out desirable activities with initiative, skill, and reliability. Certain kinds of punishment and reward have just this effect. It is misconceived, then, to ask whether the individual or society is responsible, or whether it is ever legitimate to hold the individual responsible. Not to hold individuals responsible would be the height of irresponsibility! Holding responsible is our principal teaching device. It is contrary to all fact to say that behavior changes only on the heels of social reconstruction. In some cases, it may require nothing more complex than a kind word, or perhaps a good bawling out.

The moral requirements we impose on one another are among our most important teaching devices. We require our children to behave in certain ways, for example, and we impose what we take to be appropriate benefits and penalties. Thus they learn to be moral. But we might be poor teachers, or we might make demands on them that are impossible to meet, in which case they will learn the arts of subterfuge and hypocrisy. We *should* make high demands, or they will never reach the morality of which they are capable. But we must be realistic about the possibilities of human nature.

"Ought," said Kant, implies "can." He thought of it as a cognitive claim, but it is evaluative. We *could* penalize a person for failing in an impossible task; but, normally, we don't advocate doing so. We are opposed to holding people responsible for things that they are unable to do. But it is sometimes not only reasonable, but necessary, to require of individuals more than they might be capable of producing on a given occasion. Like any good teacher, one might demand of persons that they go beyond their current limits. The fear of penalty or the promise of praise might be just the stimulus they need. If they fail, the penalty must be visited, precisely on the assumption that a better effort will be called forth next time. Thus "ought" does not always presuppose "can," but we must levy our requirements with a judicious eye to individual potentialities.

I have been stressing the importance of responsibility and how our thinking about it is dependent upon assumptions about human nature. The postulate of free will is of no help in such perplexities, theoretical or practical. Many believers in free will are inept in actual cases of being responsible themselves or in holding others responsible. A full library of treatises on free will can be of no help to them.

We are as concerned with being master of our own destiny as we are with responsibility. Indeed, we could put it that we desire to be *responsible* for our own destiny. We wish to be in control of our own life, to have the course of events develop much in the way that we want, rather than feel like a slave to circumstance. We would like, moreover, to know how to deal with *ourselves*. We want to overcome our insufferable and debilitating habits and develop more effective powers of affection and action. It would be the idlest postulate to attribute variations in these qualities to variations in free will. These are *acquired* powers; some people possess them in abundance, and others are bereft of them. Some people are out of control. Others feel that they are helpless to help themselves; they are full of excuses, and they always feel like victims. By contrast, others have a strong sense of leading their own lives and have confidence that their agency will be effective. (Just harboring these assumptions is a major step in realizing them.) These are real differences, and *they* are of the greatest moment to us—dithering about free will is either escapist or misguided. We urgently need to know how these differences come about and what arts are utilized in their accomplishment.

The Authority of Philosophy

In reviewing the preceding reasons why philosophers have slighted human nature in moral theory, a person with a cynical bent might conclude that the slight is due in no small part to professional jealousy. The stratagems reviewed above involve assumptions that tend to encapsulate philosophy from other disciplines. Once we admit that empirical studies are organic to the formulation of moral principles, the philosopher's turf is threatened, his esoteric craft imperiled. The same yearnings that drove the foundationalist of old are still intensely active.

The Presumed Malleability of Human Nature

There comes from many quarters in social science a hypothesis that excuses moral philosophers from attending to human nature in certain crucial ways. This is the assumption that all behavior is to be accounted for by variations in socialization. Human nature is plastic to the discerning touch of education: we are a moral *tabula rasa* awaiting messages from philosophers. If this be so, we could not assert that the human constitution owns inherent constraints on the possibilities of the moral life. There are no ends truly distinctive of human nature; likewise no laws or fixed instrumentalities, short of those of mere biology. The moral life is an empty canvas to be painted by the educator, upon whom our nature places no limitation.

No one holds this hypothesis absolutely. The nature/nurture controversy covers a continuum of possibilities. For about three quarters of a century, however, it has been popular in the social sciences to incline strongly to the view that most of the important traits of individual and social life are simply learned. Much of the evidence for it is predicated on recognition of the remarkable diversity of cultures. In philosophy, this view was articulated and championed by Dewey and Mead, and they have had many followers. Before them (and before the rise of the social sciences), Karl Marx had argued that consciousness is class consciousness, and class is determined by one's relation to the means of production. John Stuart Mill also argued (at times) for the omnipotence of culture,[8] as had many before him.

The further one goes in the direction of the socialization theory, the more one tends to be ambitious about social engineering—about undertaking bold and sweeping social experiments or creating "ideal" societies. Here, of course, extensive knowledge of the interactions of organism and environment *is* required. We need to know how to get human nature to take or to choose the desired formation. We may be like plastic, but even that stuff varies under specific conditions; so we must experiment with it. Ambitions to remake the world are sometimes chastened by recognizing that our knowledge may be presently insufficient to know how to do it. There are so many variables to identify that we may get all sorts of unexpected and unwelcome results.

Our belief in the educability of human nature has a great hazard: that no measure to reform it will go untried. Hence we witness, for example, the various campaigns to create "socialist man," the failures of which have been uniformly abysmal, sometimes catastrophic. When people are resistant to the desired forms of change, ever more tyrannical measures are taken to enlighten them. These regimes have had too many apologists in the "intellectual" community, who are too sentimental, or who persist in the opinion that all will be well once we identify the proper form of socialization.

The question of what human beings can learn and how they can learn it is of the greatest importance; and it is a subject about which we still have much to find out.[9] To investigate the moral bearings of such answers as we have is a further, and even more urgent, matter. In the last twenty years or so, there have been many conscientious inquirers in the fields of biology, sociology, anthropology, linguistics, neuroscience, and psychology who have concluded that there are many native constraints and requirements of human nature. They also believe that many individual differences are due in significant measure to differences in genetic endowment. Differences in culture can be accounted for to some extent by variations in gene-culture coevolution, as it is called. A given environment "selects" certain genes rather than others for reproductive success. Hence this environment produces a distinctive culture. In an embattled population, for example, reproductive success might come particularly to genes fostering warlike qualities, while a safer or more plentiful environment might select genes of different qualities. This assumption acknowledges that culture plays a vital role in behavior, but it does so as part of the evolutionary process, not (here) as part of education. That is, the selection of genes is not a deliberate process; the culture is not even aware of it.

These are exacting and somewhat unsettled questions. Even those who are persuaded of important native structures are not in agreement as to just what they are and how they vary. At the same time, the relations between native capacities and processes of socialization are not altogether clear. There are questions of the continuities of native powers and socialization. In some cases, socialization might run contrary to inborn biases; in others it might work independently of them; in still more, education might be a strengthening and directing of preexisting tendencies. Hence the mere fact that we are educable does not determine what our native stock might be. In any case, few would deny that these are inquiries of the most intense concern. Indeed, they arouse such passionate advocacy that participation in the controversy proves dangerous to one's reputation, even to one's livelihood or life. This leads me to the final suggestion of reasons why the rigorous study of human nature is discouraged in philosophy and elsewhere.

Intimidation and Fear

The norms of civility in discourse are readily attacked and abandoned when ideology is at stake. Critical intelligence is subordinated to the preservation of our fondest hopes and most passionately held convictions. Unfashionable hypotheses about human nature are a conspicuous case in point. It is very dangerous in academic and intellectual circles to make claims about innate gender or racial differences, for example, or about innate differences in intelligence. A recent case is that of Michael Levin, a professor of Philosophy at City College of New York. He cited substantial scientific evidence to the effect that the mean IQ of blacks is lower that that of whites, and he argued that the decline in academic standards is attributable in part to the attempt to accord academic success to unqualified black students. As quoted in a column by Ilene Barth, ". . . [T]he City College faculty senate passed [by an overwhelming majority] a resolution condemning Levin's 'expressed racist sentiments.' "[10] (Both "racist" and "sentiments" are gratuitous.) The chairman of the senate—one Bernard Sohmer—added that the condemnation of Levin did not constitute a threat to academic freedom because "what we were taking exception to were things said out of class." We are to be reassured by this, presumably! All we need be concerned about from the Ministry of Truth is the content of our research! But the Ministry has become increasingly watchful of what is said in class, too.[11] Levin himself was persuaded "under pressure" by the administration and the Department of Philosophy to withdraw from teaching his introductory philosophy course.

The immediate issue is not whether the claims about racial differences in IQ are correct. It is a matter of the right to investigate such questions without presupposing what the answers must be, the right to submit such inquiries to the normal procedures of test through free communication and publication, and the right to consider the bearings of supposed answers on matters of public concern. One hopes that the hypotheses about comparative intelligence would prove unwarranted, and, failing that, that the differences would be transient. In any case, it is important that we be permitted, if not encouraged, to pursue the truth of the matter. To require an orthodoxy is to put an end to conscientious inquiry, to impose a tyranny on mind and behavior. The consequences of such an orthodoxy can only be disastrous. In the case at issue, it is certain that the search for educational excellence at all levels must fail if it is not predicated on accurate assumptions about learning capabilities. Aspirations for racial harmony will likewise fall victim to the intensified hostility and recrimination that succeed unwarranted expectations, double standards, and charges of bigotry.

Intimidation of the sort mentioned is a powerful weapon against inquiries into human nature, and there are many inquirers who are afraid to speak their conscientious beliefs. For one of many possible examples, consider the report of Robin Fox in "The Seville Declaration: Anthropology's Auto-da-Fe."[12] Fox narrates the story of the Seville Declaration, a proclamation asserting that there is no good evidence to the effect that aggression and violence have substantial genetic sources. He encouraged his colleagues in anthropology to repudiate the declaration, which was more a political than scientific document. Many of them confessed to him privately that they agreed with his position, but they were unwilling to say so for the record. ". . . [M]ost of the fear expressed was of offending their 'morally committed colleagues.' . . ."[13]

The thought police—recruited from students, faculty, and administration—are attentive to the enforcement of many orthodoxies, not just those regarding human nature. Resistance to their demands is labelled racist, sexist, imperialist, and fascist. Resistance is also called "divisive," as if the enforcement of dogma were not itself divisive against all those who cannot accept it, and the university were not of all places the one upon which we are most dependent for free inquiry.

There are also fears of a different sort. We witnessed the hideous consequences of the Nazi belief in the inherent superiority of the Aryan race, and today we contemplate prospects of genetic engineering that would make the Third Reich's Dr. Mengele rub his hands with glee. Better, we think, to lock the menace of such questions in a vault and throw away the key. There *are* nightmarish potentialities in our technological prowess, and for that reason we must be extremely wary. The Nazi nightmare cannot be exorcised by ignoring it, however.

We must acknowledge, furthermore, that belief in inherent human differences *by itself* does not lead to atrocities or even injustice. It was not simply the belief in Aryan superiority that moved the Nazis to their demented adventure. They were driven by their insatiable lust for power and domination, and these are lusts that we must guard against in *any* case. Historically, most populations have thought themselves somehow superior to their neighbors—a thought that can be dangerous. But it doesn't follow that those who believe themselves to be superior are entitled to subordinate or exterminate the alleged inferiors. As a matter of familiar daily experience, we are repeatedly in situations where inequalities of talent, authority, and intelligence—whatever their source—are acknowledged, but we don't take them as license to do harm. Keep in mind as well that there are tyrannies that are not predicated on assumptions of superiority. The gulag archipelago and various "reeducation camps" are perpetrated in the name of an ideology declaring the equality of all mankind.

We might be tempted to suppress information about human nature in order to conceal a possible rationale for bad behavior of various kinds. If males, for example, have a genetic bias in favor of violence, then violence-prone men can plead that they are just doing what is natural to them. Or, if males have a genetic structure less disposed to monogamy than females, men can adopt this theory as an excuse for impulsive philandering that might spell the ruin of marriage and family. As the case may be, such episodes are entirely possible, but that hardly seems an adequate reason to eradicate one of our most precious and most fragile resources, freedom of inquiry. There are many hazards in the moral life, and many rationalizations, and knowledge is often used for despicable ends. It is also knowledge, however, that will teach us how to contend with such trials, insofar as that is possible. How many history lessons do we need before learning that the thought police are sure to make matters worse? We have no choice but to make do with who and what we are—with the passions, hostilities, virtues, talents, and sympathies characteristic of human existence. A moral philosophy that would turn on the real capacities of human nature does not credit itself by censoring the inquiries essential to its task. In short, I do not know of a defensible reason to curtail serious inquiry into human nature, certainly not as a component of moral philosophy. Our patron saint, Socrates, was not one to be intimidated, and his example is once again to be emulated.

Philosophies without Anthropology: Studies in Infertility

My intention has not been anything so ambitious as to articulate a philosophical anthropology. I have been occupied chiefly with indicating the important uses to which such a theory could be put and offering explanations for why such efforts are no longer to be found in philosophy. I shall continue by reference to a few specimens of current moral thought to illustrate how they are debilitated by inattention to human nature. I will confine myself to instrumental functions of the understanding of man—more specifically, to the demands made on us by the principles articulated in the theories selected.

The most famous requirement in *A Theory of Justice* is the so-called difference principle, according to which "Social and economic inequalities are to be arranged so that they are both (a) to the greatest benefit of the least advantaged, consistent with the just savings principle, and (b) attached to offices and positions open to all under conditions of fair equality of opportunity." Rawls summarizes, "*General Conception*: All social primary goods—liberty and opportunity, income and wealth, and the bases of self-respect—are to be distributed equally unless an unequal distribution of any or all of these goods is to the advantage of the least favored."[14] Without going into qualifications, this arrangement accepts only those inequalities that improve the condition of the least advantaged. When inspecting alternative inequalities, we are obliged to adopt that one—and only that one—that brings the most benefit to the worst off, regardless of how it might affect anyone else for good or ill. An example of this would be to raise the salaries of managers if this increase is necessary to make industry so productive that the poorest people are helped. The raise should go only to that level, and no higher, that will have the best result for the poorest, regardless of whatever advantages or disadvantages might accrue to others.

Such a scheme might be thought to threaten the interests of those persons most endowed with talent, intelligence, and ambition. Great rewards await them, and once possessed they are not graciously relinquished. The gifted or hard working can offer their abilities on the open market and provide them to the highest bidder, whose principal concern might well be the maximization of profits. The bidder might have some other end in view, however, such as the increasing prestige of an educational institution. Such bidders compete strenuously with like bidders, and scholars compete vigorously, sometimes ruthlessly, for the preferred positions. Many a man and many a woman passionately aspire to possess such things, and the passions are not to be taken lightly.

There are many types of individuality: the cautious, the adventurous, and the ambitious; eccentrics, loners, and geniuses of all kinds, those with little moral compunction, the status-hungry, the saintly, and so on. A theory of justice must be concerned with all such types. This is not because they are all equally laudable, but because they all are participants, for better or worse, in common life, contributing or undermining as conditions permit. What sort of institutions and what sort of morale tend to make the most of human potentialities? What sort of conditions discourage high attainment and extraordinary individuals? Rawls is not *wholly* unmindful of these sorts of concerns. In fact, he devotes all of half a paragraph to the condition of those better endowed with talent.

> Now what can be said to the more favored man? To begin with,
> it is clear that the well being of each depends on a scheme of
> social cooperation without which no one could have a satisfactory

life. Secondly, we can ask for the willing cooperation of everyone only if the terms of the scheme are reasonable. The difference principle, then, seems to be a fair basis on which those better endowed, or more fortunate in their social circumstances, could expect others to collaborate with them when some workable arrangement is a necessary condition of the good of all.[15]

Just in these few lines we can identify several improbable assumptions. There are obviously *plural* schemes "of social cooperation without which no one could have a satisfactory life"; so the most-favored are not stuck with the one grounded on the difference principle. And will they think the terms "reasonable"? Suppose they—as well as the less-favored, for that matter—regard desert as a principal measure of justice? Are there alternatives they would regard as more reasonable? Is this the *only* scheme under which they could "expect others to collaborate with them"? Although it is highly desirable that all the varying members of a society feel a stake in perpetuating its basic institutions, is there really *any* social arrangement that works consistently for "the good of all"? Perhaps, though, an economy unconstrained by the difference principle would be far more productive for all; the less gifted might prefer it, even if they were less equal. Could any one of moderate worldliness believe that the talented and ambitious persons who populate the (despised) world would tend to find these blandishments convincing? (This is not to mention, for the moment, whether anyone else would be convinced.)

Rawls is not a student of the world. He regards our soul as almost indefinitely pliable. But there are passionate ends and imperatives of our nature that he doesn't know. His offhand assertions represent the curse of the ivory tower at its zenith.[16] Many thinkers are disgusted and frightened by the various forms of self-seeking exhibited in social life, and no one wants to leave such conduct unchecked, but what might, or should, be done about it is another question. It is greatly interesting that egalitarians acutely conscious of the pervasiveness of such behavior nevertheless suppose that it is readily assuaged by appeals to "reasonableness."

Remarkably, it is not just the most favored who are unlikely to find the difference principle palatable. How would the least advantaged fare under its beneficences? One might assume that, by definition, they would be better off here than under any other conceivable arrangement. Regardless of what they do, the least advantaged are going to be benefitted by all inequalities. Presumably, they don't have to *earn* anything; they don't have to work hard or even show up for work at all. They can walk off the job forever. Just the same, they will get their benefits, supported by the work of others.

With Rawls, the entitlements of this particular class are unprecedented. (Marx, remember, says "*from* each according to his abilities.") Perhaps, just the same, most people would strain to rise above the status of the least advantaged. Experience suggests great caution, however. The difference principle might well create a permanent class of dependent and demoralized persons. It is very difficult willingly to stop accepting something for nothing. If the worst off fall into complete sloth, moreover, the class above them will be deeply resentful and in all likelihood hostile. Will they work less industriously? Perhaps they, too, will walk off the job. Following such a probable outcome, the economy will fall into a coma. Now the worst off are much worse off than they were before, even if they are more equal. As the condition of the worst off worsens, they might start making "unjust" demands: "We don't accept the difference principle. We want still more of what the better off have. We want complete equality!"

The reader might suppose that this scenario is predicated on nothing more than my own curbside assessments of human nature, or perhaps I have made the mistake of mindlessly accepting historical evidence at face value. Perhaps. But recall the empirical studies of justice and desert that were introduced in the preceding chapter. So far as such studies have validity, Rawlsian intuitions about fair distribution begin to look a bit woebegone. (And we have not even considered the reaction of those who are, say, above the mean in the scale of income but whose liabilities exceed their assets even so. They are told that *their* plight is irrelevant. Only the condition of the worst off is taken into account.) There are human demands and aspirations that will defeat his conjectured justice. Real individuals would object to the difference principle, would not voluntarily abide by it, and would have to be coerced to observe it. The coercion would certainly bring about further resistances of various kinds to this "well-ordered" society.

There are various studies of historical experiments and their like, and there are likewise various interpretations of the historical record.

If we take the evidence of worldly events that would be understood by scientific hypotheses, we observe a truly amazing record of human conduct, ranging from the almost unimaginably grisly and hateful to prodigies of virtue and steadfastness. Malice, deceit, treachery, cruelty, and the like are commonplace in every civilization. Individuals and groups are willing to visit unprovoked and unspeakable suffering on others. In conditions of *both* scarcity and plenty, it must be remarked, and in all manner of cultures, human beings are ambitious, petty, adventurous, competitive, domineering, possessive, ferocious, violent, jealous, vengeful, greedy, fearful, cowardly, and suspicious. We are *all* that way, more or less. We are also heroic, kind, steadfast, trusting, loyal, protective, dependable, loving, nurturing, and beneficent. No one disputes the reality of these phenomena, but many try to explain them away. They say that all these traits are the product of either bad or good socialization. We are not *essentially* violent, competitive, and possessive, they say. Such a claim is reminiscent of a favorite philosophical distinction—that between appearance and reality. The hitherto persistent and universal traits of behavior are a form of appearance; they are not really true of us, but are a kind of accident. Well, that surely is true of many variations, but it would take an extremely powerful theory to explain away the persistence of so much appearance. I know of no such theory, but I have cited theories more compatible with the experienced evidence. If Steven Goldberg is somewhere near correct, hierarchical structures could be eradicated only by draining males of their testosterone. Perhaps we *should* take history at face value.

Human beings are clannish: they are strikingly partial to their family, friends, religion, ethnic group, and local associations. When such groups are threatened, all resources are marshalled in their defense, and hostility may know no limit. How vividly this condition has been exemplified in recent years! In spite of more than seven decades of indoctrination, the multiple peoples of the former Soviet bloc persist in fiercely defending their traditional identities.

Being an integral member of a group is an acknowledged good in many ways. One main reason why membership is a good is precisely that, as members, we enjoy various forms of sustenance and defense from our fellows that are not available to outsiders. Without such partiality, the good of community would be greatly diminished.

Just because of group attachments, some of our most conspicuous virtues and vices are inseparable. One wonders whether such traits might wax and wane *because* of our particular partialities. It is plausible: both our virtues and vices might be due in large measure to our *partialities*—to our lack of "rational autonomy." We are protective of the ones we love and care about and are ambitious for them. We are hard working, willing to sacrifice, steadfast in our obligations, and heroic in providing for their security and welfare. Because we are intensely concerned for the unity and flourishing of such associations, we promote intelligence, industry, honesty, responsibility, and justice—both within the associations and more widely on their behalf. It is because of such ties that these virtues prosper. The correlate of this condition is aggressiveness to what threatens the tie or competes with its happiness. Distrust, hostility, deception, and force are deployed against a seeming danger. Natural selection wouldn't have it any other way. We are naturally equipped with the capacities for both virtue and vice. They are nurtured and triggered in various ways, of course; and they are likely to find inappropriate targets.

But the hypothesis, all the same, returns to this: we could not be without our local partialities without being at the same time rid of the very condition of our virtue and our good. Perhaps, in my terms, this is a law of human nature. There have been many communities of great strength and endurance where we find order, hard work, perseverance, sacrifice, and loyalty. Necessarily, the demands made on members are strenuous; obligations are taxing, and they must be continuously maintained against various forms of backsliding and external threat. Could groups survive, much less prosper, if these conditions were absent? In any event, given the facts of experience, it takes quite a theory to maintain that the desirable traits can be produced at will by means of a properly orchestrated process of socialization, and the undesirable traits likewise prevented from occurring.

Let these comments not be taken as an endorsement of multiculturalism, as that term is understood today. I am not saying that all cultures are equal or that communication between them is impossible. I would insist, too, that subcultures within a larger society can and must make concessions to common principles. On the other hand, I contend that there are inevitable tensions between groups. By contrast, people like Mill, Marx, Dewey, and Rawls envision human communities populated by autonomous and fully socialized agents, largely purged of vice, irrationality, and prejudice. These are voluntary associations that individuals enter freely in order to develop, sustain, and share certain values held in common; the whole of life, through all its trials and vicissitudes, would be nourished and protected by such relations. Groups of this sort, moreover, would have amicable and cooperative relations with groups of the same kind. Such thinkers assume that what is valued in such associations need not be confined to their own partisan concerns. Their virtues can be purified, enriched, and extended beyond the narrow confines in which they have hitherto existed.

But it is not clear how far such an extension can go. Actual groups have admittedly not been comprised of the desirably universalistic individuals, and it might well be that precisely the *lack* of enlightenment autonomy sustains such demanding association. It is distressing to expand upon the weaknesses of the flesh, but utopianism is one of the great soporifics of the mind. It is soothing and reassuring to hear Marx speak of "communist society, where . . . society regulates the general production,"[17] all contradictions dissolve, and partiality and oppression come to an end. We might nod agreeably, but what—short of our own wishes or Marx's theory on its own— would convince us of the possibility? In a passage that Dewey went out of his way to praise, Mill speaks eloquently of our social capacities:

> Not only does all strengthening of social ties, and all healthy growth of society, give to each individual a stronger personal interest in practically consulting the welfare of others, it also leads him to identify his *feelings* more and more with their good, or at least with an even greater degree of practical consideration for it. He comes, as though instinctively, to be conscious of himself as a social being who *of course* pays regard to others. The good of others becomes to him a thing naturally and necessarily attended to, like any of the physical conditions of our existence. . . . In an improving state of the human mind, the influences are constantly on the increase which tend to generate in each individual a feeling of unity with all the rest; which, if perfect, would make him never think of, or desire, any beneficial condition for himself in the benefits of which they were not included.[18]

We also nod agreeably at this, and in an obvious sense we should. Not only is this condition genial and desirable, but we have some experience of it. These are relations we ourselves have enjoyed. But to generalize the experience is quite another matter. The question, again, is whether the relations typical of a prized association can be extended equally to everyone—to *all* the rest, as Mill put it—through thick and thin, day in and day out. Can the work and devotion within precious local societies be extended indefinitely beyond their confines? While consideration for others is always a *desideratum,* can it include the efforts and sacrifice made on behalf of established and cherished relationships?

In assessing the capabilities of *Homo sapiens,* it is also well to remember the notorious gap between declared principles and actual behavior. The gap is, often enough, a case of simple hypocrisy. It is disgusting to hear exhortations of high moral principle from individuals and then witness their own underhanded behavior, when it suits their purposes. But the gap is also occasioned by simple lack of self-knowledge. In a heady moment, we may sincerely profess compassionate ideals, and we may live in accordance with them from time to time. But when put in competition with the pressures of local and immediate concerns, they often come out the loser. As the experiments of Stanley Milgram showed, avowed moral scruples give way with dismaying ease under varying experimental conditions.[19] The soaring enthusiasms of Mill and Dewey are unjustified.[20]

I have stressed that we are sometimes capable of great virtue, but such dispositions might be beyond the reach of the (mythical) "autonomous" man. Undeniably, too, there *are* extremely important variations in behavior due to socialization. I have insisted that becoming responsible is a function of social practice, and I have noted the indispensable socializing role of the family. It is essential to ask, however, what the limits of such socialization are. Families turn children into tolerably competent adults. That doesn't mean they—much less any other agency—can do much more than that. There is a kind of myopic logic that says, "There is effective socialization, therefore there can be *unlimited* socialization." Or, "There is great impetus to community, therefore there is great impetus to unlimited and universal community." But this is no logic at all. (For that matter, would there be anything interesting or fun in communities comprised of autonomous and universalistic agents? Would the joy and vitality, the camaraderie and devotion, survive?)

We still have much to learn about these processes, and the way will be rife with honest controversy. Our ignorance is such that it is premature to judge with confidence precisely what our prospects might be. As we proceed from one feature of behavior to another, we will find that some are more and others are less amenable to education. How are changes in, say, rationality and virtue achieved or corrupted? Are such changes more or less permanent, or do they tend to require continued incentive to prevent the recurrence of irrationality and selfishness? What are the variations in genetic endowment? Are we quite uniform in this, or are some groups different from others in say, courage, aggression, intelligence, cooperativeness, or educability?

There *are* individual and cultural differences, and we might find the means to understand and control them. Control, one hopes, will be subject to intelligent moral constraints. There is a sense, I suppose, in which a human being *is* indefinitely malleable. Given the resources, it might be possible to condition an entire population to go about on all fours, noses to the ground; but the result is in no way desirable. We want to learn under what conditions our vices tend to languish, but we don't want to mutilate human nature at the same time.

The public policy implications of these questions are of intense concern. If philosophers are to contribute effectively to public discourse and the moral life, they must engage such questions. It is not that moral prescriptions are deducible from claims about human nature, but we cannot formulate a respectable moral philosophy heedless of the ends, imperatives, constraints, and resources of the human condition. We can't have everything that we want. The moral life will have sacrifice and tragedy. But if we have the welfare of the race at heart, it is essential to know what the social arrangements might be that tend to conduce to this end. Lacking such information, our moral prescriptions are fantasy or imposture.

I have been contending that with such scientific and historical knowledge as we now possess we have strong reason to be wary of egalitarian and universalistic pretensions, even in the qualified form in which they appear in Rawls. We are flooded with a variety of moral theories that are impotent due either to inattention to vital characteristics of human conduct or to uncritical acceptance of the idea that all behavior is socially determined. An example of the latter is Kai Nielsen's *Equality and Liberty: A Defense of Radical Egalitarian-*

ism.[21] In a discussion very well argued in its own terms, Nielsen defends a view quite similar to that which he has held hitherto: Marxism. In this radical defense, with its characteristic littany of demands and complaints,[22] there is frequent allusion to the question of the feasibility of instituting and maintaining such a program; the question also receives some systematic recognition—of sorts.[23] In this regard, Nielsen has nothing to add to what was written by Marx himself more than a century ago. Blindness to the injustices and incapacities of the liberal regime is attributed to capitalistic socialization. Somehow the working class (and eventually everyone else) must be made to see through the lies and distortions of the "consciousness industry," and then a "vast majority" will "see fit to set about the construction of a genuinely egalitarian society."[24] There will be a concomitant revolution in the conditions of socialization: this community will satisfy, without deprivation, the emotional, moral, and material needs of its citizens. Remarkably, this particular version of the socialization theory is simply asserted, without evidence or argument! Yet without a sustained scientific defense of it, the book collapses into revery.

Like Rawls, Nielsen believes the justification of this system can be made today on the basis of a theory of rational choice. A more intriguing specimen of unsubstantiated moralizing is Michael Walzer's *Spheres of Justice,*[25] which disavows any recourse to such strategems. Walzer insists that moral criticism can be lodged nowhere else than in the values already resident in some form in a community. His argument, he says, "begins from our understanding—I mean our actual, concrete, positive, and particular understanding—of the various social goods."[26] (All goods for Walzer appear to be social goods. He identifies no nonsocial goods.) Political judgment sets out from "shared understandings" or "common understandings" and seeks to identify the "inner logic" or "social and moral logic" implied in them.[27] From an intitial understanding of the values of community implicitly shared in our culture, he goes on to assert in broad strokes what justice would be in the variously distinguished spheres of our common life.

There is something at least unwittingly insidious about Walzer's arguments. It turns out that the "inner logic" of the values of Americans leads inexorably to strong socialistic commitments. That is, he implies, Americans are implicitly socialists of sorts; it would be no more than an affirmation of their values to institute appropriate measures. Although the details remain to be worked out, the summation of the basic principles has a familiar ring: "From each according to his ability (or his resources); to each according to his socially recognized needs. This I think is the deepest meaning of the social contract. It only remains to work out the details—but in everyday life, the details are everything."[28] (With principles like this, it is excruciating to read "the details are everything." There are very few surprises in his own attentions to egalitarian detail, and they are deeply problematic. He foresees, for example, a sort of *corvée* labor to do the community's "dirty work.")

There are very few avowed socialists in the United States; Americans tend to think of themselves as moderate to conservative. They will no doubt be surprised to learn that they are "really" committed to a variant of socialism, and it is exceedingly doubtful that Walzer's arguments can convince them that they are. In effect, this argument has more recourse to mysterious intuitions than Walzer would like to think, but the objection that I want to make about his procedure is of a different sort.

However conjectural it might be, reflection about the "inner logic" of our values can sometimes be salutary. It might be of help in *diagnosing* current ailments or in *prognostications* about our fortunes. We might learn how incoherent values lead to incompatible demands for policy, or we might make estimates as to the particular ends toward which the state of our soul might be tending. As *prescriptive*, however, reflections on the "logic" of our values are highly suspect. Indeed, such logic is neither inductive nor deductive, and our present array of commitments might tend in many and disparate leftward and rightward directions. Surely if such tendencies are to have any rational direction, they must be informed with, among other things, some reliable hypotheses about human nature. Walzer, however, embarks on no such inquiries. His treatment of community is typical. Like many other writers, he uses it as a solving word, attributing a host of lovely characteristics to it. But he shows no recognition that communities might have their very strength and cohesiveness in their very partisanship. In any operational sense of community, it is highly problematical to suppose that the United States could be a community. If a community is a place of sustained loyalty, sacrifice, and hard work on behalf of all its members, then I am highly skeptical that any entity as large as the United States could be a community, except in exceptional circumstances. I might be mistaken, of course, but Walzer has not even ventured upon the inquiries that might convince me otherwise.[29]

As any reader of contemporary moral philosophy knows, the list of examples could be extended indefinitely. Nozick's *Anarchy, State, and Utopia* prescribes a libertarian ideal predicated on the mere postulate of certain absolute rights. There is no reference in this work to any imperatives or needs of human nature, or in the determination of what these rights are. Gauthier's *Morals by Agreement*,[30] like Gewirth's *Reason and Morality,* is predicated on a conception of ideal rational agency that is prescriptive for the moral creatures of nature and history that we contingently happen to be, and these contingencies are given no authority. How, then, do we know whether these prescriptions will be of service to the actual demands of the moral life? I have commented elsewhere, as a further example, that utilitarianism, in principle, makes impossible demands on human nature in requiring that we be impartial between the interests of those we love and those we don't even know.

The last demand has been given intelligent and conscientious study by Robert E. Goodin in his *Protecting the Vulnerable.*[31] He acknowledges that there are many occasions when we are obliged to attend to the interests of family, friends, or countrymen ahead of those of anonymous persons; but the justification for such attentions does not lie in *special* obligations that we have to the former. It lies in a *universal* obligation to protect the vulnerable. The application of the universal principle to actual cases depends upon the nature of the vulnerability: a particular person or group is *especially* vulnerable in relation to the actions of another particular person or group. In actual cases, the specification of these relations determines just who is responsible to whom. It is morally right, then, to be especially protective of your own child because the child's interests are particularly vulnerable to your conduct. The extent of your responsibility is a function of the extent of your actual power to affect the child's interests. The simple fact that it is *your* child has no bearing on the matter. We could determine specific duties to protect the vulnerable without making reference to marriage, kinship groups, friendships, social bonds, and geographical boundaries. Those relations, as such, are *morally* incidental. It is a morally incidental fact that children are vulnerable to parents. The practical upshot of Goodin's argument, as he sees it, is that what have hitherto been thought of as special obligations are left somewhat intact, but they are significantly qualified, too, by the obligation to enter into more extensive redistributivist policies, both nationally and internationally.

I admire Goodin's erudite study and perceptive distinctions, and I can hardly quarrel with making vulnerability a criterion for the determination of many duties. I have misgivings, however. It is not clear that the obligations as he specifies them can or should be met in many instances. In an important way, the human element has been left out of his equation. In the terms in which I earlier discussed the matter, it might well be that prejudicial loyalties are imperatives, or "laws," of human nature. Love, friendship, family, social bonding, have great need and force in their very constitution; such forces are not easily set aside. The moral life demands that we do set them aside to some degree. But a presumptively moral demand for such denial can become so great that it cannot be respected. If such a demand is enforced, it will at some point result in petty or gross resistances and violations, cheating, disruptive behavior, hypocrisy, or the venting of hostility on innocent and unsuspecting people. As demands become intolerable, individuals become demoralized; they fall into dissolute and destructive habits, or they break the law. The "moral" system has long since failed of its purpose and has created conflict and unhappiness instead.

Again, I don't know what the appropriate limits are, but this vital issue has no part in Goodin's treatment. He speaks characteristically of moral intuitions, which to my mind are no more than moral sentiments. If analysis of our responsibilities is to have effective application in the moral life, it would be eminently helpful to give our provisional moral judgments a functional interpretation. Instead of chasing after free-floating, disembodied intuitions, we should be thinking about forms of action that are derivative of the real demands, resources, and constraints of common life: we would regard our judgments as implying verifiable predictions about future conduct.

Much of Goodin's argument is directed against philosophies that would defend special obligations by means of *contracts* or *self-assumed* obligations. He finds that all of them fail. Symptomatic of the dilute and abstract character of moral theorizing, few of the arguments with which he contends have anything to say about human nature, about the mighty bonds and imperatives that constitute so much of life. They are concerned only with contracts and conventions. None is criticized for this lack.[32]

Anthropologies without Philosophy: The Tendency to Reduction

I have been itemizing the severe disabilities incurred by moral philosophies that in one way or another disregard human nature. I do not mean to contend, on the other hand, that human nature is our *exclusive* concern. It is a vital part of the moral condition, but not all of it. To put this concern in some context, consider a treatise that tends to the opposite of those with which I have been contending, written by an economist, not a philosopher. It attributes all our basic moral convictions to assumptions about human nature. It is that of Thomas Sowell, a thinker of courage and intelligence. He maintains in *A Conflict of Visions*[33] that all the critical differences in our moral conceptions are traceable to differences in our conception of man. He contrasts the "constrained" and "unconstrained" visions, noting a continuum between them. The constrained vision, while cognizant of positive human capacities, is deeply sensitive to our limitations. The unconstrained edition, by contrast, embraces the most flattering assumptions. Basing his study on various historical specimens of moral theory, he concludes that our ideas of equality, power, rights, reason, and justice, among others, are determined by our respective visions of human nature—our visions of the powers, needs, strengths, and limitations of the species. Depending on the specific characteristics of your vision, you will tend strongly, for example, in the direction of the moral and political ideologies of communism, fascism, or libertarianism. While defenses of such positions will often be stated in terms, say, of metaphysical principles, *a priori* reasoning, abstract right, deontology, and the like, the correlation of the substantive conclusion with one of these "visions" is remarkably close.

There is great merit in many of his contentions, but they are overdrawn. For at least two reasons, it is premature to say that the determinative values of moral theory are exclusively derivative of a conception of human nature. First, the correlations between the professed anthropology and the theory are not as consistent as Sowell claims. He (correctly) attributes to Dewey, for example, a philosophical anthropology that tends to be of the unconstrained variety. He also states that, according to the unconstrained vision, human rights are conceived and justified apart from their social functions; but this is emphatically not Dewey's view. (Neither is it Mill's, another proponent of an unconstrained vision.) Plato and Aristotle have very similar anthropologies, but there are differences of the greatest magnitude between the *Republic* and the *Politics.* Many persons have accepted a behaviorism much like that of B. F. Skinner, but exceedingly few endorse his moral utopias.

It is instructive to consider some reasons why such differences arise. The differences between Plato and Aristotle are probably due most of all to the fact that Aristotle was a better student of both history and political science. He had great respect for the facts about how actual societies have worked under varying conditions. Aristotle had a superior knowledge of the facts, not a different vision of man. Similar considerations separate behaviorists from Skinner, but they are also separated by differences in moral convictions independent of psychological theory. Even if we believe that men and women are susceptible to almost unlimited conditioning, our respect for persons might cause us to shrink from advocating a program of complete renovation. It is, moreover, a commonplace in some respectable schools of moral theory that responsible thinking about social practices must be qualified by variations in historical conditions. Human nature might remain constant, but its larger settings might not.

Neither should we overlook the fact that some theories are driven by some great hatred or passion, some colossal zeal or crusade for true virtue, some divine mission. It would be too flattering to such postures to credit them with a theory of human nature. Their differences are owing to different manias. Yet many of the more creditable theories are also tinted with some such coloration. It could be said on behalf of Sowell that a responsible vision of human nature is precisely what such theories lack, and there would be substantial merit in that contention. Still, to remedy that deficiency would not be enough.

To some undetermined extent, we also face the problem of what human nature *should* be—a normative question. We still await a verdict regarding just how changeable human potentialities are, but obviously they are subject to socialization in important ways. That is, our nature cannot be thought of as a uniformly unchangeable given. If the possibilities for change are relatively limited, then the choices for change are likewise limited; if they are great, the choices expand.[34] In whatever choice, we would be wise to survey the realities of the moral condition, but an irreducible choice confronts us just the same. The prospects of genetic engineering—both promising and terrifying—add urgency to this question.

In studying the failures of correlation between moral theory and anthropological theory, we may discover the second reason why Sowell's reduction is overdrawn. Aristotle and Plato, I noted, were informed with different *facts*. I also observed that variations in cultural conditions prompt variations in moral conceptions. This is to acknowledge, then, that we must take account of a setting substantially more inclusive than human nature alone. Ultimately, we must take account of the moral condition.

I have adverted to several of the varying conceptions of the moral condition, and they cannot be reduced to anthropology. Consider the massive influence of the most enduring metaphysical theory in Western history: the ordered hierarchy of being, in which every distinctive nature—whatever it is—has its appointed place, determined by the nature of the cosmic order itself. Cartesian dualism also had vast consequence for moral theory, as did Kant's distinction between phenomena and noumena. Hegel's dialectic of history is not reducible to psychology, yet it has had great moral implications. F. H. Bradley's monistic idealism deeply colors his moral convictions, just as James's pluralism colors his. Dewey's conclusions about nature as precarious and stable had a profound effect on his conception of moral intelligence. It seems perverse to deny that our vision of the moral life can be focused on human nature alone.

Theological and metaphysical assumptions are not reducible to anthropology or sociology, yet they typically penetrate our thinking about the assets, possibilities, and limitations of human existence. We attempt to adjust our hopes about human fate to our conceptions of the encompassing order. Our basic orientation to life has a great bearing on our apprehension and securing of a satisfying existence; many subordinate goods will be thereby qualified and our moral conceptions chastened. The concluding chapter of this book will present an extended analysis of the minimal virtues for conducting the moral life. The analysis is predicated upon assumptions about the entire moral condition. I will contend that the possession and exercise of these virtues is of great instrumental value, but I do not suppose that they necessarily constitute personal fulfillment. Regarding their suitability to human nature, I assume only that their demands are not so great that they are beyond the reach of a more or less normal person.

I do not suppose that all such views of the nature of things are warranted. The point is that we can hardly be indifferent to the nature of the inclusive realities, whatever they are. Whatever vision we have of the moral life takes into account, implicitly or explicitly, assumptions about the characteristics of the general frame of things within which we act and suffer. Part of the wisdom of life consists in taking such considerations seriously. We have only a truncated conception of the moral life—its promise, constraints, and instrumentalities—until we take account, in Santayana's words, of "the large facts" of human existence. Our vision of the moral condition is more inclusive than our vision of human nature. In addition to obviously scientific constituents, it includes irreducibly social, historical, normative, and metaphysical dimensions.

I by no means wish to minimize the contention that human nature is a vitally important constituent of the moral condition. What I stress here is that, important as it is, it is not the only variable; humanity's moral ambitions cannot be usefully conceived in a vacuum. Sowell is convincing in displaying a *high* correlation between moral conceptions and visions of human nature; that is a most significant finding. In exhibiting very considerable variations in moral theories, he demonstrates the consummate importance of conscientiously investigating the ways of man. The fact that the correlation is not perfect tells us that there are more inclusive foundations of the moral life.

Sowell's venture is most welcome, and we would hope that philosophers would share in that sort of inquiry—but they haven't. If we seek help in this area, we must look to workers from other schools. I have already cited some pertinent studies, and a further sampling would be instructive. An interesting example is provided by political scientist Robert J. McShea, author of *Morality and Human Nature: A New Route to Ethical Theory*.[35] McShea asserts that basic moral postures can be validated only by our "species nature," or "species-typical feeling pattern,"[36] or yet again, "the deep structure of the human motivational pattern."[37] These patterns are said to be common to us all, and they are determined genetically, regardless of culture.[38] Yet the ambitious announcements create expectations that are not fulfilled. Unhappily, we learn almost nothing of what these alleged "patterns" are. That is, we don't learn what behavior they sponsor; so the project is only programmatic, and we are given no convincing evidence that the patterns are universal and wholly reducible to genetics. It is not explained, moreover, just how we would deploy knowledge of these patterns in moral theory. This is a serious failing. One final point on the negative side: McShea reduces fundamental moral orientations to these patterns alone; the inclusive moral condition is given no account.

McShea's work is an attempt to argue that morality is by nature— a task that demands more sophistication than he seems to realize. The program is commendable, the execution disappointing. Saying only this much, however, does not do justice to the book. Two of its most telling chapters (8 and 9) provide devastating critiques of what he calls culturalism: the thesis that human nature is reducible to socialization. He points out that there must be an antecedently distinctive being upon whom the socialization is conferred. Otherwise, we could literally be socialized into anything. To assert that socialization is all in all is to claim that there is nothing in the object of socialization that would cause the outcome to be one way rather than another—an absurd claim indeed. So long as there are predictable outcomes to human interactions, there must be an antecedent nature. The Marxian posture, for example, that the nature of consciousness is reducible to the agent's relation to the means of production turns out to be self-contradictory. It is only a creature *of a definite sort* of whom it can be predicted that it will behave in specifiable ways under specifiable conditions.

Roger D. Masters, another political scientist, explores some similar pathways in *The Nature of Politics,* which provides a good summary of the pertinent biological research.[39] Admirably resistant to reduction, the work aims for a synthesis of evolutionary biology, social science, and political philosophy. Masters assumes that our biological makeup is resistant to acculturation in important ways. He supports the Aristotelian view that political institutions come into existence in order that people may fulfill a basic repertoire of propensities. Institutions can neither create nor annihilate those propensities, but when social arrangements are uncongenial to our natural endowment, they cause deviant behavior. "Just as a computer can be rendered inoperable by certain contradictory problems, an organism can be seriously disturbed, if not destroyed, when genetic and learned behavioral programs are in radical contradiction."[40] There are, then, discoverable imperatives of human nature; much deviance and social conflict is attributable to incoherences between these imperatives and imposed forms of conduct. Regrettably, Masters provides very little here in the way of example, so his hypothesis is not well verified. There is, however, a suggestive discussion of how it has happened that life in the modern state can be "consistent with the needs of humans formerly living in less centralized communities."[41] His chapter 7, "The Biology of Social Participation," urges that of all modern political forms, democratic institutions best suit our biological inheritance.

The Nature of Politics is admittedly programmatic, but it is not altogether clear about how the proposed synthesis might be used to determine moral and political principles. Masters assumes that the linchpin of the project would be the effective solution of the is/ought problem. On the contrary: our obsessive concern with the problem effectively obscures the inquiry into the many ways in which our knowledge of human nature might be put to good account in the moral life. The analysis of human nature and democracy, for example, will not yield a cognitive claim to the effect that we ought to be democratic. Yet it would be the height of impertinence in actual problematic situations, where human fate is at issue, to deny that the welfare of human nature need be taken into account. Admit that advocacies for political systems are determined in part by assumptions about their suitability to our nature; then we may be justly contemptuous of an argument to the effect, say, that the differences between fascism and democracy are morally arbitrary.

The marshalling of scientific knowledge with moral pertinence is explicit in the work of still another political scientist, Charles Murray. I am thinking not only of his important work, *Losing Ground,* which documents some major failures of welfare systems,[42] but also of *In Pursuit of Happiness and Good Government,* which utilizes current research in psychology to great effect in discussing the good of human nature.[43] *Losing Ground* is full of graphs and charts correlating variations in welfare programs with variations in social distresses.

The most important of Murray's theses regarding the welfare state is that government interventions into community and family life have the effect of undermining the natural human mechanisms for contending with social pathologies. By means of government action, we wish to remedy such ills as illegitimacy, educational failure, occupational failure, and crime. But government programs rescue individuals from the consequences of their acts; so the designated populations do not develop and exercise the normal responses to their problems. A family with a dependent unmarried daughter, for example, does not readily tolerate being responsible for any children she might have, thus posing powerful resistances to illegitimacy. Murray contends that government policies, by contrast, have the effect of facilitating illegitimacy (as well as other ills). He does not put his inquiries in the context of conceiving morality according to nature. Instead, he is concerned to identify truly efficacious means for contending with various social problems. In this ambition he has, in effect, appealed to nature.

Thomas Fleming, a classicist by training, investigates a number of pressing moral issues in his *The Politics of Human Nature*.[44] Deploying extensive historical knowledge, research in the behavioral sciences, and evolutionary biology, Fleming offers sometimes compelling evidence that human beings are most apt to flourish when the nuclear family enjoys considerably more autonomy and responsibility than it does at present. He likewise makes a strong defense of the federal system in politics.

Fleming presents himself as an Aristotelian and wants to hold, very much after the manner of Aristotle himself, that morality is by nature. But Fleming does not observe that Aristotle had a complacent view of nature. Assuming, with Plato, that existences in their true nature are always good and mutually harmonious, Aristotle could dismiss the wicked and conflicting as not truly by nature. He could also take the traits he judged best—such as the virtues—and declare them to be our true nature. An Aristotelian analysis today would have to be much more discerning and tentative, and it would have to confess that what is by nature is not necessarily good. As Murray contends, however, many of the effective responses to hurtful indulgence of our natural impulses occur as a natural corrective. The vital forces characteristic of real communities are the best natural resource for contending with "social" problems.

234	Rediscovering the Moral Life

It is plausible, too, that many happy arrangements in human life are by convention. Even so, there are vital imperatives, consummations, and restraints intrinsic to mortal life in its own nature; if we neglect to investigate them, or scoff at them, we put life in needless peril.

Morality by Nature: A Necessary Constituent of Moral Philosophy

Inescapably, the moral life is lived on a slope with footing that is sometimes uneasy, but it is most unlikely that the slope is as steep or as slippery as many would like to suppose. The moral condition, including the nature of its inhabitants, has its characteristic constraints and goods. If we are students of our condition, we will attain to some order and wisdom, but we will never suppose that we will put an end to perplexity, tragedy, and conflict.

It is important to seek the truth about human nature. Acceptance of the assumption that moral behavior is nothing but the product of socialization is both complacent and dangerous. We already have plentiful evidence to discredit various egalitarian ambitions. This is the evidence of both experience and scientific research. The interests and needs of human beings necessarily exist in priorities. We are interested in the welfare of family, friends, colleagues and comrades, our immediate community, our country. We are also, in many cases, interested in the welfare of starving Somalians and oppressed Yugoslavians. But we cannot be interested in the fate of all these people equally. If we had the same concern for Somalian children as for our own, we would quickly be driven mad with despair and suffering. If our child has a life-threatening illness, we are beside ourself with anxiety and distress; all other concerns are for the time cast aside. We cannot replicate this experience for all children whose lives are threatened. There appear to be powerful forces rooted in our nature that go far toward determining what the order of our priorities tends to be. These forces are at once conditions of some of our most intensely precious experience and of our moral limitations. Whether sponsored by a moral philosophy or not, a social system that requires continued sacrifice of our greater interests to our lesser ones is certainly headed for disaster.

If "community" be defined operationally to refer to those relationships within which we will over time be steadfast, helpful, cooperative, and willing, as the demand arises, to subordinate our immediate interests to those of the group, then large populations cannot be communities, except in times of emergency. Even in strong, enduring communities there is recurrent resistance to fulfilling obligations, and the solidarity of the group is frequently under stress. How much more difficult is it to sustain such relations in large, anonymous groupings? We do not find, however, that communities are threatened by the condition in which inequalities are perceived to be proportionate to contributions and responsibilities. Indeed, it is the egalitarian community that readily dissolves. Among other things, a moral system requires that we do show concern for anonymous persons, but there are powerful limitations in the human capacity to carry on unreciprocated beneficences indefinitely.

I have indicated ways in which knowledge of human nature can be incorporated into the formulation of our advocacies of how we ought to live, and I have insisted that a philosophy failing to take heed of such concerns must be an arid and unconvincing affair. Worse, if it *is* convincing, that is due to the sentimental appeal of intuition—unenlightened and unchastened by the hard or alluring realities of life experience. Even though the morals industry is thriving inside the academy, it should not be surprising that its numberless products barely seep outside the boundaries of professors' libraries. Surely its innocence of the realities of the moral condition has something to do with that.

Whether by way of concocting theoretical critiques or of moral exhibitionism, professed moral idealism is cheap. Anyone can denounce the regime, or march in a demonstration, and remain nonetheless self-indulgent. Idealistic moral sacrifice, however, is dear. We rightly revere it, but we should recognize that it is a limited commodity; in its extremes it occurs only in special circumstances, and not everyone is equally responsible to exercise it. Fortunately, given the right conditions, human beings can do quite well for themselves. Acknowledgment of limitations in human charity needn't be a counsel of despair. We have many highly serviceable resources, and the demand for universalistic moral heroism can be exaggerated. Neither is the demise of the idea of rational, autonomous man to be lamented. As I have suggested, much of the real good of life is found in traditional, partial, and natural associations, which persevere only because of their internal goods and obligations.

The last thing I wish to defend is heartlessness. I am defending a scarce resource, realism, wherever it might lead. Without it, there is no way to investigate and realize our best possibilities. Reality is sobering. Many moralists are already so ideologically committed that they are impervious to experience uncongenial to their doctrines. They wander the domains of morality like a veritable Dr. Pangloss. There are further ways in which they tend to neglect reality than have been pointed to so far. The next chapter will consider some of them.

Notes

1. An excellent book has opened up this topic somewhat. The author does not address quite the same concerns that I do in this chapter, but, like myself, he regrets the inattention to human nature in current moral thought. See Christopher J. Berry, *Human Nature* (Atlantic Highlands, N.J.: Humanities Press International, Inc., 1986).

2. Dewey, *The Public and Its Problems,* in *Later Works,* Vol. 2, p. 369.

3. Robert H. Frank, *Passions within Reason: The Strategic Role of the Emotions* (New York: Norton, 1988).

4. Steven Goldberg, *The Inevitability of Patriarchy* (New York: William Morrow & Company, Inc., 1973/74). Goldberg concludes that male dominance is attributable primarily to differences in the hormonal systems between males and females. If the intellectual environment had not already burst aflame, it would not be necessary to repeat the obvious: (1) Sexual differences, so far as they exist, represent statistical variations, and these variations are attributable in part to socialization. (2) They have no bearing on the right to equality of opportunity or equality of respect. (3) There are extremely valuable traits possessed more by women than men. (4) Women have in fact suffered widespread adverse discrimination solely on account of their sex.

5. The nature and existence of human universals has been carefully studied by Donald E. Brown in *Human Universals* (Philadelphia: Temple University Press, 1991.) While Brown is confident that there are many important universals, he does not inquire into their bearings on morals and politics.

6. For a statement of the main thesis and a sampling of references, see R. J. Herrnstein, "Lost and Found: One Self," *Ethics* 98, no. 3 (April 1988): 566–78.

7. Daniel C. Dennett, *Elbow Room* (Cambridge, Mass.: MIT Press, 1984).

8. See chapters 3 and 4 of my *Excellence in Public Discourse* for an analysis of Mill's philosophical anthropology.

9. For example, the state of the art study of crime by James Q. Wilson and Richard J. Herrnstein investigates a staggering number of variables in the incidence of crime. While the authors present confident conclusions on many issues, on many others they are admittedly more tentative, and on others they are undecided. (*Crime and Human Nature* [New York: Simon and Schuster, 1985].)

10. *Newsday*, Sunday, November 13, 1988. The principles at stake in this academic horror story are of the greatest consequence, yet the scandal was not even reported by the newspaper that covers "all the news that's fit to print."

11. The long arm of the moral censor *does* reach into the classroom, of course, and beyond, with increasing frequency. The spread of speech codes to enforce political correctness in universities, for example, has become epidemic. Academic freedom is fragile at best, and it will not endure under such intrusions. The desire to sanitize all language in the classroom will be fatal to good and honest teaching. It also provides a lethal weapon for any student or teacher with an ideological axe to grind. Numerous instances of intrusions into academic freedom and excellence have become widely cited in the media and in such books as *Illiberal Education*, by Dinesh D'Souza (New York: The Free Press, 1991) and *The Hollow Men*, by Charles J. Sykes (Washington, D.C.: Regnery Gateway, 1990). The journal *Academic Questions* is an excellent source of well-documented information about the deterioration of American higher education.

12. *Academic Questions* 1, no. 4 (Fall 1988): 35–47.

13. Ibid., p. 39.

14. Rawls, *A Theory of Justice* (Cambridge, Mass.: Harvard University Press, 1971), pp. 302 and 303.

15. Ibid., p. 103.

16. Rawls has the additional argument that to accept the principles of justice is to express our true nature. This fancy will be examined in the next chapter. Here it is enough to comment that his conception of our "true" nature is not predicated upon any empirical studies.

17. Marx, *The German Ideology*, in *The Marx-Engels Reader*, 2d ed., edited by Robert C. Tucker (W. W. Norton & Company, Inc., 1978), p. 160.

18. John Stuart Mill, *Utilitarianism* (New York: The Liberal Arts Press, 1957), pp. 41–42.

19. Stanley Milgram, *Obedience to Authority* (New York: Harper and Row, 1974).

20. A recent account by a distinguished biologist, so far as it is correct, is enough by itself to dash the hopes of all but the most committed utopians. See Richard D. Alexander, *The Biology of Moral Systems* (New York: Aldine De Gruyter, 1987). But Alexander's study requires substantial rethinking in light of Frank's *Passions within Reason.*

21. Kai Nielsen, *Equality and Liberty: A Defense of Radical Egalitarianism* (Totowa, N.J.: Rowman and Allanheld, 1985).

22. To quote without comment: "I do not think that at this historical stage capitalism benefits the most disadvantaged. Indeed, I think it is plain that it does not. In fact I would go beyond that and argue that it hardly can benefit more than 10 percent of the people in societies such as ours. (Ibid., p. 87.)

23. Ibid., pp. 65–67 and chap. 10, esp. p. 224.

24. Ibid., p. 65.

25. Michael Walzer, *Spheres of Justice* (New York: Basic Books, 1983).

26. Ibid., p. 18.

27. Ibid., p. 75.

28. Ibid., p. 91.

29. Walzer's emoting about community pales before that found in *Habits of the Heart,* an ideological tract presented as sociological analysis. The authors of this work presuppose without argument that the United States and indeed the world can become virtually as communal as a kinship group. (Robert N. Bellah, Richard Madsden, William M. Sullivan, Ann Swidler, and Steven M. Tipton [New York: Harper & Row, 1985]).

30. David Gauthier, *Morals by Agreement* (Oxford: Clarendon Press, 1986).

31. Robert E. Goodin, *Protecting the Vulnerable* (Chicago: The University of Chicago Press, 1985).

32. In one way, an exception to this neglect of human nature is Bernard Williams, who has been critical of utilitarianism for its insistence that the claims of utility override the very qualities of human relations that give life meaning and substance. See esp. *Moral Luck* (New York and Cambridge: Cambridge University Press, 1981), chap. 1. Williams's most recent work in ethics, *Ethics and the Limits of Philosophy* (Cambridge, Mass.: Harvard University Press, 1985), contends that the scientific and universalistic ambitions of moral philosophy are in vain. He does not consider alternative ways in which philosophical reflection might contribute to the effective

prosecution of the moral life. He simply concludes that philosophy has very little to say about ethics.

33. Thomas Sowell, *A Conflict of Visions* (New York: William Morrow and Company, Inc., 1987).

34. This issue has been seized upon by Barry Schwartz in his polemic, *The Battle for Human Nature* (New York and London: W. W. Norton & Company, 1986). Schwartz argues that the sciences of evolutionary biology, psychology, and economics, as we know them, are inherently tilted in favor of the assumption that human nature is selfish, uncaring, and intolerant. Hence, in effect, they deny the possibility of much realistic choice between policies. Frank's *Passions within Reason* constitutes a refutation that these sciences are *inherently* tilted. Schwartz believes we have a wide freedom of choice of possible institutions, but the implementation of his preferred choices would in fact diminish our freedoms.

35. Robert J. McShea, *Morality and Human Nature: A New Route to Ethical Theory* (Philadelphia: Temple University Press, 1990).

36. Ibid., p. 76.

37. Ibid., p. 87.

38. Ibid., p. 261.

39. Roger D. Masters, *The Nature of Politics* (New Haven and London: Yale University Press, 1989).

40. Ibid., p. 139.

41. Ibid., p. 112.

42. Charles Murray, *Losing Ground: American Social Policy 1950–1980* (New York: Basic Books, 1984).

43. Charles Murray, *In Pursuit of Happiness and Good Government* (New York: Simon and Schuster, 1988).

44. Thomas Fleming, *The Politics of Human Nature* (New Brunswick, N.J.: Transaction Books, 1988).

7

Prejudicial Simplifications
of the Moral Condition

Reductive analysis has been a plague in modern philosophy. At least since the time of Descartes, philosophers have delivered themselves of theoretical conceptions about nature and experience, offering up these abstractions as full and true characterizations of reality. So, they have said, nature is nothing but matter in motion, or perhaps it is a mass of unrelated particulars—or, possibly, nothing but a rational order of ideas. Experience, philosophers had us believe, consists only of discrete, unrelated, altogether passive bits and pieces, none of which can have any significance whatsoever. Acceptance of such an account has led many to assert that experience is mere appearance. Given the premise, it was a logical conclusion. But in order to accept such abstractions, we are forced to deny the reality of ordinary life. Philosophy, accordingly, has often obscured, rather than enlightened, matters of deepest concern.

The tendency to reduction has been prominent in many fields of philosophy, and moral philosophy has been no exception. Moral experience has typically been bleached and fractured at the hands of philosophers, with highly adverse consequences. The emotivist analyses, for example, fell far short of indicating the sort of experience that is actually expressed in moral discourse or of suggesting its resources for the moral life.

In preceding chapters I have remarked on other ways in which philosopers have obscured the salient characteristics of moral experience, such as the reduction of all moral value to utility. Another prejudicial simplification is to take one phase of moral experience and declare it to be the exclusively relevant phase—as in the assumption that the moral value of an event can be determined independently of its continuities with other events. One of the most prominent examples of oversimplified thinking occurs in *moral rationalism*. This mode of thought, in moral theory as elsewhere, aims at the formulation of virtually self-contained systems of ideas. In moral theory, it proceeds by isolating one or a few moral values and declaring them to be exclusively relevant to moral decision. In doing so, it rejects much that is of consequence in the moral life.

I will not summarize the many ways of thought that willfully, naively, or even conscientiously (but effectively) misrepresent moral reality. I will concentrate on rationalism and transcendental philosophy, and give just passing reference to a subtle form of irrationalism. Irrationalism, in its great variety of forms, usually makes a different appeal, but it, too, is steadfastly oblivious to characteristics of humankind and the world, both of which we ignore at the price of crippling the possibilities of our precarious span of years. Each of these philosophies perpetrates its unwarranted simplifications of the moral condition.

Kant: The Archetypal Moral Rationalist

On the face of it, the moral life is complex and diverse, often deeply problematic. It is rife with conflict and uncertainty. Many of us, perhaps most of us, would like to eliminate what is vexing and tragic in moral experience. No doubt it is possible to achieve such a simplification to some extent. Moral rationalists pursue this aim to a fault. In order to construct a rational system, they must—wittingly or not—introduce drastically simplifying assumptions. Thus they produce a neat universe of ideas that can succeed only at the expense of sacrificing many precious moral values. They do so needlessly, and to our detriment. Even worse, moral rationalists do not regard their system as a prejudicial simplification. Indeed, they declare that they have given us the final and absolute truth about things just and unjust. Kant is the greatest exemplar, but I will give only summary attention to him. My principle aim here is to analyze some characteristics of the work of John Rawls.[1] Even in this I am constrained to be more hurried than the subject deserves, but I intend at least to suggest some of the serious difficulties attending this form of reductive philosophy.

Kant is the author of the much-revered lines, "Now, I say, man and, in general, every rational being exists as an end in himself and not merely as a means to be arbitrarily used by this or that will."[2] In the following sentences he asserts that man necessarily thinks of his existence as an end in itself, and concludes, "The practical imperative, therefore, is the following: Act so that you treat humanity, whether in your own person or in that of another, always as an end and never as a means only."[3] In the quoted lines, Kant refers to "man" and "humanity." Humanity has absolute worth. This is edifying. But what does it mean?

At the outset of *Foundations of the Metaphysics of Morals* he presents the all-important distinction between laws of nature and laws of freedom. Morals proper, he insists, are concerned only with the latter; it is an exclusively rational and *a priori* discipline:

> Is it not of the utmost necessity to construct a pure moral philosophy which is completely freed from everything which may be only empirical and thus belong to anthropology? . . . [One] must concede that the ground of obligation here must not be sought in the nature of man or in the circumstances in which he is placed, but sought a priori solely in the concepts of pure reason. . . .
>
> Thus not only are moral laws together with their principles essentially different from all practical knowledge in which there is anything empirical, but all moral philosophy rests solely on its pure part. Applied to man, it borrows nothing from knowledge of him (anthropology) but gives him, as a rational being, a priori laws.[4]

Why is it of "utmost necessity" to be *a priori*? The key to Kant's moral philosophy is found neither in the *Foundations* nor in the Second *Critique*. It is in *The Critique of Pure Reason,* specifically in the division of all beings into phenomena and noumena and the antinomies of pure reason. The distinction is that between nature, including human nature, and things in themselves, including the noumenal self. The latter, which alone possesses the possibility of freedom of the will, includes rational nature. In the third antinomy,

Kant reasserts that the phenomenal world, as such, is wholly determined by causal law; hence it is devoid of moral quality. Unconditioned freedom is a necessary condition of an act being distinctively moral, and such autonomy is possible only in the noumenal realm. On these terms, the sentences quoted just above become intelligible: our phenomenal nature—the domain of "anthropology"—must be devoid of moral quality. He likewise insists that a moral law must express universality and necessity. It must apply to *all* rational beings, and it must be unconditional: no ifs, ands, buts or maybes—no excuses, no qualifications. A moral imperative cannot be derivative of the contingencies of natural existence. An empirical proposition makes assertions about the contingent phenomena of nature; it is subject to falsification and revision. The moral law must come from pure reason. As a "synthetical a priori practical proposition," it could not express the contingent conditions of appearance, only the conditions of free and rational nature as such, in whatever empirical conditions it appears.

When Kant says "humanity" is an end in itself, he means *rational nature* is an end in itself, as he explicitly declares: "The ground of this principle is: *rational nature* exists as an end in itself."[5] He had said moments earlier, "The inclinations themselves as the sources of needs, however, are so lacking in absolute worth that the universal wish of every rational being must be indeed to free himself completely from them."[6] And from his *Lectures on Ethics*: "Moral laws must never take human weakness into account, but must be enunciated in their perfect holiness, purity and morality, without any regard to man's actual constitution."[7]

Why is rational nature an end in itself? The moral worth of reason has a twofold source: it legislates universal law, and it is subject to that law. "[T]he will of every rational being must always be regarded as legislative, for otherwise it could not be thought of as an end in itself."[8] The worth of the person, then, is derivative of the worth of law, law as such. "All so-called moral interest consists solely in respect for the law."[9]

Man *wants* happiness, to be sure, but on no account could happiness as such be a moral aim. It is the object of inclination, desire, and as such it is a heteronomous end. The imperative that commands happiness is assertorical, not categorical, Kant says.[10] The rational will could not act morally for the sake of a contingent end. The will cannot have moral worth due to services rendered to the inclinations in their own nature. Whenever a maxim to promote happiness is universalizable, however, it is *therefore* a duty to promote it. Universality only as such establishes duty.

Has such love of abstraction ever been equalled? One might object that Kant's elaboration of his position avoids sheer abstraction. Does he not say there are ends valid for every rational being? Does he not say that we ought to treat rational nature as an end in itself? These formulations, however, amount to no more than reasserting, as he himself insists, the original categorical imperative in a new form. There is only one way to treat rational nature as an end in itself, and that is to act always in conformity to the concept of law as such.

In strict fidelity to his assumptions, Kant must be a pure formalist: If a maxim can be logically universalized, then there is no other moral criterion than universalization as such. His philosophy cannot be modified without destroying his own intention. Suppose, for example, we admit contingent ends and obligations into moral consideration, and we assume that some of these ends and obligations are appropriate for human beings and some are not. What we have done is to abandon universality and necessity; we have admitted indeterminacy and variation in the matter of what is befitting a moral being.

Many students of Kant have been critical of such an interpretation, and there is textual evidence that Kant himself at times assumed criteria additional to and even other than sheer universality. His own examples, for instance, are notoriously ambiguous and inconclusive. They evidently seemed perfectly sound to him, however. It might well be that he was so convinced of the intuitions of his own reason that it never occurred to him to put such intuitions to the test he himself prescribed. *Of course* it is in accordance with rational nature, for example, to develop our talents rather than indulge in pleasures. No need to give it a second thought, much less to see if the maxim is formally universalizable!

It is possible to argue for a more "embodied" conception of rational nature in Kant, but only if you can explain away his unqualified insistence on the independence of the moral self from nature. Those who would ascribe a substantive test to Kant's categorical imperative must show how such a test is compatible with the views so meticulously set forth in the First *Critique*.

In retrospect, what are we to make of the statement that *humanity* is to be treated as an end in itself? Taken at face value, it is highly misleading. When Kant says "man," or "person" or "humanity," he actually means *rational being* and nothing else. The concrete person with the specific culture and history, specific fears, aspirations, and loyalties peculiar to himself is not at issue. He is morally irrelevant. This is said again and again by Kant in various ways, but the typical reader seems not fully aware of the import of what he sees. We don't treat a moral person as an end in himself by catering to his particular hopes, needs, and strivings, however earnest they might be. To treat humanity always as an end has no such meaning. The moral law prescribes no end given by inclination. Such ends can be neither free, universal, nor necessary. Rational nature, not human nature, is worthy of respect.

To rule out human nature from moral relevance is certainly a simplifying stroke. It makes the moral condition very tidy indeed. Morally, one acts only in accordance with reason, and the law of reason is in no way contingent upon knowledge of nature.

This simplification is purchased at great expense. Not only are the natural strivings and bonds of human beings consigned to ir-relevance in the moral life, but reason is left with no criterion for determining choice. The categorical imperative commands rational nature to act in accordance with a maxim that can be universal law for all rational beings. Kant evidently failed to realize that a great diversity of maxims can be universalized without contradiction. Which universalized maxim are we to follow? That which serves an end in itself, Kant says. The only end in itself is rational nature in itself, and the only consistent way to treat rational nature as an end in itself is to conform to law as such. The notion of rational nature will not discriminate any particular universalized maxim. Thus we remain helpless—an ironic result for a philosophy intended to be so austere. This is a conceptually elegant and coherent system, yet it fails altogether to have any import. Here is one rational system, at least, that "succeeds" at the expense of actual moral life.

Kant's ethical theory is a classic example of taking certain moral values exclusively and pushing them to their limit. It is a philosophy of, by, and for what is alleged to be rational nature and only that nature. Absolute impartiality, universality, and unconditionality are all-sufficing. Everything historical, cultural, everything individual, distinctive, or idiosyncratic is ruled out of the moral test. There can be no moral conflict or uncertainty, no cases where something valuable or valid can be said for two or more incompatible positions. Moral beings cannot be pulled in two directions, cannot feel the tug of competing moral demands. In principle, there can be no trade-offs, compromises, or adjustments—only total solutions.

What adoration of the eternal and unchanging! The moral condition is more complex, indeterminate, and tragic than Kant supposed. It is also much richer. Hegel, in effect, recognized this right away in holding that each culture has its own moral validity. Nietzsche's reaction was stronger still. He praised what is most individual in humans, and he jeered the idea that all persons will universalize the same maxims—indeed, that they should universalize them at all. Not surprisingly, Kant was not admired as a moralist by Mill, Santayana, or Dewey. He has always had devoted admirers, of course, especially today. Leading current thinkers in moral philosophy are not all explicitly Kantian by any means, and they rarely suppose that Kant's ethics, just as it stands, is successful; but they share a devotion to the Kantian project. They share with him, then, the grievous fault of prejudicial simplification of the moral condition.

Rawls: The Poverty of Rationalism

No treatment of contemporary moral thought can disregard Rawls. Directly inspired by Kant, John Rawls created an industry: interpreting, analyzing, praising, and criticizing *A Theory of Justice* and the handful of articles that accompanied it. Is it possible to say anything fresh about this theory twenty years and millions of words after its birth? I think there is. Both critics and admirers of Rawls, like Rawls himself, are unusually gifted at highly abstract thinking, and they love to indulge their gift. When such theorists get down to their first love, really hard-core thinking, they become engrossed in the intense logic of it all and never find their way out. Accordingly, the attentions lavished upon this particular system have been of a kind: questioning how it fares as a theoretical order of ideas. What logical structures are inherent in the entire edifice, and how do they hang together? No doubt if there is coherence in it all, justice will have been done. Such have been the preoccupations, but precious little attention has been given to the concrete implications of these ideas.[11] What I intend to show is that Rawls's theory, due to its simplifications, overlooks crucial traits of the moral condition and hence would ravage the moral life itself. It is a dangerous philosophy and *mode* of philosophy. Its generally enthusiastic acceptance betrays much about the nature of philosophy and ethics today.

Methodology first, then the principles themselves. The method consists in getting "our" intuitions, or considered judgments, into coherent order. The result is a construction, not a correspondence to an alleged moral reality. The construction is regarded by Rawls to be valid if it consists of an order that we accept in what he calls wide reflective equilibrium.

The first major task of *A Theory of Justice* is to define the ideal conditions of choice. The process is that of ordering our intuitions. With that accomplished, we may determine what principles would be formulated under such circumstances, and these would be the ideal principles. This is a two stage procedure, with the two dialectically related. Our ordinary intuitive judgments give us a provisional characterization of the preferred choice conditions. We then determine what principles would be established in the conditions so described. It might be that the principles in the provisional instance would be somehow unacceptable; they might conflict with at least some of our considered judgments. If such an incompatibility occurs, we might revise one or more of such judgments, or we might revise our conception of the conditions of choice, or both. We might also find that our intuitions about ideal choice conditions are inconsistent with each other, so we must find the consistent set that yields principles acceptable to "our moral sense" in "reflective equilibrium." One might believe, for example, that choice conditions ought to be such that the deliberative process would turn out to favor, in effect, those especially capable of amassing great wealth. (One might favor, that is, choice conditions that would yield strong property rights.) But such implications would conflict with the intuition that justice should negate the advantages of "the natural lottery." Accordingly, we look for a way to conceive the preferred conditions of choice in a way to preclude such inequity. So the dialectic continues. This attempt to refine our various moral judgments revises our provisional intuitions and the conception of choice conditions alike. In the final analysis, the judgments creating the original choice position, that position itself, and the principles derivative of it must be judged together. We finally determine the package that provides the most coherent representation of our considered judgments. On the face of it, this promises to be a Herculean effort to be fair to the many dimensions of moral experience in respect to justice and its cognate relations.

A particular cluster of moral intuitions is crucial to the formation of the original position, and—so it turns out—it survives the entire construction project intact. One of them is the judgment of what constitutes "moral personality"—"the ideal of the person" or "a free and equal moral person." In abbreviated form, such a person is free because his or her judgment is clouded by no historical or natural conditions—a perfectly Kantian conception of the noncontingent rational being. He or she is equal because identical to all the rest in the relevant traits of moral personality. Moral persons possess "the capacity for an effective sense of justice, that is, the capacity to understand, to apply and to act from (and not merely in accordance with) the principles of justice."[12] They also possess a rational conception of the good, and they are conceived to possess "highest order" interests in attaining and exercising these powers. "[A]s the model-conception of a moral person is specified, these interests are supremely regulative as well as effective."[13] A rational conception of the good implies, among other things, that such a good is always subordinate to the requirements of justice. For a moral person, the good is always subordinate to the right.

Another crucial idea is that of a "well-ordered society." It is "a society in which (1) *everyone* accepts and knows that the others accept the same principles of justice, and (2) the basic social institutions generally satisfy and are generally known to satisfy these principles." The citizens' "public sense of justice makes their secure association together possible. Among individuals with disparate aims and purposes a shared conception of justice establishes the bonds of civic friendship; the general desire for justice limits the pursuit of other ends."[14]* Especially noteworthy is the requirement that the principles of justice be unanimously acceptable to the citizens governed by them.

A third moral assumption of consequence is that we "look for a conception of justice that nullifies the accidents of natural endowment

---

*Hereafter, all references to *A Theory of Justice* will be given in parentheses following quotations.

and the contingencies of social circumstance as counters in quest for political and economic advantage . . ." (p. 15). This point might be conceived as an implication of the very notion of a free and equal moral person, but it is well to cite it explicitly. In general, there is an assumption throughout of Kantian impartiality, but it is not self-evident that such moral rigor entails the nullification of natural assets as means to legitimate inequalities.

With such intuitions, Rawls arrives at an elaborate description of the preferred choice conditions. This is what he calls the original position, which yields precisely formulated principles of justice. Its most striking feature is that the agents participating in it are conceived to deliberate behind a "veil of ignorance," as he calls it. The existence of the veil satisfies the demand for perfect Kantian impartiality. It is by definition impossible for anyone to devise or advocate principles that would be to his particular benefit. Not one of the agents behind the veil *has* an individuating identity. Each is conceived as being ignorant of who he or she is. They don't know whether they are rich or poor, smart or dull, talented or incompetent, educated or ignorant, old or young, weak or powerful, passive or active, ambitious or lazy, and so on. They don't know their nationality, sex, race, religion, culture, or historical period. No one has any notion of his own particular good, and no one is encumbered with any antecedently held moral convictions. Neither are they animated with envy or altruism, either of which would also introduce bias into the discernment of principles. Each deliberates without intent to help or hinder anyone, except to help himself, whoever he might turn out to be. Inasmuch as he enjoys not the slightest hint of what that outcome will be, his self-concern is not of a sort that allows him to advantage himself relative to others. Inescapably, then, each actually thinks for everybody in the original position.

Strictly speaking, the occupants of that assembly are not themselves free and equal rational beings. Rather, their nature and circumstances are such that their judgments represent, or model, the considered intuitions of ideally moral persons. This elaborate device gives voice to conceived moral persons under conditions that are "fair and impartial."

Their ignorance would make the denizens of the original position even more incapable of choice than a Kantian rational being. Rawls endows them, however, with some indispensable knowledge: They all know that they want to have access to certain so-called primary goods, the more the better. These are goods, presumably, that any rational person would desire to have, whatever else might be desired; and it is only these goods that are taken into account in the deliberations concerning the rules of their distribution, the rules of justice. "[T]he chief primary goods at the disposition of society are rights and liberties, powers and opportunities, income and wealth," and "the bases of self-respect" (p. 62). These are distinguished, Rawls believes, because they are instrumental to any other goods that anyone might want.

The agents also possess knowledge that would be the envy of any philosopher king. "[T]hey know the general facts about human society. They understand political affairs and the principles of economic theory; they know the basis of social organization and the laws of human psychology" (p. 137). Finally, they are also invested with knowledge of all the main theories of justice hitherto formulated. Significantly, they are *not* endowed with knowledge of history or literature, and, of course, personal experience—even if conveyed anonymously—is excluded.

With this combination of self-ignorance, science, mutual disinterest, theories of justice, and moral innocence, and with an agenda of primary goods, the parties determine principles to which they know they will be subject in the contingent, non-ideal world. The contractors must bear in mind that any implied system will be inhabited by ordinary mortals. Whatever the character of the principles, they must be such that they can be understood and followed in the historical world.

To grasp Rawls's intent, we must be clear that the ignorant/ learned bargainers are not concerned with whether worldly contingent beings, *as such,* would extend their moral approval to a given form of justice. Rather, the concern of the postulated agents is whether the understanding and operation of the principles is *feasible* in the everyday world. Given the feasibility, the moral acceptability of the principles is a function of whether they are suitable to the nature of the bargainers *as* modeling free and equal rational persons. Under these constraints and assumptions, each of the contracting parties projects the likely consequences of alternative systems of justice. Their self-interested but unavoidably impartial reaction to these consequences in the real world, as seen from the vantage of moral personality, determines the ultimate choice of principles.

Whether in defining the original position or in establishing its implications, the ordering of moral intuitions is not determined exclusively by their coherence. As we have just seen, the projection of consequences from behind the veil has recourse to what Rawls usually calls "social theory." His explanation is highly indicative of the bent of his thought:

> [T]he way justice as fairness is set up allows the possibility that, as the general beliefs ascribed to parties in the original position change, the first principles of justice may also change. But I regard this as a mere possibility noted in order to explain the nature of the constructivist view. . . . I distinguished between the roles of the conception of the person and of a theory of human nature, and I remarked that in justice as fairness these are distinct elements and enter at different places. I said that a conception of the [moral] person is a companion moral ideal paired with the ideal of a well-ordered society. A theory of human nature and a view of the requirements of social life tell us whether these ideals are feasible, whether it is possible to realize them under normally favorable conditions of human life. Changes in the theory of human nature or in social theory generally which do not affect the feasibility of the ideals of the person and of a well-ordered society do not affect the agreement of the parties in the original position. *It is hard to imagine realistically any new knowledge that should convince us that these ideals are not feasible,* given what we know about the general nature of the world, as opposed to our particular social and historical circumstances. . . . *Thus such advances in our knowledge of human nature and society as may take place do not affect our moral conception,* but rather may be used to *implement* the application of its first principles of justice and suggest to us institutions and policies better designed to realize them in practice.[15]

Hence, given this (astoundingly complacent) "social theory," Rawls's position is driven essentially by intuitions and their coherence. He does not regard his theory to be in fact liable to serious change. The chastening effect of social knowledge pertains to nothing more than the mere feasibility of principles for human action. Given appropriate educational techniques, a great variety of principles might be feasible in the minimal sense Rawls requires. Yet this is the only empirical limiting condition of the moral quality of his principles.

Incorporating this permissive limitation, the *final* test of a theory of justice is the coherence of our considered judgments in wide reflective equilibrium.*

When I studied *A Theory of Justice,* I kept wondering who "our" refers to—not only the "our" in "our considered judgments," but in "our sense of justice," which the considered judgments are said to describe (pp. 46–48). The reference was far from obvious, and it was never specified. In subsequent articles, Rawls characterized his efforts as an attempt to describe the "latent," "implicit," or "deeply embedded" principles espoused by persons inhabiting constitutional democracies. So, presumably, "our" refers to just such persons. Rawls's theory, then, is an identification, articulation, and systematization of the principles of justice that "we" already hold, or would hold, upon sufficient reflection.

Accordingly, the intuitions allegedly "congenial to . . . [the] deepest tendencies" of our culture are determinative of the substance of the principles. Were such intuitions to undergo change, then the theory would change. Characteristically, however, Rawls always insists that the original position be conceived *in any case* as ahistorical and nonexperimental. The intuition supporting *this* conception seems to be timeless. It also seems to be a timeless intuition that both the method and ultimate test ought to be that of bringing coherence to intuitions. The critical assumption of the ideal of the moral person does not determine the *method* or *structure* of Rawls's theoretical edifice. It is incorporated within the theory *after* he has adopted the elaborate intuitive procedure.

What are the deliberations of the inhabitants of the original position? Their condition is such that everyone will be motivated to ensure that their worst possible outcome in the real world would be as good as possible. Safety first! In our contingent identity, we might be intelligent, talented, vigorous, and comely; but that identity is on the other side of the veil. We also might be solitary, poor, nasty, brutish, and short! So why take a chance? Hence the difference principle. There is also no home for the notion of desert. We deserve, Rawls says, neither the native talents that might carry us to pre-

---

*The state of mind of a fully free and equal rational being, as defined by Rawls.

eminence nor the sometimes happy family and social circumstances that might nurture talent to fruition. Hence also we do not deserve whatever success such endowments might bring us. A just society, then, has no place for distribution according to desert. This reasoning is presented by Rawls without a trace of a suggestion that there is anything problematic about it. "It seems to be one of the fixed points of our considered judgments that no one deserves his place in the distribution of native endowments, any more than one deserves his initial starting place in society." Hence there is "no basis" for permitting the exercise of our abilities in a manner that draws power and wealth to their possessors on the basis of desert (p. 104). The rejection of the notion of desert satisfies the demand that justice nullify the "accidents of natural endowment." Apparently, it is rejected in the original position because persons there have no idea of how "deserving" they might be according to conventional standards. Another case of safety first.

Giving just the conclusions and no more of the argument, these are the principles: Each individual has an equal right to fundamental liberties. Any person's liberty is to be limited only insofar as it infringes on the liberty of others. These liberties include freedom of speech, assembly, thought, and conscience, freedom from arbitrary arrest and seizure, something called freedom of the person, and the right to vote and hold office. Free trade—free enterprise—would not be included in the system of guarantees by the parties to the original contract. (On the other hand, they do not *prohibit* private ownership of productive property. That issue is contingent upon the implementation of the difference principle.) Assuming a society in which the basic material needs of all can be satisfied, liberty is not to be limited for any reason except to secure a larger system of liberty. It is unjust to secure economic plenty at the expense of liberty.

The second principle has two parts: first, social and economic inequalities in the possession of primary goods (except liberties) are justified only when these inequalities have the effect of increasing the supply of these goods for the least advantaged individuals. That is, for example, it would be justified to pay higher salaries to some individuals only if the increase had the effect of improving the condition of the worst-off members of society. Any distribution of primary goods other than liberties is to be established by determining which distribution among the possible alternatives will best serve the condition of the lowest stratum, regardless of the other consequences of the disposition. If it should happen, then, that salaries of $100,000 to a certain group had the effect of affording $10,000 for unskilled workers, while salaries of $11,000 to the first group had the effect of providing $10,500 for the unskilled, then the second arrangement is just, the first unjust. (I use this contrived example in order to make the meaning of the principle clear.) Presumably, the principle holds regardless of the number of persons in each group. It is "better" for ten persons to make $11,000 and one hundred persons to make $10,500 than for one hundred persons to make $100,000 and ten persons $10,000. Your one thought in the original position: "I'd rather make $10,500 than $10,000."

The first part of the second principle is the famous difference principle. The second part prescribes that any inequalities in regard to primary goods must be attendant to offices and positions that are open to everyone, and everyone has fair equality of opportunity to qualify for these offices and positions. The satisfaction of the second part of the principle takes precedence over the first. The least advantaged are not entitled to an improvement in their position if that improvement is contingent upon denying anyone fair equality of opportunity. (Fair equality of opportunity exists when persons of comparable relevant talents are also provided comparable means —primarily education—of competing for their desired stations.)[16] No considerations of general utility determine the principles of justice. Universal liberties are to be sacrificed on no account, and no accumulation of wealth or power on the part of the greatest majority could be offered as justification for even a marginal deprivation of the few.

As conceived by the ideally situated choosers, the principles are predicated not on contingent features of human existence, but on the nature of the "free and equal rational person." The beings in the original position also think of themselves as constituting the principles "once and for all" (p. 12). From the same perspective, the principles establish a "moral geometry," a deductive system; and their requirements are unconditional: "[T]he parties are to choose principles that hold unconditionally whatever the circumstances" (p. 125). Unmistakably, their principles are not experimental; they are not subject to test and revision in the light of experience. All this is consistent. We couldn't change the principles once the veil is swept aside, for then our natural biases would reassert themselves. One of the prime purposes of the veil is to ensure that principles not be tailored to support interests of contingently situated individuals.

The result, then, is justice. It is an arrangement that tends toward equality, but Rawls states his position with greatest eloquence when he speaks in terms of the status of the individual in a just society. "Each person possesses an inviolability founded on justice that even the welfare of society as a whole cannot override. For this reason justice denies that the loss of freedom for some is made right by a greater good shared by others. It does not allow that the sacrifices imposed on a few are outweighed by the larger sum of advantages enjoyed by many. . . . [T]he rights secured by justice are not subject to political bargaining or to the calculus of social interests" (pp. 3–4). And, "The two principles of justice . . . rule out even the tendency to regard men as means to one another's welfare. In the design of the social system we must treat persons solely as ends and not in any way as means" (p. 183). (This is going one better than Kant, who put it that we should not treat humanity as a means *only*.)

What do we make of this remarkable theory, said to express our considered judgments? The first principle of justice, guaranteeing liberties, expresses convictions widely held today in constitutional democracies. A great many people, however, would insist on property rights, and for various reasons—not the least of which are that they cherish the freedom and the cognate freedom of contract. They are convinced that these rights are necessary for high material productivity and are an essential bulwark against tyrannical government. (Much of the basis for such confidence lies in actual historical experience, which is not incorporated into "ideal" choice conditions.) Many would deny, then, that our considered judgments exclude property rights.

Rawls, as we shall see, has a crucial rejoinder to such reservations, and it will be considered in due course. But now we take up another element of justice, the difference principle. Insistence on property rights, as we understand them, would eradicate the difference princple as a requirement of the theory of justice. Quite aside from that concern, the principle in itself is extremely dubious, as I contended in chapter 6. To begin with, it nullifies distribution according to desert. As I argued in chapter 5, desert is an evaluative notion. It specifies a mode of equity that ought, in the judgment of many, to be operative in many forms of exchange. We are inveterate distinguishers of merit, as we must be simply to survive. We don't make such distinctions for the sake of noting them down and forgetting them. We also reward them proportionately to the degree of merit. Ought we, really, to regard the differences between persons as morally impertinent, or are they among the conditions that we must always be cognizant of in our moral reflection? Will human nature permit such differences to be negated from the moral point of view?

Reward according to merit is a relation that we *advocate,* and there is no act of willful obstinacy or ignorance in doing so. Indeed, it may well be an indispensable constituent of justice; and we reject it *in toto* at the price of being highly coercive and inviting demoralization or insurrections, both petty and great. The nullification of desert is by no means, then, "one of the fixed points of our considered judgments."

How might the principle work? As Nozick pointed out so incisively, the principle requires a certain end-state, and deviations from it cannot be tolerated. A rather carefully measured ratio of inequalities-tending-to-equality must be maintained. This arrangement effectively abolishes a vast range of values. It is not merely a more-or-less libertarian view that is threatened by the requirement of maintaining the end-state. Marxists, too, would regard a fixed end-state as tyrannical. The classless society, after all, would have no political instruments. Many philosophies (such as that of Dewey) advocate that social decision be made by a method of free and deliberate choice at the point of decision, rather than by conformity to antecedently fixed principle.

The difference principle would have even more radical effects on the private sector than Nozick recognized. On this formula, the just reward for achievement could not exceed whatever is necessary to improve directly or indirectly the condition of the least advantaged. Increments in reward without such benefits would be unjust. Accordingly, "excessive" wealth could never be accumulated. A person would get only enough differential reward to keep him at a job that benefits the worst off; no further benefit, no further reward. This arrangement would undermine the private sector (if, indeed, it could be called private at all). Much is done in and by means of the private sector in addition to accumulating personal wealth. Much "excessive" wealth is used to create and/or support private organizations that do not exist for profit; e.g., philanthropic foundations, religious institutions, symphony orchestras, recreational facilities, museums, libraries, theaters, and—above all—universities.

As I understand Rawls's position, a just society would have no private educational institutions, since the discretionary wealth that creates and sustains them would not exist.[17] Indeed, any private association that functioned inconsistently with the difference principle would have to be abolished. Many such associations do in fact tend to be inegalitarian, for they are supportive in many ways of their own membership in preference to other groups. Rawls does not flinch at the possibility. In discussing the family (in the context of equal opportunity), he asks,

> Is the family to be abolished then? Taken by itself and given a certain primacy, the idea of equal opportunity inclines in this direction. But within the context of the theory of justice as a whole, there is *much less* urgency to take this course. The acknowledgment of the difference principle redefines the grounds for social inequalities as conceived in the system of liberal equality; and when the principles of fraternity and redress [corollaries of the difference principle] are allowed their appropriate weight, the natural distribution of assets and the contingencies of social circumstances can more easily be accepted. (pp. 511-12; emphasis added)

I intimated in chapter 6 that the difference principle would probably work out badly even for the least advantaged. *Regardless of what they do,* they are the intended beneficiaries of all inequalities. Such an arrangement would very likely be hurtful to them and intolerable to others. There might be increasing sloth and dependence, and increasing rancor on all sides, and very little could be done about it. (Remember, you can't change the rules once the veil of ignorance is removed. The rules are unconditional.) It could very well happen, then, that the attempt to observe the difference principle would be the bain of the underclass.

What further questions can be raised about the implications of the principle? When everything in society is judged exclusively by its effects on the worst off, what might happen to the arts and sciences, the quality of life, and human excellence? Would great individualities emerge? Would there be increased or diminished self-respect? (The family is the cradle of self-respect, but Rawls regards it as a marginal institution. Self-respect may be tied as well to feeling *deserving*.) These are vitally important questions, but no answer awaits in *A Theory of Justice.* What sort of government apparatus would be necessary in order to maintain the end-state? With the effective demise of the private sector, the state would perform many, if not most, of the functions now undertaken by private initiatives; there would be few, if any, independent sources of power and authority counterpoised to the state. It is reasonable to believe that the enforcement of the principle would require regulation that would bring a blush to even the most hardened bureaucrat. Imagine the laws, the controls, the petty tyrannies, the reports, the accounting, the corruption, the costs, the depressed productivity, and, yes, the cries of injustice! It could be a nightmare. One might be prompted to say, "My considered judgments are (a) I'm against the difference principle and (b) I'm against any principle not subject to revision in the light of experience."

Rawls is aware that the principles of justice developed in the original position might be obnoxious to many actual persons; and he could not deny that the principles are at variance with those of many serious philosophers. Classical liberals find him far too egalitarian; socialists find him insufficiently egalitarian; and these are but two of many moral/political configurations. Who knows how many millions of people believe, in contrast to the difference principle, that we *deserve* what our talent and industry will bring us? How many cries of injustice are predicated on the assumption that we are entitled to the product of our labor? It would be difficult to overestimate how much the relationships between persons incorporate relations of desert. Are we simply to discard them out of hand? How many believe that private property and freedom of contract are cornerstones of a free society? We needn't persist in the point that enforcement of the principles of *A Theory of Justice* would violate the actual moral values of numberless individuals.

How can such principles be liberal or just? Rawls has an answer. It is one of noble ancestry: These principles are not really alien to us; they are the principles we ourselves would choose if we were in the initial position. They're not an imposition; they represent our true selves:

[W]e can say that when persons act on these principles they are acting in accordance with principles that they would choose as rational and independent persons in an original position of equality. (p. 252)

[W]hen we knowingly act on the principles of justice in the ordinary course of events, we deliberately assume the limitations of the original position. One reason for doing this, for persons who can do so and want to, is to give expression to one's nature. (p. 253)

[A]cting from such principles . . . is sufficient to express one's choice as that of a free and equal rational being. . . . Thus if a person realizes his true self by expressing it in his actions, and if he desires above all else to realize this self, then he will choose to act from principles that manifest his nature as a free and equal rational being. (p. 255)

On the face of it, at least, this answer is unacceptable. The creatures in the original position—"zombies," as Robert Nisbet has called them—seem to be totally unlike flesh-and-blood human beings. Stripped of all individuating characteristics, they aren't like us at all. We are the diverse, complex, passionate beings of nature and history. We are members of communities, traditional associations, with their varied and profoundly affective legacies. Contingently imbued with a skein of virtues and vices and loyalties, we have deeply cherished moral values and commitments. We are, for better and worse, striving within an existing scheme of ends, rights, and obligations that guarantee certain expectations. We each have "our own bright good," in Santayana's phrase, and we have promises to keep.

Into this scene enter the legislators of justice. They tell us to make a wholesale renunciation of our contingent moralities and to take up the unconditional principles they have fashioned for us. "Whose life *is* this?" one might ask. But we must take up these principles, Rawls says, because we are only acknowledging what we ourselves would adopt under the appropriate conditions. What we really seem to be told, though, is this: "You would choose these principles if you were beings of a much different sort than you are." It is absurd to say that we are "really" like the spectral legislators. We are not they; it is tyrannical to say that they may legislate in our name.

Rawls won't give in to this argument. He can concede the difference between contingent and noncontingent beings, yet insist, as he does, that the latter is our true nature, our true self. In *A Theory of Justice,* deliberately taking up the terminology of Kant, he calls it our "noumenal" self (pp. 255–57). What are we to make of such a claim? What is the evidence for it? What science or inquiry would establish such a hypothesis: psychology, anthropology, history, biology, theology? The assertion that our true nature is what is presupposed and described in the original position would find something less than universal acceptance.

In subsequent essays, Rawls clarified his position.[18] He said the notion of moral personality was really a *normative* and *political* ideal rather than a descriptive account of the self, but he insisted at the same time that the ideal is in fact that which is implicit in the culture of constitutional democracies. Hence, those who do not already hold such an ideal explicitly can be convinced with appropriate reflection and philosophical argument to embrace it—indeed, to recognize that it has been latent within them all along. This claim is put in the most categorical terms, as it must be, in keeping with his companion idea of a well-ordered society. It insists that virtually universal acceptance of the political ideal of moral personality and its implications is implied by the requirement of a well-ordered society.

How did Rawls reach the conclusion that these ideals are implicit in our culture? It would be a formidable task to achieve such discernment, yet he presents no research—*none*—into the culture of any constitutional democracy, whether by way of study of founding documents, customary behavior, history, philosophy, judicial decisions, institutions, literature, or popular thought and culture. The ideal is *his* intuition, and he is blandly confident that it is that of others as well. This is the "defense" of the most crucial assumption within his theory. In fact, he effectively denies his own intuition in his claim that his theory is offered as a replacement for the dominant utilitarian philosophy of our recent tradition. If we have been utilitarians, we could not have been implicit Rawlsian deontologists. (How good a student of American culture is he? Our tradition is in fact heavily dosed with a seemingly odd amalgam of natural rights and pragmatism, with a strong willingness throughout to revise theory in the light of experience. There is little utilitarianism there.)

These posited implicit ideals run up against mighty opposition. We must give up, for example, belief in property rights and freedom of contract, desert, experimentalism, and regard for the values of contingent persons. These beliefs cannot be negated by taking recourse to Rawls's ideal of the free and equal rational person, for precisely that ideal is in question. *It* is to be discarded if it is radically uncongenial to many of our treasured and durable values. These values must be subjected to critical scrutiny, of course, but they are hardly to be cast aside by theoretical fiat.

Consider further the notion of respect for persons. The following statement is significant:

> We see then that the difference principle represents, in effect, an agreement to regard the distribution of natural talents as a common asset and to share in the benefits of this distribution, whatever it turns out to be. (p. 101)

One's talents, in other words, are common property; and their fruits are to be disposed as suits one group alone. Everyone's talents are hostage to the worst off. This, Rawls has us to understand, is to treat persons as ends, not means. It is one thing to make provision for those who need help and can't help themselves. It is quite another to make the improvement of the worst off the exclusive criterion for the proper exercise of human abilities. Yet if one were to protest the implications of the difference principle, Rawls's simplifications permit such objections to be brushed aside. In a sentence that could have been written by Kant, he says, "As we have seen, a certain ideal is embedded in the principles of justice, and the fulfillment of desires incompatible with these principles has no value at all" (pp. 326–27). In much the same vein he declares, "[T]he contract view requires that we move towards just institutions as speedily as the circumstances permit irrespective of existing sentiments" (p. 451). Another forthright claim: "A person's conscience is misguided when he seeks to impose on us conditions that violate the principles to which we would each consent in that [original] position. . . . We are not literally to respect the conscience of an *individual*. Rather, we are to respect him as a *person* and we do this by limiting his actions, when this proves necessary, only as the principles we both acknowledge permit" (pp. 518–19; emphasis added).

For Rawls, the object of respect is not the concrete individual, i.e., people like ourselves with real identities—friends, lovers, strangers, accomplices, antagonists, baseball players, Aunt Ruth, people who live in New York or Beijing and the like—doing what they can. He does not attempt to discriminate between such individuals to determine which are more worthy of respect and which less, but respects only a concocted noncontingent being. The person possessing the "inviolability founded on justice," then, is the free and equal rational being, not your Aunt Ruth. Aunt Ruth may well be violated if she doesn't behave in accordance with the philosophic confection known as the difference principle.

The notion of respect is also critical to the notion of a well-ordered society, which postulates that agreement on principles of justice be unanimous. No one may be subject to principles to which he does not subscribe. Here, majority rule is forbidden. Inasmuch as every creature in the original position is identical to every other, unanimity could hardly be avoided. However, as we might suppose at this point, Rawls believes that unanimity in the original position implies unanimity—or something very close to it—in the workaday world. The requirement of unanimity "enables us to say of the preferred conception of justice that it represents a genuine reconciliation of interests" (p. 142). "[T]his unanimous agreement . . . in *no* way overrides a person's interests as the collective nature of the choice might seem to imply" (p. 257; emphasis added). Are these statements simply harmless? Not really. The requirement of unanimity is in fact a deadly Trojan Horse. Inasmuch as the principles express our putative moral nature, it is entirely appropriate that they and their intrinsic rightness be taught to everyone in society. For an individual in a well-ordered society,

> moral education itself has been regulated by the principles of right and justice to which he would consent in an initial situation in which all have equal representation as moral persons. As we have seen, the moral conception adopted is independent of natural contingencies and accidental social circumstances; and therefore the psychological processes by which his moral sense has been acquired conform to principles that he himself would choose under conditions that he would concede are fair and undistorted by fortune and happenstance.

> Nor can someone in a well-ordered society object to the practices of moral instruction that inculcate a sense of justice. For in agreeing to principles of right the parties in the original position at the same

time consent to the arrangements necessary to make these principles
effective in their conduct. . . . Thus no one's moral convictions are
the result of coercive indoctrination. (pp. 514–15)

Extending the requirement of unanimity to this side of the veil means
that the educational system will guarantee that even here moral
diversity in regard to justice will be reduced to homogeneity. Although
such a program would be regarded by Rawls as teaching each person
to do no more than agree with himself, we can be confident that
success in it would require quite a Ministry of Education. Is no one
aghast at the prospect? Noting that in the original position the deliberations of one will be typical of all, Rawls adds that "the same will
hold for the considered judgments of the citizens of a well-ordered
society effectively regulated by the principles of justice" (p. 263).
Effectively regulated indeed!

   This is a fair example of the philosopher's will to excogitate
a blueprint for a "just" society. Could an act of etiolated reason
revolutionize what time and nature have laboriously wrought? Again,
I have no wish to shield any moral norms or practices from careful
attention. I am objecting to a mode of philosophizing whose effect
is precisely to withhold such attention. Man is not by nature a free
and equal rational being, nor even a liberal. Given the right conditions,
on the other hand, he can more often than not become a tolerably
decent and rational and even democratic sort of person, and he can
become a more or less effective critic of laws and institutions. But
Rawls's blueprint would under no circumstances be accepted in a
free plebiscite.

   Apart from tyrannies and tiny, highly homogeneous societies,
the problem of politics is everywhere to devise means whereby a
plurality of interests can live reasonably well with each other. For
this it is necessary to have a good measure of consensus about justice;
we couldn't carry on without it, and we are incessantly working at
it. But one of the legacies of our history is to recognize that the
consensus is never perfect, absolutely stable, or final; and the attempt
to make it so assures violations of our respect for democratic citizens.
Something of a democratic system of decision is a good means for
reconciliation, but it always embodies compromises, tensions, and
adjustments; dissent is always possible, and remedies of novel sorts
are never ruled out. Our conduct, indeed, must tolerate a certain

amount of *in*coherence. We trade off, for example, a sharp definition of desert for, say, the extension of public education. Freedom and public security are likewise in tension, as are conditions of equal opportunity and the autonomy of the family. Property rights and social benefit clash on occasion. Countless adjustments, great and small, must be made every day. We *accept* tragedy, loss, and controversy as part of political life; the result is precisely that we *are* able to effect a considerable, but never total, reconciliation of the interests of contingently moral persons. One's moral and political orientation is not determined by accepting some coherent set of universal principles, as such. Principles may well guide our experience, but we subscribe to a more-or-less provisional complex of *practices,* which is more or less in disturbance and in need of watchful adjustments. We move toward one complex or another as worldly lessons and searching reflection suggest. Total "reconciliation" requires the thought police.

As I urged in chapter 5, the notion of respect for persons is both very important and highly problematic. One sort of respect may well be prejudicial to another. In order to get any specific principles out of some supposedly ideal choice condition, the postulated choosers must have some determinate nature and constraints. As we have seen, this situation can be—and is—defined in different ways, depending on the contingent beliefs and values of the designer. As the nature of the postulated moral agents varies, so also do their choices vary. Each phantom population determines principles suitable to itself and, hence, prejudicial to others. For all his talk of free and equal rational beings, Rawls has in fact constructed a position that creates a bias in favor of the cautious and timid. His creatures do not attempt to identify with all types of real human beings; they are not equally concerned with all stations in society, much less the mavericks, eccentrics, adventurers, and dissenters. The occupants of the original position are so situated that they are concerned above all with the fate of the least advantaged.

A choice situation can be so conceived that it would be impossible for anyone *in those conditions* to be prejudicial to anyone else *in the same conditions.* But this absence of prejudice pertains only to persons with just those characteristics and constraints. The contrivance of "perfectly impartial" choice conditions is necessarily prejudicial to the principles that would be chosen in different "perfectly impartial" conditions. Stock the pond of the original position according to your predilections and land any fish that you like! Real-life choice conditions, however, are never so simple—especially in constitutional democracies, where we can expect no notion of "perfect impartiality" to be universally accepted.

To conclude with Rawls, I return to the notion of moral intuition. He never explains what the meaning of an intuition is, how its meaning might be articulated, or what historical experiences might have generated it. Intuitions like "You ought to keep your promises" or "Slavery is wrong" in Rawls's rendering are, in effect, no more than expressions of sentiment. (Expressions of our moral nature, he says.) We do not, then, investigate the consequences of honesty or slavery *for moral experience*—for the achievement or destruction of real values in the actual course of life. There does not seem to be even a provisional test in experience for the adequacy of a moral judgment. Yet if we don't know what such intuitions mean, then we don't know what real-world contingencies we are actually contending with. Insofar as these intuitions are said to be typical of a certain population, we are given no indication of what sort of conditions and experiences caused them to be generated and to be revised. As historical fact, the causes had little or nothing to do with the coherence of intuitions as such. They had to do with the effects of *implementing* moral judgments; surely the coherence of their *effects* has been potent in formulating and defending them. We do not desire, after all, that behavior be mindless, uncoordinated, and self-defeating.

The question 'What will happen?' is confined to the matters of generic feasibility and to figuring out what the best outcome would be in terms of the primary goods for the least advantaged. On these questions, Rawls uncritically adopts an extremely dubious "social theory," on the merits of which he perceives no need for experimental test. There is nothing left to do, then, but render intuitions coherent. A moral intuition is neither certified in experience, however broad and humane, nor self-certifying. Certification has another source: the panoply of considered judgments has to be brought into internal consistency. Their coherence *among themselves* is the test, and once the system is established, its principles are treated as unconditional. A lonesome judgment is not self-accrediting, but a gang of them somehow is. Just as Kant had made law as such the supreme criterion, Rawls comes close to so anointing coherence as such. We're still floating on the winds of intuition. Think of it! We are enjoined to live irreversibly according to a particular selection of moral sentiments coherent in and of themselves—sentiments regarding noncontingent beings at that. The consequences of these sentiments for experience are irrelevant.

What we gain, however, is a rational system, the beloved of certain kinds of philosophers. Such a system is achievable only by introducing drastic and prejudicial simplifications. Rawls's thinking excludes all values that are not organic to his particular notion of the moral person or that otherwise fall outside his system. It is the very demand for system that must exclude such values; yet the system itself is demanded not in the nature of things, but only in Rawls's intuitive judgments. In *A Pluralistic Universe,* James half-whimsically, but with great effect, introduced a generic philosophical distinction between the thick and the thin. This is a distinction between ideas that are close to the throbbing realities of lived experience and those abstractions with little if any discernible connection to them. Moral rationalism would be a case of the thin. For that reason, it must be ineffectual. In the nature of things, a society of contingent beings will not live by the rules of noncontingent beings. If we think of moral philosophy as a disciplined attempt to attend to the very conditions of life experience that prompt moral reflection, then we must identify Rawls's theory as a spectacular impertinence.

Rawls is the most famous and influential exemplar of this reductive and prejudicial mode of thought. The many tributes paid to him are testimony to the weakness of philosophers for seemingly self-sufficient systems of ideas. To my knowledge, no philosopher so much as gives passing attention to this simplifying *mode* of thought, as such, to see what its virtues and vices might be; so I have seen fit to give it protracted attention.

We must make moral decisions in any case. We take action while recognizing the weight and merit of convictions other than our own, and we are sometimes painfully aware of uncertainty about our own criteria; so we think of them as open to revision. We might somehow come around to the position of the other fellow, or he to ours. An experimental treatment of moral issues must be to some degree tentative, inconclusive, and controversial. Such a procedure is altogether different from that of the rationalist, who is bent on consigning alternative convictions to oblivion. By introducing simpli-

fying assumptions, the moral rationalist is delivered from the perplexities and torments that attend the moral life. At the same time,
he enjoys the sentimental and intellectual satisfactions of an orderly
and elegant system of ideas. But the product is not *just* a rational
system. The lives of people are being "simplified" in a manner to
cram them into the theoretical order.

The moral condition is more diverse, complex, and uncertain
than rationalists will allow. They try to deny the reality of the moral
condition; they want to reduce it to something much more manageable
than it really is. What begins as an attempt to grasp moral reality
under the aspect of eternity ends as a kind of philosophic tunnel
vision.

Transcendental Communicative Ethics:
The Case of Habermas

We could compile a long list of philosophers who have been neglectful
of the moral condition. Jürgen Habermas would not be the worst
offender. A conscientious, catholic, and polymathic thinker, he is
vitally concerned with the moral life of the contemporary world,
which he has analyzed with the resources of a remarkable variety
of intellectual disciplines. Nevertheless, there are crucial blind spots
in his work. Because of his distinction alone they merit scrutiny.

Habermas has been on a crusade to rescue the very idea of
practical reason. While sharing the general disaffection with the Enlightenment notion of reason, he resists the concomitant disaffection
with the idea of universal norms of rationality, especially moral rationality. Contemporary variations of skepticism are the consequence,
he urges, of the stubborn hold of the assumptions of the Cartesian/
Kantian "philosophy of the subject." The skeptic holds that to abandon
this paradigm, as we must, is to abandon everything. Habermas,
in contrast, turns to and develops a systematically *inter*subjective notion of reason and knowledge. In this he acknowledges his resemblance and indebtedness to American pragmatism, especially Peirce,
Mead, and Dewey. On first inspection, Habermas's theory of communicative action seems to resemble Dewey's theory of social intelligence.

While there is some resemblance, there are also crucial differences,
and these should be remarked. In most ways, truth to tell, Habermas

is closer to Rawls than to Dewey. There is also a transcendental turn in his thought that is foreign to Dewey and unconvincing to boot. This "turn," as well as his similarities to Rawls, betray a flight from moral reality.

Human action predicated on individual reason yields no universally valid norms. To attain the latter, we must appeal to *communicative* action; that is, we must arrive at norms and action by means of free and equal rational discourse. Here we have what evidently amounts to Habermas's operational (but nonetheless stipulative) definition of moral rightness: whatever would be determined by free and equal rational communication. "[T]he basic institutions of the society and the basic political decisions would meet with the unforced agreement of all those involved, if they could participate, as free and equal, in discursive will-formation."[19]

Such discourse implies universal communicative competence, however, and such competence does not yet exist. Communication as we find it is distorted in two inseparable ways. The objective conditions of socialization are themselves distorted—fundamentally due to class conflict—and the subjective condition of individuals thus socialized is likewise distorted—principally because the capitalist class has generated several devices for maintaining its undeserved power. It has exerted the power of private property to keep the working class in a state of subordination. It has produced the welfare state in order to disguise, or at least to make palatable, the essentially unjust nature of capitalist institutions. In addition, it has organized the instruments of education and communication in a way that makes class domination appear to be just. But by its nature, capitalism cannot produce common interests. In reference to the persistently impervious quality of the attachment to private property, Habermas says, "I would explain this unassailability by the systematic restrictions placed on communication."[20]

Undistorted communication, according to Habermas, would take place between autonomous persons. These are individuals who have internalized the notion that morality implies acting in conformity to universal norms and who are motivated to act accordingly. In thinking about 'right,' as distinguished from 'good,' they transcend the limitations of culture. Their ego development, nevertheless, would be such that their personal good is organic to a universal morality. Habermas believes, indeed, that the motivating force of sacred traditions will be surpassed by the appeal of a truly communicative ethic. "The concept of God is transformed (*aufgehoben*) into the concept of a *Logos,* which determines the community of believers and the real life context of a self emancipating society. 'God' becomes the name for a communicative structure that forces men, on pain of a loss of their humanity, to go beyond their accidental, empirical nature to encounter one another *indirectly,* that is, across an objective something [the transcendental structure of intersubjectivity] that they themselves are not."[21]

The generic moral aim of his social thought is "emancipatory." He develops extensive theories about the inseparable processes of social evolution and ego integration. Neither a revolutionary nor a historical determinist, Habermas sees a gradual development of universalistic consciousness in the modern world, in spite of efforts to hinder it, and he is convinced that bourgeois culture is riven with self-disintegrative contradictions. His theories are typically couched in terms of the nature and development of communicative competence, which is obviously something more than the ability to speak, read, and understand a language well.

The communicatively competent are emancipated, autonomous, properly socialized. Such individuals would address their moral and political problems by a process of thorough consultation and inquiry in which their aim would be the realization of interests that can be universally agreed upon. They will seek and find generalizable interests.

> Since all those affected have, in principle, at least the chance to participate in the practical deliberation, the "rationality" of the discursively formed will consists in the fact that the reciprocal behavioral expectations raised to normative status afford validity to a *common* interest ascertained *without deception.* The interest is common because the constraint-free consensus permits only what *all* can want. . . . The discursively formed will may be called "rational" because the formal properties of discourse and of the deliberative situation sufficiently guarantee that a consensus can arise only through appropriately interpreted, *generalizable* interests, by which I mean needs *that can be communicatively shared.*[22]

If such universality cannot be attained, compromise would be permissible, but only if there were an equal balance of power between the compromising parties. "Compromise" effected in consequence of unequal power would not be legitimate in the ideal communication community.

One might wonder what, if anything, obliges us to adopt the norms of communicative competence. Does Habermas simply make an appeal to our good will, moral sentiment, or to welcome consequences? Hardly. He has something presumably more potent in mind: self-contradiction. If I ask why I must accept the norms of the ideal communication community, Habermas replies, "You already have!" The universal and unavoidable ground of these norms is transcendental. That is, they are always and necessarily presupposed every time we speak. We accept them whenever we engage in discourse of any kind.

> The problematic that arises with the introduction of a moral principle is disposed of as soon as one sees that the expectation of discursive redemption of normative validity claims is already contained in the structure of intersubjectivity and makes specially introduced maxims of universalization superfluous. In taking up a practical discourse, we unavoidably suppose an ideal speech situation that, on the strength of its formal properties, allows consensus only through *generalizable* interests. A cognitivist linguistic ethics (*Sprachethik*) has no need of principles. It is based only on fundamental norms of rational speech that we must always presuppose if we discourse at all.[23]

This is the transcendental turn. (Although he frequently deploys the expression, Habermas is worried about using "transcendental," because it is loaded with connotations of the Kantian "philosophy of the subject" that he wishes to avoid. Habermas's is a transcendentalism of the *inter*subjective.)

The "universal and unavoidable" presuppositions of speech are in fact four: (1) The statement is *comprehensible*; it has an intelligible meaning. (2) It is *true*; it can be verified by inquiry. (3) Insofar as it is normative, it is morally *right*. In the sense that it can be "redeemed" in competent discourse, it is universally acceptable. (4) It is made *sincerely*; the conveyer of the statement means what he says.[24] However much we might in fact be liars and obfuscators, our participation in discourse implies our commitment to universal norms. Given the transcendental nature of these norms, "we are not free then to reject or to accept" the normative validity of truly rational discourse.[25]

But observance of the norms is frustrated by devious forms of socialization that conceal class conflict. Discourse is distorted due to power and intimidation. To understand Habermas well, it is essential to understand that in these conditions the judgments of ordinary people (including unemancipated workers) are *not* acceptable; they are permeated with false consciousness. Indeed, the judgment of any person with the incorrect ideology is automatically nullified. Those who have "already successfully completed processes of enlightenment" recognize the "incapacity for dialogue on the part of the strategic opponent," making free and equal discourse "impossible under the given circumstances."[26] The determination of the right thing to do can be accomplished only by those persons who are already emancipated.

The similarity to Rawls's posture is evident. Ideally situated persons—unlike ordinary persons—are alone fit to judge, for themselves as well as for the rest. "An agreement counts as rational, that is, as an expression of a general interest, if it could only have come to pass under the ideal conditions that alone create legitimacy."[27] Since those conditions do not now exist, it is necessary to determine what *would* be chosen if they did exist. "[G]enerality is guaranteed in that the only norms that may claim generality are those on which everyone affected agrees (or would agree) without constraint if they enter into (or were to enter into) a process of discursive will-formation."[28] Habermas explores various strategies for determining what would be determined under the only admissable choice conditions. The reliance is primarily on "simulated" choice conditions. Although their outcomes cannot be identified with certainty, such limitation is not sufficient to "paralyze the determination to take up the struggle against the stabilization of a nature-like [i.e., capitalist] social system *over* the heads of its citizens, that is, at the price of—so be it!— old European human dignity."[29] That is, "over the heads" of the actual populations of bourgeois societies and, in fact, many populations that dearly want to be bourgeois. What dangerous games to play with our lives! "This does not exclude the necessity for compelling norms, since no one can know (today) the degree to which aggressiveness can be curtailed and the voluntary recognition of discursive principles attained."[30]

Unmistakably, Habermas's analysis begs many problematic questions. Not only does he insist that any moral judgment rest upon a formally universal principle, but the content of the judgment must prescribe a policy that is acceptable to all. It prescribes a common interest. Or, if there is compromise, it must take place between agents of equal power. Any valid moral deliberation must be transacted between persons of equal power and autonomy. They must, in the familiar phrase, stand in equal relation to the means of production. In other words, a moral person is *by definition* an emanicpated egalitarian socialist of some description, and the judgments of those who do not satisfy the description are disqualified.

As indicated in chapter 5, the demand for universality in moral prescription must be approached in a guarded fashion. A particular demand might well exceed our ability to perform and bring many unintended and unwanted consequences. Persons are certainly unequal in their ability to meet moral demands, and to some extent allowances must be made for such differences. Under normal circumstances, there are actions that have to be almost universally prohibited, but it is hard to argue that there should be entitlements and requirements that are invariant across all conditions. Habermas repeatedly insists, as we have seen, that any legitimate moral interest is generalizable. But the notion of a literally common interest is wildly unrealistic. While it is unproblematic to unite interests *so far as possible,* in real life the problem is more often to adjust and adjudicate interests, *if we can.* Unanimity typically requires the Ministry of Truth.

Habermas is confident not only that our parochial deficiencies are eradicable through socialization, but also that full communicative competence will bring forms of self-realization surpassing any goods hitherto achieved. With unqualified approval, he quotes a remark from George Herbert Mead: "I think all of us feel that one must be ready to recognize the interests of others even when they run counter to our own, but that the person who does that does not really sacrifice himself, but becomes a larger self."[31] Now it is a wonderful occasion when conflict leads to growth; but, Hegel aside, how often does this happen, really? If it were as easy as all that, it could hardly make a difference which side of a conflict happened to succeed. Tell that to the Palestinians and Israelis! Tell the Irish in Northern Ireland! Tell the Yugoslavs! Even under favorable circumstances, we endure our share of conflicts, and we're not happy about that. When they don't turn out in our favor, we may well be hurt and unconvinced after all. This happens with colleagues, associates, and lovers, and we just accept it. How much more often does it happen with people we don't admire or don't like? There may be positive growth of some sort on such occasions, but there may just as easily be heightened resentment and animosity. Any other view subordinates experience to theory. It cloaks the moral condition in philosophic abstractions.

Perhaps all Habermas is looking for is a sort of impartiality, but even that takes the Kantian-Rawlsian form of impartiality in regard to human beings only as conceived in a certain way. Those not in the embrace of egalitarianism need not apply.

He takes it as virtually self-evident that in capitalism the relation between classes is inherently unjust. (We read such phrases as "privileged appropriation of socially produced wealth," which as it stands is a mere slogan.) And he has defined the ideal communication community in such a way that the relative merits of capitalism and socialism are not even subject to debate. Inasmuch as inequalities in ownership of productive property negate autonomy, that "debate" has been decided before actual discourse gets underway.

There are many serious and intractable problems regarding any political economy or social order. They constitute many eminently debatable issues. But they *are* debatable. Habermas wants to rule out certain positions from the beginning, charging them off either to greed for wealth and power or to false consciousness—never to conscientiousness. There *is* much false consciousness. We are besotted with it. We are prejudiced beings, and intellectuals are especially susceptible to being seduced by high-flown ideas. But given that false consciousness is a fact, what ameliorates it, insofar as that is possible? When we evaluate political economies, for example, our assessment depends largely on determining the behavior of what it is that we are assessing. To take just a few variables, we might compare general productivity, or increases in productivity and employment; the relative wealth of different groups; the condition of the poor regarding wealth, political activity, health care, and education; the real opportunities and mobilities exhibited in the systems; both the explicit and symptomatic expressions of satisfaction or dissatisfaction by various groups; the correlation between economic and political institutions; cultural vitality. And we must observe the tendencies of these variables over time and in comparison to other forms of political economy. Marx spoke eloquently of the progressive immiseration of the working class. If his claims had substance, we would have the most powerful indictment of liberal capitalism. To what, however, does Habermas appeal? He certainly can't bring out the immiseration theory. He speaks rather emptily of "justice." He falls back on false consciousness. In a seemingly more eligible vein, he claims that all major social problems in the capitalist world are owing to its "fundamental contradictions." This is the thesis of *The Legitimation Crisis*. The thesis is not defended on the basis of field studies or other sorts of empirical evidence, however, but is an application of his preestablished social theory. Of course there are problems with capitalism, as there must with any mortal enterprise, but Habermas's response is in effect to condemn it *a priori*. In truth, his condemnation is sentimental, cloaked in protestations of reason.

There is an obvious sense in which Habermas sidesteps, rather than contends with, the moral condition. One of the most conspicuous traits of the moral life is the recurrence of conflict, ambivalence, and uncertainty. One way of addressing these traits is, in effect, to dismiss them. Instead of conceiving ways to approach conscientious conflict or to marshall data pertinent to a debate, we simply say the debate is spurious. This is not an effective way to contend with moral problems. If we have some respect for real persons, we cannot just dismiss their serious and thoughtful convictions; and when their loyalties are strong, we cannot expect they will sacrifice them without a fight. Better that the fight be intellectual than physical, but if the ground rules of debate are established in a way to preclude what are otherwise regarded as arguable (and highly cherished) positions, then we simply are not going to get people to accept these rules. They won't participate in our "free" discourse. If moral philosophy is conceived as the formulation of assumptions and distinctions responsive to the very conditions that occasion moral reflection, then one of its first responsibilities is to take moral conflict and disagreement seriously. Habermas neglects these aspects of moral reality by defining them out of existence. This is prejudicial simplification.

The centerpiece of his thought is the notion that we already necessarily subscribe to certain fundamental moral principles. What does it mean to say that these norms are "contained in the structure of intersubjectivity," that they are "universal and unavoidable" presuppositions of communication? Intersubjectivity has many structures, and communication has many functions, including those of deceit and intimidation. In a given speech situation, the speakers might have differing presuppositions in the sense of recognizing that they intend to use language for a variety of purposes. But what could it mean to say that there are universal and necessary normative presuppositions? Could this mean that I would be literally unable to engage in discourse at all without these transcendental conditions? But that is patently false. I can engage in a variety of speech acts without entertaining any such notions. So why *must* they be presupposed? It is by no means obvious that these alleged transcendental conditions have any role in accounting for either the existence or functions of linguistic interactions, nor do they account for the moral assessments we make of the manner in which persons use speech.

When we help our children learn to use speech, with good reason we teach them to be truthful, and the like. In many forms of effective communication there is a reasonable presumption that the persons engaged will speak intelligibly, truthfully, sincerely, and with good moral intent. Without such a presumption, our typical intercourse would be far more laborious, and the results in the universe of action typically hateful; so we are normally inclined in this way. We want others to speak in the same manner, but there are many occasions when we must exercise various tests to see whether they actually do so. None of this suggests, however, that everyone must be at least implicitly and unavoidably committed to these norms just because they talk. It seems a mystification to say we have "always (already)" subscribed to such rules when, try as we might, we cannot perceive that we have. The situation is analogous to that in which the philosopher tells us that what we contingently happen to will is not what we truly will, regardless of our insistence to the contrary. Habermas's declarations have an aprioristic ring to them. It is as though God or Nature or Platonic Forms had somehow bestowed a changeless essence on communicative behavior even before such behavior occurred in the temporal realm; when it does appear it is already and necessarily invested with characteristics neither of its evolution nor our choosing.[32]

Habermas's stated position is also *pointless*. Suppose that there are necessary presuppositions of communication, or of anything else, for that matter. Even if we must do or presuppose something, that doesn't make the something morally desirable. Just because they exist, presupposed entities are not therefore good or right. To assume that they are is tantamount to saying that the inherent nature of things is necessarily good. I must presuppose death, heartbreak, ignorance, and failure. Maybe I have to presuppose Kant's twelve *a priori* categories of the understanding. It is a further matter to judge the *desirability* of the existence of such conditions. They might be helpful or hurtful as the case may be, and we might well wish that they were otherwise. Accordingly, the mere existence of transcendental conditions, just because they are transcendental, would not constitute a determination of the moral merit of their existence.

If we survey the various *functions* that language has, or might have, in the moral life, *then* we are in a position to appraise them. We can learn how they promote or retard our urgent concerns, how they might be conducive to discord or concert, to well-being or confusion and frustration. Perhaps Habermas is outwitting even himself with his transcendental arguments. He has great concern for the welfare of modern man and alarm about the stupid and destructive tendencies active in human societies. He is convinced that the best way to address them is to renounce our individualistic ways of thought, to renounce our vain hostilities and greeds, and to launch a shared and cooperative venture to try to secure universal human flourishing. *These* concerns and the pursuit of *these* ends give moral import to his particular version of social intelligence. If we believe it could function effectively, *then* we could commit ourselves to it, but certainly *not* on the basis of the transcendental argument with which he labors. Regrettably, he imposes so many *a priori* moral constraints on the process of communicative action that he makes it obnoxious, and his utopian assumptions about human capacities invite tyrannical means to make them come true.

In any case, there has to be something suspect about an argument to the effect that just by virtue of the fact that we use language, we are therefore egalitarian socialists. Once again, the moral condition has been left forlorn.

Irrationalism: Rorty as Social Thinker

There are many ways in which the study of the moral condition might be blocked and prejudicially simplified. One of them, as we have seen, is to regard the study as irrelevant. Another is the embrace of irrationalism. A straight-out irrationalist is simply opposed to the exercise of intelligence, making for disaster. Yet there are forms of thought—if we can call them that—which are in effect irrational. Endowing a *Führer* with divine powers of intuition accessible to no one else is a too-familiar case in point. Another form of blockage, slightly less dangerous, is dogmatism. Still another—sometimes respectable—form is skepticism in one of its many incarnations. One might conscientiously hold that our possibilities of knowledge are so slight that it is vain to pursue them. There is yet a subtler way to "block the way of inquiry," to use Peirce's phrase. Some may hold that we cannot possess intersubjectively verifiable knowledge and insist at the same time that we can get along just as well without it. In a very sophisticated version, this seems to be the position of Richard Rorty. It denudes the moral condition of some of its prominent characteristics and effective instruments. I will attend to it briefly.

Rorty does not say that we have no knowledge whatever. He just says that what "knowledge" we have is sociologically determined. It is a function of the "vocabulary" that a group has happened to adopt in order to "cope." To cope, however, does not imply that we have come to grips with certifiably determinable properties of "the world," and we cannot claim that our "knowledge" is testable in reference to worldly "facts" acquired by ourselves or by other groups, be they ever so "scientific." *A fortiori,* the same analysis applies to our moral convictions. In regard to moral thought, then, Rorty works wholly within the tradition of what he has called "postmodernist bourgeois liberalism."[33] On his premises, there is nothing else to do. Why get hysterical looking for a nonexistent black cat in a dark room? My intent is not to contest Rorty's position but to present a few of his most recent ideas and to point out the calamitous implications of taking them seriously.

Any phenomenon, Rorty says, can be "redescribed," and the only limit to redescription is our ability to formulate new vocabularies. "What was glimpsed at the end of the eighteenth century was that anything could be made to look good or bad, important or unimportant, useful or useless, by being redescribed."[34] This would hold true, we need hardly add, for societies or individual human beings. There is, then, no human nature or essence; no innate propensities or regularities lurk within the self. The "self" is sheer contingency. The process of creating an entire personality and character he calls socialization. We are what we are socialized to be, and societies begin with the upper hand. As society goes—whatever it might be—so goes the man. "Socialization, to repeat, goes all the way down, and who gets to do the socializing is often a matter of who manages to kill whom first."[35] But, as we are about to see, there is a possible salvation from such servitude.

This theory cannot be regarded as scientific, of course, or derived from science. It is a product of Rorty's views about language. In creating a language, or vocabulary, we create the self. The initial vocabulary that creates us is impressed upon us; it is neither our choice nor our invention. "[T]he human self is created by the use of a vocabulary, rather than being adequately or inadequately expressed in a vocabulary."[36] "[H]uman beings are simply incarnated vocabularies."[37] And language, the almighty Creator, is also a matter of sheer contingency.[38] This condition, however, allows us to create ourselves. We may create new vocabularies and thereby a new self. This is the characteristic venture of what Rorty, following Harold Bloom, calls the "strong poet." By inventing new narratives, "the hope of such a poet is that what the past tried to do to her she will succeed in doing to the past: to make the past itself, including those very causal processes which blindly impressed all her own behavings, bear *her* impress. Success in that enterprise—the enterprise of saying 'thus I willed it' to the past—is success in what Bloom calls 'giving birth to oneself.' "[39] Once you have given birth to yourself, you can go on to create yourself. Redescribe yourself and you *are* a new self!

No one can say Rorty is bashful. What he says contradicts all experience, science, and common sense. Nor can we say he is inconsistent. He has invented a philosophy that permits him to cast such constraints aside with impunity. There *are* no facts to puncture his ideas, as he understands them. *Others* may disbelieve him, but *he* is impenetrable. As I promised, I shall offer no refutation. But before proceeding to speak of the danger in his philosophy, I offer this preliminary comment, which is more in the way of a speculative diagnosis: Rorty is surely right, I think, in his dismissal of inherent essences, as they were bequeathed to modern philosophy from the ancient and medieval traditions. That's old hat. But he seems to suppose that the dismissal leaves nothing but sheer contingency, and that is a non sequitur. He always poses the alternatives as either sheer contingency or—to use one of his favorite phrases—a condition "beyond the reach of time and chance." But there assuredly is a space between this dichotomy for natural constraints and instrumentalities. Conditions that are not beyond time and chance are still persistent and consistent enough to prevent our redescribing them at will or acting with them in any way that we might wish. Water, to take a homely example, possesses no essence, but it has many certifiable functions owing to its various and distinctive properties. Water is a distinguishable and singular phenomenon, not precisely like any other, and hence its behaviors are not precisely like those of anything else. And that is enough. It doesn't need to have an essence in order to have a sufficiently determinant nature to structure our behavior in reference to it. We bathe in it, drink it, and cook with it; we would not do so with hydrochloric acid, and we would not use water to start fires. Claims of a parallel sort could be made in regard to the properties of *Homo sapiens*. Ironically, Rorty still owes much to the despised essentialists. He seems to believe their argument that, without good old substantial forms, there is chaos.[40]

These conjectures suggest my complaint: Rorty's belief that everything bends to redescription is complacent and, as such, a menace. As we find in every context of life, nature has definite constraints and powers, and to neglect them is fatal. It is likewise fatal to believe that the very idea of inquiry into such constancies is misconceived. All discipline and direction of life come from respect for the conditions that nature and social life impose on us; and, when it is not luck, all successful adventure is a consequence of identifying the predictable relations between processes of change.

A philosophy that obscures such conditions is of no help in the moral life. To confine our attention to matters of his own choosing, self and society, Rorty has us believe that we can create ourselves by creating a new vocabulary. A cruel, if inadvertent, hoax! Changing ourselves is arduous work, and it usually doesn't get very far, in spite of our best efforts. We don't control alcoholism, cowardice, cruelty, stupidity, or pigheadedness by adopting new metaphors. We don't usually change *ourselves,* in the sense of asserting command and directly instituting a difference, whether by creating a vocabulary or by some other means. Dewey's notion of growth as primarily a social process is more like it. To recall an observation quoted earlier from Santayana, "[T]he objects in which that satisfaction may be found, and the forces that must cooperate to secure it, lie far afield, and his life will remain cramped and self-destructive so long as he does not envisage its whole basis and co-operate with all his potential allies."[41]

Here is a sample of Rorty's social observations: "[R]ecognition of a common susceptibility to humiliation is the *only* social bond that is needed"[42] (emphasis in original). It's that easy! This may be one of the most inaccurate and reductive statements in the history of social theory. As if warring groups do not recognize such a common susceptibility, and do battle just the same. Such adversaries love to humiliate each other, knowing how subject each is to feelings of disgrace. Ties of kinship, tradition, obligation, affection, and inter-dependence are evidently not needed for the social bond. Perhaps we need take no account of them in considering the imperatives, constraints, and opportunities of the moral life.

If one believes, as Rorty does, that (with the exception of the "strong poet") political reality creates human reality, then he is apt be more willing to support wholesale social reconstructions. The myth of socialization can be destructive. If Rorty is wrong—if human beings prove insufficiently malleable—reeducation camps are not far off. His view also supports the myth of equality, which is anything but benign. The myth tells us that there is no intrinsic reason why any person should not be able to accomplish any more than any other. Then, when differences in outward circumstance are observed, it is easy to conclude that they can be attributable *only* to injustice and exploitation. "The only reason I am not better off is because I am being cheated by . . . (name your scapegoat)." It is such a myth that is seized upon by the Robespierres and Lenins to enlist thousands into bloody campaigns. Armed with the myth, we divest productive persons of their material instruments and achievements, denouncing them as oppressors. We take inequalities in outcome as sure evidence of undeserved status, and we set about to rectify the injustice. If demogogues are unavailable to lead such crusades, one may have no recourse but petty hostility, resentfulness, or perhaps he will just sulk. Few are greater believers than I in encouraging people to be adventurous and enterprising. Nevertheless, part of the final wisdom in life is "know thyself." We must either settle accounts with our own limitations or be embittered.

It is needless to say more of my concern with Rorty's particular philosophy. But it is a part of a very dangerous trend. It is representative of the current movement among intellectuals to deny the authority of any *impersonal* epistemic test. Authority will reside with the intelligentsia *as such*. This is a form of irrationalism. Not uncommonly, it takes an insidious guise: intellectuals preach a form of extreme skepticism, if not irrationalism, while not practicing it. If they keep their wits about them, they may bamboozle others in a manner to promote their own political agenda. (I do not believe this cynicism is true of Rorty.)

Nothing is more threatening to our endeavors than to disregard, willfully or not, the lessons, efficacies, and possibilities of mortal existence. Inquiry into the conditions of life, both generic and particular, is an invaluable constituent of moral philosophy and the moral life. There is not the slightest reason to believe that these conditions are equally conducive to the flourishing of just any way of life. Nature is not that permissive, nor is human nature; both (together) provide resource and direction for definite sorts of human success and fulfillment. Hence my animus to prejudicial simplifications or distortions of the moral condition. Rawls excludes much that is vital, persistent, and urgent in that condition. Habermas does the same, and both are therefore led to artifices that are of little relevance to our moral experience. Rorty obscures the moral condition by denying that there is any nature of things to be known, that there is any intersubjectively valid method of inquiry, and—for a parting shot—that we are well rid of such pretensions anyway.

Whatever Rorty might believe, there is invaluable information about the moral condition for the conduct of life. I have tried to draw attention to some of it and to indicate its bearing on problems of reflection and action. Enlisting James and Dewey, for example, I focused attention on the pervasive realities of change and contingency and their continuity with order, noting as well a conception of the functions of intelligence organic to these realities. I tried to demonstrate the irreducibly evaluative nature of any norm for conduct, the inevitably plural nature of such norms; and, in light of such conditions, to analyze the nature of moral disagreement. A characterization of the real efficacies of discourse followed. The naturally generated relations of moral experience and their interrelations were surveyed; and the arbitrary character of any attempt to amalgamate them into a unity or a fixed priority was urged. Some gesture was made in the direction of suggesting the strengths and limitations of these relations. The functions of philosophical anthropology in moral theory and reflection were canvassed, and the need for unsentimental knowledge of human nature was stressed. At the same time, I have been critical throughout of leading lights in moral philosophy for the futility and irrelevance of their paradigmatic exploits.

Such inquiries as these do not leave us with a shapeless prospect. Rather, they suggest real and effective instruments for prosecuting the moral life. These instruments will not satisfy those who accept nothing short of perfect uniformity and certainty. But that demand is the enemy, not the friend, of human striving. In any case, it is time to see whatever harvest this investigation of the moral condition might yield.

Notes

1. Rawls's rationalistic pretensions have dwindled a bit since the publication of *A Theory of Justice,* but his whole philosophy is still a fine specimen of a simply excogitated system.

2. Immanuel Kant, *Foundations of the Metaphysics of Morals,* translated and with an introduction by Lewis White Beck (New York: The Liberal Arts Press, 1959), p. 46.

3. Ibid., p. 47.

4. Ibid., p. 5.

5. Ibid., p. 47. Emphasis added.

6. Ibid., p. 46.

7. Immanuel Kant, *Lectures on Ethics* (New York: Harper & Row, 1963), p. 66.

8. Kant, *Foundations,* pp. 52–53.

9. Ibid., p. 18*n.* Not only does sheer consistency demand this conclusion, but Kant spells it out somewhat himself. Law, he says, is the *only* ground (moral determinant) of will (*Foundations,* pp. 17, 45). The ground

of the rational will is also characterized as *end* (p. 45). If both law and rational end are the only moral ground, then law and end are identical. Kant says (p. 65) that universal law is the object (end) of the will.

10. Pages 35ff of *Foundations* discuss the contingent (empirical, heteronomous) quality of happiness. Page 33 gives an account of the assertorical imperative, which is in sharp contrast to the categorical. "The absolutely good will, the principle of which must be a categorical imperative, is thus undetermined with reference to any objects. It contains only the form of volition in general . . ." (p. 63).

11. A noteworthy exception to the tiresome theoretical quality of Rawls studies is Michael J. Sandel's *Liberalism and the Limits of Justice* (Cambridge: Cambridge University Press, 1982). Sandel concentrates on Rawls's concept of the moral person, urging that it is too abstract or "metaphysical" to represent a real person. Rawls replied in "Justice as Fairness: Political not Metaphysical," *Philosophy and Public Affairs* 14, no. 3 (Summer 1985): 223–51. Rawls here denies that his concept of the person was ever intended to be "metaphysical," declaring that the "free and equal rational person" of *A Theory of Justice* was intended to represent a normative *political* ideal. Rawls was certainly ineffectual in making this point in *A Theory of Justice,* where he repeatedly refers to this alleged moral being as "our true self." (See my text for documentaion of this observation.) In my judgment, Rawls's reply is unsuccessful no matter how it is read. (This, too, is documented in my text, which will cover a somewhat broader range of issues than those selected by Sandel.)

12. John Rawls, "Kantian Constructivism in Moral Theory," *The Journal of Philosophy* 72, no. 9 (September 1980): 525.

13. Ibid.

14. Rawls, *A Theory of Justice,* p. 5 (emphasis added).

15. Rawls, "Kantian Constructivism in Moral Theory," p. 566 (emphasis added). In a footnote he adds that advances in our knowledge "might be relevant" at stages of *implementation,* "as opposed to the adoption of principles in the original position," *ibid.*

16. The principles also include a provision for justice between generations. No generation is entitled to indulge its present natural resources at the expense of succeeding generations. Neither may a current generation be sacrificed for the sake of the future.

17. Faculty salaries at all schools would have to be set in accordance with the difference principle. Would Rawls have to undergo a salary cut—or nullification—if it were determined that his theories would fail to aid the least advantaged, or would even hurt them? I think that would be unjust!

18. His "clarifications" were in large part implicit retractions and revisions.

19. Jürgen Habermas, *Communication and the Evolution of Society,* translated and with an introduction by Thomas McCarthy (Boston: Beacon Press, 1979), p. 186.

20. Jürgen Habermas, *The Theory of Communicative Action,* Vol. 2, *Lifeworld and System: A Critique of Functionalist Reason,* translated by Thomas McCarthy (Boston: Beacon Press, 1987), p. 189.

21. Jürgen Habermas, *The Legitimation Crisis,* translated by Thomas McCarthy (Boston: Beacon Press, 1975), p. 121.

22. Ibid., p. 108.

23. Ibid., p. 110.

24. See esp. chapter 1 of Habermas, *Communication and the Evolution of Society.*

25. Ibid., p. 177.

26. Jürgen Habermas, *Theory and Practice,* translated by John Viertel (Boston: Beacon Press, 1973), p. 39.

27. Habermas, *Communication and the Evolution of Society,* p. 187.

28. Habermas, *The Legitimation Crisis,* p. 189.

29. Ibid., p. 143.

30. Ibid., p. 87.

31. Quoted on p. 94 of vol. 2 of *The Theory of Communicative Action.* Habermas quotes from George Herbert Mead's *Mind, Self, and Society* (Chicago and London: The University of Chicago Press, 1934), p. 386.

32. Karl-Otto Apel has pursued the transcendental argument more systematically than Habermas. Apel argues that when we acknowledge that meaning and truth are socially determined, we must also acknowledge what he calls "the *a priori* of the communication community." But I could concede—even insist upon—the socially determined character of meaning and truth without accepting the rest of the argument. Meaning and truth would be social regardless of the moral qualities of the social relations in which they developed. See esp. chapter 7 of Apel's *Towards a Transformation of Philosophy,* translated by Glyn Adey and David Frisby (London, Boston and Henley: Routledge & Kegan Paul, 1980).

33. This is the expression Rorty uses in his article "Postmodernist Bourgeois Liberalism," in *The Journal of Philosophy* 80, no. 10 (October 1983): 583–89. Rorty fails to appreciate the pluralism of "our" tradition. He holds that Rawls's (highly dubious) account of our tradition accurately represents it. See his "The Priority of Democracy to Philosophy," in *The Virginia Statute for Religious Freedom,* edited by Merrill D. Peterson and Robert C. Vaughan (Cambridge: Cambridge University Press, 1988).

34. Richard Rorty, *Contingency, Irony, and Solidarity* (Cambridge: Cambridge University Press, 1989), p. 7.

35. Ibid., p. 185.

36. Ibid., p. 7.

37. Ibid., p. 88.

38. Ibid., esp. chap. 1.

39. Ibid., p. 29.

40. I make no claim that Rorty's argument is reducible to such an assumption. The explicit resource for his position is philosophy of language.

41. George Santayana, *The Life of Reason,* Vol. III: *Reason in Religion* (New York: Collier Books, 1962), p. 156.

42. Rorty, *Contingency, Irony, and Solidarity,* p. 91.

8

Ways of Life

There are various reasons for engaging in theoretical moral reflection. Not the least of them is simply to partake of the enjoyable intellectual exercise of analyzing and straightening out the conceptual muddles that others have got themselves into. But there are also less academic and more serious motives. If we determine universal and rationally incontrovertible principles, then we have the indispensable standard for knowing always how to act rightly, and seeming moral disagreements evaporate in the bright light of reason. We might also aim for the discernment of the true good, thereby to identify—and perhaps to achieve—the highest happiness. If such are the goals of moral theory, and if we become convinced by the heterogeneity of absolutes, by their morally selective premises as well, that such ambitions are in vain, then we might suppose that the whole enterprise is without merit.

These are the controversies of absolutists and relativists. Philosophic moral reflection typically oscillates between versions of these two stances, which are the opposite sides of the same coin. Partisans of both camps, as well as neutral observers, suppose that the purpose of moral theory is to *try* to arrive at universally valid moral principles. Both schools come in various guises, but the following definitions seem to be inclusive of each. The absolutists purport to establish moral principles that are both precise and certain: precise in what they require in the way of conduct, and certain in that their validity is thought to be established in a manner that withstands rational controversy. These are the "scientists" of moral theory as described in chapter 3. Relativists are those who are convinced that there are no intersubjectively binding constraints on the determination of moral norms. They give up normative moral theory as a lost cause.

Absolutists are subject to many embarrassments. The more precisely they articulate their conclusions, the more restrictive must their premises be, and the more readily are they refuted, or simply ignored. But they are not easily discouraged, as we see from the dazzling variety of closed (and prejudicial) systems that have rolled from the presses in recent years. The embarrassments that befall them do not uniformly still the absolutistic impulse. There seems to be an insistent need in human beings for exactitude and certitude in morals.

The goal of theorizing could be more modest, however: the historicists believe that all we can do is articulate the moral assumptions and ideals resident in a given culture. Success here, however, gives us no purchase on the vexatious questions that arise when cultures are in conflict. Indeed, it is impotent within a pluralistic culture, or one in transition, or one whose norms might otherwise be thought to be odious. In effect, the historicist is a sophisticated relativist.

The historicist position is similar to that of the relativist in that it agrees that there is no universal and objective moral standard against which we can measure the comparative worth of various codes. The historicist compounds the problem by adding that the language used in one code is incommensurable with that of another: the proponents of different principles cannot even carry on intelligible discourse with each other. Such a condition evokes a feeling of helplessness, and experience gives evidence to suggest that it might be an accurate characterization of the state of moral communication. Everywhere, it seems, the champions of varying camps defend their points of view with closed systems of rhetoric. Worldly events that might seem to call a system to account cannot even penetrate it. Consistent with the historicist position, there seem to be no facts that are not determined by the antecedently given system. The theory defines the very reality that would test it. This is a solipsistic nightmare, where cultures rather than individuals are impervious to any instruction foreign to their existing assumptions. In daily experience, we find convincing support for relativism of any kind. Moral controversy and conflict are pervasive, and the discord is not confined to fanatics, the uneducated, and the irrational. Intelligent and conscientious people exasperate each other with interminable moral debate.

In Defense of Pluralism

For many, the lesson in all this is to resign themselves to the conclusion that whatever discontents they might have with a different moral position must take the form of simply opposing it with their own moral bias. They find themselves so typically at impasse that they abandon efforts at persuading others, and they form parties to seek recruits to their cause. Ethics descends into routine politics. There is even more at stake than the suffering and frustration occasioned by moral conflict. Failing to unearth the philosopher's stone, if we struggle and sacrifice in behalf of our values, we must conclude that we do so for no other reason than that they happen to be ours. However, if the scruples of our ethic just happen to be such that we don't feel justified in struggle unless we have irreproachable warrant, then we will not in fact work and sacrifice, while other populations do not hesitate to come to the defense and aggrandizement of their own cultures.

Persuaded that our alternatives are exhausted, we might well decide to give it all up and tend to the garden. But the alternatives are not exhausted. There is pluralism. This is the doctrine that there can be a range of defensible positions regarding a given moral issue. From issue to issue, different persons situate themselves at different points on the spectrum, and there is no ultimate criterion to put the plurality of stations in an unchallengeable order of priority. Though indeterminate, the range varies in scope from question to question, and sometimes it virtually disappears. All this is a matter of persistent experience; I have argued that the nature of the moral condition makes it inevitable.

This will sound too permissive—soft in the head, perhaps—to the absolutist. All the same, everyone is intimately familiar with this condition, which must be accepted in some measure in the most precious forms of association: families, friendships, voluntary groups of all sorts, where give and take is necessary for perpetuating shared life. Spouses, good friends, comrades, and allies never find themselves in complete accord—they also endure discord—but they do not allow their relationships to unravel. Pluralism incorporates distinctions between virtue and vice, the permissible and the impermissible, the constructive and the destructive; but it insists that the boundaries between these differences cannot always be marked with exactitude, and it recognizes that our specific discernments of the virtuous, permissible, and constructive will undergo variation and cannot be aligned in faultless priorities. Yet it remains resolutely out of the embrace of sources of human misery like corruption, wickedness, dogmatism, and destructiveness.

Pluralism is a fact. There is an inevitable plurality of responses to moral situations, an irreducible plurality of types of moral relations, and a plurality of moral criteria without fixed priorities among them. But the inference that community is impossible is absurd. *Acceptance* of pluralism is the condition of any free and sustainable community. We must and we do find perfectly good ways of living together, even though there are earnest differences in moral judgment. We typically tolerate and even respect many instances of difference, and we must in any case accommodate ourselves to them if community life is to go on.

Relativism is obviously incompatible with tolerable social life, and so is absolutism. A community of radical absolutists is impossible, if the members hold divergent absolutes. The United States could not sustain many conflicts of the sort we witness in our tragedy over abortion. An absolutist society is possible only if there is one set of absolutes. It requires a führer or an ayatollah. Hence there is an operational definition of pluralism: it is the condition of a moral community where there is sufficient consensus to carry on its life to the satisfaction of its members. When relativism prevails, concerted action is impossible. When absolutism prevails, there is either a tyranny holding everyone in line, or warring groups of absolutists glare immovably at each other. Integral to pluralism is a certain conception of virtue, and virtue is the condition of maintaining a steady and ordered life.

Absolutists might contend that the indeterminacy of pluralism is incompatible with moral resolve. They say we will be paralyzed with doubt, in moral action, until we know exactly what to do. Pluralism is viewed as a prescription for indecision. Amidst all the contentions centering on abortion, for example, how could anyone conscientiously decide where to stand, unless one position was shown to be clearly correct? The matter of being morally resolute will be the next topic. It will be followed by an exposition and defense of the pertinent virtues, and the chapter will conclude with some observations about moral justification.

Pluralism and Moral Resolve

Even though pluralism rarely gives us the sort of certitude beloved by the absolutist, it by no means makes a Hamlet of us all. In the context of action, we do not really need ethical norms that will give us *certainty* in what we are doing. Simple *confidence* will suffice. If Peirce is right, what we seek is a readiness to act, though we may deceive ourselves that only a putative absolute can provide this for us. We want to be *sure* of what we do, sure enough to proceed with resolve and dedication. In a pluralistic, changing, and precarious world, resolve and dedication are sometimes hard to come by, and when we achieve them conscientiously, that is enough.

To insist that certainty is a required foundation of moral action surely represents a misunderstanding of the nature of steadfast attachment and perseverance. A man is devoted to his wife, but he doesn't think that she is perfect. Neither must his devotion waver just because he learns that some men do not regard her as attractive. It is a common fact that we have many powerful loyalties predicated on much less than an assumption of perfection in the object of allegiance. We are beings of great passion, capable of great devotion, and we become affixed with alacrity to some cause. It is passions that move us, and they are all too ready to ignite. In many cases, the problem is to restrain, not stimulate, them.

What garden-variety absolutists are really thirsting for, I suspect, is dedicated allegiance to the values they regard as indispensable to a precious form of life, and they are alarmed when they see the allegiance eroded or ridiculed. Their aim and concern will surely be laudable on many occasions, and the pluralists might well share them. If the case at issue is judged deserving, the pluralists can dedicate themselves to it even unto death. To do so, they need not believe that there is no conceivable contingency that could modify their loyalty, nor must they suppose that their object of devotion is beyond improvement. We don't need moral absolutes, for example, to defend a free society. We need devotion, to be sure, as well as knowledge, intelligence, courage, honesty, and persistence.

Moral experience precedes, rather than follows, the formulation of supposed absolutes. Absolutes have their origin in conditions that men find supremely valuable. They are contrived to preserve and defend such conditions. But the conditions have *already* been found supremely worthy, and an observer sensitive to them could explain why—perhaps with insight, vigor, and eloquence. Hence he provides reason enough for devotion to them, without incurring so great a risk of inviting intolerance, fanaticism, and the stilling of critical powers.

The assurance to act with intelligent conviction is neither the helplessness of relativism nor the certitude of rational finality. It does not imply that others will have no grounds to act other than we do. It doesn't mean that moral conflict and perplexity can be banished. (Very often, uncertainty and reserve are virtues.) Neither does it imply that we can necessarily persuade others to our view of things, or even that our own standpoint is immovable. But it does imply that when a decision has to be made, we can make it in good conscience, in the conviction that we need not regret the way we made it; indeed, that we might celebrate our purposes. The virtues of the pluralist by no means preclude steadfastness, sacrifice, and heroism.

While there are neither axiomatic nor unexceptionable principles, there are virtues—enduring dispositions to behave in certain sorts of ways—that are appropriate to the moral condition and are defensible in just that capacity. The nature of these virtues does not entail invariant rules of conduct or eradicate moral uncertainty. That, surely, is one of their virtues, if I may put it that way. The obsession to wield a moral fine-tooth-comb is symptomatic of the zealot. Possession and use of the virtues at issue would be more adequate to the vicissitudes and challenges of the moral life than would any of the dreams of the absolutist, and their exercise would provide whatever confidence the case might deserve. No more is needed: no social contract, no logical demonstration, no certification of ideal rationality.

The Virtues Appropriate to the Moral Condition

Virtues are not philosophic constructs. They are born of the demands and opportunities of associated life in varying environments. Courage, truthfulness, constancy, reliability, cooperativeness, adaptability, charity, sensitivity, rationality, and the like are distinguished because of their great efficacies in the life of a people. We could not live at all well without them. This is not to say that all of them are uniformly and impartially recognized. Differing cultures honor differing virtues. Socrates is neither St. Francis of Assisi nor Ralph Waldo Emerson.

Yet virtues must be philosophically examined. Their critical discrimination and analysis depend on more than observance of local conditions. There is also a reflectively analyzed environment, and these reflections have reached differing conclusions. For the universe as conceived by St. Augustine, faith, hope, and charity are the necessary virtues; while Nietzsche exults in the adversities of natural existence, which will generate the supreme virtues of the *Übermensch.* Russell taught "unyielding despair" in the face of a hostile universe, while Dewey stressed the many positive habits that human beings can develop with the *support* of natural conditions.

The rationalist supposes a fixed and finished moral world, furnished with the solemn authority of inflexible principle. He tailors his virtues accordingly: they consist in the ability to stick to the rules. Pragmatists are struck by the contingencies and limitations of the moral life and would likewise have a sense of openness, exigency, and adventure. Rationalists solve moral problems in the study; pragmatists would attend to them by helping to deploy the resources of intelligence and virtue that are organic to actually problematic conditions. Both reason and courage would have more limited roles in the rationalist scheme of things than in the pragmatic.

Such analyses are anything but arbitrary. The realities on which the formulations of virtue are predicated are subject to cognitive test. My claim throughout has been that philosophy cannot address the moral life without investigating these realities; that is, it must investigate the moral condition.

There is a distinctively moral discernment in reflective analysis. If we conceive of particular goods to be achieved, rights to be maintained, or distributions to be honored, we will devise the appropriate virtues accordingly. To do so in a scientific and cultural vacuum, however, is folly. A reflective study of virtue must take into account the varying possibilities of human nature and society as functional parts of the more inclusive wholes of nature and history. Owing to differing apprehension of such considerations, the conceived virtues of the socialist, for instance, are unlike those promoted by the fervent individualism of Ayn Rand.

The moral life includes conditions of order, constraint, and resource. It is also precarious, in process, and plural—plural in its natural imperatives, tensions, and opportunities. It is plural in its moral relations and standards of judgment, and plural in the advocacies that it generates. Plural, too, are its distinctive forms of life. There is a plurality of environments in which the drama is developed, each of which has its distinctive benefits and challenges. We find in tightly knit communities the conditions for the formation of great loyalties, mutual support, and a deep sense of attachment to a people, place, and tradition. We also find suffocating authority, implacable bias, and hostility to outsiders. As such bonds become attenuated, there is greater chance for the exhilaration of individualism and growth, for the exercise of creative intelligence, for new and voluntary association, for cosmopolitanism and tolerance—for true enhancements of life. Such liberation provides increasing chance, too, for *anomie* and loneliness, nagging uncertainty and spiritual homelessness. It often promotes as well an illusion of freedom from moral prejudice, taking form in reductive philosophies, with their consequent disregard for signs of vital life. In highly privileged conditions, some people become parasitic upon the work of others and easily forget the devotions that are necessary to sustain an ongoing community; or they suppose that the conditions of life are indefinitely plastic and subject to ready manipulation. We can build Utopia, where sacrifice and tragedy will be things of the past.

The individuals who contend with such varying circumstances are themselves varying. They are nurtured by differing traditions, and they protect different allegiances. They struggle for incompatible ends, and have heterogeneous assumptions about what gives life meaning. They possess, and are possessed by, great passions and lusts. Their sensibilities range from the barbaric to the mindlessly sentimental, and they are endowed with unequal capacities and talents.

This is not to say that we have nothing in common. Of course we do, both by nature and nurture. Such commonality sometimes works to help us understand each other and to live compatibly; it provides invaluable clues about the possibilities of the moral life. But a common trait is not tantamount to peace and harmony. We humans are extremely protective of our families and communities, for example, and are typically ambitious for them: we thereby fertilize the ground of competition and antagonism. We likewise cling tenaciously to traditions, but they are not the same traditions.

Caught up in such contingencies, we try to give them some sort of recognition, order, and direction. The consequent relations go by such names as rights, obligations, and goods, which no one will find fully satisfactory just as we find them. Satisfactions and dissatisfactions will vary somewhat from group to group, individual to individual; the means and criteria of thinking about them will likewise vary. The life of the community cannot be brought to a standstill; so some version of what we call moral reflection and discourse becomes organic to the life of at least some groups within it. What are found to be the most durable and important principles in the life of the group must be memorialized in art and myth, celebrated in ritual, and sanctified in religion; but whoever supposes that finality in critical discourse is attainable has not glimpsed the nature of the moral condition.

Such are the contingencies upon which we might helpfully ply our wit. We must be realistic, suppressing both our resignation and our sentimental exhortations for universal love. The philosophical response to the moral condition is to consider how to understand and address it in a practicable way. As I shall urge, certain virtues constitute that way. The virtues called forth by the moral condition are not those that are most comfortable for human beings to acquire. They are not easy, but they are often highly rewarded; their possessors are justly celebrated. Moreover, they are not just constraints; they are powers of attainment as well. Our moral condition is not just one of duty. It has resource and promise to be identified or created.

One could reasonably compile an elaborate list of virtues. I will confine myself to what might seem an astonishingly short and inadequate list: *rationality, courage,* and *respect for persons.* Following Aristotle (which is usually the best thing to do), we will find that they are interconnected, sometimes inseparable. In fact, they suggest forms of behavior that might themselves be regarded as virtues. They are practices, or habits, that one exercises across a wide range of contingencies. They are *dispositions* to behave virtuously, but what that behavior might be will vary with the context, and it will also vary with the antecedent requirements and entitlements of given agents. Virtuous behavior cannot be invented out of thin air. For just such reasons virtues should not be seen as implying exact and invariable rules of conduct.

In addition to their being vital to the moral life, the virtues are distinctive, in my account, for being in crucial ways rather permissive. Their permissiveness is part of their excellence. Moreover, their defense at the level of discourse would be more compelling to a broad spectrum of persons than are the scrupulously fine-tuned demands of the typical moralist, whose obsession guarantees that he will have little more than a cult following.

We are tailoring these virtues to the moral condition, not to abstract reason or to moral sentiment. We look for behavior that will address our problems, not compound them. One of the keys to this aim is to think of dispositions suitable to *beginning* and *sustaining* moral discourse and action, not to bringing indisputable finality to them. They should be effective in the *processes* of the moral life, not in determining an inflexible outcome to them.

The shortness of my list is appealing in the same way. We should not wander into the absolutist's self-defeating strategy of trying to prescribe a virtue to satisfy every moral sentiment. These three make great enough demands, and they would accomplish much in the moral life. And their observance, insofar as that might occur, comes to encompass still further traits of character, the desirability of which is obvious in any case, such as truthfulness and dependability. The virtues of the pluralistic point of view might not find universal endorsement, but they will provide confidence, not necessarily certainty, for their possessor.

Rationality

Philosophers labor night and day to deliver the true normative characterization of rationality. In respect to physical science alone, we have found that rational inquiry cannot be reduced to just one form, and the forms proliferate when we move into social science, law, history, and the humanities. When we assay *moral* rationality, the floodgates burst. Every philosopher has a remarkable aptitude for defining moral rationality in a way to yield the prescriptions that he or she already prefers.

I have something far more modest in mind. It is a minimum condition for anyone who would support any notion of rationality. For the virtue of rationality I ask no more than a sincere attempt to seek the truth relevant to a given situation. If the expression "truth" is too quaint, I'll accept "a sincere attempt to achieve assertibility," or "a sincere attempt to get at the facts." Even these phrases are not unproblematic, but what I wish to emphasize is the *motive* of rationality. The operative term here is *sincere*. The crucial need is that individuals caught up in moral controversy be willing to make an honest effort to get at the facts, which might be complex and wide-ranging. Rational individuals must be apprised, for example, of the deep tensions, resistances, and loyalties resident within a situation.

The effort also implies getting at the truth, so far as possible, regarding the assumptions in terms of which we try to *predict* facts. We make assumptions about human nature, for example, in accordance with which we anticipate behavior contingent upon certain conditions. Rationality would include as well an acknowledgment of logic as the means to determine the formal relations between statements.

It seems clear that all who are rational in the minimal way would sooner or later be constrained by the overwhelming evidence to recognize that they are fallible. This simple recognition alone is a great advance in our moral and intellectual life, for it precludes the conspicuous vices of dogmatism and the closed mind. It encourages conscientious inquiry, a willingness to rethink ideas, and a disposition to consult and listen to other persons and to take their views seriously. It disposes us to contrive and consider alternative plans of action.

What I am talking about is a persistent intellectual honesty. There may well be all kinds of dispute regarding how to go about our investigations, but if the will is present, we have at least eliminated the dogmatist, ideologue, and deliberately irrational; and that is no small achievement. We might find ourselves engaged with persons relying upon occult religious doctrines or special intuitive powers, but if such persons are *conscientious* truth seekers, then discourse with them has some future.

There are problems of course with what facts *are* relevant to a given moral predicament, an issue to be sincerely addressed. To my mind, as I have indicated hitherto, the relevant facts are legion. If we are wondering what to do, for example, in Eastern Europe, South Africa, or the Middle East, we have to know what is really happening in those places: who are the agents, what are their ambitions, their claims, their constraints, and their powers. We have to speculate about the behavior to be expected from the peoples who are implicated in the situation; we have to know what options are realistically open to us, and what their ramifications might be. A formidable task.

Some success in it does not entail a particular choice of policies. One's *reaction* to the panoply of presumed facts and predictions determines choice. Every relevant fact is a constraint in that it is a condition that resists our will in specifiable ways. It also is a definite power in that it has ascertainable potentialities that can be utilized to produce predictable outcomes. The inquiry to remedy our ignorance by itself, moreover, has the effect, more or less, of modifying the values that occasioned it. We might, say, gain increased respect for the capabilities of one of the engaged factions and therefore abandon a desire to resist them. Hence a determination of relevant facts serves both to modify our antecedent interests and to constrain and direct action.

It is no ordinary task to be adequately informed. It is often a massive labor, and extensive resources are needed to fulfill it. The impediments to inquiry are not only its magnitude and the physical difficulties of acquiring on-site information. Responsible inquirers come to different conclusions, just as they entertain conscientious differences about appropriate methods and criteria. Such problems must be acknowledged. It might be supposed, then, that my rather unspecific notion of rationality invites interminable epistemological wrangling—as if a specific one wouldn't!—but in practice this rarely happens. If we are trying to get at the facts about the Arab/Israeli conflict, for example, we are not delayed by disputes in theory of knowledge. We are delayed by incomplete, inaccurate, dishonest, and conflicting news reports; and relevant intelligence is insufficiently disseminated. We do not have sufficiently trustworthy data to make confident predictions. We are all pretty sure that people who are of a certifiable character will act in that character, but the certification itself may well be uncertain or ill-grounded.

For such reasons, getting at the facts is often very difficult, and the problem is compounded by an *unwillingness* to get at them. With dogged tenacity, we cling to what we want to believe. I referred earlier to moral argument that proceeds by way of interpreting the world according to a closed system of concepts. Perhaps what makes the system impenetrable is not incommensurability, but ordinary stubbornness; a completely conventionalized mind; or an assortment of laziness, passivity, fear, dogmatism, and intellectual complacency.

Perhaps the hard-core historicist is guilty of the latter. Does Rorty really believe that no one could carry on mutually helpful discourse with an open-minded person from another culture? Does he really believe that it is inherently impossible to do so? There is plenty of experience to the contrary, although not as much as one would like. Sometimes conflicting cultures understand each other only too well, as in the case of Arabs and Jews; that is why they are in such intense conflict. And somehow the rhetoric, if not the practice, of democracy has spread 'round the world to heterogeneous cultures. Although fine distinctions can get lost in translation, varied peoples with differing vernaculars are insisting that they are weary of tyranny, that it must perish, and that they can command their own fate. We understand them, and they understand each other, well enough.

It is a virtue of the minimalist account of rationality that it doesn't rule out *a priori* any of the more specific characterizations of rationality, while it permits their scrutiny, if need be, in ongoing discourse. If, as so often happens, a moral theory begins with one of these specific accounts—be it that of a MacIntyre, Rawls, Habermas, or Gauthier—it then leads inexorably to certain moral conclusions. The result is that the whole argument is rejected by all those who have a different model of rationality, with its own moral presuppositions. The moral convictions of those who don't accept the model are threatened from the outset; discourse, then, begins at an impasse.

The looser notion of rationality casts a wider net; it encourages a more heterogeneous array of persons to participate in what appears to be a less question-begging procedure. It is thus more suitable to the actual problems that the moral life presents. It is appropriate to a contingent and pluralistic environment. If we are not to be mutually intransigent, we have to enlist cooperation and exchange, not discourage them.

Few people, if any, seriously espouse outright irrationality. With the exception of the dogmatic (and doubtless posturing) irrationalist, we all accept, I suppose, at least the minimalist notion of rationality. It is a virtue that is not at all difficult to defend convincingly. Everyone accepts it: *being* rational is the problem.

One might object, however, that not enough is built into my notion of rationality: there isn't enough there to be of any serious help in moral controversy. On the contrary, there is inestimable value in the observance of this virtue, especially when it works in conjunction with other traits of character. This is a matter to be considered more fully at a later juncture. For the moment, consider only the merit of a notion of rationality that, in contrast to philosophic subtleties and sects, gains almost universal acceptance. For my part, I would consider moral discourse that displayed this minimal rationality to be vastly more adequate to the moral life than the communication that now routinely takes place, where ignorance, inflexibility, and dogmatism prevail. Again, I am looking for virtues to sustain the processes of the moral life, not to clamp finality upon it.

It is tempting to equate this virtue of rationality with simple honesty in inquiry. How long has it been since any of us has had the pleasure of conversing with someone who honestly and sincerely wanted to get at the plain truth, whatever it might turn out to be? No salesmanship, no proseletyzing, no hidden agendas. How honest! How refreshing! And how fruitful such conversation might be! But of course such discourse is as unreal as a Platonic Form. We are not all that well suited to being untarnished and honest inquirers; there are too many aspects of our nature that we want to protect from the facts. The passion of antecedent commitment makes honest inquiry repugnant. Nevertheless, we at least *subscribe* to minimal rationality.

Courage

Everyone agrees that we should get the facts, but very few do much about it. There are further virtues requisite even to approximate honest inquiry. The one I wish to stress is courage, which has many functions in the moral life. Our cherished biases and ideas are part of our very identity, and we want to protect them. It is easier to shrink from the truth than to surrender our defenses. It takes courage. Courage is the name we give to, among other things, the disposition to question our beliefs, to ask for the evidence that supports our favorite dogmas. Bathed as it is in the reassurances of comforting beliefs, the psyche could not be widely rational without courage.

The power of honest thought is also eroded, if not swept away, by peer pressure. This is not just a problem for adolescents. Intellectuals, as Nietzsche and others have observed, are cowards and herd animals. There is as much at stake for an intellectual to hold the "correct" opinions as there is for an adolescent to hang out with the "right" crowd, use the accepted lingo, and wear the approved clothes. Intellectuals are as unforgiving of betrayal of the party line as are teenagers of deviation from "cool" deportment. How needy we are for approval! Cowardice turns intelligent persons into party hacks. University faculties and administrators stampede on behalf of "politically correct" moral sentiments. Many would-be dissenters are afraid to murmur against them. Better to remain silent, or even to dissemble.

Our intellectual honesty can be stupefied by other, less dishonorable factors. Utopian idealism is one of them, unreflective compassion another, tunnel vision yet another; but in any case, a kind of courage is implied in their overcoming.

It is a bit simplistic, of course, to speak of the sheer presence or absence of a virtue. We not only possess them in different degrees, but they are ordered in different priorities. A given individual might have some courage, but he accords highest priority to being clever or "with it." Hence his analyses subordinate courageous reflection to the opportunity to share with friends a witty ridiculing of their rivals.

I do not mean to neglect the more traditional roles for courage in the moral life. We all know that it is one thing to advocate a brave line of action or to favor an unpopular opinion, and quite another to carry it out or to express it. Courage in the face of hardship, obstacles, and harm is always admired and often envied. It takes courage to implement our advocacies. Hence, as the preceding observations suggest, a further aspect of courage as a virtue, as a disposition, must be stressed. The idea is suggested in the Latin precedent *fortitudo* (fortitude): the capacity to endure through a protracted challenge or difficulty. Courage implies a sustained, not episodic, dedication to a course of conduct.

There is a subtle but no less important role for courage in the very formation of moral judgment. If a moral judgment were simply a cognitive act, rather than an evaluative response, then we could arrive at the truth of it simply by deploying our rational powers. But our prescriptions for conduct are not deduced from factual assertions. They are complex reactions to a moral situation. The nature of the response depends very much on our understanding of the nature of that situation, *but it also depends on our character.*

A courageous response to a certain body of information will be unlike a cowardly one, and the proposed judgment of what ought to be done will then be different. If you and I encounter the same situation and are equally apprised of its implications, you might decide to fight and I to run.

Courage is organic not only to the reaction to an existential condition, but also to its understanding. Recalling our needs for evasion, we are reminded that our understanding is skewed by our emotional constitution—for example, by a fear of uncovering some unwelcome facts. Cowardice is a good source of wishful thinking. If I am a fearful person, I have a strong inclination to "understand" the situation in a way that caters to my fear: Hitler is not really preparing for conquest. *Anschluss* with Austria will give him all the *Lebensraum* he could ever want. We can remain secure in our comforts. We need not build up our defenses.[1]

Rationality requires courage, and courage requires rationality. It is crucial that courage be informed with knowledge. Otherwise our actions might, by inadvertance, be rash or timid. Dangers might be either more or less than supposed; our ignorance could bring about an unintended underreaction or overreaction. For courage to be rational, we must make a realistic estimate of threats, resources, opportunities, and limitations. And when such estimates are made, rationality is in vain without courage.

No one would deny that the moral condition requires courage. Like rationality, the problem with courage is not to provide it with a credible defense, but to have it and use it wisely. Everyone is in favor of it, yet it remains rare. It is not part of this discussion to investigate how people become virtuous. Certainly our relevant native capacities vary, and there are limits to what can normally be expected of human flesh. Though sometimes terminal, the rewards of virtue are great; nobody wants to be irrational or to be ruled by fear. Yet if the rewards are uncertain, or if they are distant, abiding dispositions will not develop. Only when the disposition is already established can there be gratification in the mere doing of a virtuous deed. Given such reservations, and given our penchant for evasion, we could not be wildly optimistic about the dawning reign of goodness. Mere prudent self-interest would seem to carry us far in matching our wits against self-destruction, but even such a minimal expedient is too little in evidence. It readily succumbs to passion. If we are to be somewhere near equal to the demands and opportunities of the moral life, we must cultivate whatever incentives we can to encourage the growth of our more admirable qualities. Whether we can do so is problematic, but the minimal virtues advocated here are less elusive than the unrealistic demands of many moralists.

Respect for Persons

Another virtue needed in the moral life is the disposition to show respect for persons. This is a more subtle and protracted case to make than that for rationality and courage. As with rationality, the analysis depends on not defining the characteristic too stringently or in isolation from other virtues. Three points will be critical. First, respect for persons is a condition that everyone cherishes in various forms of association, so there is no question whether it should exist at all. The more critical matter is to study the traits of the moral life that would move us to extend respect universally, in some sense. Second, the conduct organic to showing respect in any situation will vary with differences in the relations between the persons involved. Third, of utmost importance is the *disposition* to show respect. United with rationality and courage, the disposition prompts conduct that is at least intended to exhibit moral regard.

As the discussion in chapter 5 concluded, the notion of respect for persons is elusive and problematic, and it can be formulated in distinctively different ways. Questions of exactly what it is about us that is respected (or is perhaps worthy of respect) and what sorts of conduct actually exhibit respect seem to raise more problems than they solve. I sponsored what I called a democratic version, and I will stay with it, not least because it is in some ways rather undemanding, and it seems appropriate to the actual condition of human beings. Respect should be characterized realistically. This means, again, a minimalist accounting. Even then, as we shall see, it does lots of moral work.

Respect, as I will use it, implies a kind of impartiality, or moral equality. In an important but difficult sense, it is impersonal. It implies in many instances the existence of consistently applied rules in place of the vagaries of personal authority. Yet in addressing moral problems, including the formation of policy when need be, it means giving an equal hearing to competing claims with the intent of endorsing what seem the most meritorious of them, or of contriving alternatives that might go some way in bringing them together. But it does not mean that the claimants are treated as indistinguishable rational ciphers. Each one has a particular urgent business, in many instances in behalf of others; and everyone who tries to be impartial is likewise invested with personal moral convictions and is often caught up in varying sorts of relationships with those who are in contention. I am speaking, then, of the living persons of nature and history, as I think I must; for these, and not Kantian artifacts, will have their way in the end. It is their (our!) moral life that is to be bungled, steadied, or enriched. But then being impartial carries no assurance that all interests will be equally served or given unproblematic priorities.

So long as explicit rules and regulations are not read into it—after the manner of Rawls, for example—I am willing to call this disposition a rough sense of fairness or fair play. My own thinking about this virtue is pulled strongly in the direction of regarding respect for persons as consisting largely in giving each person his due. It will be important, however, not to insist on that formula. This is not because it is vague (that tends to be an advantage), but because it might not be pertinent in every context. Given the complexities of human association, the drafting of policies cannot always give everyone their due, whatever it is; but we can still treat everyone with respect. We might think of respect as sometimes including charity and mercy, too. The formula would be well regarded as provisional, for there may be conscientious objection to it from time to time. It will compete with other moral priorities, and perhaps it can be regarded as derivative of a more permissive sense of respect anyway. Accordingly, strict maintenance of relations of desert might sometimes be regarded as a violation of respect for persons.

It is important that the virtue be conceived in a manner to be less specific rather than more, more *in*clusive than *ex*clusive. A highly serviceable account of it can be given nevertheless. Although our notions of fair play differ, *our respect for a person would in any case mean that we acknowledge that he is included among those to whom this rough sense of fair play applies.*

There is a vital corollary to this rendering of respect: it prohibits the infliction of unmerited ill-treatment. If one is not yet found guilty of offense, he does not deserve to be abused. Just minimal respect rules out the infliction of gratuitous harm. It means as well, then, that one be honest and truthful with others. There are strongly positive reasons for such behavior, of course, but here we include them simply because deceiving, cheating, and so forth are hurtful, not respectful.

I call this a *rough* sense of moral equality because it is not freighted with any particular entitlements or rules of conduct. The action that would express respect is by no means uniform and changeless, and it does not imply that everyone's interests will be equally served. Orders of precedence and systems of authority also inform the moral life. Compromise and tragedy are sometimes inescapable, and values in addition to equality of regard must be recognized. For all of us there are forceful limits, natural and moral, to putting all interests on a par with each other. I advert once more to the power and glory of our more local bonds. This is a condition that everyone except philosophers acknowledges to be just. I do not treat my family, my comrades, and my countrymen as interchangeable with other families, with strangers, and with people across the globe. These other people do not expect me to do so, just as I do not expect it of them. Indeed, an obvious sort of impartiality is evidenced in the nearly universal belief that we owe more to some people than to others just in virtue of our established relations with them. This does not mean that a state of total indifference, much less hostility, toward distant persons is warranted. How much local concerns should crowd out more extended ones is always problematic. Hence a precise meaning for respect for persons is likewise problematical.

I am trying to capture an attitude, a disposition, that we would bring to the moral life—a *disposition* to show respect for persons, without overwhelming it with impossible demands. It could be *strongly* characterized as a universal positive regard for others or even general good will, but a less ambitious approach is more true to life and will serve us better in the end. In its reduced sense, the attitude is one of recognition or acknowledgment of others as fellow petitioners in the moral life; so they are included in whatever we regard as fair.

Moralists, both lay and professional, will be apt to say that this notion is too thin, too unspecific and undemanding. It is pertinent to ask not only what a notion of respect can do, but what it should do as well. What do we want it to accomplish? If we formulate it with a laundry list of specific duties and principles, then it will create more controversy than convergence. We must ask what good it would be in light of the characteristic constraints, imperatives, and opportunities of the moral life. If one must sell the farm in order to take up the virtue of respect, we can be sure that respect will be the loser. Given the problematic nature of our predicament, it seems more sensible to look for broadly acceptable but nonetheless fertile conditions from which we may proceed to contend with our more specific dilemmas.

Certainly one of the first things we might ask of a notion of respect is that its observance simply exclude obvious cases of oppression, exploitation, and neglect of obligations. This is no small matter. The curse of the world is not so much in the failure to maintain fine distinctions of justice as it is in the work of tyrants, murderers, liars, cheaters, parasites, and the invincibly callous. On the most minimal reading of respect, all such persons lack it. In addition, a conception of respect has to be permissive enough to be functional across the wide spectrum of contingencies found in moral experience and to be acceptable to a variety of moral orientations. If its requirements are too stringent, they will not be respected, and one set of stringent demands will be counterpoised to another. The subdued demands are tough enough, and suitable to the moral condition. Within the permissive constraints of respect, anyone is free on a given occasion to press for a given policy. Insofar as respect is shown to him, others will listen, and he might be persuasive. And minimal virtue does not preclude the display of still more virtue.

In my rendition, respect calls for nothing so grand as universal brotherly love; it entails no specific rules of conduct; and it is not burdened with a metaphysical concept of the person. Respect would not begin with the hypothetical eradication of the concerns and convictions of the persons who have reached moral stalemate. Regarded as a virtue, it is a disposition, an attitude, that one routinely expresses in relations with others, but it cannot of itself determine the outcome of any moral deliberation. These are matters to be worked out, when necessary, and if possible, in league with rationality and courage.

Yet respect still performs essential moral functions. It rules out the victimization of persons. Its observance also requires that persons treat each other as moral equals, rather than consigning some to the status of untouchables. In addition, if we respect real people, their actual interests must be consulted or identified, and considered in earnest. There are several good reasons why moral deliberation should in many instances be explicitly communicative, but at least one of them is that we can't show respect for persons without hearing from them in some way.

Respect, and likewise rationality and courage, are excellent dispositions with which to begin moral inquiry and discourse, to conduct them, and to honor their verdicts. In themselves, out of any context, they give us no conclusions, no finality, but they are the best means for arriving at whatever conclusions we can in a given moral predicament. Respect is not omnicompetent. It obviously needs to be united with rationality and courage. Who can be sure where it might lead when, in specific circumstances, it is in concert with these other dispositions? Surely, if we can put our trust in anything human, we can do so with such a concourse of virtues.

The last comment is not an endorsement of some form of contractarianism. My opposition to that has been made clear. It does not show respect for persons, and it is not a way to contend with the contingencies of the moral life. I am not speculating about what principles would be adopted by anonymous persons invested with nothing but rationality, courage, and respect. I am investigating the sorts of realistic dispositions that would be effective for actual people to contend with their life situations—situations permeated with plural and particular exigencies, including the normal human weaknesses, and endowed with powerful allegiances, commitments, and aspirations.

As with any virtue, respect for persons is generated by the demands and rewards of the moral life. Just as a matter of simple prudence, most people must take up a stance of honest reciprocity with others. If not, they will find themselves ostracised from associated life. Our parents taught us this sort of elementary behavior. They wanted to prepare us to get along comfortably with others; they wanted us to recognize that other people have the same feelings that we do; and, more than this, they wanted to enable us to share the pleasures and resources of common life. Great rewards await those who characteristically display this basic virtue: they are trusted, relied upon, admired. Other individuals will desire to be in their company and will wish to be allied with them in common ventures.

The lessons of any tolerable family life must include the exercise of respect. No child could be brought up to a remotely sufferable adulthood if he or she were not treated with recognizable fair play.

Think of the child's horrors, for example, if the treatment received from parents were unrelated to the youngster's guilt or innocence. Or think of the paranoia that would ensue if siblings were governed by rules other than those applicable to the child in question. Presumably, it is a condition of any child's growth and happiness that the young person be treated by the parents as an individual, rather than as a cipher.

Such teachings are anything but morally arbitrary. Being the recipient of respect is one of the imperatives of any good life. We cherish the condition of being consulted as specific individualities. Even if we are not accorded personalized attention, we are extremely dependent upon the impersonal administration of rules. The virtue of this condition would be taught to the members of any social group, from the aristocracy on down. Typically, however, these are teachings that confine their requirements to a circumscribed sex, race, group, or class. Nevertheless, hardly anyone escapes exposure to the disciplines and resources organic to some society of moral equals. Such society is always a bulwark against capricious and arbitrary treatment; it safeguards the expectations and work that we take upon ourselves in social life. Without it, we would be insecure at best, psychotic at worst.

There are additional resources in normal social existence to support the willingness to accept and exhibit this virtue. Respect can be more than prudent impartiality and trustworthy relations with peers. Although there is much in our makeup that sabotages such practices, or competes with them, we seem to possess an inherent capacity to extend their scope. This is the power of sympathizing. Other persons have their own needs, aspirations, biases, attachments, and loyalties, just as we do. They rejoice and grieve, love and hate, dare and fear, just as we do, and for much the same reasons. We can, as we say, identify with them—*feel* with them, as "sympathy" implies. We can *share* that experience.

We are by no means equally capable of sharing in this manner. But even the most hardened or unfortunate have *some* sympathies in their life: perhaps for their children, if they have any; or perhaps they have some exposure to friendship; they might have had a dog, for all that. They might have had some feeling for a parent or a parental figure. Maybe there has been some trace of tenderness in their life, or some longing for it. Most of us possess the gift in some measure. It is not an unmixed blessing, for we share pain and loss along with joy and triumph. Nevertheless, it is still a blessing—no doubt one of our greatest blessings. Life would be empty without it, a hideous form of solipsism. Indeed, there can even be something blessed in sharing pain, in *sharing* pain. Accordingly, just as we want to be heard, to advance our own claims, and to be given care and consideration, others have a similar need, which we can understand and appreciate, and we can extend this sympathy to them. We have a capacity to extend sympathy to persons we do not know but have only heard about.

The dynamism of human sympathy is not that of a subjective whim or random humanitarian impulse. It is an invaluable constituent of our very makeup as human beings. The capacity to sympathize, to identify, is part of our innate inheritance. The fact that it is extended beyond the most immediate circle of associates is not mysterious. As noted, the virtue of respect for persons is something less than a demand for saintliness. It is a demand that others be sincerely acknowledged as real participants in the moral life and hence that they be included in what we regard as fair. Our power to sympathize energizes this acknowledgment.

As a virtue, then, respect for persons is born and nurtured in the moral life, and we have the strongest incentives to cherish its observance. It cannot be seriously questioned whether respect should exist at all, but serious issues do arise when we ask to whom respect should be accorded and what behavior it implies. Given the inestimable value of respect, each of us wants it as part of our life, and we know that others want it. Why, then, we ask further, should respect be confined to only this person or only that family—why to only this race, sex, clan, religion, or social class? If we admit respect at all, we are compelled to ask such questions.

The questions are vitally important and inescapable, and we have serviceable means of addressing them. If and when they are fielded, there seem to be at least three possible sorts of response. The first is positive: we take the question in earnest and consider why indeed we should limit the ambit of fair play. If we find no satisfactory answer, we are prepared to adjust our behavior accordingly. A woman believes, let us say, that orientals, as such, are lazy and untrustworthy. But she is sufficiently openminded to be convinced otherwise by the evidence. So she concludes that orientals are not possessed of these faults. Hence she no longer treats them as she treats unreliable persons; they are accorded the new status. At least she tries to accord it, and accepts responsibility for failure. Happily, this sort of response is not unexampled. The behavior was predicated on ignorance. One might conscientiously believe that those excluded from a particular form of respectful behavior are beings of another sort and hence not entitled to the same status. Women, as women, for example, have been believed to be insufficiently intelligent to participate in politics and the professions; atheists can't be trusted; blacks, as such, aren't fit for self-government; orientals are incapable of honest dealing; to be a member of the working class means that one hasn't the self-restraint to be democratic; and so on.

Such stereotypes are easily punctured, and when they are, the scope of a particular form of respect is in principle extended. This is not a denial that there are qualifications for participation in a given activity. Quite the contrary. But when the qualifications for admission or exclusion regarding a practice are spelled out, we find that members of the excluded groups meet them, and we also find that members of the excluding groups do not. We find that "inferiors" are endowed with the qualities of which their "superiors" had claimed a monopoly, and members of the "superior" group are found wanting.

This might not be what respondents to our question expect. They might be ordinary bigots, and now they have fallen upon their own swords. The respondents can mend their ways, as in the first case. They could, on the other hand, be *confessed* bigots. This is the second general response. It needn't surprise us, and it needn't shake our allegiance to respecting persons. The bigot can say orientals *are* devils and say no more about it. An individual who simply denounces a particular group—says he hates Jews, Catholics, blacks, whites, as such, and that's the end of it, without argument—has no pretense of making a claim on our convictions.

Alternatively, we could join those who would make the third sort of reply: a rationalization. We can find some sort of justification for persisting in our accustomed ways. We can agree that equals should be treated equally, but find a way to deny that there *is* equality. We can convince ourselves, say, that the credentials of those who present the unwelcome facts are worthless. Other, and better, authorities are easily found. If there are people we don't like, we will decide that they are subhuman, incompetent, depraved, and the like.

We will teach this to others, who will naively believe it. That's all it takes. When the falsehood is exposed, rationalization is easy. Note, however, that it *is* a rationalization. The principle of respect for persons has been accepted; the hate-filled individual is desperate to find a way around it.

Anyone this side of the confessed bigot acknowledges that in specific cases there are criteria for inclusion in respectful treatment. But what should the criteria be? Their determination is under some constraint simply by the nature of the status for which people are to qualify. Women were excluded from the professions on the grounds that they were insufficiently *intelligent.* Intelligence is the stated criterion. Likewise (as in some typical examples itemized above) *trustworthiness, capacity for self-government,* and *self-restraint* are among the pertinent announced criteria for assuming certain roles. In any case of qualification, there are specific talents, virtues, and skills at issue; this is how the matter is typically stated. The need is great for such things as good workmanship, reliability, energy, endurance, education, intelligence, knowledge, expertise, honesty, decency, and amiability; and there are good evidences for their existence in particular instances.

There is controversy about the appropriateness of various criteria. Kinship, race, sex, class, religion, ethnicity, or nationality are often given high priority; and sometimes they are judged to be appropriate. We rarely quarrel with the idea of a small family business, for example; and we typically assume that established loyalties often serve as warrant for active regard in a way that anonymous relations do not. Advocates of affirmative action regard race and sex as necessary considerations. (A white male is *not* like a black or a woman in the allegedly pertinent respects.) In the typical egalitarian scheme of justice, the morally relevant way in which one individual is like another is in being a "free and equal rational person." The empirical ways in which people are unlike each other have no place in the scheme. These are arguable questions, and I have argued some of them, but my point is not to look for final moral conclusions. As I have suggested, there are natural constraints and imperatives in the determination of criteria, and many pertinent considerations. The *disposition* to show respect for persons, together with rationality and courage, is more than sufficient to address these problems when they arise.

People who fail to meet the criteria for a particular status are presumably owed respect as well. We think that just being a human being qualifies one for respect of some sort. What of those who are not candidates for some specific status or office, who may be simply fellow citizens or fellow human beings, or who are in competition with us? Are they not also objects of respect? What sort of behavior exhibits regard for them?

One may extend meaningful respect in ways that do not necessarily require unrealistic exertion or sacrifice. Once again: we should not assume that it is appropriate to display the same behavior in different cases. Showing recognition of persons should *not* mean that each one indifferently is accorded the *same* treatment. If we construed respect to mean that, then we would have abolished the point of the distinction between stranger and brother; and the virtue would never be honored. It would be too demanding, and no doubt catastrophic as well. Even when we keep everyone's interests conscientiously in mind, we distribute attentions discriminately, and with good reason.

Sincere consideration and courtesy may be all that are required, certainly not contempt or cruelty, which are incompatible with any notion of respect. Moral equality can be accorded to any individual in the sense that the person will be included in what is judged to be fair, whatever fairness turns out to be, so far as we may be successful in bringing it to life. It *in*cludes taking him seriously; it *ex*cludes mistreating him. The requirements of respect need not always be threatening. Highly effectual in any case, they will vary with the contingencies at issue.

It would be antagonistic to the entire import of this book to attempt to be fastidious about what the similar treatment for similar cases ought to be, or to judge concretely of policies that might be worked out where there is respect for persons. These are matters that are addressed with a multitude of considerations. It is not evasive on my part to say again that such matters are best determined, as the case will be, by the exercise of these fundamental moral dispositions.

The basic point after all is this: respect for persons is one of the indisputable goods of associated life. Understood in a minimal but still highly consequential sense, it can be endorsed by almost anyone. The typical conditions of the moral life are such that there is little rationale for anyone not to extend it, in its minimal incarnation, universally. It asks only that people be treated with a kind of decency and accord what is fair, without any abstract rules about what that might be. Like rationality and courage, it is a splendid virtue for *addressing* moral problems, not for deciding their outcome in advance. It is suitable for the character of the moral condition. As with rationality and courage, the problem with respect for persons is not so much subscribing to it but practicing it. It might be the hardest to practice, but here, at least, it has been characterized in a way to keep its demands within reason.

Disrespect does not evaporate when it is exposed. Tyrants, thugs, and parasites, great and small, have respect neither for persons nor moral discourse; one is not likely to move them with argumentation. People cursed with hate and fear, with ravenous greeds and envies, or who are deeply threatened are not on the brink of practicing virtue. As with any virtue, advocating it is not having it. Respect is made possible by our need for impartiality, by our reliance on congenial social relations, by the many rewards for practicing this virtue, and by our capacity for identification, which is unevenly possessed and developed. There are many other human traits—some vicious, some commendable—that compete with it within the same breast. Some people are more selfish than others; some are more hard-pressed; some love unwisely; some are monumentally ambitious. There are limits to our virtue, and most people never get near the limit anyway. No doubt this condition will persist.

The preceding discussion has been simplified in a deliberate way. Three virtues have been treated, but others might have been added. Anyone who actually possesses the three would in fact possess others as well: for example, honesty and truthfulness. My aim has not been to present a complete rendition of the virtues appropriate to the moral condition. Dependability—the importance of which would be difficult to overrate—and *sophrosyne* could hardly be neglected in such an account; nor could wisdom. Love, charity, and mercy would have attention as well. Then justice would hold pride of place as the inclusive virtue.

These virtues cannot be tested or measured on written examinations; they are manifest in conduct. Few features of existence are as precious as these basic dispositions to think and act. They are mutually supporting and fructifying. In isolation they can be hurtful, as courage without rationality, or intelligence without character. But the inclusive treatment is not critical for the present venture, where the point is to represent the virtues minimally indispensable for conduct in a world that presents irreducible pluralities, change, and contingency, yet a world that also exhibits constancies, uniformities, imperatives, constraints, and consummations in their own right.

Use and Justification of the Virtues

If the moral condition bears much resemblance to the portrait offered here, then the virtues of rationality, courage, and respect for persons are conspicuously well suited to it. One of the virtues of these virtues, I might say, is that there is a limited permissiveness about them. They are not demands for rigidly specified rules of behavior. This characteristic makes them attractive in a way that neither absolutism nor relativism can be. Absolutists tell us that we must accept their well-defined position without reservation or exception. Their position threatens, therefore, much that is precious in the moral life; and for that reason, any given system will have few subscribers. If the choice we are given is to take it or leave it, we leave it. History displays a profusion of absolutistic systems; the profusion persists today. If the world were populated by consistent absolutists, social action would be paralyzed, just as it would be with persistent relativism.

In contrast to these extremes, the minimal virtues are the Aristotelian mean for carrying on the moral life. Happily, they make demands on us, but limited and flexible ones. We could subscribe to this philosophy without placing nearly so much in jeopardy as we would if we were to subscribe to a version of either absolutism or relativism. Given the contingencies of the moral life, the plurality of its values, and its uncertain but powerful constraints and opportunities, the consequence of exercising such virtues would surely be more satisfactory than adhering to either doctrinaire systems or the counsels of relativism.

Although these virtues are presented as minimal conditions for conducting the moral life, they should attain whatever realistic returns our moral condition affords. Such a notion may bring a scowl from the austere philosopher, who will say that these virtues are so indeterminate that too many varieties of behavior are compatible with them. Intolerable to the Cartesian impulse! Intolerable to the obsession with moral exactitude!

The pluralistic position does imply that the moral life is often something of a makeshift, but it is anything but living every day like it was our first. Pluralists with the requisite virtues certainly believe in maintaining rules and principles, but they are not absolutistic about it. They can be "persons of principle" in that each can stand firm as a minority of one, if need be. They might well be counted upon to do their duty, sustain their obligations even under conditions of hardship, and devote themselves to the preservation and growth of cherished institutions. Pluralists do so not because they have pledged themselves in a hypothetical contract, but because of actual pledges and because of the precious bonds that unite them with others. Pluralists are much less apt than either rationalists or relativists to try to remake the world every day, for they are deeply cognizant of the constraints of the natural world and the heavy investment that peoples have in their forms of life. Pluralists know that moralities cannot be invented anew and out of whole cloth. Yet, imbued with some measure of rationality, courage, and respect for persons, they can identify moral calamities or remediable deficiencies and can dedicate themselves to try to do something about them.

The resourcefulness of these virtues can be made evident, if it is not so already. Their adoption expels what are by far the most destructive and self-defeating modes of action. Although rationality is not conceived in a way to fix upon one rigorous method or criterion, it nevertheless excludes such features as irrationality, dogmatism, and the substitution of propaganda for education, all of which are greater banes of human existence than any conscientious attempt at rationality. Likewise respect for persons is divorced from all forms of behavior that are deliberately antisocial, callous, or otherwise vicious. Those who embody this minimal condition are not murderers, liars, or thieves; they are not willfully negligent or malign. We can disagree about whether a specific treatment is in fact prejudicial or gratuitous, but of unyielding importance is the *disposition* to respect the claims of others.

Respect must be combined with a like disposition to rationality. In the absence of that, respect degenerates into ineffectual or even destructive sentimentality. With rationality, respect is a virtue tending to potency, inclusiveness when possible, and to conciliation. Those without courage—and those who are actually cowardly—are much more susceptible to all manner of vice and weakness than are the brave. Admittedly, there could be a courageous villain, but courage in concert with rationality and respect can only have a synergistic effect for the good.

The disposition to "get at the facts," as I have called it, has much greater consequence in both moral theory and judgment than most people suspect. Unless the ambitions of this book are all in vain, to "get at the facts" about the moral condition can only be salutary for our meditations on the substance and functions of moral theory. When we contemplate the substantive moral issues of the day, great and small, we find that our respective positions on them have been affected far more by cognitive beliefs than by ethical theory. (At least one hopes that this is true; otherwise we are wafted along on the heady perfumes of moral sentiment. Instead of making our moral ideas clear, we smugly follow intuitions undisciplined by experience.) In part, these beliefs concern the constituent variables in actual moral situations, such as arms control policy, strategic defense, the war on drugs, and the effectiveness of welfare programs. At a more general level, the comparative study of cultural, economic, and political histories will have a forceful effect on our evaluations of a wide range of practices. Variations in institutions portend variations in what they deliver. Our allegiances to political and economic arrangements are necessarily (but not wholly) predicated upon what they promise by way of results for the lives of those caught up in them. Hence it is vital to know what promises they make and whether they can be kept. It is equally vital to know what side-effects the implementation of these promises might have, for they might dwarf the intended effects.

The loyalties of many are predicated on unexamined assumptions about what certain institutions do and do not deliver. Many of our moral devotions are likewise organic to assumptions about what human nature can and cannot deliver under varying circumstances. We urgently need to know what the direct effects and the side-effects of observing particular moral requirements might be.

The great moral systems with which we are familiar depend in great measure on cognitive claims. Consider, as examples, the role of Plato's theory of forms, Aristotle's "metaphysical biology" (as

MacIntyre aptly calls it), the religious and theological beliefs of Augustine or Aquinas, Locke's or Rousseau's concept of the individual, Kant's dualism of laws of nature and laws of freedom, Bradley's Absolute, Marx's laws of capitalism, or Dewey's philosophical anthropology. In each case, a distinctive shape is imparted to the moral system by just such considerations, all of which are *subject,* at least, to cognitive resolution. Examples could be multiplied and given in detail. It is impossible to judge precisely the extent to which moralities and moral theories are determined by cognitive beliefs, but the influence is considerable, even decisive. It is such cognitive beliefs, more than anything else, that differentiate one view from another. An instructive history of moral thought could be written by focusing on the question of the degree to which historical change in moral advocacy has varied with developments in knowledge. Empirical studies on the determinants of moral change in mature individuals or groups would be likewise instructive.

I do not neglect the power of bias or emotion in the formation of moral belief and advocacy. Such forces are mighty. One's morals might be intensely affected by, say, hatred of the bourgeoisie. But a hatred does not have a virgin birth. Unless it is a *completely* blind revulsion, it is predicated on explicit beliefs about what this class *does* and what other classes might do. For its detractors, bourgeois culture is not identified with freedom, growth, and opportunity, but with greed, selfishness, consumerism, exploitation, vulgarity, and struggle for survival. Maybe the bourgeoisie does, willfully or not, perpetrate hateful conditions; but in any case those charges are subject to empirical confirmation. We might make the honest attempt to find out in what sort of economic systems are greed, corruption, and exploitation—as well as more admirable traits—most likely to turn up. We might learn *to what effect* the characteristics of human nature occur in alternative orders. What are the effects, for example, of natural human ambition and competitiveness in socialist bureacracies and in private economies? Admittedly, such inquiries are difficult and controversial, but their importance could hardly be overestimated for the convergence of moral advocacies.

How could there be this importance? If evaluation is not reducible to cognition, and if human beings are invested with fluctuating and heterogeneous sentiments, why should it happen that some moral order should occur? The first answer is that convergence and order are *desirable* to the great majority of persons, who succeed more often than not in sustaining a tolerable structure. But, more deeply, the answer has to be that we suffer the same moral condition. The natural constraints and promises that haunt the moral life are there for everyone. They are not there equally, of course, or felt in quite the same way. Some persons' lives are much less cramped, more encouraging, more protected and nurtured, than those of others. Their happy condition does not of itself shield them from the generic lessons of experience. These fortunate souls can learn respect for impartiality and fair play, rationality, and courage from the moral life. In all probability, moreover, there are constraints and imperatives within us as part of our nature.

Just the same, the lessons of the moral life are not equally accessible, for various reasons. Many persons do injury out of desperation, malice, greed, and the like. But even they must have some regard for the restraints of common life. Tyrants are toppled and thugs put away, or perhaps done in by their accomplices. The fact that the lessons are not always learned does not diminish their importance.

I hardly wish to deny that there have been all manner of unspeakable and unavenged crimes and endless cases of unrewarded virtue. The moral condition does not possess the essential perfections imputed to it by Plato. On the other hand, it *must* have its powerful efficacies all the same. As I have remarked, we are not primarily indebted to philosophers for whatever direction and success with which we are blessed. The lessons of life itself—however muted, confused, and unsystematic they have been—have provided for us.

As a final note on this point, it must be said that moral philosophy does not exhaust itself with the hopeless tasks of refuting all evil and proving that somehow everything can turn out all right in the end. It can address morally earnest persons—seekers of the good, if you will—already committed to a decent life of some sort and hopeful of improving it for themselves and others, but groping for insight and direction. Philosophers could try to equip them with methods and ideas that would facilitate and enrich their efforts. They would be helpful to such persons, for example, by indicating some of the positive efficacies of the moral life and how we can become allied with them.

At issue has been the question of the constraint that the virtue of rationality exerts on our advocacies. This disposition is not so permissive as one might assume. Indeed, the case is stronger than has been suggested. Hardly anyone will deny that it is essential to "get at the facts," so why do I make such a spectacle of it? I do so because this is a virtue that gets more flattery than honest service. It has been said that facts are hard to deny, but they are not. When they threaten our loyalties and weaknesses, it is easy to refuse to look them in the face. With our gifts of imagination, we can, with the ingenuity of a paranoid, explain away or discount almost any fact. If necessary, we can contrive spanking new methodologies and criteria of knowledge in order to be rid of it, or we can find authorities more likely to support what we already believe. If a fact will still not go away, we can have faith that somewhere, somehow, sometime, someone will come up with a theory that will give another explanation of it; we needn't have a bad conscience about ignoring it.

This inventive, if pathetic, capacity has its limits. They are not in intelligent discourse, as such. Discourse functions to make us aware of the real rewards and penalties that await our conduct. Hence informed and intelligent discourse is invaluable. But getting advice and information *about* pending experience can never be as effective as *having* it. The principle constraint on our evasions and irrationality is experience itself. If the promises of policies and institutions continue to fail, again and again, time after time, then they will be believed only by intellectuals ensconced in very protected environments. But it is a pity that we must suffer so much in order to be convinced. The suffering can be reduced insofar as the virtue of rationality is more served than flattered.

Given my characterization of the moral condition, it would be easy to conclude that social intelligence is the best procedure for an effective engagement with our moral problems. If moral problems are by nature interpersonal, and if there is no one right answer or perfect solution to them, then, assuming some respect for persons, an interpersonal method presents itself as the most suitable manner for contending with them. It is attractive, among other reasons, because it does not come with preestablished answers. Answers remain to be worked out, if they can be, with the active participation of those who are engaged with them. Perhaps it is more apt than other methods to enlist the support and participation of differing groups.

Discharged with virtue, social intelligence represents the consummation of the powers of discourse. I am not, then, speaking of anything so mindless as the mere counting of heads. We cannot be reminded too often that nonauthoritarian methods of social action will perish without virtue. They will turn into acrimonious and greedy struggle and will be supplanted by tyranny. Persons with significant traces of rationality, courage, and respect, however, can converge, if not unite, in maintaining social relations in which the many values of the moral life can be well served.

But the conditions in which social intelligence is possible are anything but universal. Rationality, courage, and respect for persons are difficult. Intelligence did not evolve in order to sacrifice the interests of its possessor. Intelligence is instrumental to the preservation and enhancement of the interests of the organism, whatever they might be. These interests can be rather generous and inclusive; and often the critical reexamination of our position and the exertions of virtue can lead to a greater good.

But very often, too, persons have no wish to put their goods in jeopardy. Human nature holds fast to the possessions and dispositions with which it is already endowed. If too many of them are put on the line, social intelligence will founder. The occasion for this form of discourse occurs, patently, just when values are divergent or in conflict, so our defenses tend to be up. An honest effort at social method requires a good measure of mutual trust, yet we are often suspicious of one another, sometimes with good reason. There may be hidden agendas, deceit, dishonesty, or great discrepancies in power. There may be very good reason for simple obedience to authority, too. Accordingly, to enter into democratic discourse naively can be a fatal trap. Those who lack the virtues for such communication, or who have contempt for it, will use the occasion to exploit their counterparts.

This is a counsel to use social intelligence cautiously. It is exercised as rationality, courage, and respect might dictate. Sometimes it is better to play it tough instead. Rather than depending on rational persuasion, we would often do better to set limits to the behavior of others. Intelligence is the faculty that has evolved to preserve and enlarge our interests. If those interests are threatened, and if there is no acceptable alternative to them, then the time for negotiation has ended. Guile perhaps, or threat, deceit, or defense might be in order.

It is not a counsel of despair, however, but one of realism. It is not *un*realistic to believe that our best powers may sometimes have happy employment and fruition. Many occasions for honest discourse are needlessly shunted aside on the assumption that we can decide moral perplexities within our conscience alone, or in obedience to authority, or by following the dictates of an abstract system. Earnest invitation to discourse does not necessarily bring about its exploitation. Trust, honesty, and cooperation are sometimes brought forth instead.

It is worth noting that the practice of social intelligence—like the rationality, courage, and moral equality of which I have spoken—has a basis in common life. It is not just abstractly "rational," but a function of normal social relations. Every one of us is brought up within a preexisting family or group. In such contexts, in our nonage, we must satisfy others that our behavior is acceptable to *them*. It is difficult to see how it could be any other way. We begin and sustain life only with care and tutelage from others. If we are fortunate enough to have an accommodating but not overindulgent environment, then some give and take will occur, and we find the process congenial. But in any case we were not, and could not have been, anointed emperor and made invulnerable to all answerability. It would be a disaster both for others and ourselves if we were. The adults in our life expect us to be answerable to them, as part of both their good and ours; as we mature we rightly expect other persons to be answerable to us as part of any normal and sound social process. We learn, then, that in any stage of life we live in relation to others; and we typically acquire the habit of engaging in discussion with them in anticipation of overt conduct. Because of the benefits of consultation, the give and take can become routine. It is both natural and appropriate that we feel disposed to consult with others—*some* others, at least—and to take their concerns deliberately into consideration. We make the earnest effort to accommodate them, just as they attempt to accommodate us. *This effort is as intrinsic to the social bond as honoring our promises or sustaining our obligations.*

For very good reason, then, this mode of conduct becomes an ingredient in our nature. It is a natural imperative, developed in the inescapable pressures and benefits of ordinary life. We do not honor it in every context, of course; and we might confine its practice to a select few. There are ways of getting around it. We could appeal to a convenient source of authority instead, disregarding the appeals of others. Or we could rely, perhaps, just on abstract theory, as such. My point, again, is to exhibit the natural origins of consultative deliberation. Those who would be included in vital relations, who have regard for them and want them to prosper, would also teach and encourage such behavior. They respect this fundamental bond of social life.

The moral life is sometimes well served by social intelligence, and it is always well served by our virtues. But that life will never be utopia. The exercise of virtue does not yield uniform and invariant behavior. Nothing short of thought control can change this, if even then. In addition, there will always be absolutists and relativists in some measure, just as there will always be plenty of more-or-less vicious people. I don't make the claim that proposals of the sort I have made will be invariably compelling. That is not my paradigm of moral theory. I am persuaded, however, that they will answer to the realities of the moral condition more effectively than others that have come to my notice.

For most of those engaged in ethical theory, their point of departure is the current state of academic philosophy: the very latest arguments in books and journals. That state is also the point of return; that's the complete loop. If our contributions are well received in the professional literature, that makes us a success. I have been contending, by contrast, that moral theory draws its purpose and sustenance from the moral life. *That life* is its problematic situation, and theory directs its efforts to *its* concerns. Systematic reflection would be validated by real experience rather than congeniality to up-to-date philosophy. The discernment of the traits of the moral life must be faithful to its actual conditions and powers. The elaboration of these traits yields a vision of the moral condition. A justified prescription of a way of life would have to be suited to the moral condition.

What does "justified" mean? We might suppose it means justification *überhaupt*. Can there be such a thing as literally unqualified justification? I see no reason why we must look in such directions. Justification is always in reference to some standard among others, and it is relative to certain populations and problems, and not others. The choice of a mode of moral defense is itself an evaluative determination.

Yet philosophers have typically thought of justification as an appeal to such things as a Platonic form, a rational principle, a divine command, a self-evident truth, the characterization of a rational agent, the delineation of an ultimate good, or even the structures of a vernacular language. They believe, at least, that that sort of justification alone would really justify. Hence all other attempts are dismissed. They have likewise tended to put an insurmountable burden of proof on whomever would defend a given moral view. They want demonstration, certitude. This is a reversion to the assumption that a moral position is like a theorem in geometry or is somehow certifiable in and of itself. This policy invites needless skepticism and, in fact, evasion of what is morally important. A philosopher is appalled, let us say, by slavery. He contrives a social contract theory to give final credence to his opposition: An individual without an identity—he is *only* rational—faced with policy alternatives would not countenance the institution of slavery, for he might turn out to be a slave, and he wouldn't like that. Well, we already know that slavery is extremely obnoxious, but our opposition to it is due to more than the fact that *we* don't want to be enslaved. Our repugnance is predicated on many considerations. We recognize that to be enslaved is a thoroughly hateful condition, and we sympathize with those who suffer such tyranny and with their family and friends from whom the enslaved has been wrenched away. We despise the slaveholder for his complete disregard for such concerns. One of the most telling reasons for our opposition is that the slave is *innocent*: he does not *deserve* to be enslaved. We recognize, too, that protection of the innocent is essential to any endurable social order. In all probability, such concerns were what turned the philosopher against slavery in the first place. Why should he seek considerations of a completely different nature in order to be convincing to ordinary mortals, deeply caught up in the moral life? Who does he think he can persuade with his constructions? The slaveholder certainly won't care a straw for his contract theory.

If the conflicts between moral positions were all reducible to cognitive claims, then we could settle such matters by appeal to familiar procedures. They are not reducible, so additional considerations must be deployed. In many instances one of the cases is flagrantly ill-willed, inept, ignorant, or dishonest; we need do no more for our persuasion than to expose it as such. But in other cases it is often difficult to judge one advocacy over another, and on such occasions we should reflect and inquire further, bringing within range whatever relevant powers we can identify.

In the final analysis, a particular advocacy may rest on the grounds that we have reached it by faithful exercise of a certain complex of virtues. An awareness of the operative conditions, resources, tensions, and deeply held commitments, coupled with courage and moral regard, have been our sword and shield. These virtues, in turn, are justified on the grounds that they are forms of thought and action that are most suitable to the generic and persistent problems of the moral life. "Most suitable," no doubt, is an evaluative expression, but we are not philosophizing in a hermetically sealed chamber. We are responding to the real exigencies, demands, and promises of our moral existence.

What is finally at stake, then, is not the elaboration of a system of moral principles, but a *way of life*—a life with a certain character and quality. Any life, no doubt, is a *way* of life. We can't reinvent ourselves each morning. Even the selfish opportunist, the manipulative "pragmatist," has a way of life, from which anyone else wants to be as far removed as possible, making that life typically odious to its owner, too. Virtue as well comes in various shapes and degrees. No life has an altogether tidy definition, but we know the differences between one approximation and another. The point here is not to canvass all the options in ways of life, showing what condemns or commends each in turn. Again, I make a minimal but forceful claim: I urge that whatever we take to be morally good ways of life, they would be more effective with the virtues I have been discussing.

For legions of moralists it is an article of faith that principles are the ultimate justification of conduct. Yet, as I have remarked, they are decidedly awkward as premises for moral deductions. When unthinkingly observed, they are unsuited, too, to the novelties, contingencies, dilemmas, and opportunities of the moral life. The value of principles is *derivative* of the offices they perform in real situations. They have force and pertinence when utilized to identify, order, and protect our characteristic values, to make their recognition more conspicuous and consistent. They are justified on just that account. Moral experience is often complex and disordered; we can be forgetful of its patterns and unmindful of the responsibilities and pitfalls that lie within it. In such a condition, principles are means of keeping us alert to matters of consequence; they keep us from being diverted to peripheral occupations; and they help us to be impartial. In that vesture, however, they are not the sort of thing to be taken as self-sufficient just as they stand. They are among the instruments of our virtues for contending with the demands and opportunities in which we are immersed. The virtuous analysis and exercise of principle (along with other moral concerns) would take precedence over stark principle.

Would not recourse to the exercise of the virtues be more fundamental to the moral life? Would not a defense of the virtue of virtue be defense enough for our decisions and policies? We may address the moral life with rationality, courage, and respect for persons, more or less as introduced here. What can plausibly be said *against* these virtues? What sort of considerations purporting to be of a moral nature can be entered to convict them? What can be presented with a straight face as a moral reason to condemn them? Will anyone be willing to say that they are impertinent or immoral? Will anyone be willing to defend a position that flaunts them?

If no such candidates come forward, and if someone wishes to take moral issue with us, then that person might hold that a given advocacy does *not* display the requisite virtue. Our adversary might be right, and we might learn from him; or it could be that conscientious moral disagreement would persist. But notice that the question has shifted. We are no longer in discourse about the virtues in their generic function of providing moral justification. We are considering whether they have been duly exercised in a given case. The *authority* of the virtues has not been called into question.

Philosophers, of course, will leap from their armchairs to make a deadly strike: the justice of the virtues has not been *demonstrated*! No, it hasn't, but the allegedly fatal instrument is just smoke. We are asking what would count as authoritative in actual moral life and discourse, with its real imperatives and urgencies. Granted, this is an *advocacy* for virtue, not a proof; but all other claimants are advocates, too. Each must show its comparative merits in light of the nature of the moral condition, or admit to philosophizing in a vacuum.

The philosophers might also complain that the virtues lead to no *univocal* decisions: they are commendable, but inadequate. I would repeat (once more) that such decisions are purchased only with more smoke, or with tyranny. Just let it be acknowledged that there is no putatively moral reason to judge the conscientious exercise of virtue to be other than a blessing for humankind. If a decision is virtuous, if not intersubjectively conclusive, that is enough. That is the best that the moral condition permits.

To be virtuous is rarely easy or uncomplicated. Still, it is a way of life adaptable to the real contingencies of human existence and answerable to the reasonable kinds of demand nurtured in the moral life. We can believe that the way of life manifest in the virtues of rationality, courage, and respect is answerable to the conditions of mortal life, including the realistic claims of others.

The virtues are derivative of the moral life. They are conceived in a manner to be suitable to it. They possess an aptness for the characteristic problems and opportunities of conduct. The torments and ambiguities of moral life will not vanish. They are unavoidable. The issue is whether our way of life, our virtues, are befitting of our circumstance as moral beings. If we believe that they sustain us as well as anything could through the fortunes of life, that is all the justification the moral condition affords. It is justification enough.

Note

1. "It is my purpose, as one who lived and acted in these days . . . to show . . . how the malice of the wicked was reinforced by the weakness of the virtuous . . . how the counsels of prudence and restraint may become the prime agents of mortal danger; how the middle course adopted from desires for safety and a quiet life may be found to lead direct to the bulls-eye of disaster." Winston S. Churchill, *The Gathering Storm,* vol. 1 of *The Second World War* (Boston: Houghton Mifflin Company, 1948), pp. 17–18.

Bibliography

Alexander, Richard D. *The Biology of Moral Systems.* New York: Aldine De Gruyter, 1987.

Alexander, Thomas S. *John Dewey's Theory of Art, Experience, and Nature: The Horizons of Feeling.* Albany: State University of New York Press, 1987.

Apel, Karl-Otto. *Towards a Transformation of Philosophy.* Translated by Glyn Adey and David Frisby. London, Boston, and Henley: Routledge & Kegan Paul, 1980.

Aristotle. *Nicomachean Ethics.* Translated with introduction and notes by Martin Ostwald. Indianapolis and New York: The Bobbs-Merrill Company, 1962.

———. *Politics,* in *The Complete Works of Aristotle.* Vol. 2. Revised Oxford Translation. Jonathan Barnes (ed.). Princeton, N.J.: Princeton University Press, 1984.

Bellah, Robert N., et al. *Habits of the Heart.* New York: Harper & Row, 1985.

Berger, Peter L. *The Capitalist Revolution: Fifty Propositions About Prosperity, Equality, and Liberty.* New York: Basic Books, 1986.

Berlin, Isaiah. *Four Essays on Liberty.* Oxford: Oxford University Press, 1969.

Berry, Christopher J. *Human Nature.* Atlantic Highlands, N.J.: Humanities Press International, 1986.

Boisvert, Raymond D. *Dewey's Metaphysics.* New York: Fordham University Press, 1988.

Brown, Donald E. *Human Universals.* Philadelphia: Temple University Press, 1991.

Cassirer, Ernst. *The Myth of the State.* New Haven, Conn.: Yale University Press, 1946.

Cavalier, Robert, James Gouinlock, and James P. Sterba (eds.). *Ethics in the History of Western Philosophy.* London: Macmillan; New York: St. Martin's Press, 1989.

Churchill, Winston S. *The Gathering Storm,* Vol. 1 of *The Second World War.* Boston: Houghton Mifflin Company, 1948.

Danto, Arthur. *Nietzsche as Philosopher.* New York: Macmillan, 1965.

Dennett, Daniel C. *Elbow Room.* Cambridge, Mass.: MIT Press, 1984.

Dewey, John. *The Early Works, 1882–1898,* 5 Vols. Jo Ann Boydston (ed.). *The Middle Works, 1899–1924,* 15 Vols. Jo Ann Boydston (ed.). *The Later Works, 1925–1953,* 17 Vols. Jo Ann Boydston (ed.). Carbondale and Edwardsville: Southern Illinois University Press, 1967–1989.

D'Souza, Dinesh. *Illiberal Education.* New York: The Free Press, 1991.

Dworkin, Ronald. *Taking Rights Seriously.* Cambridge, Mass.: Harvard University Press, 1978.

Edwards, Paul. *The Logic of Moral Discourse.* Glencoe, Ill.: The Free Press, 1955.

Erasmus, Charles J. *In Search of the Common Good.* Glencoe, Ill.: The Free Press, 1977.

Fleming, Thomas. *The Politics of Human Nature.* New Brunswick, N.J.: Transaction Books, 1988.

Fox, Robin. "The Seville Declaration: Anthropology's Auto-da-Fe," *Academic Questions* 1, no. 4 (Fall 1988): 35–47.

Frank, Robert H. *Passions Within Reason: The Strategic Role of the Emotions.* New York: W. W. Norton & Company, 1988.

Gauthier, David. *Morals by Agreement.* Oxford: Clarendon Press, 1986.

Gewirth, Alan. *Reason and Morality.* Chicago: The University of Chicago Press, 1978.

Goldberg, Steven. *The Inevitability of Patriarchy*. New York: William Morrow and Company, 1973/74.

Goodin, Robert E. *Protecting the Vulnerable*. Chicago: The University of Chicago Press, 1985.

Gouinlock, James. "Dewey's Theory of Moral Deliberation," *Ethics* 88, no. 3 (April 1978): 218–28.

———. *Excellence in Public Discourse: John Stuart Mill, John Dewey, and Social Intelligence*. New York: Teachers College Press, 1986.

———. *John Dewey's Philosophy of Value*. New York: Humanities Press, 1972.

———. "What Is the Legacy of Instrumentalism? Rorty's Interpretation of Dewey," *Journal of the History of Philosophy* 28, no. 3 (April 1990): 251–69.

Greenberg, Jerald, and Ronald L. Cohen (eds.). *Equity and Justice in Social Behavior*. New York: Academic Press, 1982.

Habermas, Jürgen. *Communication and the Evolution of Society*. Translated and with an introduction by Thomas McCarthy. Boston: Beacon Press, 1979.

———. *The Legitimation Crisis*. Translated by Thomas McCarthy. Boston: Beacon Press, 1975.

———. *Theory and Practice*. Translated by John Viertel. Boston: Beacon Press, 1973.

———. *The Theory of Communicative Action*, Vol. 2, *Lifeworld and System: A Critique of Functional Reason*. Translated by Thomas McCarthy. Boston: Beacon Press, 1987.

Hancock, Roger L. *Twentieth Century Ethics*. New York and London: Columbia University Press, 1974.

Hare, Richard M. *The Language of Morals*. Oxford; Clarendon Press, 1952.

———. *Moral Thinking*. Oxford: Clarendon Press, 1981.

Herrnstein, Richard J. "Lost and Found: One Self," *Ethics* 98, no. 3 (April 1988): 566–78.

Homans, George C. *Sentiments and Activities*. Glencoe, Ill.: The Free Press, 1962.

———. *Social Behavior: Its Elementary Forms*, rev. ed. New York: Harcourt Brace Jovanovich, Inc., 1974.

Hudson, W. D. *Modern Moral Philosophy.* London: Macmillan, 1970.

Hume, David. *David Hume: Philosophical Works.* T. H. Green and T. H. Grose (eds.). Aalen, West Germany: Scientia Verlag, 1964.

James, William. *A Pluralistic Universe.* Cambridge, Mass.: Harvard University Press, 1977.

————. *Pragmatism.* Cambridge, Mass.: Harvard University Press, 1975.

————. *The Principles of Psychology,* 3 Vols. Cambridge, Mass.: Harvard University Press, 1981.

————. *The Will to Believe and Other Essays in Popular Philosophy.* Cambridge, Mass.: Harvard University Press, 1979.

Kant, Immanuel. *Critique of Pure Reason.* Translated by Norman Kemp Smith. London: Macmillan, 1958.

————. *Foundations of the Metaphysics of Morals.* Translated and with an introduction by Lewis White Beck. New York: The Liberal Arts Press, 1959.

————. *Lectures on Ethics.* Translated by Louis Infield. New York: Harper & Row, 1963.

————. *The Metaphysics of Morals.* Translated and with an introduction by John Ladd. Indianapolis and New York: The Bobbs-Merrill Company, 1965.

Kaufmann, Walter. *The Future of the Humanities.* New York: Thomas Y. Crowell Company, 1977.

Kerner, George. *The Revolution in Ethical Theory.* New York and Oxford; Oxford University Press, 1966.

Larmore, Charles. *Patterns of Moral Complexity.* Cambridge: Cambridge University Press, 1987.

Lerner, Melvin J. *The Belief in a Just World: A Fundamental Delusion.* New York and London: Plenum Press, 1980.

Livingston, Donald. *Hume's Philosophy of Common Life.* Chicago: The University of Chicago Press, 1984.

MacIntyre, Alasdair. *After Virtue,* 2d. ed. Notre Dame, Ind.: University of Notre Dame Press, 1984.

MacIntyre, Alasdair. *Three Rival Versions of Moral Enquiry.* Notre Dame, Ind.: University of Notre Dame Press, 1990.

———. *Whose Justice? Which Rationality?* Notre Dame, Ind.: University of Notre Dame Press, 1988.

Marx, Karl. *The German Ideology,* in *The Marx-Engels Reader,* 2d. ed. Robert C. Tucker (ed.). New York: W. W. Norton & Company, 1978.

Masters, Roger D. *The Nature of Politics.* New Haven, Conn., and London: Yale University Press, 1989.

McDermott, John J. *The Culture of Experience: Philosophical Essays in the American Grain.* New York: New York University Press, 1976.

———. *Streams of Experience: Reflections on the History and Philosophy of American Culture.* Amherst: University of Massachusetts Press, 1986.

———. (ed.). *The Writings of William James: A Comprehensive Edition.* Chicago and London: The University of Chicago Press, 1977.

McShea, Robert J. *Morality and Human Nature: A New Route to Ethical Theory.* Philadelphia: Temple University Press, 1990.

Mead, George Herbert. *Mind, Self, and Society.* Chicago and London: The University of Chicago Press, 1934.

Melden, A. I. *Rights and Persons.* Berkeley: University of California Press, 1977.

Milgram, Stanley. *Obedience to Authority.* New York: Harper and Row, 1974.

Mill, John Stuart. *On Liberty.* Indianapolis and New York: Bobbs-Merrill, Inc., 1956.

———. *Utilitarianism.* New York: The Liberal Arts Press, 1957.

Murdoch, Iris. *The Sovereignty of Good.* London and New York: ARK Paperbacks, 1985.

Murray, Charles. *In Pursuit of Happiness and Good Government.* New York: Simon and Schuster, 1988.

———. *Losing Ground: American Social Policy 1950–1980.* New York: Basic Books, 1984.

Nagel, Thomas. *Mortal Questions.* Cambridge: Cambridge University Press, 1979.

Nielsen, Kai. *Equality and Liberty: A Defense of Radical Egalitarianism.* Totowa, N.J.: Rowman and Allanheld, 1985.

Nozick, Robert. *Anarchy, State and Utopia.* New York: Basic Books, 1974.

Peirce, Charles S. *Collected Papers of Charles Sanders Peirce.* Vol. 5. Charles Hartshorne and Paul Weiss (eds.). Cambridge, Mass.: Harvard University Press, 1934.

Pepper, Stephen G. *The Sources of Value.* Berkeley: University of California Press, 1970.

Perry, Ralph Barton. *The Thought and Character of William James.* 2 Vols. Boston: Little, Brown and Company, 1935.

Peterson, Merrill D., and Robert C. Vaughn (eds). *The Virginia Statute for Religious Freedom.* Cambridge: Cambridge University Press, 1988.

Plato. *Philebus,* in *The Dialogues of Plato.* Vol. 2. Translated by Benjamin Jowett. New York: Random House, 1937.

―――. *Republic.* Translated with introduction and notes by F. M. Cornford. Oxford: Oxford University Press, 1945.

Quine, W. V. *The Time of My Life.* Cambridge, Mass.: MIT Press, 1985.

Randall, John Herman, Jr. *The Making of the Modern Mind.* Boston: Houghton-Mifflin, 1940.

Rawls, John. *A Theory of Justice.* Cambridge, Mass.: Harvard University Press, 1971.

―――. "Justice as Fairness: Political not Metaphysical," *Philosophy and Public Affairs* 14, no. 3 (Summer, 1985): 223–51.

―――. "Kantian Constructivism in Moral Theory," *The Journal of Philosophy* 77, no. 9 (September 1980): 515–72.

Raz, Joseph. *The Morality of Freedom.* Oxford: The Clarendon Press, 1986.

Reck, Andrew J. *Recent American Philosophy.* New York: Pantheon Books, 1964.

Rorty, Richard. *Contingency, Irony, and Solidarity.* Cambridge: Cambridge University Press, 1989.

―――. "Postmodernist Bourgeois Liberalism," *The Journal of Philosophy* 80, no. 10 (October 1983): 583–89.

Rousseau, Jean-Jacques. *Social Contract*. Translated and with an introduction by G. D. H. Cole. New York: E. P. Dutton, 1950.

Russell, Bertrand. *Mysticism and Logic*. New York: W. W. Norton, 1929.

Sandel, Michael J. *Liberalism and the Limits of Justice*. Cambridge: Cambridge University Press, 1982.

Santayana, George. *The Life of Reason*. 5 Vols. New York: Collier Books, 1962.

Schwarz, Barry. *The Battle for Human Nature*. New York and London: W. W. Norton & Company, 1986.

Sher, George. *Desert*. Princeton, N.J.: Princeton University Press, 1987.

Sleeper, Ralph. *The Necessity of Pragmatism*. New Haven, Conn.: Yale University Press, 1986.

Smith, John E. *America's Philosophical Vision*. Chicago and London: The University of Chicago Press, 1992.

———. *Purpose and Thought*. New Haven, Conn.: Yale University Press, 1978.

———. *The Spirit of American Philosophy,* rev. ed. Albany: State University of New York Press, 1983.

Sowell, Thomas. *A Conflict of Visions*. New York: William Morrow & Company, 1987.

———. "Affirmative Action: A Worldwide Disaster," *Commentary* 88, no. 6 (December 1989): 21–41.

———. *Preferential Policies; An International Perspective*. New York: William Morrow & Company, 1990.

Stevenson, Charles L. *Ethics and Language*. New Haven, Conn.: Yale University Press, 1944.

———. *Facts and Values*. New Haven, Conn., and London: Yale University Press, 1963.

Sykes, Charles J. *The Hollow Men*. Washington, D.C.: Regnery Gateway, 1990.

Thayer, H. Standish. *Meaning and Action: A Critical History of Pragmatism*. Indianapolis and New York: The Bobbs-Merrill Company, 1968.

Walzer, Michael. *Spheres of Justice*. New York: Basic Books, 1983.

Warnock, G. J. *Contemporary Moral Philosophy*. London: Macmillan; New York: St. Martin's Press, 1967.

Warnock, Mary. *Ethics since 1900*. London: Oxford University Press, 1960.

West, Cornel. *The American Evasion of Philosophy*. Madison: The University of Wisconsin Press, 1989.

White, Morton. "Value and Obligation in Dewey and Lewis," *The Philosophical Review* 58, no. 4 (July 1949): 321–30.

Williams, Bernard. *Ethics and the Limits of Philosophy*. Cambridge, Mass.: Harvard University Press, 1985.

———. *Moral Luck*. New York and Cambridge: Cambridge University Press, 1981.

Wilson, James Q., and Richard J. Herrnstein. *Crime and Human Nature*. New York: Simon and Schuster, 1985.

Index

335